The Soul of Jewish Social Justice

THE SOUL *of* JEWISH SOCIAL JUSTICE ☐

Rabbi Dr. Shmuly Yanklowitz

URIM PUBLICATIONS

Jerusalem · New York

The Soul of Jewish Social Justice

by Rabbi Dr. Shmuly Yanklowitz

Copyright © 2014 by Shmuly Yanklowitz

Typeset by Ariel Walden

Printed in Israel

First Edition

ISBN 978-965-524-156-3

Urim Publications, P.O. Box 52287,
Jerusalem 9152102 Israel

www.UrimPublications.com

Library of Congress Cataloging-in-Publication Data

Yanklowitz, Shmuly, 1981- author.
  The soul of Jewish social justice / Rabbi Dr. Shmuly Yanklowitz. – First
Edition.
    pages cm
  ISBN 978-965-524-156-3 (hardback)
  1. Social justice–Religious aspects–Judaism. 2. Social
service–Religious aspects–Judaism. 3. Jewish ethics. 4. Judaism and
social problems. I. Title.
  BM645.J8Y36 2014
  296.3'8–dc23   2014001164

This book is dedicated to our first child, our dear daughter AMIELLA RACHEL.

Sweetie, may you be blessed to always be spiritually connected to AMI (your people) and ELLA (your God). May you live with strength, grace, courage, blessing, and inspiration in all of your endeavors and journeys.

I love you from the depths of my heart,   ABBA

CONTENTS

SPIRITUAL PRACTICES
AND HOLY COMMUNITIES

JEWISH NARRATIVES AND CUSTOMS
RECONSIDERED

SUPPORTING THE ALIENATED

PRESSING POLITICAL ISSUES IN OUR TIME

ADDRESSING SCANDALS AND SOCIAL WRONGS

GREAT LEADERS OF OUR TIME

ISRAEL AND SOCIAL JUSTICE

CHILD ADOPTION

BUSINESS ETHICS

SOCIAL JUSTICE –
CONSIDERING THE FUTURE

INTRODUCTION

I N 2012, I RELEASED MY FIRST BOOK, *JEWISH ETHICS & Social Justice: A Guide for the 21st Century* (Derusha Publishing), and in 2013, my second book, *Epistemic Development in Talmud Study* (ProQuest U M I Publishing). I see this third book as a continuation of that work to apply Jewish values and laws to the most pressing contemporary moral and spiritual issues of our time. My intentions and hopes with this work are to foster further discourse, research, and activism around these core issues. These articles have appeared in *The Jewish Week*, *The Jewish Journal*, *The Jewish Press*, *The Jewish Forward*, *HaAretz*, *Milin Havivin*, *Conversations*, *Jewish Educational Leadership*, *Sh'ma*, *The Times of Israel*, and *The Huffington Post*. I am grateful to all of the editors for their support.

Through our building the Orthodox social justice movement, Uri L'Tzedek has become an American center of Torah social justice thought, and leads, inspires, challenges, and supports the Orthodox community to raise our ethical bar to a higher standard. At The Shamayim V'Aretz Institute, we are working to inspire deeper commitments to animal welfare, veganism, health, and the environment. At the Valley Beit Midrash, we are furthering learning and discourse about our unique obligations and responsibilities as American Jews. I have written this book in response to many of the issues we are addressing to create social change on.

The book addresses one core issue: how do our traditional Jewish ethics translate into contemporary Jewish social justice responsibilities? How do the virtues required for each Jew become converted into commitments to creating more sustainable and systemic social change for the most vulnerable in our society? Here I offer frameworks and questions to launch a broader discourse about these responsibilities.

While I am a moral philosopher and developmental psychologist by disposition and training, I am primarily a rabbi and activist by conviction and commitment. While the academic research and insights are implicit within these articles, it is the rabbinic and activist voice that is made most explicit. I believe that there is currently a greater need for inspiration and guidance than for drawn-out analytical essays on these issues. These essays are mostly short and devoid of overly-extensive analysis and apologetics.

My hermeneutic approach is to show how Jewish wisdom is relevant to our most pressing moral problems. Today, two prevalent trends have emerged. One is to read text with a fundamentalist orientation, with literal application ignoring other interpretations and sensitivities. The other is to make text irrelevant and merely confine it to its historical context. One ideological camp attempts to limit the scope of meaning while the other attempts to nullify its potential for relevance. It is my contention that the most complex and meaningful interpretation of text requires intellectual rigor, a concern for the moral consequence of an interpretation, integrity to the meaning of the text, and the consideration of all prior interpretations.

With a lens focused on Jewish social justice, I explore issues of spirituality, ritual and holiness, narratives and traditions, education, ethical consumption, alienation, leadership, Israel, child welfare, and business ethics, among many other moral and political issues. While there is a constant dance between the parochial and universal, my hermeneutic is clear: the particular informs the universal. It is our Jewish texts, values, and laws (while leaving room for conscience and natural morality) that inform how we are to respond to our greatest moral challenges; it is also clear that we must respond. It is my conviction that of the typical and knee-jerk responses, e.g., "these issues are too complex" or "only a council of great sages can address these issues," are inadequate. I take a grassroots rather than a top-down approach. This is to say that all Jews must engage in social justice thinking and activism and that all must make their own informed choices on how to proceed. Just as I believe all Jews should be engaged with ritual commitments, so too must be they be engaged in the pressing moral issues of our time.

I would like to humbly offer a *bracha* (blessing) to all my readers, that you continue to search for the true voice of your calling to improve the world and stay focused and earnest in pursuing those goals to create the change that is so sorely needed in our world.

GRATITUDE

THIS BOOK COULD NOT HAVE BEEN WRITTEN without the core support of family, friends, teachers, mentors, colleagues, and supporters.

I am very thankful to Urim Publications, in particular Tzvi Mauer, for enabling me to publish this book.

I am in gratitude to those who have offered ideas and helped in the editing of articles over the years such as Batsheva Pomerantz, Dr. Peter Geidel, Ze'ev Sudry, Shlomo Bolts, Ari Siegel, Jonathan Henkin and Abraham J. Frost.

I feel so fortunate to have so many intellectual, spiritual, and activist partners who give me strength and inspiration to continue to work each day for a more just world.

Nothing would have been possible at all without the love and support of my family: my father Stephen Yanklowitz, mother Sandra Yanklowitz, and brother Scott Yanklowitz.

Most importantly, my lovely wife and partner in life, Shoshana Yanklowitz, has provided me more support and inspiration than any person could ask for. I am so deeply fortunate and full of love and gratitude.

I thank the Creator for giving me life, hope, and strength to empower me to share my Torah based upon the Divine word.

☐ THE INNER WORLD
OF SOCIAL JUSTICE

A FLOOR AND NOT A CEILING:
MY RELIGIOUS PRACTICE

TWO MOMENTS DURING MY EARLY TWENTIES stand out, each enlivened by religious sensibilities. The first moment occurred in the middle of an African desert, when a tribal chief said that the Israelites serve as a "light in the world." After that, while I volunteered in small villages around the world by day, I spent my nights reading Jewish books under a lantern. The second moment occurred late one night on a hilltop in Efrat, Israel, where I was studying at a yeshiva: That's where and when I finally let my soul open to Talmudic law. I felt extreme urgency at both moments and in both settings to do more and to be more. Jewish values and community became the foundation of the mission for my public life and personal quest.

These are the values that guide my halachic reasoning: Judaism is neither a science nor an art; it is neither logical nor perfectly beautiful. Judaism is messy, complicated, and incomplete; it provides more questions than answers; it is more of a yearning than a finding. Halacha is a floor and not a ceiling. Ironically, Jewish law helps me to fly – frees me rather than confines me, inspires me rather than weighs me down. Rather than restrict me, the laws of Shabbat enable me to carve out time for prayer, meditation, reflection, conversation, and learning like no other time in my week.

I also embrace Jewish values beyond Jewish law in a very serious way. For example, on our wedding day, my wife and I chose to become kosher vegans. The tradition inspired us but didn't mandate this life choice. Obeying my conscience is a crucial part of my attempt to fear and serve God.

Rabbi Moshe ben Nahman, known as the Ramban (Nahmanides), a thirteenth century Spanish scholar, explains that it takes more than halachic observance to live a holy life. He suggests that one could keep every minutiae of Halacha and yet live an unholy life. For example, one could follow the laws governing the relations between husband and wife and yet treat one's spouse disrespectfully. And while one could observe the laws of *kashrut* and eat meat, one could still eat unethically. Ramban explains that we can become an abomination with the permission of the Torah (*naval b'reshut ha-Torah*). To live with holiness, then, we must go above the requirements of the Torah (*she-ni'hi'yeh perushim min ha-mutarot*).

Some things have come easy for me, such as making autonomous moral decisions. My early education and family challenged me to think for myself. While my theology is complex, my faith in God — an early gift from my parents — remains simple. Other aspects of my adopted religious life have been more challenging. Most days, I am more in love with God and Torah than I am with the Jewish people. My struggle with *ahavat Yisrael* (love for the Jewish people) has been a weight on my heart.

One of my primary religious goals is to strengthen and deepen my internal world in order to address more deeply the messiness of the outer world. For me, this is primarily done through *tefillah* (prayer), *hitbodedut* (isolated meditation), *Talmud Torah* (learning and challenging myself intellectually and personally to think and feel more deeply), and *mitzvot* (mindful traditional Jewish observance). Deepening my connection to God, my community, and my inner self cultivates my approach to social justice work. This is my "calling" – to help the most vulnerable by making society more just, fair, and holy.

I've changed a lot over the last decade. I have taken more ownership of the tradition. While Orthodoxy often poses barriers to taking ownership, the more "Open Orthodoxy" charges us all to learn and encourages us to develop confidence in our own interpretations of texts and tradition. I am inspired by the relevance and urgency of our tradition. I feel called each day to serve, give, and reflect. I've been told I have an "intense" and "urgent" personality; this may be the result of the religious choices I have made. □

AN APPROACH TO SOCIAL JUSTICE

I WALKED UP TO NELSON MANDELA'S FORMER prison cell on Robben Island (just off the coast of Cape Town, South Africa) wondering what I would feel. Mandela, due to his political and ethical convictions, was locked away for decades. Somehow, after all that pain and sorrow, he kept faith in mankind. He writes in his autobiography:

> Because of the courage of the ordinary men and women of my country, I always knew that deep down in every human heart, there is mercy and generosity. No one is born hating another person because of the color of his skin, or his background, or his religion. People must learn to hate, and if they can learn to hate, they can be taught to love, for love comes more naturally to the human heart than its opposite. Even in the grimmest times in prison, when my comrades and I were pushed to our limits, I would see a glimmer of humanity in one of the guards, perhaps just for a second, but it was enough to reassure me and keep me going. Man's goodness is a flame that can be hidden but never extinguished (*Long Walk to Freedom*, 457).

A commitment to social justice consists precisely of this optimism: that no matter how dark times get, we see the dignity and potential in every human being. All individuals have rights and obligations. In times of despair, a people can only look toward their personal and national self-interest, but this leads to greater universal tragedy. It is in the most trying times that we must especially remember the other.

Social Justice – a Jewish Ethic

Defending the vulnerable is a core Jewish value which draws upon our highest values and laws such as *pikuah nefesh* (saving the life of another), *Kiddush*

Hashem (sanctifying the Name of God in public), and loving the stranger. "God upholds the cause of the orphan and the widow, and befriends the stranger, providing him with food and clothing. You too must befriend the stranger, for you were strangers in the land of Egypt" (Deuteronomy 10:18–19). Ibn Ezra teaches the extent of our collective responsibility: "Do not oppress . . . for anyone who sees a person oppressing an orphan or a widow and does not come to their aid, they will also be considered oppressors." We must intervene and emulate God (*halachta b'drachav*) and be compassionate in all of our ways. But this cannot stop at *hesed* (one time acts of kindness) and must enter in the realm of *tzedek* (systemic change). We must get to the root of problems if we truly wish to have a lasting impact.

Based on the verse Leviticus 25:35 that we must "strengthen him" (the one who has stumbled), Rashi teaches: "Do not wait until he has gone down and fallen, because it will be difficult to raise him up. Instead, strengthen him at the time where his hand is slipping. What is this like? To a load upon a donkey. When it is still on the donkey, one can support it and make it stand. Once it falls to the ground, even five cannot make it stand." Rashi is teaching that we must embrace preventive justice attacking the root cause of social ills ensuring a society that is just for all. Further, Rashi teaches that this is not only the most moral path but also the most cost effective.

The Jewish community has apparently integrated values of social justice into its very being. The Nathan Cummings 2012 Jewish Values Survey asked American Jews how important Jewish values are. The core findings include in Table 1.

The number of Orthodox participants was less than ten percent, representative of their numbers in Jewish America. From this survey, it is unclear what the numbers were for the Orthodox community. Anecdotal evidence suggests that it would be less than for that of the Jewish community, and to fill that gap is why Uri L'Tzedek and an Orthodox social justice movement needed to be founded.

Social Justice – an Orthodox Jewish Ethic?

Uri L'Tzedek, the Orthodox Social Justice movement, was founded to apply the wisdom of Jewish law and values to the most pressing moral issues of our time based on the premise that observant Jews have unique obligations toward the vulnerable (poor, sick, abused, oppressed, alienated). The Torah prioritizes the language of obligation to the language of rights to ensure

Statement	Somewhat/Very Important (percent)
The pursuit of *tzedek*	84
Caring for the widow and orphan	80
Tikkun olam	72
Welcoming the stranger	72
Political beliefs and activities are informed by a belief that every person is made in the image of God	55
A commitment to social equality is most important for Jewish identity	46

Table 1

that we are all empowered as agents of responsibility. The Orthodox community has an enviable commitment to Jewish life, Torah study, prayer attendance, and *mitzvah* observance. Religious idealism (messianic fervor, perhaps) is matched by the pragmatic charge to daily ethical leadership. The Orthodox community is a natural and fitting home for social justice leadership because of its commitment to consistent ritual practice. This consistency allows for the structure and reflective space that empowers the activation of values learned through rituals. Leon Wieseltier writes about a child who walks onto a stage. If the child does not have lyrics, he or she will spend energy thinking of the words. If the words are set, the child can focus on singing as best as possible. When ritual is set, we can sing in life better. Psychologists have shown that when children have a large backyard without fences to play in, they play in only a small section, but when there is a fence, they play in much more of the backyard. Structure and foundation provides us stability, and thus courage.

This combination of factors – Jewish law and values, commitment to *mitzvah* observance, strong ritual and structure, religious idealism – has practical relevance regarding how to build a religious social justice movement. The Orthodox social justice movement begins by building on our strong commitment to our obligations *bein adam la'Makom*, which serves as a foundation to actualize our ethical commitments of *bein adam l'havero*.

But it goes further, ensuring that those prior commitments become a foundation for service on the level of *bein adam la'kehilla* (between the person and the community) and *bein adam la'olam* (between the person and the rest of the world).

Indeed, Jewish tradition understands that God, on some level, is at the center of social change, yet the burden is upon us to humans to enact that change. We need not perfectly understand the nature of the world to fully throw ourselves into creating change. Rabbi Jonathan Sacks explains this point well:

> If we were able to see how evil today leads to good tomorrow – if we were able to see from the point of view of God, creator of all – we would understand justice but *at the cost of ceasing to be human.* We would accept all, vindicate all, and become deaf to the cries of those in pain. God does not want us to cease to be human, for if he did, he would not have created us. We are not God. We will never see things from his perspective. The attempt to do so is an abdication of the human situation. My teacher, Rabbi Nahum Rabinovitch, taught me that this is how to understand the moment when Moses first encountered God at the burning bush. "Moses hid his face because he was afraid to look at God" (Exodus 3:6). Why was he afraid? Because if he were fully to understand he would have no choice but to be reconciled to the slavery and oppression of the world. From the vantage point of eternity, he would see that the bad is a necessary stage on the journey to the good. He would understand God but he would cease to be Moses, the fighter against injustice who intervened whenever he saw wrong being done. "He was afraid" that seeing heaven would desensitize him to earth, that coming close to infinity would mean losing his humanity. That is why God chose Moses, and why He taught Abraham to pray (*To Heal a Fractured World*, 22–23).

Challenges Facing Orthodox Social Justice

While the opportunities for a powerful Orthodox Social Justice movement are immense, there are also barriers:

- The observant community often values study over action. While this yields a great commitment to Torah scholarship, it tends to create a vacuum in change leadership.

- The Orthodox community, and particularly its more right-wing segment, tends to suffer from a parochialism and insularity that comes from the historical experience freshly emphasized in the traditional mind. The Orthodox community focuses heavily of protecting, tending to, and taking care of its own needs. Even when broadened, those needs extend to other members of the Jewish community.
- The insularity is often connected to a general conservatism, one of whose markers is a trend toward preservation of the past and stagnant thinking.
- The top-down power structures in rabbinic authority also at times perpetuates a culture of disempowerment and a lack of critical autonomous thinking.
- Committing to live an observant life and to have one's children educated in the day school system requires a tremendous amount of time and resources, which leaves little for other types of commitments.

As a religious global citizen, it is not enough to seek mere personal piety. That commitment must be converted into altruism. We must zoom out of the minutiae and see the bigger picture. A personal example, which was transformative for me, exemplifies this challenge.

A few years ago, I led a Yeshiva University service-learning volunteer trip to rural Thailand through the American Jewish World Service. A few days into the trip, the students were informed that there was going to be an anti-HIV parade in the village. The custom is for adults to serve as educators and models by wearing costumes that promote safe sex through the use of condoms. Some of the YU students approached me and asked whether or not it was appropriate for them to wear these outfits as the village leaders requested. I told them it was up to them to decide on their own, based upon their values and comfort levels. Two or three of the students decided that since HIV was such a rampant problem in this developing country, it was appropriate for them to take part in this educational initiative. What they didn't expect was to return back to their campus with pictures of them posted on classroom doors demeaning their experiences and articles questioning whether they should have been serving "idolaters" in the first place. The response shook me at the core. These students bravely went beyond their comfort zones to serve others and their yeshiva peers mocked (and some faculty reportedly condemned) their service. It was one of many experiences I have had that reminded me how much courage it takes to be an

Orthodox social justice activist swimming against a stream of complacency and insularity.

While the Orthodox social justice movement has learned much from other social justice organizations and continues to have much to learn from their decades of experience, much has also been learned from the pedagogical approaches of the well-established traditional Orthodox institutions. While the explicit existence of the organization is very new, the ethos of the movement is with Avraham, who was chosen because of his commitment *laasot tzedaka u'mishpat* (to do justice and righteousness). It stands to argue that if this was the rationale for God's choice of Avraham, then this value of justice and righteousness is the Jewish people's *raison d'etre* – to be the global leaders in fighting for justice. While the Jewish people have often been disempowered to stand on the front lines for change, there are new opportunities provided by our return to our homeland and the establishment of a nation on Jewish principles. Our newfound power must be exercised not only to provide security for the Jewish people, but to serve as a platform to create a more just world based on Jewish principles and ideals.

Study Can Interfere with Action

Sometimes study can get in the way. The Rabbis concluded that "Study is greater because it leads to action" (*Kiddushin* 40b). Today, unfortunately, study sometimes actually *impedes* action. Sometimes, when the study of Torah is done wrong, it prevents necessary action rather than enabling it. Rav Aharon Lichtenstein (the *Rosh Yeshiva* in Yeshivat Har Etzion) writes powerfully about an experience that influenced his perspective on balancing learning with action:

> A couple of years after we moved to *Yerushalyim*, I was once walking with my family in the *Beit Yisrael* neighborhood . . . We came to a corner, and found a merchant stuck there with his car. The question came up as to how to help him; it was a clear case of *perika u-te'ina* (helping one load or unload his burden). There were some youngsters there from the neighborhood, who judging by their looks, were probably ten or eleven years old. They saw that this merchant was not wearing a *kippa*. So they began a whole *pilpul*, based on the *gemara* in *Pesahim* (113b), about whether they should help him or not. They said, "If he walks about bareheaded, presumably he doesn't separate *terumot*

u-maasrot, so he is suspect of eating and selling untithed produce . . ." I wrote R. Soloveitchik a letter at that time, and told him of the incident. I ended with the comment, "Children of the age from our camp would not have known the *gemara*, but they would have helped him." My feeling then was: Why, Ribbono shel Olam, must this be our choice? Can't we find children who would have helped him and still know the *gemara*? Do we have to choose? I hope not; I believe not. If forced to choose, however, I would have no doubts where my loyalties lie: I prefer that they know less *gemara* but help him (*By His Light*, 249).

Thus, Rav Aharon teaches that when we do not act instinctively on our values, our Torah education has failed us. We have not cultivated a truly religious personality. The purpose of our learning is helping to develop the right instincts based upon our cherished values. Learning Torah and internalizing our cherished values properly should ensure that we are public exemplars at home and in the streets. The paradigmatic case of *hillul Hashem* (desecration of God's Name) is in the financial realm (*Yoma* 86a), since this classically is the main realm where Jews would interact with non-Jews and thus convey their values and integrity. Religion is truly lived in the streets, not in the sanctuary. It is at work, in the checkout line, and in our leisure time where we put our values into practice. It is about how we vote, what we buy, and how we spend our free time.

The Jewish tradition is full of values and laws concerned with justice and we must bring integrity and rigor into that learning and appropriation process. If we wish to take a position and understand that Torah is meant to be lived and internalized with a subjective experience, then we need to leave our insular worlds and experience the suffering of others. The story is told by the Baal HaTanya who heard a baby cry in the house. When he went to soothe the infant, he noticed his grandson still deeply engrossed in study. "Why did you not go to soothe the child?" asked the Rebbe. His son responded, "I was so deeply engrossed in my learning that I did not even hear the child." The Rebbe retorted, "If the cry of another does not cause you to pause in your learning, then your Torah is null and void." Religious life is not a naïve intellectual exercise. It requires engagement with the world and a deep responsiveness to the suffering of others. This experience will look different for each of us as we will be surrounded by and called toward different social justice responsibilities. Thus, we must further a respectful and sophisticated discourse around the plurality of our values, commitments, and experiences. □

JUSTICE IN THIS WORLD

Where do we look for justice?

The *Kitzur Shulhan Aruch*, the nineteenth century work of Jewish law by Rabbi Shlomo Ganzfried, teaches that "it is prohibited for a person to appeal for judgment from Heaven (i.e., Divine retribution) against his fellow who wronged him. This prohibition applies only if he has recourse to attain justice here on earth. And anyone who cries out to Heaven about his fellow, he is punished first" (29:14).

The lesson we take from this law is that while it is true that there is an ultimate judge after this life, it's during this life that we must do the hard work to make peace and pursue justice. Throughout history, there were times where we had no access to fair procedural justice, but today we live in a different era. We have religious courts, secular courts, and effective grassroots justice potential.

However, there are times when even wise people in authority make the wrong decision. There is a tragic Talmudic episode where the sages decreed after the destruction of the Temple that Jews should no longer marry, since it was the end of the Jewish people. The people, however, ignored this decree and were insistent on continuing to build their families (*Bava Batra* 60b).

There are other times when we must defy decrees because they do not represent true justice. The Talmud tells a story about how Moses's sister, Miriam, convinced their father, Amram, to have children with her mother, Yocheved, in spite of Pharaoh's decree that all Hebrew male children were to be killed at birth. Amram had insisted that they should have no more children to avoid more death. However, Miriam rebuked him, saying that even worse than Pharoah's decree was a decree that children should not be given life at all (*Sotah* 12a). The government was extremely unjust, and the Hebrews were determined to win out in this world over that injustice. This concept was expressed in the modern era by Henry David Thoreau, in his 1849 essay on civil disobedience, who writes that if injustice "is of such a nature that it requires you to be the agent of injustice to another, then I say, break the law." From Mohandas Gandhi's campaign for Indian independence to civil rights struggles in the United States, millions have been stirred by this idea in the fight for social justice.

In the United States, tolerance for racial segregation was the law of the land for over fifty years starting in 1896. During the last century, courageous people on multiple levels, from lawyers working within the system to nonviolent demonstrators who were arrested, beaten, and even murdered, worked to change the law. The Civil Rights Act of 1964 and the Voting Rights Act of 1965 eradicated many of the obvious abuses; however, the 2012 election, in which voters in predominantly black and minority areas had to wait up to eight hours to vote due to state government efforts to discourage them from voting, illustrates that the struggle is far from over. In President Obama's 2013 State of the Union address, he cited the case of Desiline Victor, a 102-year old black woman from North Miami, Florida, who endured a wait of six hours to vote in 2012, and then proudly wore a sticker that said, "I Voted." She attended the President's address and received a standing ovation for her determination to stand up for justice. Today, we look to our government to uphold the right of all Americans to vote, but we reserve the right to challenge a government that does not respond to demands for justice.

The "Torah is not in heaven" (*Torah lo ba'shamayim hi*), and the sages taught that we must accept human responsibility for law and ethics in our lives (*Bava Metzia* 59b). When the Hebrews arrived at the sea, there were four choices: 1) Go back and become slaves again; 2) fight; 3) commit mass suicide; or 4) pray to God for salvation. None of these were the right answer; Nahshon ben Aminadav's response, "Go forward, into the sea!" was the right one. From God's response to the Hebrews' prayers, "Why do you cry out to me?" (Exodus 14:15), we see that this was not the right course, and we learn the important lesson that we must take human responsibility and go forth with courage.

We take responsibility and pray for strength from our Creator, but we do not cry out to God for justice. We must take issues of justice to our religious courts and secular courts, we organize on a grassroots level for change, and we do the hard intellectual and spiritual work to take courageous responsibility for injustice in our society. Sometimes that is in line with law and sometimes it is acting against the legal system. In either case, pursuing justice in this world today is the value that triumphs.

Toward a Brighter Future

It is all too easy to neglect global suffering when it is remote. The eighteenth century Scottish philosopher David Hume once suggested that individuals care more about a pain in their finger than about the loss of a life on the other side of the planet. Suffering and injustice become erased from our consciousness when it is not right before our eyes. Elie Wiesel, in a speech in 1986, said: "The opposite of love is not hate, it's indifference. The opposite of faith is not heresy, it's indifference. And, the opposite of life is not death, it's indifference. Because of indifference one dies before one actually dies" (*US News & World Report*). The prophetic voice and *halachic* mandate do not allow us to retreat from responsibility.

Rambam (Maimonides), the twelfth century philosopher, writes that cynicism is the antithesis of the religious impulse. He explains that we must ultimately view every life choice as if our choice will tip the scale of the salvation of the world or the destruction of the world one way or another (*Hilchot Teshuva,* his work dealing with Rosh Hashanah and repentance). There is no room for cynicism or disengagement if the world and fate of all humanity rests upon our shoulders.

For years, I was the only observant Jew struggling to pray, keep kosher, observe Shabbat, and continue learning Torah on my own during service missions abroad. It was always lonely in the desert with my Gemara and shovel. Today, we have a growing culture of young observant Jews committed to creating grassroots change in society to better protect the vulnerable and attack injustice. We have many more obstacles to overcome but I remain very hopeful that the next generation of Orthodoxy will see social justice activism as a top fulfillment of the Torah's calling.   □

PASSION, POWER, AND PARTNERSHIP

We are commanded to save the life of a non-Jew and to save him from harm, that if he was drowning in a river or if a stone fell upon him, then we must use all of our strength and be burdened with saving him and if he was sick, we engage to heal him.
                  — Ramban (notes on *Sefer HaMitzvot*, Mitzvah 17)

Introduction

I CAN RECALL THE RESTLESS NIGHTS OF MY FIRST job! Upon completing college and just prior to starting rabbinical school, I worked as a corporate consultant, advising employees on their benefits packages. Frantically, many would call struggling to make ends meet as they needed to choose their health insurance packages. Every choice had serious risks and potential for immediate costs. Confined by my role and tools from my corporate training, I felt restrained in sharing my empathy and spiritual concern. While I knew that I was making a contribution to these workers, I was aware that much more needed to be done. I needed to step back to reflect upon my career path and my life directions based upon my interests, skills, and capacity for influence. Should I rise in the corporate ranks in order to increase my worth and donate more to those in need? Should I spend two years in developing towns volunteering? Should I become an educator? In the past, I may have been more inclined to look toward family, authority figures, and mentors to answer these difficult questions for me. Now, I realized that as an adult I needed to take ownership of this existential dilemma of how best to make my positive mark in the world. "*U'vacharta ba'haim!*" (Choose Life!, Deuteronomy 30:19): I recalled the Jewish responsibility of autonomy in selecting one's moral mission and calling. *Aharayut* (responsibility) comes from the root "*aher*" (other). To take responsibility means to cultivate the "ability" for "response" to another. This responsibility to another is born in the moment when no one else is present to assist. As Hillel said: "In a place where there is not someone (of moral courage taking responsibility), strive to be that person," (*Pirke Avot* 2:6, *"u'vi'makom sh'ain anashim hishtadail li'hiyot ish."*) The Rabbis learned this lesson from Moses's moral interventions of speaking up and rescuing innocent individuals who were attacked (Exodus 2:12–17). One must ask oneself: What positions in life am I in and what special points of access do I have that make me uniquely responsible and uniquely capable of giving? In my search, I found Ramban's argument, quoted above, to be a compelling and persuasive argument: One must give all of one's strength according to one's unique positioning in the world. It is my contention that to actualize one's potential and to fulfill one's Jewish duties, one should address three central issues: identify one's core passions, build upon one's power base, and cultivate partnerships for success.

Passion

David Hume famously argues that "it is not contrary to reason to prefer the destruction of the whole world to the scratching of my finger," and the "sympathy with persons remote from us is much fainter than with persons near and contiguous" (*A Treatise of Human Nature*, 2:128). In an age where apathy to the most pressing global issues of our age can, at times, almost seem to be sanctioned; there is a tremendous shortage of justice seekers who are radical passionate visionaries like our previous civil rights leaders (Martin Luther King, Rosa Parks, Heschel). More than we need perfectly measured giving, we need more radically inspired activism and community service where enflamed souls pour their love, tears, sweat, and resources into making systemic and immediate change possible thus fulfilling the mandate of the *Shema* to give according to all of one's resources *("uvchol meodecha")*. The Jewish people were born with the mission of being the guarders of justice. God came to love and choose Abraham because he and his children *"Shamru derech Hashem laasot tzedakah u'mishpat"* (Genesis 18:19, the Jewish people followed God's ways as guards for justice). Maimonides explains the virtues of excess in one's ethical pursuits:

> The *hasid* is the wise man who has inclined somewhat to an extreme in his ethical attributes . . . and his deeds are greater than his wisdom. Therefore he is called a *hasid*, in the sense of excess, because exaggeration in a matter is called *hesed* . . . (Commentary on *Pirke Avot* 5:6).

A personal calling to one's choice of *tzedek* mission (justice work) as inspiration cannot be inherited. In addition to seeking and invigorating one's general commitments to altruism, human rights, and activism, one is charged to find her or his unique passions to pursue in contributing to the world. When young people are demanding their autonomy, determined to make a difference, authorities can no longer answer the moral dilemmas of triage nor can outdated programs be thrown at our community of young professionals. The options for social justice and action that one embarks upon can neither be calculated by some consequential science nor by any religious dogma. Rather, one whose heart is stirred to make life better for others should follow one's conscience and reasoning as to how to assist and should join communities that are striving in similar ways to improve society. Creating open spaces of discourse around how our narratives and identities can inspire responsibility enables enthusiasm to emerge and commitments to be owned. In order to ensure sustainability in this work, one's choices of projects and commitments to improve the lives of others should feel right and should speak to one's soul.

Power

As we saw earlier, Ramban argues that when a life circumstance puts one in a position of influence, one is obligated to use that power to save others. The *Shulhan Aruch,* the great sixteenth century Jewish legal authority, even ruled that one must "expose oneself to possible danger (*safek sakanah*) to save a human life" (*Hilchot Rotzeah, Kesef Mishnah; Hoshen Mishpat 426, Beit Yosef*). Rabbi Shlomo Zalman Auerbach argued:

> In relation to the obligation to pay the costs of saving the life of a sick person who is in danger of dying: From the straightforward reading of *Sanhedrin* 73a, we see that one is obligated to do everything to save him, and if not, one transgresses the negative commandment: "Do not stand idly by the blood of your neighbor" (*Leviticus 19:16 in Minhat Shlomo*, Volume 2, 86).

The central problem is that each of us must operate within the limited resources of time, money, location, and relationships and we tragically can't help everyone. Given these limitations, in our attempts to make the world a more just, safe, moral, and holy place, who are the needy that we prioritize and what methods are most appropriate to do that work? When considering the amount of people in the world who need our help, we can't help but be overwhelmed.

While emphasizing the styles of social action that affect the most change we should also promote multiple methods to cater to the various careers that our diverse Jewish population chooses to embark upon. Many choose to serve as great philanthropists, some as community organizers and lobbyists, while others have chosen careers to work directly with those who are in need as social workers, educators, or rabbis. We must encourage all of these options to build our power base of partnership while adhering to the famous Jewish education principle of "*hanoch la-naar al pi darko*" (*Proverbs 22:6*) – *education based on the path of the particular student.*

After identifying one's core values and concerns, one must learn to actualize one's spheres of influence and skills in the most effective way possible. If one is well connected to power, to wealth, or with certain knowledge, then that should be accounted for in their unique decision-making process. In addition to an assessment of self, being in touch with one's environment and capabilities in that environment ensures that one can respond to crises in the most precise moment of need. At times one is placed in a situation of power and has no opportunity to postpone action. The Rabbis teach in Tractate *Taanit* 21a:

> A poor man came and stood before me on the road, and said to me: "My teacher, sustain me (give me something to eat)!" I responded to him: "Wait until I unload some food from the donkey." I did not have a chance to unload the donkey before his soul departed (he died of hunger). I went and fell on my face (fell into depression based on my insensitivity at having not prevented this man's death at the chance I was given)

We are all confronted with theses chances! But sometimes, even our decisions with the best intentions don't necessarily have the greatest effect. Peter Singer, as a moral consequentialist, has demanded a life of asceticism in which one donates all that is beyond one's basic needs. I would argue that this is likely not a lifestyle that affects the most change in the long-run. It does not enable the dynamism of sustainable giving or the more eclectic possibilities for ways in which one can contribute. Financial contribution is only one way to fuel social change in addition to the giving of time, social entrepreneurship, political influence, and education. While donating the high majority of one's income and wealth as Singer has advocated seems religiously and philosophically pious, it cannot be done at the expense of creating more change in other necessary ways. A CEO may, in fact, be able to create more significant change by being persuaded to reform her company labor practices than she could by merely writing a check. Power dynamics are laden in every relationship, as explored in the thought of Michel Foucault, and one should take a holistic power analysis to assess where they can best use their influence for positive social change.

Partnership

One can best contribute where one has the most potential for influence and where one has the most passion to make a difference. However we cannot go at it alone. This work cannot succeed as an individual cavalier journey but rather in partnership with one's own community, the affected population, co-religionists, and experts. Being in face-to-face relationship with others is a necessary element of working for social change. With limited time and resources to contribute, one should ensure at a minimum that one remains in personal relationship with the population to be helped and understands their needs on their terms own terms. Seeking partnership, however, does not preclude justification for self-interest. Rabbi Joseph B. Soloveitchik (The Rav), the great twentieth century Jewish philosopher and Talmudist, argues:

> What one is longing for is his own self-fulfillment, which he believes he will find in his union with the other person. The emotion leaves its inner abode in order to find not the "you" but the "I." . . . It only indicates that, because of self-interest, the person is committed to a state of mind which, regardless of one's self-centeredness, promotes goodwill and unites people (*Out of the Whirlwind*, A Theory of Emotions, 200).

Self interest, concomitant to a desire to create good, should not be condemned.

In addition to supporting one another, there is a mandate to challenge one another. The Rabbis expected that we would hold others in our sacred communities accountable for our collective responsibility. The Talmud says in Tractate *Shabbat* 54b:

Whoever has the power to protest against members of his household but does not protest is punished for the transgressions of the members of his household. Against the people of his town, but does not, is punished for the deeds of those in his town. Against the entire world, and does not, is punished for the deeds of the entire world.

Jewish ethics is, of course, not only about avoiding wrongs. Rather we have a greater mandate to go beyond the ethics of "do no harm" and to actually repair the world from its brokenness. We are even to "protest" when another is not actualizing their potential. Encouraging growth for those in our communities and setting positive examples is a vital part of the Jewish moral enterprise and creating a vibrant just society.

The Torah seems to make *Talmud Torah*, the study of Torah, a pinnacle responsibility for Jews and yet addressing community needs is considered to have an equal weight (*Shulhan Aruch* 93:4). In addition to our high educational standards and intellectual rigor, challenging one another to higher commitments to justice, charity, service, volunteering, and interpersonal ethics is what makes our Jewish education matter. The Rabbis explain in Tractate *Taanit* 11a that one cannot be content and comfortable when there is suffering that exists:

> At a time when the community is steeped in distress, a person should not say: "I will go to my house and eat and drink and peace be upon you, my soul."

In the United State, over forty-seven million people don't have access to medical insurance. We live in a world where over two billion, out of a global population of six billion (one-third of the world population), live on less than $2 a day. Poverty, AIDS, war, and genocide are spreading throughout various regions of the world and there is too much at stake to live or work in solitude. The Jewish community, amidst all of our differences, must unite to address these pressing issues.

Conclusion

To make the greatest contribution, one must take a *heshbon hanefesh* (self-accounting) of one's spheres of influence and one's personal calling. Acting on issues one is most passionate about while contributing where one has the most potential for influence will likely ensure the greatest sustainability for the giver and the highest societal contribution. To be sure, there are traditional basic minimum prescriptions for *tzedakah*, core responsibilities to family and community, and hierarchies of Jewish values. Rabbi Moshe Sofer, the early nineteenth century author of the *Hatam Sofer*, however, maintains that a very great need overrides the traditional hierarchy of priorities altogether (Hatam Sofer, *Yoreh Deah* 234). Rav Yechiel Michel Epstein (the nineteenth century thinker and author of the *Aruch HaShulhan*) was even more explicit arguing that everyone must give to poor people, not only their relatives and neighbors:

> There is something about this that is very difficult for me because if we understand these words literally – that some groups take priority over others – that implies that there is no requirement to give to groups lower on the hierarchy. And it is well known that every wealthy person has many poor relatives (and all the more so every poor person), so it will happen that a poor person without any rich relatives will die of hunger. And how could this possibly be? So it seems clear to me that the correct interpretation is that everyone, whether rich or poor, must also give to poor people who are not relatives. . . . (*Aruch HaShulhan, Yoreh Deah* 151:4).

We will find no adequate absolute prescriptions that help us to choose between lending our efforts to the dispersed in Darfur or to fighting malaria, the uncared-for elderly or for the malnourished newborn, to immediate disaster relief or to sustainable development, to those lacking health care or by contributing to AIDS research. This said, beginning to take a power analysis, to assess one's skill set, and to identify one's core convictions will put one on a path to make the right choices of where to contribute and to organize power through diverse partnerships. The Rabbis taught "*Lo alecha ha-m'lacha ligmor v'lo atah ben horin l'hibatel mi'menah*" (*Pirke Avot* 2:21, Though you are not obliged to finish the task, neither are you free to desist from it). For each individual to actualize their full potential to ensure a world that is repaired with both pragmatic and messianic values, the efficacy of one's work must be measured to ensure that it is making measurable impact. Together as a Jewish community, may we reach new heights in creating measurable change that brings dignity to all human beings and peace to all corners of the earth!   □

MORAL CONSCIENCE
OR ABSOLUTE DUTY?

FOR YEARS, I HAVE BEEN INSPIRED BY THE words of the great Talmudist and Jewish philosopher Rabbi Joseph B. Soloveitchik in his magnum opus, *Halakhic Man*:

> There is nothing so physically and spiritually destructive as diverting one's attention from this world. And, by contrast, how courageous is halakhic man who does not flee from this world, who does not seek to escape to some pure, supernal realm. Halakhic man craves to bring down the divine presence and holiness into the midst of space and time, into the midst of infinite, earthly existence (41).

In my spiritual activism and leadership, I receive tremendous inspiration from the mandate of Jewish commandments and of the eternally ringing voice of God from Sinai, and it is through the lens of the Jewish tradition that I view my deep commitment to synagogue community organizing. Being a traditional Jew does not for a moment exclude me from the larger pluralistic Jewish discourse or the American political discourse on social change and welfare. Thus, I am moved to engage in Congregation-based Community Organizing (CBCO) and its methodologies of one-to-one meetings, house meetings, power analyses, and actions.

While much of my social justice leadership – in organizing, service learning, education, and advocacy – has been among the broader Jewish community where we can flourish among the beautiful collage of Jewish diversity, as an Orthodox rabbi, I must admit that I find tremendous satisfaction and encouragement from facilitating this discourse in the *halachic* community.

One of the great appeals for me when I joined the Orthodox community many years ago was the strong sense of unquestioned duty that members typically embrace. A discourse of law, absolute obligation, and concomitant ethics provide structure to a day of service to God, the Jewish people, and humanity. The questions are most often not "Is there a God?" or "Am I obligated?" but rather "How am I obligated?" and "How can I best fulfill these duties?"

It is precisely for this reason that I feel compelled to work for justice from within Orthodoxy. In a community that is often times so dedicated to text study and yet also sadly passive in social systemic change beyond the parochial, it is my conviction that our sense of duty for laws of ritual must apply with an equal force to laws and ethics of *kavod ha-briot* (honoring all people), *tzelem Elokim* (serving with the consciousness that all people are created in the image of God), and *v'ahavta l're'echa kamocha* (loving another like oneself). This conviction resonates in the practices of community organizing, and also underlies the work I've undertaken with several others in building *Uri L'Tzedek,* the Orthodox Social Justice organization. In our *Tzedek Batei Midrash,* we explore the Bible, Talmud, Rabbis, and philosophers in order to understand the tradition's wisdom on social issues such as immigration and workers' justice. But as *Shammai* teaches, "Make your study of Torah a fixed habit; say little and do much," and so our work seeks to build on the learning transition from rigorous hermeneutics of texts and human narratives to the language of community organizing and social change.

There are times when my personal inspiration and sense of commitment to fighting injustice stems from the core existential self of my raw humanity. Ideally, that fire would always be lit, but I feel blessed that on the days when my conscience simply isn't enough to move me to respond to the call of duty, there is a growing Modern Orthodox community that challenges, supports, and inspires me to engage in this work. At the Yeshivat Chovevei Torah Rabbinical School, I was surrounded by inspirational peers who were trained by Jewish Funds for Justice (now a part of Bend the Arc) in community organizing and who are seeking to walk in God's ways by pursuing justice wherever we are called as rabbis and as humans to act.

Rabbi Soloveitchik later wrote: "The actualization of the ideals of justice and righteousness is the pillar of fire which halakhic man follows, when he, as a rabbi and teacher in Israel, serves his community" (*Halakhic Man*, 91). It is my dream and mission to build my rabbinate around fighting for justice for all people. □

MARTIN LUTHER KING DAY, THE PRESIDENTIAL INAUGURATION, AND A REFLECTION ON CONSCIENCE

ONE OF THE KEY TESTS OF THE QUALITY OF one's faith is whether it moves us to live in accordance with our conscience. Faith cannot cover up our innate moral compass. Rather, it should enhance and refine our spiritual conscience. Our faith should provide us with the fuel to charge forward with what we already know in our essence we must do.

No one in the twentieth century taught this message more powerfully than the Rev. Dr. Martin Luther King, Jr. King taught again and again that we must not be passive, but put our values into practice to create a just society. He even argued that "to accept passively an unjust system is to cooperate with that system." In 2013, Martin Luther King Day coincided with the second inauguration of America's first (and re-elected) black President, Barack Obama, and the President took the oath of office with his hand on King's Bible. To some, this was an affirmation of King's legacy; to others, it was an inappropriate attempt to moderate King's radical vision. Who is correct? Perhaps both sides have evidence to support their case.

Martin Luther King did not begin as a radical. He had earned his doctorate in Boston and became pastor of a church in Montgomery, Alabama. Then in December 1955, Rosa Parks refused to move to the back of a bus there, sparking the Montgomery Bus Boycott. King soon emerged as the leader of the campaign, and established the nonviolent, civil disobedient character of the early civil rights movement, based on his reading of Thoreau and Gandhi. From then until his assassination in April 1968, King was the leading civil rights figure in America, for which in 1964 he was awarded the Nobel Peace Prize. Whenever a new campaign emerged, from the lunch counter sit-ins of 1960, the Freedom Rides of 1961, or the Birmingham civil rights campaign of 1963, King was called on to lend his presence and often risk arrest along with the protesters. Before his death, he had traveled six million miles and given 2,500 speeches for civil rights.

Maintaining faith through such a period would be difficult for anyone. In 1960, after having been arrested five times (eventually, more than twenty times), beaten often, stabbed once, and had his home bombed twice, King reflected on his faith: "I could respond to my situation either to react with bitterness or seek to transform the suffering into a creative force. I decided to follow the latter course." Commenting on the question of "unearned suffering," which has long troubled theologians, King found solace in religion: "I am more convinced than ever before that it is the power of God unto social and individual salvation. . . . The suffering and agonizing moments through which I have passed over the last few years have also drawn me closer to God" (*A Testament of Hope: The Essential Writings of Martin Luther King, Jr.*, 41–42).

Perhaps the most significant event of the entire movement was the "March on Washington," when hundreds of thousands of civil rights advocates gathered in Washington, D.C. on August 28, 1963. On this day, King walked a tightrope, as President John F. Kennedy, fearing the alienation of southern Democrats, tried to dissuade King from having the march, while young activists were upset that King and other leaders had promised there would be no civil disobedience at the march. However, King's "I Have a Dream" speech, one of the most powerful in all of human history, easily eclipsed any controversy that day, and played a huge role in the eventual passage of the Civil Rights Act of 1964. In 1965, King's leadership in the march from Selma to Montgomery, Alabama, interrupted when state troopers trampled and beat hundreds of marchers, helped pass the Voting Rights Act of 1965. (President Lyndon B. Johnson's skill and courage in pushing this bill in spite of the risk of losing southern Democrats should also be acknowledged).

One of the great rabbinical followers of King was Rabbi Abraham Joshua Heschel, who was present at the 1963 rally and marched with King in Selma. Shortly after returning from the march, Heschel wrote to King: "The day we marched together out of Selma was a day of sanctification. That day I hope will never be past to me – that day will continue to be this day. . . . May I add that I have rarely in my life been privileged to hear a sermon as glorious as the one you delivered at the service in Selma prior to the march."

Perhaps the greatest human freedom is the freedom to hear one's inner truth and to strive to live by it. Heschel wrote: "Freedom means more than mere emancipation. It is primarily freedom of conscience, bound up with inner allegiance" (*The Insecurity of Freedom*, 1966).

While King often worked with President Johnson and other white political leaders, he rejected the idea that he was moving "too fast," and increasingly became frustrated at white racism and the government's abandonment of the War on Poverty in favor of the Vietnam War. He began to focus more on economic issues as well. As early as 1964, he wrote: "The Negro is still the poorest American – walled in by color and poverty. The law pronounces him equal, abstractly, but his conditions of life are still far from equal to those of other Americans" ("Negroes Are not Moving too Fast," 177, 180). He called for a "grand alliance of Negro and white" that would seek to eradicate "social evils" such as unemployment, which affected all youth. In April 1967, precisely a year before his assassination, King dramatically broke his political alliance with President Johnson, stated his open opposition to the war in Vietnam, and further advanced his evolving social justice message: "When machines and computers, profit motives, and property rights are considered more important than people, the giant triplets of racism, materialism, and militarism are incapable of being conquered" ("A Time to Break Silence," 240).

The culmination of this campaign was to be the "Poor People's Campaign," a nationwide gathering of poor people who would camp out in Washington until the needs of the poor were met by the federal government. King was prepared to go against all his former political allies in this campaign. However, on the way to Washington, King stopped in Memphis, Tennessee, to help striking garbage collectors gain a fair wage. At this point, he was assassinated on April 4, 1968. While many commemorations today stress the early, seemingly moderate political views of King, his later career shows that he was always pushing for a just society, regardless of the consequences. He still challenges us today: "To end poverty, to extirpate prejudice, to free a tormented conscience, to make a tomorrow of justice, fair play and creativity – all these are worthy of the American ideal" ("Showdown for Nonviolence," 71–72).

The great French philosopher and Talmudist Emmanuel Levinas taught: "The Torah itself is exposed to danger because being itself is nothing but violence, and nothing can be more exposed to violence than the Torah, which says no to it. The Law essentially dwells in the fragile human conscience which protects it badly and where it runs every risk. Those who accept this Law also go from one danger to the next. The story of Haman irritated by Mordecai attests to this danger. But this irresistible weight of being can be shaken only by this incautious conscience" (*Nine Talmudic Readings*, "The Temptation of Temptation," 37).

This is the message of the Jewish tradition, that each day we must embrace ritual, prayer, and meditation that elevates the soul and awakens the human conscience to put our eternal values into practice today and every day. We are grateful as American Jews to have the inspiration of Dr. Martin Luther King as a role model committed to overcoming injustice.   □

THE SHOES WE WEAR: A STATEMENT OF IDENTITY AND VALUES

How beautiful are thy feet in sandals.
> — *Song of Songs* 7:2

I N THE ARGENTINEAN SHANTYTOWN WHERE WE were volunteering, a four-year old boy said he liked my *zapatos* (shoes). Our shoes can reveal much about our socio-economic status, as I have been told many times while traveling in developing countries. While I am always surprised by this, since I think of my shoes as utterly basic, never have I been as affected as I was this time. This boy, was not wearing shoes at the time, and it was unlikely that he would ever wear them, opened up my heart.

Shoes are symbolic in Jewish thought. On Yom Kippur, Tisha B'Av, and during *shiva* (seven days of mourning for an immediate relative), it is prohibited to wear leather shoes. Similarly, Jewish priests (*kohanim*) take their shoes off when they give their Priestly Blessing. Today, some Hassidim still remove their shoes before approaching the gravesite of a holy person. One Talmudic passage even implies that shoes are more important than a home: "A person should sell the roof beams of his house to buy shoes for his feet" (*Shabbat* 129a). Shoes contribute to our basic sense of human dignity: Rabbi Akiva instructed his son Joshua never to go barefoot.

The most famous biblical stories about shoes are about the importance of removing them before God. Joshua encounters an angel of God, and the angel tells him to take off his shoes, since he is standing on holy ground (Joshua 5:13–15). We see the same behavior with Moses at the burning bush

(Exodus 3:5). The head of a synagogue in India where I spent Pesach a few years ago told me that they do not wear shoes in the synagogue because of the latter story. There is a humility that comes with being shoeless. As one's skin touches the earth, one can feel the frailty of one's humanity. Seeing the dirt upon one's toes is a reminder of our inevitable return to that earth.

Personally, when I enter a home, especially my own, I always take off my shoes. It is a sign that I feel that I am in a special place. Home is a place where I have a lower voice, speak more intimately, and open myself up. Taking my shoes off is an expression to all that I have removed myself from the chaotic and tough outside world and have entered a more soft and humble mode of being.

There is an ancient Jewish practice called *halitza*, in which a woman whose husband has died is absolved from the obligation to marry his brother by pulling the shoe off his foot and spitting in his face (Deuteronomy 25:5–10). This is meant to shame him for not taking responsibility for her. Shoes represent power, and to remove another's shoe is to humble him. There are many parallels in other cultures, such as Cinderella's glass slipper, which wins her the hand of the Prince, or Dorothy's ruby slippers in *The Wizard of Oz*, whose magical power is to resist the attempt of the Wicked Witch of the West to seize them, and later return Dorothy to Kansas.

The *halitza* ceremony also reminds us that shoes for many are symbolic of suffering. Millions have suffered and continue to suffer from the practice of foot binding, an incredibly painful and debilitating custom in which a young girl's feet are broken in multiple places (four toes are folded under the foot until they break, and the arch is broken to shorten its length to about 3 inches), and then maintained by binding the feet with cloth. In spite of opposition from the Manchu dynasty and the Nationalist (Kuomintang) government, the practice persisted until 1949, when the Communist government finally stopped foot binding for young girls. However, many women age sixty and older still keep their feet bound, as the process of allowing the foot to grow would involve further bone breaks and pain, and because some are loyal to the old ways. We should not encourage anyone, especially women, to inflict such pain in the pursuit of a perverted sense of the erotic.

Some have begun to address the importance of the shoes we wear. Toms Shoes, a shoe company based in Santa Monica, CA, will donate a pair of new shoes to a child in need for every pair of shoes you buy from them. Of course, with millions more wearing shoes, the issue of killing more animals to get the leather for shoes also becomes an issue for many. As a result, there is now also a whole industry of vegan shoes. Finally, there is even a shoe museum in Toronto, which my wife Shoshana and I had the pleasure of visiting, dedicated to the history of shoes. On a more serious note, we stand in awed reverence and deep introspection when we gaze upon the discarded shoes at Yad Vashem and the US Holocaust Museum.

When I was in Senegal, a young boy named Mamadou was persistent that I repair my shoe after it tore. I would have discarded these shoes, but Mamadou taught me about the importance of valuing the shoes I own. It is said that the Kotzker Rebbe used to wrap up his worn-out shoes before throwing them away and saying, "How can I simply toss away a pair of shoes that have served me so well over the course of years." He understood that there was almost a holiness to something so basic that has enabled us to be mobile and fulfill our life missions. As Forrest Gump famously said about his shoes, "They were my magic shoes, they would take me anywhere." Shoes truly are a magical blessing.

We take shoes for granted, but in many societies shoes are a luxury, and have symbolic significance. The *Shulhan Aruch*, the great Jewish code of law, lays out the order of how shoes are to be put on and taken off. This is not just purposeless legal minutiae. Rather, it is a way of reminding us, every time we put our shoes on or take them off, just how blessed we are. The Rabbis teach that one should say the blessing "Blessed are You Who has provided me my every need" when putting on shoes, and thus Rashi explains that there is nothing more degrading than walking barefoot in public (*Shabbat* 129a). An act as simple as putting our shoes on can remind us of human and animal suffering, inspire us toward humility, help us to transition to a more personal space, and remind us of our countless blessings. □

BECOME AN INSPIRATION ADDICT

I N MY SENIOR YEAR OF HIGH SCHOOL, I DRANK the juice of inspiration, and all of a sudden everything in the world started to matter. I used to think inspiration could be found anywhere, but I learned there are indeed bad books, pointless movies, and invites worth turning down. These comprise the "cold zone." They take energy from you, as compared with the "hot zone" – people and activities that you leave with more energy. Our task is to fine-tune our spiritual antennae to detect the hot zones that charge us.

Our end goal is not to be perfectly rested or on an artificial high. The goal of the inspiration addict is that we can do good works, pour out positive energy, and give inspiration wherever we go. Just as we need food to keep our bodies going, we need inspiration – "food" to keep our souls burning.

With fake inspiration, we run between counselors, movies, books, and houses of worship without ever feeling spiritually satiated. But with deep human inspiration that truly touches and changes us, we leave the experience overflowing. Personally, I tend to be very inspired by deeply human stories – those who overcome obstacles, those who commit their lives to serving others, the limits of human possibility, self-transformation, love, etc. For example, I have been inspired by Margarita, the leader of a movement to support the poor in rural Argentinean villages. As an inspiration junkie, I found myself writing down every word she shared about how she would work for the redistribution of wealth. My notepad again was full of scribbles when I went to hear the young, talented writer Jonathan Safran Foer describe his reasons to write a new Haggadah to reconnect with his Jewish roots.

Our bodies instinctively transfer food into energy. But we must learn how to intentionally transfer inspiration into energy. Otherwise, it remains entertainment and not inspiration-food that we pass along and truly live by. The art of living inspired is to learn how to keep our inspiration tank full enough that we do not burn out, yet outpouring enough that we live with the holy fire.

I would identify three primary types of inspiration: moment-inspiration, encounter-inspiration, and soul-inspiration. In moment-inspiration, given the conditions of one's life at the moment, one is uniquely able to understand a truth more deeply. In encounter-inspiration, one experiences an event that is transformative. In soul-inspiration, the most powerful, one does not need a particular moment or experience to have a deep inspirational moment. Rather, it is self-cultivated. One gains the tools to provide self-discovery and self-motivation without external stimuli.

At one time, the Jews relied upon God for inspiration. The prophets would be filled with *Ruah HaKodesh* (Divine inspiration) and the ability to understand higher truths. But the Rabbis teach that this type of inspiration ended with the deaths of Hagai, Zechariah, and Malachi (*Sanhedrin* 11a). The root of inspiration is spirit, since it is a spiritual process that also has a respiratory connection. God breathed the first breath into man to provide the capacity for inspiration, one that is deeply internal. Today, we must take it upon ourselves to open our hearts and allow ourselves to be inspired each and every day by infinite possibility.

When you find environments and people that inspire you, hold them close! We can learn to generate our own inspiration wherever we are if we cultivate the right life lens. When you find that you just cannot get enough, you will know that you have become an inspiration junkie! □

EXPOSED ROOTS: THE IMPORTANCE OF FAITH-ROOTED SPIRITUAL ACTIVISM

ONE DAY, AS MY WIFE AND I WERE WALKING, we passed a massive tree and marveled at how its roots were exposed above ground. These roots can still fulfill their function to absorb water, store nutrients, support the tree, and prevent erosion of the soil, but the tree seemed exposed, perhaps even naked.

Similarly, our roots are private. We share our branches and leaves with the world, even our trunks, but our roots remain underground to be clandestinely nourished and protected.

Upon reflection, I realized that this tree was strong and beautiful enough that it could expose its roots to the world. There was no shame. Too often, we leave our deepest selves below ground, so no one can see. When we hide our depths from those close to us, we often hide from ourselves as well. To be sure, most private things are appropriately shared privately; this is modesty. But what would a world look like if everyone kept the holy and meaningful below ground? Conversely, what would a world look like if we all put some of our roots above ground to share our sources of nourishment and empowerment?

Most of our roots stay below ground due to insecurity and the fear of exposing our deepest longings, dreams, fears, and weaknesses. Here, there is a clash between aspects of our modesty (keeping things private) and our humility (willingness to show our weaknesses). But perhaps even more, we leave our roots below ground because we ourselves question whether or not they are good. On some level, perhaps we disbelieve in the goodness of our own souls and belief systems.

To create change today, we must move from a faith-based activism to a faith-rooted activism. In faith-based activism, we as Jews merely act together based upon our collective cultural values, but in faith-rooted activism, we bring our deep spiritual and emotional wisdom to the surface. Our faith informs not just why but how we engage with the world. We bring our roots to the surface to share, discuss, inspire, and mobilize.

Most Jewish social justice activism remains comfortable on the faith-based level leaving spiritual depth below ground. Today, we must return to faith-rooted activism. We must not enter Capitol Hill as cultural Jews but as representatives of God, Torah, and our tradition. It takes soul power to keep the flame of social change alive and thus we must not keep our deepest roots below the earth.

Teaching about social change, Rabbi Avraham Yitzhak HaCohen Kook, the first Ashkenazi Chief Rabbi in the Land of Israel, taught the importance of "bringing up the sparks" to make all holy.

The general conception of striving for equality, which is the basis of kindness and the pure love of people, is seen in the mystical interpretation as bringing up the sparks that are scattered among the husks of unrefined existence, and in the great vision of transforming everything to full and absolute holiness, in a gradual increasing of love, peace, justice, truth, and compassion (*Orot HaKodesh* 2, 322).

It is the "husks of unrefined existence" where we can find the sparks to transform the world. Rav Kook continues that if we neglect our spiritual roots keeping them hidden from the surface of reality, while dealing with material justice issues, then we merely act like children unaware of our very existence.

Should a man want to build a completely structured cosmology without the aid of any spiritual emanation, by the calculation of material necessities, we may watch this child's game in perfect ease, since it builds a shell of life without knowing how to build life itself, whereas we can draw closer and be strengthened more in the bond of the inner light of holiness (*Igrot HaReayah* 1, 45).

Faith is not merely our motivation for acting, as the word of God must do more than just awaken our conscience. The role of religion is to agitate us to courageously go deeper into our spiritual and emotional existence, bringing those deep truths into the public sphere. Only when we share our roots can we truly change the fabric of our society and the depths of our world. □

AFFIRMING LIFE: "THE ETERNAL RECURRENCE"

I N HIS WORK *THE GAY SCIENCE* (APHORISM #341), the renowned nineteenth century German philosopher Friedrich Nietzsche (1844–1900) explains his theory of "the Eternal Recurrence":

> What, if some day or night a demon were to steal after you into your loneliest loneliness and say to you: "This life as you now live it and have lived it, you will have to live once more and innumerable times more" . . . Would you not throw yourself down and gnash your teeth and curse the demon who spoke thus? Or have you once experienced a tremendous moment when you would have answered him: "You are a god and never have I heard anything more divine."

Nietzsche has us imagine what our reaction would be, if we were told that we were to relive our lives repeatedly for all time, and whether this would be heaven or hell, based on the life we had lived, including all the choices we had made in life and their consequences. Nietzsche believed that we must learn to embrace the radical freedom we have in every life choice we make, so that we can make the right choices. To Nietzsche, the possibility of living life to the fullest was critical, as this was the only life, and eternal recurrence measured one's progress. Ironically, shortly after his revision of *The Gay Science*, Nietzsche suffered a severe physical and mental breakdown and never wrote again.

In contrast, the classic and controversial text of Jewish mysticism, the *Zohar* (70, 132a), explains that we will indeed return to this world in a state of reincarnation as many times as are needed until we have perfected ourselves, and thus made ourselves fit to return to our Creator:

> If there is even one organ in which the Holy Blessed One does not dwell, then he (the person with such organ) will be brought back into the world in reincarnation because of this organ, until he becomes perfected in his parts, that all of them may be perfect in the image of the Holy Blessed One.

In order to perfect ourselves and affirm our lives, we must heighten our awareness of ourselves through deeper contemplation and affirmation of life, gradually rising in levels of spirituality through a mystical study of the Torah. In doing this, we must also be perpetually aware of new ideas, senses, and emotions, always ready to reinvent or reawaken ourselves. Interestingly, the Zohar may be compared with Buddhist ontology, where a soul is reincarnated until it is extinguished into the oneness of the universe. In the Zohar, however, the gradual rise leads to the Creator.

The prominent Transcendentalist American Henry David Thoreau (1816–1862) expressed a similar vision in his seminal work *Walden* (1854):

> We must learn to reawaken and keep ourselves awake, not by mechanical aids, but by an infinite expectation of the dawn, which does not forsake us in our soundest sleep. I know of no more encouraging fact than the unquestionable ability of man to elevate his life by conscious endeavor. It is something to be able to paint a particular picture, or to carve a statue, and so to make a few objects beautiful; but it is far more glorious to carve and paint the very atmosphere and medium through

which we look, which morally we can do. To affect the quality of the day, that is the highest of the arts. Every man is tasked to make his life, even in its details, worthy of the contemplation of his most elevated and critical hour.

Thoreau's approach was from a belief system closest to the Unitarian church, along with a prophetic love of nature. In spite of long periods in isolation at Walden, Thoreau did believe in active reform. He was a prominent abolitionist, and his short pamphlet on civil disobedience greatly influenced Dr. Martin Luther King, Jr., and the tactics of the American civil rights movement in the twentieth century.

To live a contemplative life, then, we must affirm not only the major things, such as family, health, and happiness; we must rather affirm all of our life decisions and actions. This idea of recognizing the importance of all of our actions is expounded in *Pirke Avot* 2:1:

> Rabbi (Judah HaNasi) said: "What is the proper path that a person should choose to follow for oneself? . . . Be as scrupulous in observing a minor mitzvah as in a major one."

All of these major thinkers stressed the importance of our life decisions. Nietzsche challenges us to approach each moment of our lives with full freedom and responsibility, as if we were to relive each moment for eternity, an idea later espoused by the existentialists. Thoreau tells us to make every moment in the life of a person "worthy of the contemplation of his most elevated and critical hour," which has inspired people to cultivate inner spirituality in addition to causes such as nonviolent resistance and ecology. While these thinkers offered powerful insights, Judaism reminds us that all of life is important, both the big things and the seemingly small things. The Rabbis tell us that nothing is insignificant, that both minor and major *mitzvot* merit our full attention and dedication. We need not wait for the next life, as the Zohar says we might, to affirm our lives; we can take the next step toward perfection in every single moment in this life.   □

MARRIAGE IN THE AFTERLIFE: GROWING TOGETHER IN THIS WORLD FOR THE NEXT WORLD

THE JEWISH TRADITION TEACHES THAT THERE will be reward and punishment for how we live in this world. In many ways, the afterlife is central, but nonetheless we must focus on our work in this world. The Ramhal, Rabbi Moshe Chaim Luzzato, the prominent eighteenth century Italian kabbalist and philosopher teaches:

> Man was created solely in order to delight in God and derive pleasure from the glory of His Presence, which is the truest delight and the greatest possible pleasure. And the place of this pleasure is truly the World to Come, for it was created with that very design. But the way to arrive at this our desired destination is the Present World, as our Rabbis of blessed memory said: "This world is like a corridor to the next." And the means which bring a man to this end are the *mitzvot* which were commanded to us by God. And the only place where *mitzvot* may be fulfilled is the Present World (*Mesillat Yesharim*, Chapter 1).

We must work hard in this world to be the best we can be and we need partners to achieve that. Our strongest life partner should ideally be our spouse.

I am so in awe of my dear wife and all her virtues, and feel so deeply fortunate every day that she is my wife and life partner. I want to be sure that I am with her eternally and I often think about the afterlife and our connection in the next world. Will we be together? How can I best ensure we'll be eternal soul mates? How can I reach a spiritual and moral level even close to hers?

The thirteenth century Tosafist, Rabbi Moshe Taku, addresses this issue:

> And (after the resurrection) the righteous will take wives in accordance with their deeds, for each one will not marry the wife he had in

this world unless the two of them are of equivalent righteousness . . . A wholly righteous man (who had been married to) a non-wholly righteous woman, or a wholly righteous woman (who had been married to) a non-wholly righteous man, will not be rejoined in the future, for death severs their bonds. When they are resurrected, each person will marry the partner who is appropriate for them, in accordance with their deeds (*Sefer Ketav Tamim, translation by Dr. David Shyovitz*).

What an inspiring idea – that we must grow together to stay together. Spouses need to strive to raise each other up so that both can grow together. Rabbi Joseph B. Soloveitchik writes about the power of marriage to achieve our ethical aspirations. The Rav noted that the great covenant has been compared to a "betrothal of Israel to God," and the marriage betrothal has been elevated to a "covenantal commitment" (*berit*). Thus, when we look at the meeting of the spouses in marriage,

> . . . the objective medium of attaining that meeting is the assumption of covenantal obligations which are based upon the principle of equality. Hence, we have a clue to the understanding of the nature of matrimony. All we have to do is analyze the unique aspects of covenantal commitment and apply them to the matrimonial commitment (*Family Redeemed*, 41–42).

The Rav sees marriage situated within covenant (mutual partnership and commitment). He continues to explain the ethical foundation of marriage:

> Within the frame of reference of marriage, love becomes not an instinctual reaction of an excited heart . . . , but an intentional experience in reply to a metaphysical ethical summons . . . . Love, emerging from an existential moral awareness, is sustained not by the flame of passion, but by the strength of a Divine norm . . . . Since our eternal faith in God is something which defies rationalization, the mutual temporal faith of man and woman united in matrimony is just as paradoxical (*ibid.*, 41–42).

Here, science and romantic literature are in perfect agreement with religion. Harvard psychologist Daniel Gilbert notes that studies have long confirmed that married people are happier, live longer lives, and have more financial security than their unmarried counterparts. Two of the most prominent seventeenth century French dramatists illustrate this point. Jean Racine writes: "Happiness held is the seed; happiness shared is the flower," while Pierre Corneille put it more succinctly: "Happiness seems made to be shared." William Shakespeare also seems to approve of marriage, having one character tell another in *Much Ado About Nothing*: "Thou art sad; get thee a wife, get thee a wife!" In the lesser-known *Henry VI, Part I*, he writes that an unforced marriage "bringeth bliss, And is a pattern of celestial peace."

While pundits may tell us to avoid working with our spouses, history shows many contrary examples. Often, when American husbands went to war, became disabled, or died, their wives took over inns, did chores at farms, and kept their families together. In the modern era, the pattern is sometimes reversed. Arizona Representative Gabrielle Giffords married former astronaut and Navy Captain Mark Kelly in 2007, and everything seemed ideal. Then in January 2011, Rep. Giffords was shot and severely wounded along with many others in a mass shooting. Her husband has been instrumental in helping her achieve her remarkable recovery; can anyone imagine how much more difficult it would have been for her to recover by herself, or that they are equally righteous?

We raise each other up to be our best. Of course we do not know what will happen in the next world (whether or not we'll have corporeal bodies, whether or not we'll have identity and memory, whether or not we'll be physically together with loved ones), but Rabbi Taku teaches us that the best shot we can give is to strive to meet our potential and to help our life partner to meet his or her potential. After all, there may be eternal ramifications.

My dream is to be hand-in-hand with my soul mate, so I know I have a lot of work to get to that level. May we learn to convert our love into righteousness and merit eternal love. □

☐ SOCIAL JUSTICE AND SPIRITUALITY

CONFLICT RESOLUTION:
A SPIRITUAL APPROACH

I T SEEMS AS IF THERE IS DISAGREEMENT AND TEN-
sion everywhere. Most days, I feel surrounded by
conflicts that emerge globally, nationally, locally,
professionally, and personally.

Conflict is not something that exists outside of us. Fundamental to our
existence, we are embedded in lives of disagreement and tension. It is in
the nature of the self and society. We may hold the utopian ideal that war
and famine should come to an end, but we can never hope for the end of
conflict, for that would spell the end of the human condition. I often search
for spiritual insight on the nature of conflict that is so endemic in the self
and society.

Rebbe Nahman of Breslov, the great eighteenth century existentialist
rabbi, explains a deep truth about the spiritual nature of conflict:

> The whole world is full of controversy, between countries, towns,
> neighbors, and even within a household, between husband and wife,
> or with servants and children. No one pays attention to the ultimate
> fact that each and every day we come closer to death. Know that all
> these controversies are one: the conflict between a man and his wife
> is the same conflict as that which exists between kings and nations.
> For each one in the household represents a particular nation; their
> challenges to one another are like the wars between the nations . . .
> even one who has no desire to quarrel, but prefers to dwell in peace,
> is drawn into controversies and battles. Just as one sometimes finds
> among the kings and nations a country that wants to live in peace,

and is forced to enter the war on one side or another (despite its will-ingness to be a subject nation), so it is with household "wars." For man is a microcosm, and he contains the whole world within him. Surely this is true of a man and his household, who contain all the warring nations. That is why a person who sits alone in the forest can sometimes go mad. This happens because he is alone, but nonetheless he contains within himself all the nations which are at war with one another, and he keeps having to switch back and forth, taking the role of whichever 'nation' has the upper hand. This turmoil of the mind can drive him completely mad. But when he is in a settled place, among people, this war can spread out among his household or his neighbors. (*Liqqutim* II, 20)

Rebbe Nahman explains that we are not only embedded in political and communal conflict, but also spiritual conflict. Further, our personal exis-tential conflicts mirror external global conflicts. We must first learn to ex-amine the conflict and exist in this tension and discomfort. If we do not do this, we risk externalizing our conflict into interpersonal and social tension.

The Jewish matriarch Rebecca felt a great conflict within herself (*va-yitrotz'zu ha-banim*). The Rabbis explain that this internal stirring was not only the wrestling of her sons, Jacob and Esau, but the conflict of two great nations. The personal conflict within Rebecca modeled a national and global religious conflict.

Once God created and separated the first two humans, it was inevitable that in addition to unity there would be separation. Although separation makes conflict inevitable, we also see that it is part of the divine plan. Emmanuel Levinas explains that conflict is not only with the other, situated outside of ourselves, but also with the other that is inside ourselves – he calls this "internal alterity." The Kabbalists often describe these tensions as being between our masculine and feminine sides.

In addition to internal personal conflict, the Rabbis caution us not to avoid social conflict, as well:

If a person of learning participates in public affairs and serves as judge or arbiter, he gives stability to the land . . . But if he sits in his home and says to himself, "What have the affairs of society to do with me? . . . Why should I trouble myself with the people's voices of protest? Let my soul dwell in peace!" – if he does this, he overthrows the world. (Midrash Tanhuma, *Mishpatim* 2)

When one avoids social conflict and does not take responsibility for communal and global problems, he or she "overthrows the world." Once again, the individual is a microcosm for the global human experience. The twentieth century Jewish thinker Rabbi Abraham Joshua Heschel also struggled with and protested against this communal apathy:

> O Lord, we confess our sins, we are ashamed of the inadequacy of our anguish, of how faint and slight is our mercy. We are a generation that has lost its capacity for outrage. We must continue to remind ourselves that in a free society all are involved in what some are doing. Some are guilty, all are responsible. ("A Prayer for Peace," 1971)

By embracing the conflicts inside and outside of us we can be a part of the transformation of self as well as the world. We can, and must, pursue conflict and peace, one of the holiest endeavors within the human experience. Rav Kook explains that the most sustainable and meaningful peace is one that arises from disagreement and conflict. Ultimately, it requires deep toiling and wrestling to find a spiritual and global peace, a peace that transcends borders and intertwines souls.   □

EMBRACING THE LOST ART OF CREATIVITY

I WAS FIVE YEARS OLD AND MY FATHER WAS THE President of Crayola Crayons. This gave me significant popularity points as a kindergartner. One day, my parents came home to find that I had taken my Crayola markers and painted all over all of the white walls in the house. As protocol for this type of normal occurrence, my mother scolded me while my father, as a marketer of ideas, stood back and thought. It was in this precise moment that the washable marker was invented. (I take some credit for this invention.)

Only a few months later, I decided to help my father by washing his car. Unable to locate a rag, I decided to use Brillo pads. I never claimed I was the cleverest lad of the 1980s. I was shocked when I washed away the soap suds to find that I had scratched the paint off of the entire 1985 Buick. Unfortunately, this one didn't spur an invention.

My justification in both of these incidences was that I was expressing my creativity. Growing up, I tended to confuse the virtue of creativity with the vice of destruction. Creativity simply meant exploration and experimentation albeit with good intentions even if it happened to destroy.

"*Bereishit bara Elokim et ha-shamayiim v'et ha-aretz*" is the first line of the Bible. In the beginning, God created heaven and earth. *Bereishit bara Elokim* – God creates. God is a being of creativity.

Why does the Bible want to be sure that we recognize creativity as the first divine virtue of all? This is based on the two primary foundations for ethics. Firstly, Jewish law guides us and can set moral and spiritual boundaries. Secondly, *halachta b'drachav* – Imitatio Dei – we must strive to imitate the ways of God.

God creates and then God sees that creating is good. If we are to emulate the ways of God, then we are asked to create – to become agents of creativity – as an ethical and spiritual necessity. In essence, man is a creative being.

What is the one mitzvah that we learn from the Torah? According to the *Sefer HaHinuch*, a thirteenth century Spanish legal work, it's *peru u'revu* – to be fruitful and multiple. On a halachic level, this means that we need more Jewish babies. But on a broader plain, it means that humans were created in order to become agents of creation – to be fruitful and multiply. However, the mitzvah might mean even more. The Me'am Loez, the great eighteenth century Turkish Torah commentator, has a radical interpretation suggesting that *peru u'revu* is not only fulfilled through procreation but through *hiddushei Torah* (novel Torah interpretations) and the necessary new ideas that each person much create on their own. *Peru u'revu* is a general command for religious creativity: perpetuating what is just and good and holy in the world. We are constantly commanded to fulfill *peru u'revu* to an infinite extent as we can always seek to be more intellectually and spiritual creative.

We're not asked to be creators just once in our lives but as daily creators. As we say twice in our morning prayers each day: "*u'b'tuvo mehadesh b'chol yom tamid maasei bereishit*" (God creates daily, constantly, the work of creation). We should all yearn in our professional and private lives to be *mehadash* (creative) – to have our own effect on the world.

When a writer is up late at night trying to finish an article on deadline: "*mehadesh b'chol yom.*" When parents struggle to learn a more effective way to discipline their child: "*mehadesh b'chol yom.*" When a person realizes that they just don't understand the Talmudic passage after a few hours of concentration: "*mehadesh b'chol yom.*" When someone gains a new understanding for the suffering of others in the world and is seeking the best way to help: "*mehadesh b'chol yom tamid maasei bereishit.*" Everywhere in life, there is room for innovation and creativity creating a deep impact.

Creativity as the purpose of our existence is what Rabbi Joseph B. Soloveitchik called the charge of "majesty and humility" – that the religious personality must be humble but also seeking to live like a king – as a radical creator in the world. He writes:

> The power stored up within man is exceedingly great, is all-encompassing, but all too often it slumbers within and does not bestir itself from its deep sleep. The command of creation, beating deep within the consciousness of Judaism, proclaims: Awake ye slumberers from your sleep. Realize, actualize yourselves, your own potentialities and possibilities, and go forth to meet your God. The unfolding of man's spirit that soars to the very heavens, that is the meaning of creation. . . . . Action and creation are the true distinguishing marks of authentic existence.

This is the great challenge placed on each of us. Yet, while creativity can at times be such a rewarding spiritual process, it can also involve a complex array of feelings: fear and hope, discord and harmony, discomfort and determination, exuberance and angst. Creativity is not merely the moment of finding a solution (the light bulb moment). Rather it is the moment of finding the problem – all of our days, all of our lives we can remain in a creative process when we're focused on the problems to be addressed.

It's at the moment of despair – when it seems that there are no answers left when our unique human capacity for perseverance and creativity can kick in. This is when we have experienced failure and struggle – but we keep looking.

After all, Thomas Edison had to try thousands of different types of light bulbs before the first one finally worked. Leonardo da Vinci destroyed many of his own canvasses. Albert Einstein once said: "I have not failed. I've just found 10,000 ways that won't work."

For even the best musicians, there are a lot of flubbed notes. Failure and confusion is a necessary part of the creative process but it can be so scary to think of ourselves failing. Also, we often think of creativity as requiring the most brilliant and grand innovations. It requires serious courage, therefore, to create, where courage is not about the absence of despair and doubt but the capacity to move forward in spite of despair. We must conquer the fear that our creations will fail, will be rejected, and will be irrelevant.

So many of us, over the years, have really struggled and lost. For some of us, we're struggling financially. Some of us lost almost all we had saved. For some, our big plans were destroyed. For others relationships simply disappeared. So much despair, nothing feels quite as complete or whole like it used to, our past plans have not all come to fruition.

Yet, in this way, we can perhaps also emulate God. The Midrash teaches us a very profound lesson here regarding creation. The Midrash teaches that God created ten worlds, destroyed each one, tried again, until finally this world was created. Our universe emerged only after other unsuccessful attempts (Genesis Rabbah 3:7, *Esh Kodesh* p. 114).

Now, of course, we never know if the text is actually speaking of God and a historical reality, or just teaching us a moral value for human experience.

This world may have been the most perfect of the ten created but still the world was left unfinished so that humans could have a part in creation. When we wake up to the realities of existence, we can participate in the creative process.

As emulators of God in creation, we are called upon to see problems as opportunities where we can respond to challenges as positive opportunities for creation. We do not just sit and complain at challenges – we create partnerships and solutions.

When life is seen as a series of moments of creation through speech, through relationships, ideas, and love, we can reimagine possibility in our lives. It is only by being present in the moment and by acting in the moment that we can truly be creative to create new possibilities in the world as Jewish theology is a performative theology where the act (the mitzvah) is central to creating. Even further, Jewish theology is a transformative theology – in creation, in fulfilling *mitzvot*, we recreate ourselves and our world.

As George Bernard Shaw once said: "Life is not about finding yourself but about creating yourself." I'd go one step further: Life is about creating yourself but also creating space for others to create themselves: every person is full of creative energies and potentials. But to what end can we really seek creativity – after all, who has time to break from the routine thinking to challenge their norms and assumptions? The prophets taught us that to be a visionary, and to change the world, requires significant creativity. We are called upon to inspire in ourselves the courage to create.

Ramban explains in the Creation story a brilliant idea about the human condition based upon the use of language in the Torah. He explains the significant difference between the terms *bria* and *yetzira* (creating vs. forming). The Torah uses the language of *bria* to describe the initial creation of the world and the creation of humans. This is a creation called *yesh m'ayin* – a creation out of no prior existence. Other creations, the Torah describes as *yetzira*. This is a creation called *yesh m'yesh* – a creation from existing substance and existence. We say this every morning "*yotzer ohr u'vorei hoshech*": light comes from other light so it is the language of *yetzira* (forming), but darkness is a creation from nothingness so it is the language of *bria* (creating).

Being that humans were uniquely created from nothing, we too have this capacity through the intellectual and spiritual realm to be creative beyond anything ever imagined. Now perhaps we may only create something from nothing (*yesh m'ayin*) on a grand level a few times in our lives, but *yesh m'yesh* (creating from something) is constant throughout our day. This constant *yetzira* (constant forming process) can be holy work as such that it transforms mundane parts of our lives. This is where religious life becomes transformative for us – when it informs how we form our daily realities based on the tools we have. It can be so scary to think that all creativity must be totally innovative and that with our creative potentials we must only create the most grand ideas. Rather, we need just to maintain a steady commitment and focus by living a life of creativity and a life of possibility.

It is the constant process of creation that we as humans are engaged in that Rav Kook believed to be at the core of spiritual life. He writes in *Orot HaKodesh*:

> Every fleeting moment we create, consciously and unconsciously, multitudes of creation beyond measure. If we would only condition ourselves to feel them, to bring them within the zone of clear comprehension, to introduce them within the framework of appropriate articulation, there would be revealed their glory and their splendor. Their effect would then become visible on all of life.

For Rav Kook, the mandate is not only seeking to perpetuate our creative energies but to become aware that at each moment we are engaged in a creative process (spiritually and practically).

When the High Holidays come to a close, it is so easy for us to just move back into our daily routine. The story of creation comes at the right time to remind us of our potentials that we are full of immense potential put in this world with the purpose to create with our unique capacities. In the face of losses and defeats, we can have the courage to create. In working to build our community, to create change in the world, and in each and every career and type of work, we have unique and vital creative energies and gifts to share at every stage of our lives. We were brought into the world specifically to offer our gift, to be partners with God in creation in our own unique way. When God says, "Let us make man," it has been suggested that God is actually talking to man as a partner. God transcends nature and we are asked to do the same, to acknowledge that what is does not necessarily have to be. As the Kabbalists explain, God works through us to create change in the world. To actualize God's creative potential, each of us must create.

While sometimes our creative energies may unintentionally lead us to paint marker on the walls or accidentally scratch paint off of cars – and this can make us fearful of striving to continue to create – it is this creative potential that needs to be fostered and then courageously channeled in the most holy and noble of endeavors.   □

DISTRACTIONS AND THE SPIRITUAL ART OF FOCUSING

I N THE TECHNOLOGY ERA, WE ARE ALL FINDING IT increasingly difficult to concentrate for long periods of time on one task. Between text messages and phone messages, email, Facebook and other social media, we are constantly responding to communications from all directions. Our brains must continually adjust to these different technologies and forms of communication. Gloria Mark of the University of California at Irvine found that in the workplace, the average employee gets around eleven minutes to focus on a task before being interrupted. It then takes around twenty-five minutes to return one's focus to the original task!

This has been a long-term trend, and there are many suspected culprits. Some believe that television, with commercials interrupting programming every eight minutes or so, lessened our attention span. Later, popular music videos, where the camera angles changed every few seconds, were blamed for a generation of teenagers who had difficulty concentrating on anything, and still later our obsession with Twitter and texting has created a world in which few people appear to be able to concentrate on any topic for more than a minute. Consider: In 1858, Abraham Lincoln debated Stephen Douglas for an Illinois Senate seat; Lincoln's opening statement comprised more than 8,750 words, and he still had about thirty minutes left if he wanted to continue. Even in the 1960 Presidential debates, John F. Kennedy and Richard Nixon each opened with statements lasting at least seven minutes. In contrast, during the 2012 presidential primaries, Texas Governor Rick Perry was unable to remember the name of the third Federal Department that he would eliminate, and in general most candidates had difficulty speaking for two minutes without looking up in the air or repeating themselves. While brevity can be a virtue – Lincoln's Gettysburg Address is one example – the downward spiral of attention spans is a reality.

Research by Carnegie Mellon University's Human-Computer Interaction Lab has shown that we pay a serious cost for these distractions. Another study conducted by Alessandro Acquisti and Eyal Peer, also from Carnegie Mellon, shows that that those who are interrupted are not only slower to complete a task but make 20 percent more mistakes than those who are interrupted less frequently; that's the difference between a B student (80) and a D student (60). In medicine and other fields, this effect of distraction can lead to fatal mistakes. Think of what can happen if someone behind the wheel in the car behind you decides to start texting to avoid the tedium of driving, or if a clinician is too bored to read a patient's medical history and symptoms. There are severe physical dangers when people are distracted and bored.

The Rabbis also taught about the spiritual dangers of distractions. For example, *Pirke Avot* 3:9 records the following teaching: "Rabbi Yaakov said: One who walks on the road while reviewing (a Torah lesson) but interrupts his review and exclaims 'How beautiful is this tree! How beautiful is this plowed field!' – Scripture considers it as if he bears guilt for his soul."

Losing focus in our intellectual endeavors can lead to spiritual damage. On the other hand, in *The Gay Science*, Nietzsche explains the importance of intellectually interacting with the world and the value even of distractions:

> We do not belong to those who have ideas only among books, when stimulated by books. It is our habit to think outdoors – walking, leaping, climbing, dancing, preferably on lonely mountains or near the

sea where even the trails become thoughtful. Our first questions about the value of a book, of a human being, or a musical composition are: Can they walk? Even more, can they dance?

We miss so much when we immerse ourselves in our own mundane activities. In January 2007, the *Washington Post* conducted an experiment in a DC Metro station lobby. The *Post* persuaded Joshua Bell, a violinist who has recorded about forty albums, won several Grammys, has played at the most prestigious music festivals and with the finest orchestras in the world, and has appeared in more popular venues (such as on *Sesame Street*), to play for forty-five minutes during the morning rush hour. The purpose was to see how people would react to one of the world's finest musicians playing his Stradivarius violin while wearing jeans and a baseball cap. Bell played several pieces, including a portion of a Bach *Partita*, that did not contain catchy tunes but did reward the listener who stayed for any period of time. The compressed YouTube video documented that more than 1,000 people passed the noted violinist without paying any attention, and only seven people stayed for even a minute. One person finally recognized him from his concert at the Library of Congress. Are we so immersed that we cannot recognize artistic genius? Are we so tied to appearances that we cannot hear? Do we tune out music if it does not have an instantly recognizable tune, or because we are glued to our own ear buds? We can speculate on the reasons, but it does not bode well for our society if people are so concerned with their immediate activities that they ignore the rest of the world. Can we remake the world if we are too distracted to notice it?

There are clearly some benefits to cultivating the new art of hyper-multitasking and there are times and places where we should lose ourselves in the great distractions of the world, but to be effective and successful we also need times of great focus. Even further, to be spiritually attuned, we need times of wholeness without constant fracturing interruptions. In fact, the Ramban argues that we miss some of the most significant revelations in our lives because we have not prepared our hearts (Exodus 3:2). To truly be spiritually alive, we must take the time in transitions to emotionally prepare ourselves to have periods of intense focus and concentration or we risk missing precious gems below the surface of reality. We need not get rid of technology, or dismiss its incredible value. We do not need techno-abstinence. But what we must learn is techno-moderation and how to reduce external stimuli at times to awaken our internal worlds.   □

RECOVERING THE TRANSFORMATIVE AND ETHICAL POWER OF MUSIC

AFTER DECADES OF PIANO, VIOLIN, AND GUITAR lessons, I finally retired without any real merits forfeiting my hopes of ever becoming a rock star or fiery composer. It took me some time to realize that music is still at the core of my Jewish spiritual and ethical passion. Singing at protests, including melodies of activist storytelling, and opening my heart to new ideals while listening to powerful symphonies have changed the way I feel and interact with the world.

Some rabbis argue that music is really only an ancient relic of the past reserved for the Temple and is generally prohibited today with only a few exceptions. Others suggest that there is some spiritual value that we can derive from contemporary music. I would suggest, most importantly, that there is an ethical value to can be attained when we allow ourselves to be elevated by music.

Music has a very early origin in the Jewish tradition. Right at the beginning of the book of Genesis we learn that the harp and flute were created by our first musician Yuval (Genesis 4:21). The Torah teaches us to be proud of the creation of music as one of man's great early accomplishments. After the splitting of the sea, Moses led the people in a song of liberation and Miriam led the women. Further, we're commanded to continue to make music on our festivals: "And on your joyous occasions, your fixed festivals and your new moon days, you shall sound the trumpets over your burnt offerings and your sacrifices of well being" (Numbers 10:10).

In the Mishnah we learn that there was an orchestra in the holy Temple that consisted of twelve instruments and a choir of twelve singers. In addition to singing in prayer, the Rabbis of the Talmud encourage us to sing the Torah we study (*Megillah* 32a). The Mishnah itself originally had trope and was learned as a song and the Torah is also a song that we sing each week.

Yet, after the destruction of the Temple, the primacy of music in Jewish worship was challenged. We must understand this. There was an early tabbinic position that it was forbidden to enjoy music after the destruction of the Temple since we should not experience joy in such a time of loss (*Gittin* 7a). The danger of inappropriate music is told through a story about Elisha ben Avuha who lost his way because he got too caught up in Greek music. "Greek music never ceased to emerge from his mouth" (*Hagigah* 15b). The Rabbis are teaching us how powerful music is and that we must be very careful which music we allow into our souls. Lyrics matter, the meaning matters, and the energy created inside of us by music matters.

While many Jews refrain from listening to music during the three weeks of mourning, in the *Shulhan Aruch*, the Code of Jewish Law, Rabbi Moshe Isserles informs us that both vocal and instrumental music are permitted, at normal times of the year, for the fulfillment of a mitzvah (560:30). The Maharshal (*Yam Shel Shlomo*) goes even further explaining that listening to music "to hear pleasant sounds or to hear something fresh" is permitted. Rabbi Soloveitchik taught that the prohibition applies only to music of profane revelry but not to classical music or the like.

The concern was that if the world is broken, we cannot just sit in peace and allow music to be lessened to a mere outlet for blissful complacency. Music enjoyment at its worst can just be a form of hedonism. However, music can be used deliberately to inspire, to elevate, and to help refine one's sensitivities to the next level.

There is an element of ethical and spiritual refinement that one can achieve through music. By embracing an elevated peace and harmony, one can be opened up to creation and a sense of the transcendental. Discovering harmony within oneself can assist one to find it in others and in the world. Where do we begin?

Cynthia Ozick, the twentieth century American writer, explains beautifully that if one attempts to make music from the wide end of a *shofar*, it makes no noise. One must blow the *shofar* from the narrow end. To express ourselves as part of a collective, we must begin with who we are as individuals. To actualize ourselves as humans, we must first sing as Jews. Particularism is the channel toward a universalism that has depth. Our music must contain our unique essence before we join a communal "choir." The Kuzari describes the Jewish people as an orchestra where each instrument and voice is needed to actualize the potential of our destined song. The change that we can create in the world as a collective is much greater than what we can do alone.

As Jews, we have our own song and when we master it, we have a greater talent to create our own personal song. Mozart was an extraordinary composer because he mastered the classical form. Beethoven, on the other hand, broke through the classical form and changed music forever. Beethoven is a model for us. We master the particular songs that we've inherited in order that we can then create and innovate more deeply. To sing in solidarity with humanity, we must first master the song of our people. By understanding ourselves, we can better understand others.

There is, of course, a responsibility that comes with how we collectively engage in music. Rabbi Nahman of Breslov taught that the word *hazan* (song leader) comes from the word *hazon* (vision). A song leader has the opportunity to be a visionary and to lead others to a new place through music. This is a great responsibility. What are the words we advocate? Where do we lead others with our seductive melodies?

Further, Rabbi Nahman explains that each of us has a *niggun* (a melody) inside of us and that we are to spend our lives in search of that lost melody. Each day, we are learning to refine ourselves to connect with our own unique inner music.

To reiterate an earlier point, Leon Wieseltier explains this well in his justification for praying from traditional liturgy. If one goes on to stage with no lyrics, the entire time one thinks about what words to sing. But if one already has the lyrics, then one can focus on how beautifully one sings. We have a Jewish liturgy that can inspire us to live more compassionately. Do the words of our song truly affect us?

All these words aren't outside of us, but within our spiritual depths. Rabbi Avraham Yitzhak HaCohen Kook explains that songs are an expression of our essence. He proposes that we unite our potential through four songs: our personal song, our Jewish song, our human song, and our global song.

> There is one who rises toward wider horizons, until he links himself with all existence, with all God's creatures, with all worlds, and he sings his song with all of them. It is of one such as this that tradition has said that whoever sings a portion of song each day is assured of having a share in the World to Come. And then there is one who rises with all these songs in one ensemble, and they all join their voices. Together they sing their songs with beauty; each one lends vitality and life to the other. They are sounds of joy and gladness, sounds of jubilation and celebration, sounds of ecstasy and holiness. The song of the self, the song of the people, the song of humanity, the song of the world all merge in her at all times, in every hour (*Orot HaKodesh*, Volume II, 458–459).

In doing this, Rav Kook explains that we actualize the true meaning and purpose of Yisrael (the Jewish people) as *Shirat El* (the song of God). This is a moral choice with eschatological implications.

Music can not only be pleasurable and relaxing. At its best it can offer us the potential to strive for state of being and becoming. Finding our own music is a crucial part of our own religious journeys since music can take each of us to a new place that we have never been before. Music can pull us beyond ourselves and into ourselves at the same time. Spiritual activists must find their inner song and learn to merge it with the song of others in the world to achieve an eclectic yet unified global orchestra. Life is a song worth singing at our best.   □

THE ROLE OF THE DIVINE IN SOCIAL CHANGE: WHERE IS GOD IN TIKKUN OLAM?

WHY IS IT THAT AT A TYPICAL AMERICAN Jewish social justice event, no one invokes one of God's names? When our movement openly accepts the role of the Divine in social change and in moral development, we embrace the most powerful part of our tradition.

There are seven primary inspiring reasons why Jews engaging in social justice should embrace God in activism. When the Jewish social justice movement neglects the Divine, it may be intellectually dishonest since we deny the primary source of our sense of responsibility and we also deprive the social justice movement of the passion it would otherwise inspire.

The mitzvah of *v'halachta b'drachav*

The Torah tells us that God is merciful, and commands us to emulate God's ways. The Talmud makes this connection explicit (*Sotah* 14a). The Rabbis explain that God is ultimately not a vengeful power-hungry dictator but rather a merciful moral healer and this is the path we must follow. We must attend carefully to the means of social change (our character) in addition to the ends (assisting the vulnerable in society). Further, it means that being like God requires action. Our ultimate role model is no less than the Creator of heaven and earth. The bar is set high.

The value of *Tzelem Elokim*

The Talmud teaches that to save one life is to save the world (*Sanhedrin* 4:5). This is an essential Jewish message: Humanity is created in God's image, and is therefore sacred. Rav Kook goes so far as to argue that there is no such thing as an atheist, since God is in each one of us, and our souls long for their eternal source (*ikvei ha-tzon, eder ha-yakar*). We need not go this far, but when we embrace that each human is created in the image of God, we have the strongest model for ensuring the absolute unshakeable human dignity to all people.

The virtue of Humility

We must remember that the position of God has already been filled. The realization that in no way can we play the role of God should inspire humility in us. All too often, there can be arrogance in change-makers who see themselves as the heroes rather than as humble servants. The greatest Jewish leader, Moses, was described as "exceedingly humble, more than any person on the face of the earth!" (Numbers 12:3).

A perspective of History

The Torah says "*mi'beit avadim*" (from the house of slaves) describing when God took the Israelites out of the land of Egypt (Exodus 13:3) in order to show that God enters history in order to abolish slavery. God is the master liberator of the oppressed. Over time, God empowers humanity more and more with this role but still enters the global stage at crucial historical turning points.

A notion of Obligation

The responsibility to practice social justice is not optional or reserved for a ceremonial mitzvah day. When we embrace the notion that we are divinely commanded to heal the world each and every day, we raise the bar. Religion serves to remind us that at the end of our lives, we are ultimately held accountable for whether or not we fulfilled and exceeded our obligations. God cares whether or not we have lived up to our end of the partnership. Even further, embracing our obligations and commitments grants us dignity. Heschel explains that our dignity is not only a result of our rights but of our divine obligations. "Our commitment is to God, and our roots are in the prophetic events of Israel. The dignity of a person stands in proportion to his/her obligations as well as to his/her rights. The dignity of being a Jew is in the sense of commitment, and the meaning of Jewish history revolves around the faithfulness of Israel to the covenant" (*God in Search of Man*, 216).

Walking together with the Divine

When we are struggling for justice as part of our relationship with God, we do not walk alone. When we look at evil in the face to combat it with love, God stands with us. "As I walk through the valley overshadowed by death, I fear no evil for You are with me" (Psalms 23). Embracing religion is not comfortable conformity, but rising to a challenge. Embracing God is not believing blindly, but empowering oneself.

God is everywhere. The Me'Or Einayim (Rav Menahem Nahum of Chernobyl) explains that Avraham didn't depart from God when he left the Divine Presence to greet the three wanderers. Rather God is present in the ethical encounter as well because "The whole earth is filled with God's glory!" (Isaiah 6:3). When we realize that the Divine is present in all places and moments, we can only feel compelled to embrace the holiness of each moment and the concomitant ethical demands.

A vision of the Ideal

The notion of progress is rooted in the messianic vision: we hold paradigms of the perfect, like the heavenly realm, and we progress toward those ideal models by bringing them down to earth. There is a Temple located in the heavens that sits directly above the Temple on earth (Genesis Rabbah 69:7). The same God who makes the heavens radiate also illuminates our earthly existence.

For the religious maximalist, there is no room for cynical determinism. Rather, we are free and empowered to bring about real progress in the world. The Kabbalists explain that the world is saturated with Divinity that longs to return to its Divine source. This happens through good acts (*tikkunim*). Messianism, however, embraces not only the end (messianic times) but also the process (repairing the world each moment).

Rabbi Jonathan Sacks says it well:

> In Judaism, faith is not acceptance but protest, against the world that is, in the name of the world that is not yet but ought to be. Faith lies not in the answer but the question – and the greater the human being, the more intense the question. The Bible is not a metaphysical opium but it's opposite. Its aim is not to transport the believer to a private heaven. Instead, its impassioned, sustained desire is to bring heaven down to earth. Until we have done this, there is work still to do (*To Heal a Fractured World*, 27).

One can obviously be moral and effective in social justice work and not embrace God just as one can be devout religiously and not create any serious social justice impact. However, as a guiding principle, embracing God offers the potential to raise the bar set for what we must achieve and for how we must achieve it. God is the most powerful reality ever encountered, and like no other idea, embrace of the Divine can inspire humankind to ideal goodness and transformative justice. Merely embracing our own human authority represents a failure to recognize the power of and truth of our calling, destiny, and command. Embracing the humility to acknowledge a power beyond us demands social protest, not Divine submission. Together, as servants, we serve God by healing the world. □

SKYDIVING THROUGH LIFE: OUR RESPONSIBILITY FOR THE PRESENT

WHEN I WAS IN COLLEGE, I WENT SKY-diving over the plains of Texas. Three years later, wanting to relive that unique moment of transcendence and tested limits, I went skydiving again, this time over the Swiss Alps. Ten years later, I've learned to embrace a spiritual alternative to jumping out of planes.

The reason that most engage in adventure sports such as rock climbing, car racing, bungee jumping, and skydiving, I believe, is not so much the actual love for these activities, but the unmatched power they have to awaken an individual to the present. No one is worried about paying their taxes when falling out of a plane at a high velocity, nor is one considering their morning meeting when one false step could lead to a plunge over a mountain cliff. Some think this thrill is the way to give life meaning.

Contrary to this thrill-seeking approach, we must embrace that we are already bursting with life potential at every moment. If we live more present to the spiritual realities of our world each day, we will find a meaningful life that is sustainable and empowering. Most of us are trapped in regret, guilt, and resentment over what is behind us, or in in anxiety, stress, and worry over what is yet to come. The most important life resource every human has been blessed with is the present.

Further, we cannot sacrifice the welfare of the needy today for the promise of a better tomorrow. To further communism, fifty million people were murdered to bring about a "better world." Redemption starts today, not tomorrow, and the present can't be neglected.

To be responsible for the now necessitates that we must ensure a healthy inner life. If we pollute our souls, it will spill over into global pollution. The most important first step to healing our world is to tend to our spiritual lives and to our deepest inner spaces. When we are morally focused and spiritually healthy, we can transcend ourselves for the other in their moment of need.

Perhaps the most profound statement that our forefathers give in the Torah on numerous occasions is *hineini* (here I am), the most important spiritual response to any problem we encounter. No matter what comes up, we should strive to be present to that which is in front of us, and be appreciative of the moment, ready to take action.

This is not so easy; even Moses, our greatest prophet, struggled with this. Ramban explains: "Moses didn't see the presence of God at the burning bush right away, because he hadn't prepared his heart for prophesy" (Exodus 3:2). We must prepare ourselves for the radical possibility of the moment, or we will miss it. We have to wonder just how much we are missing each day.

Rambam explains, even more strongly, that the greatest evils come from the spiritually blind, and if we don't open our eyes in the world – intellectually and spiritually – we will actually cause great harm to others (*Guide for the Perplexed* 3:11).

The great Jewish theologian Michael Fishbane explains the imperative of the moment beautifully:

> Perhaps this: already with the opening of eyes, the hearing of ears, and the tactility of the body – already from such inadvertent moments the world imposes itself on us. It is always already there for me, just as I become there for it. There is no gap to be crossed (between the cognizing ego and the world): there is miraculously an immediate, primordial thereness of reality. Already from the first, and with every act of sensation, the world is "there" as a field of phenomenality, as a world of claims imposing themselves with an ever-present and evident presence. These claims put one under a primary obligation: one can respond or not respond; heal or destroy; attend or neglect; consume or build up. We have that choice (*Sacred Attunement*, 192).

We have that real choice to respond to the call of the moment or not to. The great sage Hillel famously teaches, "If not now, when?" There is no time like now to embrace life and its concomitant sacred opportunities and responsibilities. Hillel also suggests that Shabbat is not the sole time where we fine-tune our spiritual presence, rather "*Baruch Hashem yom yom*" – spiritually is a daily endeavor (*Beitzah* 16).

In the twenty-first century, we have more distractions than ever preventing us from cultivating the spiritual art of focus to ensure we climb to the heights of our potential. The Rabbis teach that one who pauses flippantly to enjoy nature while attempting to focus on higher spiritual matters "bears guilt upon their soul" (*Pirke Avot* 3:9). "Stopping to smell the roses" is not always the prescription for living spiritually present.

The theological model to emulate is the Shechinah (the Divine Presence) as we strive to be totally in the moment and the halachic model is called "*mitzvot tzrichot kavannah*" (commandments require presence and concentration). We emulate the Divine when we throw our full selves into our greatest life commitments (*mitzvot*).

I have come to learn over the last decade that to truly feel alive, we need not seek thrills like jumping from planes; rather, the most intensely meaningful life opportunities are constantly sitting right before our eyes. By tapping into the eternal timelessness of our inner life in the now, we have the potential to encounter two core attributes of God: the eternal and the infinite.

There is no time like now to start living in the now. It is all we have.　□

SPIRITUAL TRANSFORMATION THROUGH OUR DREAM INTERPRETATIONS

For in that sleep of death, what dreams may come.

— Hamlet

EVERY NIGHT OF OUR LIVES, WE ENTER THE dream state. Sometimes we are very aware of our dreams upon waking, sometimes not at all. I often wonder about the theological implications of our unconscious thoughts that occur while we dream. How are we to interpret these ideas and how can those interpretations help us to grow to become who we need to be?

We'll frame this issue around the explanation of the fourteenth century Spanish commentator, Rabbeinu Bahya ben Asher, of three types of dreams: those caused by indigestion, those caused by daytime thoughts, and those whose source is the soul (commentary, Genesis 41:1). Dreams, therefore, come from body, mind, and soul.

Bahya's first notion that dreams come from the body accords with one of the main theories of neuroscience today, that dreams are merely the random firing of neurons, carrying with them little to no meaning at all. One Talmudic passage similarly reduces the value of our dreams explaining that "dreams neither add nor detract" (*Gittin* 52a). The nineteenth century German scholar, Rabbi Samson Raphael Hirsch, explains what happens when neither the mind nor soul are controlling one's own thoughts: "Freedom of will is bound, fettered; body and mind obey unusual laws; as in the womb, all the germs for the future of the organism are there and swim about in unformed confusion because the soul, that spark of independent individuality is missing, thoughts and the germs of ideas weave together in confusion, they join one to the other by the laws of affinity and chance contact because the conscious human intelligence does not hold the guiding reins" (commentary, Genesis 20:3). Our first view of dreams tells us that they may be nonsense, not at all meaningful, and full of chaotic contradictory information.

The second notion that dreams might come from the mind lines up with the Freudian view that our dreams reveal a significant amount about our unconscious thoughts revolving around our childhood experiences, desires, fears, and "wish fulfilment." Freud explains that much of the repressed forces in our unconscious activity represent a desire to return to the knowing state of the womb. This is similar to the Jewish notion that a fetus is fully knowledgeable of the Torah until birth when it is forgotten. Rabbi Hirsch explains how one can take a rational psychological approach to dreams. "A perfectly rational person can explain a dream quite exactly without wishing in any way to insist that it need necessarily come true. The meaning should not be read into it from outside but must come out from the dream itself. Such an interpretation of a dream is a deep psychological task" (commentary, Genesis 40:5). For Carl Jung, we can access not only our personal unconscious realm, but also the collective unconscious. When we discuss dreams as a psychological phenomenon, we can make the case for how psychotherapy can help one reach religious and spiritual clarity and development.

However, more than seeing the body or mind as the origin of dreams, Jewish thinkers have embraced the approach that dreams originate in the soul and have spiritual significance for us. Dreams are actually embraced as one of the primary ways that God communicates with humans (Deuteronomy 12:6). Whereas Moses's prophecy came in his waking hours, all other prophecy would be transmitted in a dream state. This is not merely reserved for prophets. As the Talmud explains: "A dream is one-sixtieth part of prophecy" (*Berachot* 57b). Dreams can contain some deep truths hidden within other thoughts. "While part of a dream may be fulfilled, the whole is never fulfilled" (55a). The sixteenth century Turkish thinker, Rabbi Solomon Almoli, elaborates: "Just as there is no dream without empty matters, so there is no dream without truthful matters, and if we have not found a reason for them, it is because we have not understood the dream." Whether they are on the level of prophecy or not, our dreams have spiritual meaning!

How do we learn to discover this spiritual meaning? Rabbi Moshe Chaim Luzzatto is skeptical of how much we can uncover on our own: "God manipulates man's natural power to dream, and uses it as a means to transmit a prophetic vision. This does not mean, however, that a dream and a prophetic vision are in the same category. God's wisdom merely deemed that a dream could be an adequate vehicle for prophecy. When our Sages teach us that 'a dream is a sixtieth of prophecy,' they do not mean that the two are the same. What they are teaching us is that both contain information that man could not attain with his powers of reason alone" (*Derech Hashem*, 239). For Luzzatto, we will need more tools than reason to make sense of the complexity of our dreams.

The Zohar is very direct about the power and significance of a dream for us today: "In early times, prophecy rested on people, and they were able to see the glory above. When prophecy ceased, they made use of the voice from heaven. Now that prophecy and the voice from heaven have ceased, people must make use of the dream" (Zohar, Genesis 238a). The dreams have inherent significance that we must learn to uncover.

The Hassidim have engaged the power of dreams very deeply. The great Baal HaTanya, Rav Shneur Zalman of Liady, explains that "dreams are higher than rational thought. They come from a higher, prelinear reality." We will need more sophisticated tools to access that sphere of reality and to bring it down.

Perhaps the most profound lesson can be learned from the rabbinic teaching that "all dreams follow the mouth" (*Berachot* 56a). The meaning of dreams is based upon how we choose to interpret them. In post-modern parlance, dreams are not revealing what is necessarily true; rather, we choose and will the truth of the dreams through our interpretations of them.

For example, I believe that nightmares are gifts from God enabling us to access a painful situation without really having to experience the pain of the experience. This helps us to cultivate empathy if we choose to consider our self-improvement after our bad dreams. In fact, Rabbi Zeira taught, "If a man goes seven days without a dream, he is called evil," and Rabbi Huna taught that "a good man is not shown a good dream, and a bad man is not shown a bad dream" (55b). This comes to teach us that, perhaps, on some level, we need the human vulnerability of bad dreams to remain humble, sensitive, and empathetic. We must actively choose to use our dreams as a vehicle for deepening our spiritual and ethical sensitivities.

The alternative to gaining control of our interpretations is to make a dreamland a meaningless playground where we may experiment with possible life scenarios in ways that we may not have the opportunity or courage to do so in our regular lives. It is morally important to avoid these mental experiments since they distort our realities rather than enhance them. Others suggest that dreams may provide an important outlet to help one avoid mishaps in life. Plato explains in *The Republic* that "The virtuous man contents himself with dreaming that which the wicked man does in actual life." But Jewish tradition asks us to seek purity of mind and action and we must choose to gain more knowledge and empowerment of our psychological and spiritual lives.

There is a lot at stake if we do not invest in interpreting our dreams. The Zohar reminds us that we must invest time and effort in thinking about our dreams: "A person must remember a dream that is good so that it not be forgotten. Then it will be realized. On the other hand, inasmuch as one forgets a dream, the dream is forgotten. A dream that is uninterpreted is like a letter unread. Since one does not remember it, it is as if one does not know its interpretation. For this reason, if one does not remember a dream and is not conscious of it, it will not be realized" (Zohar, Genesis 199b). To avoid losing important growth opportunities, we must actively choose to employ all resources we are given in life to become better and our dreams are important tools in the process.

Rav Kook teaches us of the spiritual importance of this dream interpretation process:

> The dream is the conception of one's direction which sent from heaven for the purpose of activating one's energies lying dormant in the soul. The Sages' words that the dream follows the interpretation were not to be taken literally, as the interpreter's function is merely

to remind the dreamer of what he already knows . . . Dreams serve as
a boost from God helping to develop the quality of the soul of man.
The dream indicates that there is a hidden quality in the soul of the
dreamer. Through the dream alone, the soul-quality lacks the strength
to bring about the event hinted at; through the meaning reinforced
by the interpreter, the vision is perfected and grows strong in the soul,
where it is ready to bring about the event befitting it. . . . By recalling a
dream one strengthens that vision and the quality inside one's soul can
become strong enough to be actualized (*Midbar Shur* 222–6, 231–2).

As a religious activity, we must listen to our dreams and share them appropriately to learn from them, and spiritually actualize their intended
potential.

Rav Kook goes on to explain the spiritual work we must do upon rising
from sleep.

Sleep and the general nature of night that brings it about, work in man
two opposite effects: Man's spiritual self rises higher. His imagination
is liberated from the pen of the sense. He can visualize that which he
cannot during his waking hours. But the body has lost its connection
with the spirit. It operates on its own, going about its functions in
the dark. Both of these phenomena produce results: Pure lights from
the soul's ascent, and clumps of impurity from the darkness in which
the body was enveloped. Every morning, we turn to two tasks: To
purify the body, and to fasten the additional lights of the soul. And
once again, there commences the work of achieving a harmony of two
extremes (*Orot HaKodesh* I, 230).

This is our work: to unite the body and soul in this spiritual endeavor.

Before sleep, we recite the traditional prayers, hoping our dreams should
be for the good. "May my ideas, bad dreams, and bad notions not confound
me." Upon rising, we recite the traditional prayer, "*Modeh Ani*," thanking
God for returning our souls to us. Many also recite a special liturgy during
Birkat Kohanim, the priestly blessing recited on festivals. These prayers each
night, morning, and holiday provide us with special opportunities to pause
and reflect on our spiritual state and to regain connection with our soul.
These are opportunities not to escape but to embrace the spiritual toil accompanying our transitions from the conscious to the unconscious realms
and back. Here we can become more connected with the latent workings of

our body, mind, and soul. By gaining awareness through reflection, meditation, therapy, spiritual writing, and dream interpretation, we gain the empowerment to take more responsibility for our complete existence by uncovering the gems hidden in our souls.

God has given us a great treasure by giving us sleep filled with dreams. As the great Irish poet William Butler Yeats said: "In dreams begins responsibility." To embrace the profundity and spiritual insight of dreams is to embrace a very significant part of Jewish tradition and spiritual life.   □

JUDAISM'S VALUE OF HAPPINESS: LIVING WITH GRATITUDE AND IDEALISM

T HE WEEKLY READER OF THE JEWISH NEWS might come to believe that Judaism opposes happiness and favors worry, guilt, and conflict. We seem to be so down and obsessed with our problems: anti-Semitism, anti-Israel propaganda, assimilation, intermarriage, scandals, and on and on. But actually, Judaism very much embraces the importance of happiness.

Much attention has been given to the biological, economical, and philosophical approach to happiness, but what about the religious approach? Can and should the great religious virtues bring us deeper life contentment? The great virtues of gratitude and idealism not only add to the lives of others, but can enrich us with a happier and more fulfilling life.

The great Hassidic Rabbi Nahman famously taught that "It is a great mitzvah to always be happy." When we are happy, we can do everything better, so religious life necessitates that we cultivate happiness when appropriate. When things were going poorly for the Jews 2,500 years ago, the prophet reminds the people of the importance of joy: "Do not mourn or weep. Go and enjoy choice food and sweet drinks, and send some to those who have nothing prepared. This day is sacred to our Lord. Do not grieve, for the joy of the Lord is your strength" (Nehemiah 8: 9–10). There is a place for mourning loss, but Judaism cherishes the celebration of life.

The Rabbis teach that "the reward of a mitzvah is the mitzvah itself" (*Pirke Avot* 4:2). Rather than some metaphysical intervention, the great feeling that comes from doing right is itself the reward. Some have suggested that no act is altruistic, since one feels good afterwards. This is not the Jewish approach. What would it say about the religious personality if one did not feel positively after doing a good act? Feeling good about doing right is an important reminder that we are on the right track and is constitutive of the ethical personality. One of the greatest contributions that Judaism makes to the potential of soul actualization is "*ivdu et Hashem b'simhah*," that we are to serve God in joy. This is what Judaism preaches: happiness must actively be cultivated if we are to thrive in this life. Pessimism and cynicism are vices in Jewish thought.

Psychologists have also found that idealism is correlated with happiness. The Israeli-born Harvard professor of positive psychology, Tal Ben-Shahar, in his book *Happier* writes:

> Being an idealist is being a realist in the deepest sense – it is being true to our real nature. We are so constituted that we actually need our lives to have meaning. Without a higher purpose, a calling, an ideal, we cannot attain our full potential for happiness . . . Being an idealist is about having a sense of purpose that encompasses our life as a whole; but for us to be happy, it is not enough to experience our life as meaningful on the general level of the big picture. We need to find meaning on the specific level of our daily existence as well.

To live Jewishly is to live inspired with the optimism that we can build a more just and holy world, with the faith that there is a promising future for all humankind.

Surely, idealism is not all happiness, as living by our ideals entails struggling. Viktor Frankl, in *Man's Search for Meaning*, explains: "What man actually needs is not a tensionless state but rather the striving and struggling for some goal worthy of him. What he needs is not the discharge of tension at any cost, but the call of a potential meaning waiting to be fulfilled by him." When we struggle to achieve our ideals, we live a life of meaning. To do this, one not only needs courage but also fellow human beings (family, friends, mentors, spiritual community). For example, research shows that national pride is correlated with happiness.

In addition to struggling to live by our ideals of the future, psychologists teach the importance of gratitude in the present. This is made most clear by the rabbinic teaching: "Who is rich? He who appreciates (or is happy with) his portion" (*Pirke Avot* 4:1). To cultivate this, the Rabbis teach that we should make 100 blessings a day (*Menahot* 42b). These are moments when we step back and reflect upon our good fortune and express gratitude.

Perhaps the most basic event that all humans can feel gratitude for is waking up each morning. There is a Jewish blessing to commemorate this daily miraculous occurrence: "I express my gratitude before You, Living and Eternal King, for You have returned my soul to me with compassion; how great is your faithfulness!" Realizing that each day is a blessing can lead to real inner joy (*sipuk nefesh*).

Another common time to express gratitude is before and after eating. In the Jewish blessing after meals, the words "*v'achalta v'savata uveirachta*" (you shall eat, be satisfied, and bless) are recited, teaching that one not only expresses gratitude on eating, but also on the feeling of being full and satisfied. Before we run to fulfill our next desire, we should pause to be full of gratitude and contentment (*histapkut*).

To be sure, happiness alone cannot be our end point. Toni Morrison, speaking to college graduates, said it best: "I urge you, please don't settle for happiness. It's not good enough. Of course, you deserve it. But if that is all you have in mind – happiness – I want to suggest to you that personal success devoid of meaningfulness, free of a steady commitment to social justice, that's more than a barren life, it is a trivial one. It's looking good instead of doing good." While we should strive to live with joy, we should balance this with other life commitments and values.

When we actively cultivate gratitude and idealism, we can become happier individuals better equipped to change the world and live inspired lives committed to doing good. The Jewish people have much to be preoccupied with, but when we infuse joy into our service and commitment, we can actualize to the next level and in more sustainable and meaningful ways.

□

WHERE ARE YOU?
KEEPING OUR DREAMS ALIVE

JEWS (AND THE 3,300 YEAR-OLD PROJECT OF Judaism) are pretty *meshugana*! We believe in the most radical way that everything we do matters, and that we can and must change the world. Even though there are only about thirteen million of us, we believe that every one of us matters in our national and global commitments to transform the world. Is it okay that we are so radically hopeful?

Edgar Allan Poe once wrote: "Men have called me mad; but the question is not yet settled, whether madness is or is not the loftiest intelligence."

We, as a people, are ambitious and strive to excel beyond the norm, and sometimes we draw credit or blame where none is due. This is perhaps why, when four Americans were murdered in Libya, there are immediate accusations that it was a Jew behind the video that agitated the rioters and terrorists.

Albert Einstein remarked: "Great spirits have always encountered violent opposition from mediocre minds." We are a people with a bold task and the rigorous ethical and religious demands of the Torah. And we believe that we are free and capable of changing the world. Animosity from small minds will always assail us, and others may remain aloof. Sometimes we may also be challenged by our own lack of personal autonomy and sense of responsibility.

Do you recall the infamous case of Kitty Genovese, who in 1964 was raped and murdered in New York City as dozens of people watched from their windows and did nothing? Social psychologists show that the larger the number of bystanders, the less likely we are to intervene to help another. Perhaps we see that others are not helping so we need not help. Or perhaps we feel that someone else has probably responded or may be better equipped to help so we need not help. We are social beings, and at times social conformity can have disastrous results. Rather than live with the bold goal of actualizing our individual responsibility, too often we live with the goal of avoiding shame, avoiding doing anything new or different than what is done all around us, avoiding risk.

The shortest question in the Torah is, remarkably, God's first question. It is a question asked in Genesis 3:9. Adam and Eve had just eaten some fruit from the forbidden tree and, sensing God's presence in the Garden of Eden, they hid among the trees. While they were hiding, God asked Adam a one-word question: *Ayeka*? "Where are you?"

This is a question that only those with courage ask themselves each year: Where am I? Am I just getting by? Eating, sleeping, working? Seeking instant gratification? Or am I driven by a greater purpose? Am I aware every day that what I do with my life truly matters? There is indeed an urgency to find ourselves. When we arise each day from bed, and we say "*Hineni*" (here I am), we know that we cannot resolve all of the problems of the world, but we know we can try our best. As we learn in *Pirke Avot* (2:21): "It is not upon you to complete the task, but you are not free to desist from it."

One of the great sicknesses thriving today in the twenty-first century is cynicism. Ever seen it? Someone who thinks that nothing is important and nothing matters and nothing needs to change. Things are really just fine as they are, or maybe terrible and not worth improving. It is perhaps the most un-Jewish approach to life and the most uninspired way to live. It is a sickness that spreads to all others around: where everything becomes a joke rather than a holy opportunity to engage.

Maimonides teaches in *Hilchot Teshuva* that we should view our lives as if we were standing on a scale and our next action will determine whether the world is redeemed or destroyed. Now how many of us really believe that our next action will have this impact? We need not believe it. But Rambam is teaching that this is a way to see the world and live our lives. We are to live as though everything matters. We live with hope and faith and possibility.

I think of my friend and teacher, Oscar in Guatemala. Oscar lost all of his family in war. His friends, all around him, gave up. There was no more meaning, no more hope, no more purpose. Somehow, Oscar found the courage and inspiration to protest this mentality. Today, Oscar travels from poor village to poor village around his country helping the leadership to build their communities. Oscar saw the bait to deny hope and to be stuck in the past. He resisted, and is a faith hero!

Rav Hayyim, a close student of the Baal Shem Tov from the town of Krosno, used to love to watch the rope dancer with awe and attentiveness. One day, his students asked him why he spent so much free time watching the man on high dancing upon a rope. He responded that this person, while risking his life, could not be thinking for even a moment about the 100 gulden coins that he was going to make, because then he would fall. And that this is how we should view our lives – we are all walking on a very thin rope . . . at any moment, it could all be over for us. If we remember this, then we'll always have to be focused on the big things that really matter. We should consider what Kafka once said: "The meaning of life is that it ends." Our lives are deeply sacred!

Rav Shlomo Karlin, of the eighteenth century, once explained that the greatest *yetzer hara* (inhibition against doing good) is that we forget that we are the children of the King (we forget *Avinu Malkeinu*). We are not without value or purpose. We are here because God brought us into being with love and gave us work to do, saying in a quiet voice, "Bring a fragment of my presence into other lives."

We are free to answer the question "*Ayeka*" with deep integrity as we say *Hineni*. We have the ability and freedom to choose our lives. After all, the absolute foundation of Jewish philosophical commitment is that we are free.

This message is not always clear because unfortunately, the three great advocates of determinism were Jews (Karl Marx, Baruch Spinoza, and Sigmund Freud). Karl Marx argued that our behavior is determined by structures of power in society, among them the ownership of property. This is called economic determinism. Baruch Spinoza argued that human conduct is given by the instincts we acquire at birth. This is called genetic determinism. Sigmund Freud argued that we are shaped by early experiences in childhood. This is called psychological determinism.

But determinism leads to excuses. We know that we are affected by our culture, by the economy, by our upbringing, by our genes, etc. Judaism comes to tell the world that there are no excuses! You are free! You have choice. You are responsible. You can transcend your reality. Adam's first response is the denial of freedom – the woman gave it to me. And Eve's first response also denies freedom – the serpent told me to do it. The Torah warns us that at the core of human nature is the need to give excuses and to deny our freedom for how we choose to live.

Rabbi Jonathan Sacks, the former Chief Rabbi of the United Kingdom, writes in *To Heal a Fractured World*:

> There is no life without a task; no person without a talent; no place without a fragment of God's light waiting to be discovered and

redeemed; no situation without its possibility of sanctification; no moment without its call. It may take a lifetime to learn how to find these things, but once we learn, we realize in retrospect that all it ever took was the ability to listen. When God calls, He does not do so by way of universal imperatives. Instead, He whispers our name – and the greatest reply, the reply of Abraham, is simply *hineni*: "Here I am," ready to heed your call, to mend a fragment of Your all-too-broken world.

May we embrace our freedom in the deepest way and may we all respond: "*Hineni*, here I am, ready to heed your call, to mend a fragment of Your all-too-broken world."   □

CAN ANGER BE CONSTRUCTIVE? A REFLECTION ON ACTIVISM AND LIFE

ANGER IS UNIVERSALLY CONSIDERED A VICE. WE are asked to emulate the Divine who is "*erech apayim*," slow to anger (Exodus 34:6; Deuteronomy 11:22). The Rabbis, in fact, refer to anger as a form of idolatry, where one worships oneself. Thus, the Rabbis teach that one must be slow to anger and easy to appease (*Pirke Avot* 5:10). Rabbi Nahman of Breslov taught: "There is no peace in the world because there is too much anger. You can only make peace with joy." The Rabbis teach us: "One who sees an idol that has not been destroyed pronounces the blessing, 'Blessed is He who is slow to anger'" (Tosefta, *Berachot* 7:2). I would suggest that this wording was chosen because God should be angry at how much evil there is in the world that is unchallenged. Yet God has humbly allowed us to be the ambassadors of truth and the defenders of justice on earth. We can emulate this divine patience frustrated at an unredeemed world while still feeling a great sense of urgency.

In a brilliant Midrash, we learn that God withholds expressing anger not only from the just but also from the wicked. "Rav Shmuel bar Nahman said in the name of Rav Yohanan: It does not say here *erech af*, but rather *erech apayim* (in plural); He delays His anger with the righteous and delays His anger with the wicked" (Yerushalmi *Taanit* 2:1; *Eruvin* 22a). We are to withhold expressing anger to any person, good or bad.

However, expressing anger can be useful. The Rambam taught that while one should not get angry, one should pretend to be angry to educate young children when they're doing wrong. On the most basic level, this emotion stimulates people to reach a goal, in the short term. Furthermore, it is a factor that can be particularly useful for social justice activists and leaders. Professor Jeff Stout, the great religion scholar at Princeton University, writes in *Blessed are the Organized*:

> Anger is one of the most important traits they (organizers) look for in potential leaders. Someone who professes love of justice, but is not angered by its violation, is unlikely to stay with the struggle for justice through thick and thin, to display the passion that will motivate others to join in, or to have enough courage to stand up to the powers that be.

In social justice work, one must be sure to respond quickly to social problems and injustices and yet also be sure not to let anger dominate one's psyche or persona. Sustained anger takes up an extraordinary amount of energy, and as activists we must preserve our energy as best we can to ensure we are effective. The Hassidic rabbis, therefore, teach that we must not subdue our anger, for that leads to lost potential. Rather, we should channel our anger into more productive and healthy emotions that increase our ability to engage in constructive organizing. Mohandas Gandhi, who led the fight for independence in India, observed that "anger controlled can be transmuted into a power that can move the world." To clarify further, Professor Stout describe his concept of "just anger," that

> . . . stands midway between despairing rage and liberal squeamishness about the vehement passions. A politics of just anger aims to restore the spirit of democracy to democratic culture, a spirit disposed to become angry at right things in the right way and use this passion to motivate the level of political involvement essential to striving for significant social change.

To Stout, "elites" that proclaim their impartiality too often support social injustice by insisting that "victims" remain passive, and view any righteous anger of the oppressed as a violation of "the elite code of decorum." The proper role of social organizers, Stout notes, is to "oppose that code" and disrupt the deceptive calm of oppression.

Finally, Stout explains that anger can facilitate the creation of a communal feeling of empowerment, which can lead to social justice.

> The experience of anger can reveal to us that we do indeed care about being treated as citizens. If we did not think of ourselves as bound together to some extent by mutual respect, then we would not be angered by the behavior and negligence of elites. To feel anger is to have the importance of the relationship and its demands drawn to our attention. Accordingly, the individual who rarely experiences anger in response to injustices . . . [shows] slavishness and apathy. A central task of a leader . . . is to help others transform themselves from slavish or apathetic victims into people who behave and feel as citizens do.

To put this differently, as the French existentialist (and French Resistance member) Albert Camus writes: "I rebel – therefore we exist."

Rabbi Abraham Joshua Heschel, in his "A Prayer for Peace," writes:

> O Lord, we confess our sins, we are ashamed of the inadequacy of our anguish, of how faint and slight is our mercy. We are a generation that has lost its capacity for outrage. We must continue to remind ourselves that in a free society all are involved in what some are doing. Some are guilty, all are responsible."

We must feel outrage, as our prophets once did, when we encounter oppression and injustice. This is what it means to be alive and to be Jewish.

Rabbi Joseph B. Soloveitchik argued that:

> Of course, love is a great and noble emotion, fostering the social spirit and elevating man, but not always is the loving person capable of meeting the challenge of harsh realities. In certain situations, a disjunctive emotion, such as anger or indignation may become the motivating force for noble and valuable action ("A Theory of Emotions," 183).

The greatest Jewish philosophers of the last century recognized the importance of this truth: Controlled and righteous anger, in defence of social justice and noble causes, is no vice.

Anger is unhealthy, but it is also human. We should dismiss rage (*hema*) when it comes from self-righteousness but when anger (*af*) is experienced in response to the pain of another we should harness the emotion to elevate ourselves by responding to a greater calling. ☐

SHOULD WE RELY UPON SIGNS?

POLLS HAVE REVEALED THAT ABOUT ONE IN eight people admit to believing that bad luck will ensue if they allow a black cat to cross their path, if they walk under a ladder, or if they break a mirror. In addition, while fewer than one in ten acknowledge seeing the number 13 as unlucky, it is rare to find a building with a thirteenth floor. The irrational belief in the significance of "signs" is prevalent in contemporary society, as it has been since the beginning of time. Jewish thought provides an array of approaches to this phenomenon, but the rational one as articulated by the Rambam is most compelling.

We find this old tendency in the book of Genesis, when Eliezer has a mission to find Yitzhak a wife. He travels, looking for a specific sign to determine who the correct bride would be. Tosafot in *Hullin* 95b questions Eliezer's methods in selecting a wife for Yitzhak, suggesting that he is violating the prohibition of *nihush* (found in Leviticus 19:26).The Gemara (*Sanhedrin* 65b) gives examples of this biblical prohibition against making decisions based on omens and random events, such as food falling from one's mouth or a deer crossing one's path, or on the supposed significance of natural occurrences such as the migratory patterns of fish or birds.

There is an important argument between Rambam and the Raavad (Rabbi Avraham ben David of Provence) on this subject (*Hilchot Avodat Kochavim u-Mazalot* 11:5), particularly as it relates to the Eliezer story. The

Raavad is lenient on Eliezer, arguing that the only prohibited cases of *nihush* are the examples explicitly enumerated in the Gemara and that the signs validated and followed by Eliezer are actually permitted. Additionally, the Raavad connects the prohibition of *nihush* with that of *kishuf* (magic), and argues that since Eliezer is using the value of kindness demonstrated by Rivka, rather than an omen or magic, as a sign, this is not a problem.

In contrast, for the Rambam, *nihush* is about a lack of faith in God, who provides good without resorting to the occult. The Rambam is not lenient on the Eliezer case, and he not only includes the specific omens brought in the Gemara but extends the prohibition to include any and every sign used to predict the future – even one based on a personal experience. He writes: "One must not say 'if the following occurs I will take a specific action and if not I will refrain.'" This activity, practiced by Eliezer, is forbidden: "Anything like this is completely prohibited, and one who commits such an action is punished with lashes." Raavad is furious at this approach: "How is it possible that he (the Rambam) thought such righteous people would have engaged in such a sin? If I were they, I would send tongues of fire into his nostrils."

One might argue (like Rambam) that attempts to predict the future trivialize the capacity for rational thought, intellectual deliberation, and thoughtful reflection, and that religious life should not be tolerant of this. On the other hand, we may note that, as some cognitive psychologists have argued, humans are unique in their capacity for planning and looking toward the future: While most of our daily thoughts are involved in memory of the past and tasks in the present, about twelve percent of our thinking is about the future. Thus, planning – setting goals, hopes, and dreams – is part of our being. Since we have this special capacity, we can ask, how do we, as religious people, think about the future, about expectations, and about dreams or desires? How do we use our memory actively to plan for our future?

In our own times, we can see the importance of forward thinking to our happiness and sense of self. The philosopher Robert Nozick imagined the possibility of a virtual reality machine, through which one could have any chosen experience and not have it ruined by the knowledge that he or she is hooked up to the machine. Nozick asked, "Would one choose to be hooked up?" He concluded, perhaps idealistically, that no one in their right mind would choose to be hooked up to this machine, even if it means constant pleasure, since it could not bring happiness at all. Fulfillment of purpose must be real and deliberate, not accidental or virtual. A meaningful life is a contemplated one that involves will, choice, planning, and perhaps struggle.

There are countless "signs" and systems in place in our lives that prompt us to act in a certain way: When I see a red light, I stop; when I hear the baby crying, I go to soothe her. I would argue here that we are mostly discussing our most meaningful life decisions and roles rather than our way of getting through daily tasks. These signs also are necessary to the task and not arbitrary. Still, there should be moments of reflection before a stimulus produces a result.

To return to Eliezer's case, even when his motives seem to be the most pure, as he was looking for positive qualities so as to find a match for Yitzhak, the Rambam teaches that one must not rely upon signs. It is not fitting for one striving to max out one's human potential as a meaning-making being to trust in omen and superstition. And so I would argue that this is the reason that Eliezer's name is not mentioned in the *parsha*. He is the generic "*eved*," or "*ish*." When one relies upon signs, one gives up one's uniqueness as a future-looking and thinking person, indeed one gives up one's very personality. Reliance upon signs transforms a person from being a religious agent into a mere sign checker.

When we use random occurrences and connect this to key decisions, we make mistakes. The fact that I saw a black cat actually has no connection to my stubbing a toe and certainly does not mean that I need to sell off my investments. Superstitions can cause one to make poor decisions or poor cause/effect connections.

Finally, what is the source of truth and good that we rely upon in life while making our core decisions? How in touch with our decision-making process are we, and do we reevaluate it from time to time? According to the Rambam, religious life demands not only the commitments of our actions and the commitments of our thoughts and intellectual strivings. It also commands the connection between the two: which thoughts lead us to which actions. The stakes are high, but God has faith in us. Do we have faith in ourselves? □

☐ SPIRITUAL PRACTICES AND HOLY COMMUNITIES

IS PRAYER FOR ACTIVISTS?

Our basic premise as activists is human responsibility. We, not someone else, must step up to create change in the world. To turn to others before ourselves is for cynics and critics, not change-makers. What about prayer? Is it a cop out? I would suggest that prayer offers us three vital opportunities as activists:

- Reflection and Self-awareness
- Reminder of Values and Recharge
- Humility

First, we know that activism can make us hot-headed, and impulses can run high. Prayer is the opportunity to check back in with our essence. As Rav Kook explains:

> Prayer is only correct when it arises from the idea that the soul is always praying. When many days or years have passed without serious prayer, toxic stones gather around one's heart, and one feels, because of them, a certain heaviness of spirit. When one forgets the essence of one's own soul, when one distracts his mind from attending to the innermost content of his own personal life, everything becomes confused and uncertain. The primary role of change, which at once sheds light on the darkened zone, is for the person to return to himself, to the root of his soul (*Olat HaRaaya*, 2).

Prayer reminds us that we must slow down, reflect upon our actions, and become very aware of our feelings and our spiritual integrity.

Second, prayer is a time to recharge, pausing to remind ourselves of core values and reaffirming our highest moral and spiritual commitments. Activists are consumed with opposing some of the most immoral forces on the planet. Prayer is a return to idealism, to hope, and to faith that justice will prevail. The twentieth century philosopher Pierre Teilhard de Chardin explains: "We are not physical creatures having a spiritual experience. We are spiritual creatures having a physical experience." By connecting with our spiritual values, we can return to the material world with a broader, fresher, and more idealistic spirit.

Third, in prayer we humble ourselves. We remember that we do not control the world. We do not naively believe that we will succeed in all of our endeavors or that God will merely fulfill our requests. Instead, we seek a humble connection above, without expectations, as we affirm that the job of God is taken. Rabbi Joseph B. Soloveitchik explains that God listens, but prayer is more about relationship and connection than wish fulfillment.

> We have the assurance that God is indeed a *shomeiah tefillah*, One who *hears* our prayers, but not necessarily that He is a *mekabel tefillah*, One who *accepts* our prayers, and accedes to our specific requests. It is our persistent hope that our requests will be fulfilled, but it is not our primary motivation for prayer. In praying, we do not seek a response to a particular request as much as we desire a fellowship with God (*Reflections of the Rav*, Vol. 1, 78).

When we seek a relationship with the Divine, we not only humble ourselves but fill ourselves with wonder. Biologist J.B.S. Haldane said it well: "The world will not perish for want of wonders but for want of wonder." Prayer reminds us of how small we are amongst the cosmos.

To be an activist is about taking responsibility for the injustices and oppressions in society. A spiritual life that embraces prayer is not at odds with this goal. Prayer may be one of our most important tools to build community, spiritually recharge, and enhance our collective efforts to create a more just world.   □

IS THE SYNAGOGUE A RELIC
OF THE PAST?

M ANY JEWS TODAY CLAIM THAT THEY ARE "spiritual not religious," that organized religion is not relevant, or that they would rather spend their free time alone than with others. Those who attend synagogue weekly often reserve the service, especially the sermon, for a special naptime. Others prefer a twenty–person basement setting for a quick prayer service rather than a formal, large gathering at *shul*. Around two-thirds of Americans claim to be members of a house of worship, which is more than twenty-five percent higher than Jewish synagogue membership. Is the synagogue becoming extinct? If so, should we seek to prevent extinction?

At its worst, synagogue is rife with factionalism and small-mindedness, a place to mumble irrelevant foreign words and snooze during an out of touch sermon, and later nosh on stale chips at *Kiddush* while discussing the stock market and the latest gossip. Synagogues spend their limited funds on plaques, high-end scotch, and a new social hall rather than on adequately paying staff and investing in learning programs. Congregants drive $50,000 cars but request assistance on the membership dues. The experience is predictable, tedious, and boring. It resembles a business transaction, where one has paid membership dues for the right to services, more than a sacred obligation. The staff and board do not lead with Jewish values but act as management as if the congregation was just another business venture. The ritual is empty and the action is either inadequate or nonexistent.

Leading such a congregation is virtually impossible. The rabbi is required to perform four full-time jobs, take 3 AM phone calls, act as the scapegoat for all failures, and also please each congregant while handling critiques with a smile. Congregants are forthcoming with complaints, but few volunteer when they can watch the football game on television. Rabbi Abraham Joshua Heschel observed: "The modern temple suffers from a severe cold. The services are prim, the voice is dry, the temple is clean and tidy . . . no one will cry, the words are stillborn."

Some see patterns of dysfunction. Professor James Kugel identified three kinds of harmful synagogues: the (1) "Ceremonial Hall Synagogue," (2) "Nostalgia Center," and (3) "Davening Club." In the Ceremonial Hall, the congregants neither care to participate nor learn about what is really going on; they just wish to be an entertained audience. Mimicking a Broadway show, *shul* becomes entertainment, and the rabbi and cantor get a score for their performance. At the Nostalgia Center, the rabbi is often the youngest one present, and Judaism is about sitting where one's grandfather sat, saying *Kaddish*, and telling stale Yiddish jokes. Everything is wrong but nothing should be changed. The congregation's traditions and customs trump shared values, meaning, connection, and opportunities for growth. At the Davening Club, there is a false semblance of prayer intensity, but it more closely resembles a mumble-festival, without any real spiritual uplift.

On the other hand, at its best, *shul* can be a transformative spiritual experience. Eager congregants roll up their sleeves to build the community, providing an open, relevant experience for all. Prayer centers can be welcoming, participatory, and collaborative. Most importantly, a strong synagogue is driven by shared values and a sense of mission and purpose. Congregants look inside the walls of the prayer community for intimate connection and reciprocal comfort, and look outside for opportunities to reach out and give back. Peter Steinke, author of *Healthy Congregations*, explains that congregations need to move from being clergy-focused to mission-focused. Rather than relying upon clergy to inspire and entertain the congregation, everyone is involved in a system of involvement, encouragement, and teaching.

A healthy congregation takes much effort to build. A diverse population attends *shul* for very different reasons: children, singles, empty nesters, intermarried families, etc. Each population must be honored and be given a seat at the table. Too often, the elderly members of the congregation complain that there are not enough young people at the congregation to "keep the tradition alive"; to improve, they must be willing to adapt the experience to invite a new audience.

For the synagogue to survive and be relevant in the twenty-first century, congregants must seek authentic prayer experiences, enrichment through learning, and a contribution to community building. One does not just show up when convenient, but to support others consistently. Do not sit back and blame a poor prayer experience on the rabbi. If you find yourself unable to achieve meaningful prayer, learning, and volunteer experiences, consider changing *shuls* (and search within yourself). The heart must actually be open if one wishes to be inspired. But do not quit the synagogue enterprise — it has survived thousands of years for a reason.   □

BUILDING HEALTHY COMMUNITIES: WHAT TYPE OF CONGREGANT ARE YOU?

M Y RABBINIC COLLEAGUES OFTEN REMARK to me how much they care about and even love their congregants. In particular, they appreciate the *compliment-giver*, *volunteer-giver*, and the *humble servant*. The compliment-giver feels deep appreciation for all the community provides and likes to express this gratitude. The volunteer-giver does not just make suggestions for improvements but jumps at the opportunity to contribute to improve the community. The humble servant is rarely seen in public leadership but is consistently contributing behind the scenes to ensure that things operate smoothly. Serving these individuals makes the strenuous work of rabbis an utter delight.

One of the most common complaints I hear from rabbinic colleagues, on the other hand, is not the long hours, stressful counseling sessions, or the difficulty of attracting new members. Indeed, worse than low numbers is the appearance of a challenging congregant. Just as there is almost always a student in the class holding a group back with constant jokes, there are often a handful of *shul* members who strain the emotional patience of the rabbi and other congregational leaders.

There are three types of tough congregants: the *kvetcher* (complainer), the *schnorer* (beggar), and the *mazik* (troublemaker). The *kvetcher* is irritated by everything — the custom should always be different, and everything is offensive. The *schnorer* always wants something — worst of all, they take your time even when there is no question or task to address. The most draining, however, is the *mazik*. This individual feeds off of conflict and tension, and always needs to be the center of attention. Anyone else, especially those in leadership, is subject to attack at any moment. The *mazik* alienates other congregants, frustrates spiritual leadership, and makes the congregation an unsafe and unhealthy place. Because of these individuals, well-meaning people searching for spiritual succor dread going to the synagogue, *beit midrash*, or community program. One rabbinic colleague shared with me that he quit leading his pulpit he loved after many years of service because a small handful of these individuals drained all of his spiritual energy.

Of course, these challenging congregants must be shown respect and love (and on occasion encouraged to seek psychiatric treatment), but we need defined boundaries for the preservation of the community. After all, it only takes one bad apple to spoil the bunch. The sage Rabbi Shimon bar Yohai tells this story: "A man in a boat began to bore a hole under his seat. His fellow passengers protested. 'What concern is it of yours,' he responded, 'I am making a hole under my seat, not yours.' They replied, 'That is so, but when the water enters and the boat sinks, we too will drown'" (*Leviticus Rabbah* 4:6).

Spiritual leaders commit to serving all congregants regardless of their moral character, but it is the job of the congregational staff, board, and lay leaders to shield spiritual leaders when this goes overboard. Most abuse goes unseen: 3 AM phone calls on issues that could wait until the morning, five-page emails with twenty questions, and complaints about the hummus brand served at *Kiddush*.

In extreme cases, a *farbisener hunt* (mean, bitter person) can threaten to turn our warm spiritual homes into dreary and toxic places. Thus, when they speak gossip, complain left and right, and abuse community privileges, everyone should work cooperatively to address the problem. Fortunately, the *kvetcher*, *schnorer*, and *mazik* are exceptions. The majority of congregants are wonderful, and they enrich and enjoy each other's company. They make the tireless rabbi's toil worth the effort.

We can all pause to ask ourselves: what type of congregant am I? Where do I operate as the compliment-giver, volunteer-giver, and the humble servant? Where do I operate in the *kvetcher*, *schnorer*, and *mazik* triumvirate? Am I adding positive energy to the congregation or am I draining the community? Am I defending congregational leaders and congregants who are being drained? Sometimes we have to inquire of others what role we play as we may have blind spots.

Spiritual homes should prioritize inclusivity so that all feel welcome but this does not mean that everything goes. To ensure that a community is inclusive, warm, and safe, there need to be limits and practices that are identified as harmful to one or all.

Congregations are not places where we seek to be served, but holy sanctuaries where we learn the art of giving to actualize our potential. □

LEVINAS AND THE TRANSFORMATIVE POWER OF RITUAL

I WAKE UP TO AN INBOX FULL OF EMAILS, GLOBAL news demanding reaction, and a daily agenda triple the size of what will prove achievable. How am I to pause to turn inward? When I put on my *tefillin* each morning, I consider what I need to become liberated from in order to fully return in servitude back to my highest callings. The straps bind me to that mission.

Rituals are non-utilitarian, symbolic acts that involve and promote the cultivation of mindfulness. The transformative power of ritual is achieved when we take the opportunity to explore ourselves, our hearts, and our ideals. We step out of this world to cultivate a meaningful experience and then to return to life changed. This is why we seek to perform ritual on our own and not by proxy. There are various explanations for, and values to, the performance of ritual.

"Ritual," in its essence and spelling, is the root of "spi-ritual" because we can only really access the depths of our minds, hearts, and souls when we perform certain physical acts with our bodies consistently as rituals. Rambam explains that the deepest human learning comes from habituation. Returning to ritual each day of our lives helps to condition us to live by our ideals.

Some explain that the great power of ritual is social since the performance of rituals indicates commitment to a group and to an identity. Rituals add stability to community and tighten social bonds through the sharing of meaningful practices. Others suggest ritual allows for cathartic, emotional purging, since in ritual one can emotionally distance oneself from certain life events and experience feelings with a degree of separation.

Time to pause

The danger in ritual is that one can use the power of the structure to avoid internalization. One can sit *shiva* as their act of mourning yet never truly embrace the grief and loss. One could embrace *kashrut* yet never seek the deeper spiritual and ethical components to the ritual. One could pray from a *siddur* every day yet never really concentrate on the deep meaning of the words recited. Ritual, at its worst, distracts us from real life. But at its best, ritual can enhance our mindfulness with which we live.

Writer Jonathan Safran Foer spoke about the "room servicing of life," how the tendency today is to prefer that others do things for us than we do them for ourselves. Ritual is the radical reminder that we live our own lives.

The greatest power of religious ritual, in my view, is the opportunity to deepen one's self-awareness about one's own moral and spiritual values. Too rarely do we pause to give birth to our dreams and visions that make our lives unique. As German social psychologist Erich Fromm writes: "Man always dies before he is fully born." Ritual gives us the chance to pause to assess how we are living and to give rise to our nascent spiritual potential. It is done with urgency since we never know when our time on this earth will run out and we will have passed away before we've given birth to our great contributions in this world.

Even further, it reminds us of our ability to slow down. A study in the *Academy of Management Journal* shows that when confronted with clear choices of right and wrong, people will take some time to think about the issue rather than make a quick decision they are five times more likely to do the right thing. Pausing to reflect provides moral clarity.

Daily ritual is an opportunity to pause, reflect, and step out of our routine to hear the voice of our inner conscience. Viktor Frankl explains that moral life exists in the moment between stimulus and response. Ritual reconditions us to make more of those crucial moments in our life that elevate us from base to noble and can be used to enhance our psychological processes and internal incentives.

On Ritual and Justice

The great Franco-Jewish philosopher and Talmudist, Emmanuel Levinas, in his book *Difficult Freedom* teaches about the power of Jewish ritural to inform and inspire our work to make the world more just, which is of paramount importance. He writes:

> The Justice rendered to the Other, my neighbor, gives me an unsurpassable proximity to God . . . The pious person is the just person. . . . For love itself demands justice and my relation with my neighbor cannot remain outside the lines which this neighbor maintains with various third parties. The third party is also my neighbor. Thus, when we pursue justice in a Jewish way, we come closer to God. This is because "[t]he ritual law constitutes the austere law that strives to achieve justice. Only this law can recognize the face of the Other which has managed to improve an austere role on its true nature . . ." (176–177).

This discipline found in religious life through ritual is needed in our daily lives: "The way that leads to God therefore leads . . . to humankind; and the way that leads to humankind draws us back to ritual discipline and self-education. Its greatness lies in daily regularity . . ." One cannot rely on an occasional, passive religious service, but on daily ritual. To Levinas, ritual tames man and calms the spirit: "The law is effort. The daily fidelity to the ritual gesture demands a courage that is calmer, nobler, and greater than that of the warrior. . . . The law of the Jew is never a yoke. It carries its own joy . . ." Far from religion as dour, drudge-like labor, ritual is joyful labor.

We can see this truth in other areas, as well. Social workers have seen the beneficial effects of rituals on youths who have grown up with poverty, domestic violence, sexual abuse, drug addiction, crime, and parents who either abandoned their families or have been incarcerated. Mark Redmond, Executive Director of Spectrum Youth and Family Services, observes: "Rituals, whether religious or not, are vital to family life. Having dinner together every night – without any television, cell phones or email present – is extremely important. Bedtime rituals are also important. And making a big deal about birthdays and anniversaries and holidays – all important." These rituals, and religious rituals, provide safety, stability, and purpose to children who otherwise would live in a world of anxiety and hopelessness.

In a similar vein, Levinas argues that the human-Divine relationship formed in ritual gives us the strength to fight for justice: "The fact that the relationship with the Divine crosses the relationship with people and coincides with social justice is therefore what epitomizes the entire spirit of the Hebrew Bible. Moses and the prophets preoccupied themselves not with the immorality of the soul but with the poor, the widow, the orphan, and the stranger." This human-Divine relationship should not be characterized as "spiritual friendship," but one "that is manifested, tested, and accomplished in a just economy for which each person is fully responsible . . ."

The Jewish sense of slavery, which we return to so frequently in Jewish prayer and ritual, defines our narrative and ethical consciousness. "The traumatic experience of my slavery in Egypt constitutes my very humanity, a fact that immediately allies me to the workers, the wretched and the persecuted peoples of the world. My uniqueness lies in the responsibility I display to the Other . . . Humankind is called before a form of Judgment and justice that recognizes this responsibility . . ." Once again, Levinas challenges the view of ritual as insular and passive, recasting it as central in raising our awareness of our commonality with all the poor and vulnerable.

Levinas reminds us that when we honor the dignity of the other we are also honoring the Other. When we embrace the Other we are preparing for our work in social justice for the other. May we return to Jewish ritual with fervor and determination, and may we allow its spiritual power to transform us to be agents of love and justice in emulation of the Divine.

Every year we return to the *Haggadah* and the *shofar*. Every week we return to candle lighting and Shabbat song. Every day we return to text study and prayer. These rituals are about religious worship, intellectual development, community building, and emotional stability. But they are also important for the creation of the just society, ensuring that we all take moments to return to non-utilitarian acts that do not advance our self-interest but challenge us to stop and listen. In an age of honking, buzzing, and texting, this may be one of our greatest moral salvations. The performance of ritual is the timeless channel back to moral purpose.   □

LIVING AND LEADING WITH SOUL

S INCE THE BEGINNING OF TIME, HUMANS HAVE sought to discover the essence and location of the soul, the divine essence constitutive of our humanity. Some scientists today claim that *le siege de l'ame* (the seat of the soul) is in the temporal lobe of the human brain ("the God spot"), and V.S. Ramachandran, a neuroscientist at University of California, San Diego, demonstrated in the 1990s that patients with temporal lobe epilepsy were particularly affected by religious experiences. Others reject this claim that the soul has a physical location, thus preserving its metaphysical mystery. But more important than knowing the soul's location is to understand the soul's value. Today, in a world flooded with external stimuli, we often forget the greatest treasure we have access to – the depths of our own souls.

To the Jew, the soul is not some esoteric mystery to wonder about, but a force to be accessed and lived with. We should neither neglect nor obsess over the body and soul. Activism requires both mental work, to understand the issues and come up with a strategic response, and physical work, to apply that response in practice, in our streets. More important than mind and body, however, sustained social justice activism needs the soul, to inspire the deeper sensitivity that ensures we help, more than harm, others. The soul is where our moral and spiritual choices leave their eternal mark. In today's world, and especially in Jewish social justice activism, the soul has in many ways been forgotten. It is of tremendous importance that we return to our spiritual essence.

The soul is our holy transcendental channel to the infinite and eternal, our source of immortality. Those who choose enlightened life can access spiritual wisdom: "For God speaks time and again, though man does not perceive it. In a dream, in a night vision, when deep sleep falls on people as they slumber in their beds, then it is He who opens people's understanding" (Job 33:14–16). Our social identities in this world are helpful but not eternal: We can embrace them but we must also transcend them. Eckhart Tolle in *The Power of Now* explains this well: "Death is a stripping away of all that is not you. The secret to life is to 'die before you die' – and find that there is no death." Remembering that we have a deeper essence inspires us to live and strip away the falsity surrounding the self.

Further, the soul serves as a reminder that this life is fleeting. "Do not rely on the mighty to save you, or on any human being. His breath gives out, then back to earth he goes – on that every day, his projects are all for naught" (Psalm 146). Our soul is on loan in order that we return it even more beautiful than how we received it. The sages of the Talmud refer to the soul as a *pikadon* (a deposit), since God has entrusted us with this divine light to use and guard during our days. Maimonides teaches that if we cultivated something very beautiful with our lives, when the body ceases to operate, the soul will continue to flourish. If we neglect the soul, nothing will continue to exist after our body is buried. The afterlife is not, God forbid, only for those with a particular religious affiliation. The Rabbis teach that "The righteous of the nations have a share in the World to Come" (Tosefta *Sanhedrin* 13:1). The soul, the foundation of human existence, is universal.

Our souls also give us accountability, serving as reminders that not only are all our actions watched, but all our motives and desires are known: "A man may do whatever he wishes, but his soul reports it back to God" (*Pesikta Rabbati* 8). From cognitive perception in this world, we live with moral ambiguity; all of us do good and evil. But the soul is more black and white. Based upon our true motives, it is known if we lived committed to good or evil, self-worship or other-serving. The options are to "choose life or death" (Deuteronomy 30:19). When it comes to the soul, there is no in-between. In our activism, the soul, the home of the conscience, can help as a guide through the morass of gray. The deepest inner voice only knows truth.

The soul is our inner light. If we can tap into our spiritual channel and access that light, we can share it with the world. This is the work we are called to.   ☐

THE PRESENT AND THE FUTURE: HEISENBERG'S UNCERTAINTY PRINCIPLE

I N 1927, WERNER HEISENBERG SET THE WORLD OF quantum physics on its ear with his Uncertainty Principle. In relation to a subatomic particle (e.g., electron), Heisenberg stated that the more precisely we measure its location, the more imprecise becomes our calculation of its momentum, and vice versa. Thus, in a physical seesaw, we cannot measure both an electron's location and momentum simultaneously, for measuring one will thwart the measuring of the other.

In practical terms, Heisenberg's Uncertainty Principle relates to knowing either where an object is or where it is going in the future. We can calculate exactly where something is in the present moment, but then its momentum (i.e., knowledge of where it is going) is completely unknown. I would like to use this uncertainty principle as a springboard to the broader question of how we live our lives.

Notwithstanding the past, is our present the electron and our future the momentum? Can we be cognizant of the present and simultaneously be aware of our future, or is there an uncertainty principle here? If so, which deserves more of our attention: being present in the moment, or being prepared for the future? We would like to fully embrace both, but our human experience seems to demonstrate that the more "present" you are, the less aware you will be about where you are going, and vice versa. Both of these mindsets are important; however, should we give more weight to being present-minded or future-minded? Is there another possibility?

Judaism has tended to place more value on the past (memory, *zachor*) and the present (observing and protecting, *shamor*) than the future. However, while acknowledging that the future remains uncertain, there are significant responsibilities upon us to plan for and consider the future. In fact, one rabbi argues that our consideration of the future outcome of our actions is the most important virtue for man to cling to (*Pirke Avot* 2:13).

God is the ultimate model for living in all times simultaneously, as is learned from the revealed Divine Name (*yud, hey, vav, hey,* "to be" in past, present, and future). But this is one of the attributes of God that we cannot emulate. We learn from the Seven Blessings recited at a Jewish wedding that at that holy moment of union, the Garden of Eden and the messianic times are connected. It is a moment of transcendence in a cosmic connection between past, present, and future. Perhaps only at a divinely embraced union of love such as this is such a phenomenon possible.

Aside from a unique moment of transcendence, we cannot simultaneously know our current position and our trajectory. However, we must strive to make the effort to consider the future implications of our actions today, and perhaps we can then achieve more balance in present and future thinking. An imbalance of present and future thought can create problems. Many are constantly late because they get so caught up in current activities that they neglect future commitments. Others struggle with present obligations because they are so consumed with upcoming events. We must learn to constantly alternate between present and future thinking. Ron Heifetz, Harvard professor of leadership studies, teaches that when we "dance" we must also be "on the balcony" watching ourselves. If we are only dancing, we are unaware that the dance is changing. However, if we are only observing, then we fail to dance properly in the present.

This cognitive exercise provides an important lesson about creating social change. We must attend to the needs of those suffering before us in the moment (*hesed*). However, if we only do this, then we risk neglecting the paradigm shifts that are necessary to understand to attack the root causes of injustices (*tzedek*). As moral agents, we must consider the current situation and the future outcome of our actions. We cannot merely embrace current obligations (deontology), nor can we merely act based upon future expectations (consequentialism). Rather, our moral lives transcend these temporal paradigms.

While we must always strive our best, Heisenberg's Uncertainty Principle reminds us that we must have the humility to embrace that we cannot fully live in the present and engage in future thinking simultaneously. The best we can do is *teshuva* (repentance and transformation): working to change the future by actively changing ourselves and our world in the present. The world is constantly changing but together we must tackle the greatest moral issues of our time. □

YOM KIPPUR: AN ENCOUNTER WITH DEATH AND LIFE

"**M**ITAH V'YOM HAKIPPURIM MICHAPRIN." THE two ways to truly atone are Death and Yom Kippur. But are the two really so different? On Yom Kippur, we reject food and drink, similar to one close to death. We say *Vidui* (our confessions) just like someone preparing to die. Many wear white on Yom Kippur – the *kittel*, the same plain shroud that one will be buried in. We remove ourselves from leather shoes, bathing, anointing, and marital relations on Yom Kippur again as though we are mourners. Our lives are lived in our bodies. On Yom Kippur we step out of our bodies as if we were gone. We visit the cemetery at this time to honor those who have passed away and to soften our hearts to our mortality. We ask ourselves on Yom Kippur in *U'Netaneh Tokef*: "Who shall live and who shall die."

One of the main objectives on Yom Kippur is to encounter death. We spend one day reflecting on our mortality. When we fully embrace Yom Kippur, we have an encounter with death (a preparation for death). We are to be transformed by it; in preparing for death, we come to more deeply celebrate life. Even more, our transformation teaches us to reprioritize what really matters. As Sogyal Rinpoche once wrote: "Death is a mirror in which the entire meaning of life is reflected."

One day of the year we accept the reality of death, but we are not like Buddhists who willingly embrace death. On all other days of the year, we mourn those who have passed, we protest the taking of lives, we prevent death by seeking cures and healing. But protesting death must not overtake us. Rather, taking ownership of life must. As the great French existentialist Simone de Beauvoir writes: "We are having a hard time living because we are so bent on outwitting death" (*The Ethics of Ambiguity*, 120).

So only on this day we let down our guard and embrace the inevitable to remind us that although our death must come someday, today we must live. We can best perform the mitzvah of *u'varchata ba'chayim*, to choose life, once we are aware of the alternative and that there is a choice to be made.

There is an intimacy we achieve with our Creator when we approach death just as those on their deathbeds who lose their theological skepticism. In fact, we learn from the Talmud (*Shabbat* 88b) that those who experienced the revelation at Sinai directly from the mouth of God perished in that moment and were brought back to life. It is only in a life/death transcendental moment that we can truly grasp certain truths.

Longtime hospice worker Kathleen Dowling Singh lays out the stages of dying in her book, *The Grace in Dying*. They are, according to her: Chaos, Surrender, and Transcendence. Yom Kippur can be modeled off these three. We are in chaos during the night, and the early morning of Yom Kippur hits us like a ton of bricks. Then we begin to surrender once we realize that we are able to transcend our hunger and personal desires. Finally, we may reach transcendence in the late afternoon when we tap into our deeper potential to understand ourselves and the world.

If we "die" on Yom Kippur, then we go to *Olam HaBa* (the next world). That next world paradoxically is actually *Olam HaZeh* (this world). We learn to live in this world as if it were the next world (in our near-death experience). We encounter death in order to live.

The Talmud in *Moed Katan* teaches the following story:

> When Rav Nahman was dying, he begged Rava to implore the angel of death not to torment him. Rava replied, "But, Master, are you not esteemed enough to ask him yourself?" Rav Nahman considered this for a moment, and then pondered aloud, "Who is esteemed, who is regarded, who is distinguished" in the face of Death Himself? Then, after he died, Rav Nahman appeared to Rava in a dream: "Master, did you suffer any pain?," Rava asked. Rav Nahman replied, "As little as taking a hair from milk. Still, if the Holy One were to say to me, 'Go back to that world,' I would not consent, the fear of death being so great.'"

On Yom Kippur, we learn that we need not fear death. Rather, we must embrace death in order that we can affirm life in the deepest sense.   □

YOM KIPPUR: EXPANDING OUR COMMUNAL ROLES

THE JEWISH COMMUNITY, AT LARGE, IS STRUG-gling to find common spaces where all can be together. After all, where can we be united as twenty-first century Jews? In religious belief? On Israel? In Jewish educa-tion? On some type of mitzvah day or day of learning? Only a small fraction of the community shows up to anything or agrees to anything; we have become remarkably fragmented.

If the Jewish community is merely a restaurant, then we come when we're hungry and like what's on the menu. We pay for our food, leave our trash, and go home. But if the Jewish community is more like a family, we show up to support things even when they do not totally speak to us, even when the meal being served is not what we would have ordered. Perhaps what has been most lost from Jewish community building is a sense of connection to the big picture, the whole, and the notion that we sometimes must sacrifice our desires for the well-being of the broader community.

In the Yom Kippur liturgy, before *Vidui*, we sing "*Ki Anu Amecha*" (be-cause we are Your people) and in this prayer we use eleven metaphors of our collective relationship to God (Nation before God, Child before Parent, Slave before Master, Congregation before Portion, Heritage before Lot, Sheep before Shepherd, Vineyard before Watchmen, Handiwork before Shaper, Beloved before Lover, Treasure before God, Designated before Designated). We are able to sustain as one people before God, since there are many divine roles. Perhaps no one role could hold the attention and trust of us all.

And yet, there is an important growth opportunity for each of us hidden in this song. One aspect of *teshuva* we focus on at Yom Kippur is learning how to connect to all of these different divine manifestations (God as shep-herd, God as parent, God as watchman, etc.). By doing so, in addition to strengthening our personal connection to our Creator, we can learn how to emulate each of these roles and how we can broaden ourselves to play mul-tiple communal roles. We do not come to *shul* just to see our three or four friends and achieve personal goals, but also to connect to the community as a whole and achieve communal goals. To do that, we must be broader in our vision.

As part of the philosophical mind-body problem, we know that we cannot know each other's essences, nor each other's minds and hearts. We come to learn about each other through our actions. Someone smiles! Someone picks up a table to help! The way one walks and talks! One reveals oneself through actions. We relate to community not through our belief but by what we give, by what we do publicly, and sometimes just by showing up.

Elie Wiesel explains that we can connect to one another through our common history:

> We are bound by tradition to believe that together we have stood at Sinai, that together we have crossed the river Jordan, conquered the land of Canaan and built the Temple; that together we have been driven thence by the Babylonians and the Romans; that together we have roamed the dark byroads of exile; that together we have dreamed of recapturing a glory we have never forgotten – every one of us is the sum of our common history.

This is true, but we are also much more than a "sum of our common history." We are the present as well.

The early twentieth century Jewish Russian philosopher Jacob Klatzkin wrote: "To be a Jew means the acceptance of neither a religious nor an ethical creed. We are neither a denomination nor a school of thought, but members of one family, bearers of a common history."

To be a family means to show up for one another and to support one another, to fulfill what the Talmud (*Shavuot* 39a) mandates as "*Kol Yisrael arevim zeh ba'zeh*" – "All Israel is responsible for one another." We do that by broadening ourselves and by building bridges, not through putting up walls.

Unfortunately, there are those who would reject this family. Israeli Chief Sephardi Rabbi Shlomo Amar has stated that if a Jew should encounter only Reform Jews on Rosh Hashanah, "it is better for him to pray in his hotel and not go near them. Moreover, it is better that he not pray at all than pray with them." In response, Reform Rabbi Uri Regev said: "It is sad that Rabbi Amar chooses the holiest time of the Jewish year, which should celebrate Jewish unity, to pursue his sectarian fundamentalist views." Rabbi Regev added that "pluralism and diversity," rather than seeking "fault with fellow Jews," should be what Judaism stands for.

There are very valid disagreements about how we should practice Judaism today. We need not agree with one another but we must respect one another and find spaces for sharing, dialogue, cooperation, and support. We need not love everyone in our spiritual family but we must support one another nonetheless.

One of the themes of Yom Kippur is that we enter alone. Each of us arises in fear for our lives, standing alone, feeble before the Creator without any good explanations for how we lived the previous year. Yet, we conclude by singing about our collective destiny, *"L'Shana Ha'baa B'Yerushalayim."* We enter as individuals, but if we truly internalize the day, we feel more connected to our whole community and people.

On Yom Kippur, we should strive to emulate the Divine to become larger presences, playing greater roles in our communities to have our own unique impact in our magnificent national story.   □

SHOULD AMERICAN JEWS CELEBRATE THANKSGIVING?

I N MODERN TIMES, JEWS ARE OFTEN WARY OF EN-gaging in non-Jewish practices, even non-religious ones, since participation could lead to assimilation or a perversion of our values. In the case of the American holiday of Thanksgiving, not only should we, as Jews, not be hesitant to participate – we should embrace the spirit of this day and lead!

It took nearly 240 years for Thanksgiving to become an annual observance. Thanksgiving was first celebrated in 1621, a century and a half before the United States of America was formed, by early pilgrims who wanted to express thanks for their harvest. During the American Revolution, the Second Continental Congress set December 18, 1777 as the first day of Thanksgiving (although not an annual observance). After the Constitution was ratified, President George Washington, at the request of Congress, issued a Thanksgiving Day Proclamation for October 3, 1789 (again a one-day observance). Finally, in 1863, President Abraham Lincoln made this a reality. While the 1777 Proclamation uses overt Christian language, neither Washington's nor Lincoln's proclamations carry a specifically Christian message, so Thanksgiving could be celebrated by Americans of all faiths.

For many Americans today, Thanksgiving is just a day for turkey, football, and beer. But for many others, the day represents much more: reconnecting with family, expressing thanks for those people and values we cherish most, and engaging in service for those in need. The continuing American commitment to family is evidenced by the estimate that in 2012, 43.6 million Americans will travel at least 50 miles to be with their families.

Thanksgiving offers an extra opportunity to cultivate the Jewish virtue of gratitude (*hakarat ha-tov*). In the Jewish blessing after meals, the words "*v'achalta v'savata uveirachta*" (you shall eat, be satisfied, and bless) are recited, teaching that one not only expresses gratitude for eating, but also for the feeling of being full and satisfied. Before we run to fulfill our next desire, we should pause to be full of gratitude and contentment (*histapkut*).

Rabbi Moshe Feinstein, the great 20th century American Jewish legal authority, said that America is a "*medina shel hesed*" (a country of kindness), and that we are obligated to express our thanks to this great nation for giving us a free and safe home. As American Jews, we have much to be thankful for. My synagogue will be saying a portion of *Hallel* at our morning prayer service because Thanksgiving is a time for us as Americans and as Jews to give thanks. When gratitude is authentic, it is turned from an emotion into song, and from song into giving outwards. On Thanksgiving, let's remember to show our thanks and take this opportunity to give! □

ORGAN DONATION:
HOLIEST OF MITZVOT

WHEN WE PASS FROM THIS WORLD AND our bodies enter the ground, do we merely wish to be remembered or do we wish to give the gift of life to others? For the medical, economic, and moral well-being of our society, the United States must change its policy on organ donation requirements.

In my community, we were shocked and relieved when one congregant received a new kidney (a 100 percent perfect match, which is quite rare). After much pain and prolonged dialysis, she and her family were able to start a new life.

When my colleague and friend Robby Berman founded the Halachic Organ Donor Society, he sought to educate and inspire the Jewish community to save lives. Many had been confused by obscure teachings that Judaism was in some way opposed to organ donation, since, as some have told me: "I will emerge in heaven without that body part," or that it is a violation of the dignity of the human corpse. Nothing could be further from the truth; organ donation is tantamount to *pikuah nefesh* (saving a life), one of the greatest of Jewish *mitzvot*.

The Nodah B'Yehuda, the great eighteenth century authority of Jewish law, teaches that saving a life is such a high priority that it overrides the prohibitions against cutting into or desecrating a cadaver. Jewish sources do not show that one must be buried with all of one's organs to be resurrected and that there is only spiritual gain, not loss, in performing this mitzvah.

Consider the current state of Americans on the waiting list for organs and other transplant needs, which grows by 4,000 every day due to the sharp increase in type 2 diabetes (the leading cause of kidney failure) and other factors:

- In a recent ten-year period, the number of people waiting for kidney, heart, liver, lung, or pancreas transplants doubled – to a total of 98,000.

- Tens of thousands of others wait for bone and joint, skin, and heart valve transplants.
- Each organ donor has the capacity to get eight people off the organ transplant waiting list, and help as many as fifty people through donation of corneas, bone and joint tissue, heart valves, and skin.

Failure of the heart, liver, kidney, or another organ no longer has to mean the end of life. Most recipients live many years after their transplant. For example, in 2009, the percentage of people still living five years after their transplant ranged from a low of 54 percent for lung recipients to 75 percent for heart recipients. However, while about seventy-nine organ transplants take place every day, another eighteen people die on the waiting list before they receive a transplant.

Princeton University ethicist Peter Singer boldly argues that it is immoral to keep both of one's kidneys, since we generally only need one and someone will die if we do not donate our kidney to them. We are not all on the moral level to donate our kidneys as living donors, but at least at the end of our lives, we all must take this step. If everyone would commit to donating their organs at the time of their death, this would help to alleviate the worldwide organ shortage and its associated abuses. According to the World Health Organization, thousands of people a year in India, Pakistan, the Philippines, China, and other countries sell their organs to mostly wealthy recipients, in spite of international efforts to prohibit these activities. If more organs were available here, there would not be a demand to buy organs from more vulnerable individuals around the world.

On the positive side, 100 million Americans have signed up to be organ donors. However, America needs to offer more incentives to draw in those unwilling to donate. Spain and Austria, to take but two examples, have adopted an opt-out approach, called presumed consent, to posthumous organ donation. An opt-out, rather than an opt-in, approach is more likely to produce a society that takes care of its own.

There is an important rabbinic debate about whether death occurs at the cessation of the heartbeat or at the death of the brain stem, but virtually all major authorities take the lenient approach, agreeing that saving lives is the highest value.

Some ultra-Orthodox Israelis have said they would accept organ donations but not give them. This is clearly immoral. In response, the Israeli government has decided to try a new system that would give organ transplant priority to patients who have agreed to donate their own organs as well. Thus, Israel has become the first country in the world to incorporate "nonmedical" criteria into the organ donation priority system. Medical necessity would, of course, still be the first priority. This is a step in the right direction. We must be a nation of givers as that is the purpose of our people. The Israeli government should continue to lead the way toward incentivizing the moral commitment of organ donation.

In the Talmud, saving a life supersedes almost all other values, and thus organ donation is one of the great religious acts according to Jewish law. Mature religious thinking requires that we consider the big picture: our spiritual existence after our physical existence has expired. We should open up conversations with our loved ones about what we want to happen with our organs after we leave this world. The Halachic Organ Donor Society is leading the way in opening this conversation, but we also need more voices to advocate for positive change. We must be proactive and "choose life!"□

A REFLECTION ON AWAKENING AND ENCOUNTERING

THE JEWISH TRADITION SEEKS TO STARTLE US, to challenge our routine and our dogmas. Slavoj Zizek, the Slovene philosopher and social critique, writes poignantly about this point:

> There is an overwhelming argument for the intimate link between Judaism and psychoanalysis: in both cases, the focus is on the traumatic encounter with the abyss of the desiring Other, with the terrifying figure of an impenetrable Other who wants something from us, but does not make it clear what this something is – the Jewish people's encounter with their God whose impenetrable call disrupts the routine of human daily existence; the child's encounter with the enigma of the other's (in this case, parental) enjoyment (Zizek, *How to Read Lacan*, 99).

This is what Emmanuel Levinas similarly calls "the ethics of alterity," and Martin Buber refers to as the "I and Thou." It is about human encounters and the responsibilities born out of them. Encountering the human face and presence is indeed the birth of the ethical moment. Poverty is not an abstraction and it can take consistent conversations with the homeless to remember the pressing needs. So too, social change does not happen from the email or the office but in the streets and in relationships. Being in relationship with God is described as being *panimelpanim* (face-to-face). How much more true for humans where the face can be taken literally. Perhaps one of the most powerful ways that one may encounter the Divine is in the face of the human, in the calling of the ethical moment of the encounter.

Zizek explains the thinking of Jacques Lacan, the twentieth century French psychoanalyst. "For Lacan, the ultimate ethical task is that of the true awakening: not only from sleep, but from the spell of fantasy that controls us even more when we are awake" (ibid., 60).

To truly live, we must break free from fantasies and from our societal torpor. To do this, we must take off the veils that block us and hide us from true encounters with God and man. When we have the true courage to see and be seen, we can awaken our deeper spirit and our authentic self.

Sigmund Freud often took a very negative approach to the human psyche and to human nature. Here is how he understood the depth of Plato's myth of the "Ring of Gyges" (where Plato ponders in *The Republic* whether an intelligent person would be moral if he or she were invisible and did not have any fear of being caught and punished):

> The bit of truth behind all this [talk of virtue] – one so eagerly denied, is that men are not gentle, friendly creatures wishing for love, but that a powerful desire for aggression has to be reckoned with as part of that instinctual endowment. The result is that their neighbor is only to them not only a possible helper or sexual object, but also a temptation to them to gratify their aggressiveness on him, to exploit his capacity for work without recompense, to use him sexually without his consent, to seize his possessions, to humiliate him, to cause him pain, to torture and to kill him; *homo homini lupus* – who has the courage to dispute it in the face of all the evidence in his own life, and in history?

But we need not, and must not, view ourselves and others in this way. Humans are capable of doing terrible acts of evil, but we are also capable of performing tremendous acts of love. With each new human encounter we must see the beautiful potential in the face of that other. □

☐ JEWISH NARRATIVES AND CUSTOMS RECONSIDERED

GENOCIDE IN THE BIBLE

IN 2006, CONSERVATIVE RABBI JACK RIEMER, President Bill Clinton's rabbinic counsel during his tenure in the White House, created a stir when he associated Islamic fundamentalism with the biblical nation of Amalek:

> I am becoming convinced that Islamic Fundamentalism, or, as some people prefer to call it, "Islamo-fascism," is the most dangerous force that we have ever faced and that it is worthy of the name: Amalek . . . We must recognize who Amalek is in our generation, and we must prepare to fight it in every way we can. And may God help us in this task.

Who is Amalek?

According to the book of Exodus, Amalek is the nation that attacked the weakest among the Israelites as they fled from Egypt. This transgression was not to go unpunished. The Bible has a harsh prescription for Amalek: annihilation.

> It shall be that when Hashem, your God, gives you rest from all your enemies all around, in the Land that Hashem, your God, gives you as an inheritance to possess it, you shall blot out the memory of Amalek from under the heaven. Do not forget it! (Deuteronomy 25:19; also, see Exodus 17:14 and Numbers 24:20)

Blotting out the memory of Amalek was no mere psychological activity. The Israelites were expected to kill every Amalekite – man, woman, and child. But was this just a theoretical imperative or was it meant to be carried out?

The First Book of Samuel implies that it required actual fulfillment: "Now go and smite Amalek, and utterly destroy all that they have, and spare them not; but slay both man and woman, infant and suckling, ox, and sheep, camel and ass" (I Samuel 15:3). King Saul struck down Amalek as he was commanded but he then took mercy upon King Agag and upon some of the Amalekite animals. God and the prophet Samuel harshly criticized Saul for not fulfilling God's word.

The point, of course, is that an invocation of Amalek is serious business. Rabbi Riemer was not issuing a literal call to arms, but by associating "Islamo-Fascists" with Amalek, Rabbi Riemer was referencing the Jewish tradition's latent genocidal proclivities. Jewish authorities have struggled with this commandment for centuries, but the issue is perhaps even more urgent now.

For the last 2,000 years the Jewish people have lacked political sovereignty. With the return to the Land of Israel, however, this is no longer the case. Invoking Amalek during the centuries of military impotency was one thing. Today, when there is a Jewish state with an army, it is quite another, entirely.

A Complicated History

The exegetical history of the commandment to destroy Amalek is painful and complicated. The Talmud argues that the attacks and exiles of Sanherib, the king of Assyria and destroyer of Samaria, "mixed up the nations" over 2,500 years ago, and thus all identity of the biblical nations has been lost (*Berachot* 28a). This implies that all commands of exterminating nations were dismissed and that it is not appropriate to label any contemporary peoples as descendants of Amalek.

However, the *Sefer HaHinnuch*, a thirteenth century Spanish legal work, claims that the commandment still exists, demanding that every individual Jew must kill each individual Amalekite man, woman, and child (mitzvah 604). Maimonides, on the other hand, argues that the command applies not to every individual, but to the Jewish nation as a whole (*Hilchot Melachim* 6).

Yet, Maimonides also stated that the Jewish nation could accept converts from any nation in the world, including Amalek (*Hilchot Issurei Biah* 12:17).

Most significantly, Maimonides contends that the Jewish nation can never launch a war with any nation (uniquely including Amalek and the seven Canaanite nations together) without first offering "a call to peace" (*keri'a l'shalom*). If in this call to peace, the seven Noahide laws are accepted and peace is made, then no war is required (*Hilchot Melachim* 6:1).

In the *Guide for the Perplexed*, Maimonides explains further that the command to wipe out Amalek isn't based on hatred, but on removing Amalek-like behavior from the world (3:41). For Maimonides, the commandment is not necessarily fulfilled through killing; it can be fulfilled through moral influence and education.

Deuteronomy 20 distinguishes between the obligatory war of conquest against the seven nations of Canaan and other wars. According to Maimonides and Nahmanides, however, the obligation to offer a call for peace is applied to both. Nahmanides, in quoting a midrash, also claims that there is an obligation of a Jewish army, laying siege upon a town, to provide an open direction to escape for those of the enemy who do not wish to fight (*Sefer HaMitzvot* 5).

Some legal authorities were more eager to remove the commandment entirely from being applicable in our era. For example, in the nineteenth century, Rabbi Avraham Sochatchover argues: "If they repent from their ways and accept the Noahide commandments, and they no longer continue in the path of their forefathers, they are no longer held responsible for the sins of their forefathers" (*Avnei Nezer, Orah Hayyim* 2:508).

The Sochatchover Rebbe, like Maimonides, suggests that Amalek is a way of being, not a genetic trait. Shouldn't it be justified, then, for us to label contemporary enemies of the Jewish people Amalek? It appears, however, according to these interpretations, that the intention of the enemy must be first and foremost to destroy the Jewish people.

In addition to the rational legalists, the mystical thinkers in the Jewish tradition also provided useful reinterpretations. Professor Avi Sagi demonstrated the claim of many Hasidic sources that the battle against Amalek was only intended to be a spiritual war.

Invoking Amalek

Even if most people would not invoke the commandment to destroy Amalek today, there are certainly those, like Rabbi Riemer, who have ventured to do so. And there has been no dearth of similar, violent quasi-genocidal invocations in reference to the Palestinians, as well. For example, Benzi Lieberman, the former chairman of the Council of Settlements, said in no uncertain terms: "The Palestinians are Amalek! We will destroy them. We won't kill them all. But we will destroy their ability to think as a nation. We will destroy Palestinian nationalism."

The general consensus among today's Jewish community seems to be that our energies can and must be used to stop the perpetuation of genocidal activity occurring throughout the world, to become agents for peace, and to dismiss any contemporary comparisons to the biblical paradigm. But clearly there are difficult texts and teaching that remain in our tradition.

☐

WHAT'S THE PURPOSE OF CREATION? ON JEWISH RESPONSIBILITY

O N ROSH HASHANAH, I FIND MYSELF CON-
sumed in the liturgy by the phrase "*Ha-Yom harat olam*" (today the world is created), and raising questions about the purpose of creation and of my personal existence. When we reflect on the direction of our lives between Rosh Hashanah and Yom Kippur, we might ask ourselves why humans – generally as well as individually – were created.

In response to this philosophical question, the great ninth century Jewish philosopher Saadia Gaon argues that we live in an anthropocentric, centripetal universe. Everything is moving in value towards the center, towards the human. Rambam, however, rejects this view, arguing instead for a teleological view that God created everything for its own purpose and for the sake of God, not for man's sake, and that the universe is centrifugal, with everything moving out in value from the center.

I feel personally challenged and inspired by Rambam's position for which there is a lot of textual support that everything has a purpose, not only humans, and that humans are not the center of reality and value. Everything has a purpose and nothing is purposeless (Ecclesiastes 3:1, 3:17, 8:6). Rav Yehuda taught, "Of all that God created in the world, God did not create a single thing without a purpose" (*Shabbat* 77b). The Maharal understood this statement as follows: "All creatures were created because of the good inherent in them, and if the beings in existence did not have some good inherent in them, they would not have been created. For whatever is not good, in essence, is unworthy of existence" (*Derech HaChaim, Pirke Avot* 1:2).

This notion of existence's inherent goodness helps us cultivate a humility that we as humans are not above the rest of creation. Sustainability of the universe and all its inhabitants must be honored. We do not downplay the unique human dignity imbued in us when we embrace our lack of centrality. Rabbi Norman Lamm puts it well: "There is no need to exaggerate man's importance, and to exercise a kind of racial or global arrogance, in order to discover the sources of man's significance and uniqueness."

When we don't see ourselves as the sole purpose of existence, we can live in a complex society as more responsible beings. I quote philosopher Emmanuel Levinas:

> If (the Other) were my only interlocutor, I would have nothing but obligations! But I don't live in a world in which there is but one single "first comer"; there is always a third party in the world . . . my central idea is what I called an "asymmetry of intersubjectivity": the exceptional situation of the I. I always recall Dostoyevsky on this subject; one of his characters says: "We are all guilty for everything and everyone and I more than all others. But to this idea . . . I immediately add the concern for the third and, hence, justice."

When the purpose of creation is all about us, we may feel entitled. When we are not at the center, we may be more responsible and perhaps even "guilty." We have responsibilities to the "other" on an interpersonal level, to the "third party" on a social justice level, and to all of existence on a teleological level.

Harvard psychologist Bob Kegan explains that adults can progress through developmental stages from the impulsive, to the imperial, to the interpersonal, to the institutional, to the inter-individual. We are always fundamentally locked into our own minds but we can also transcend our egotistical limitations to reach greater levels of consciousness, mutuality, and intimacy. The foundation of our reality can become much more interconnected and interdependent. Our personal purpose is enhanced and actualized when it is interconnected with the multifaceted purposes of other forms of existences.

Perhaps Rabbi Simcha Bunim of Peshischa demonstrated it best when he taught that one should keep a slip of paper in each of one's two pockets. On one it should be written, "The world was created for me," and on the other, "I am but dust and ashes." He taught "The true wisdom is to know which pocket to use and when one should read which slip." We can embrace both aspects of life, what Rav Soloveitchik referred to as "majesty and humility." We should feel humbled that we were chosen for life, but also empowered to fulfill our calling in this world – fulfilling our full human and individual potential.

In the days between Rosh Hashanah and Yom Kippur, we should realize our importance in creation and thus our responsibility, but we should embrace a larger perspective of our lives, of our planet, and of the cosmos. This can inspire awe, humility, and responsibility.   □

TORAH AND SCIENCE: THE JEWISH MORAL CASE FOR EMBRACING EVOLUTION

T HE JEWISH TRADITION EMBRACES A VERY positive approach toward secular wisdom. The Talmud even transforms a mundane encounter with a wise gentile into a religious experience: "On seeing one of the sages of the nations of the world, one makes the following blessing: 'Blessed are you, Lord our God, King of the universe, who has given of His wisdom to mortal human beings" (*Berachot* 58a). The leading scientists of our age have fully embraced evolution as a given, yet for some reason, a literalist approach toward the Creation story is embraced by some rabbis today.

We are overdue in responsibly making the moral case for evolution in a religious framework. A secular person may be making evolution into a form of idol when they claim that evolution is the ultimate reason that we are what we are. Religious people, on the other hand, can view evolution as a tool of God rather than our primary cause. Science has a very important descriptive value whereas religion can have a very significant prescriptive value. We can embrace the tools and wisdom of science to fulfill our religious mandate to repair the world.

We must demonstrate why evolution is an acceptable Jewish theory to embrace. I would suggest that there are three approaches to making the case for evolution: textual, existential, and moral.

Maimonides, the great medieval Jewish thinker and doctor, makes the case for the textual ambiguity of the Creation story:

> Now, on the one hand, the subject of creation is very important, but on the other hand, our ability to understand these concepts is very limited. Therefore, God described these profound concepts, which His Divine wisdom found necessary to communicate to us, using allegories, metaphors, and imagery. The sages put it succinctly, "It is impossible to communicate to man the stupendous immensity of the creation of the universe." Therefore, the Torah simply says, "In the beginning, God created the heavens and the earth" (Genesis 1:1). But they pointed out that the subject is a deep mystery, as Solomon said: "It is elusive and exceedingly deep; who can discover it?" (Ecclesiastes 7:24). It has been outlined in metaphors so that the masses can understand it according to their mental capacity, while the educated take it in a different sense (*Guide for the Perplexed*, Introduction).

Further, Rabbi Avraham Yitzhak HaCohen Kook explains in the early twentieth century:

> These hesitations (in accepting an evolutionary view of the development of life) have nothing to do with any difficulty in reconciling the verses of Torah or other traditional texts with an evolutionary standpoint. Nothing is easier than this. Everyone knows that here, if anywhere, is the realm of parable, allegory, and allusion. In these most profound matters people are willing to accept that the true meaning lies on the mystical plane, far above what is apparent to the superficial eye (*Orot HaKodesh*, 559).

Rabbi Kook further explains that we must not be afraid to bring external truths into Jewish thought and belief.

> And in general, this is an important rule in the struggle of ideas: we should not immediately refute any idea which comes to contradict anything in Torah, but rather we should build the palace of Torah above it; in so doing, we are exalted by the Torah, and through this exaltation the ideas are revealed, and thereafter, when not pressured by anything, we can confidently also struggle against it (*Iggrot HaRe'iyah* 134, 163–164).

Along these lines, Rabbi Chaim Seidler-Feller, the Executive Director at the UCLA Hillel, argues that it may be a *hillul Hashem* (desecration of the Name of God) to read the Creation story in the Torah literally. He claimed that this makes religion look silly and the wisest scholars of our time will think we're ridiculous – thus desecrating our G–d and the value of religion.

There is also an existential case to be made. Why is evolution such a burning topic that drives everyone to have a strong opinion? We are ultimately trying to figure out who we are. Who is man? We look toward our beginnings but on a deeper level, we are not only searching for the origin of man but for the destiny of humankind, an answer to "who can man become?".

The Talmud itself couldn't be more explicit when it states "There were 974 generations before Adam" (*Shabbat* 88b). Quite simply, the Midrash explains that there were other manlike creations in existence before Adam. At a certain point, man was elevated to exist in the "image of God" and this is the moment of Adam HaRishon. This is the first human imbued with a certain level of spiritual dignity and responsibility. The moment when God breathed a soul into man creating human awareness of the self and of the Divine as well as the spiritual distinction between man and animal.

Rabbi Nissim ben Reuven, the great fourteenth century Spanish Talmudic scholar, suggested that all creation evolved from one substance:

> At the beginning of creation, a unified substance was created for everything under the lunar sphere. . . . this was because the will of God was to continue the nature of existence according to the possibilities, and not to create many things *ex nihilo*, since it is possible to make one substance that includes everything. . . . the creation of two substances

in the lower world *ex nihilo* would be without benefit; it suffices to have this wondrous and necessary origin.

In addition to evolution being an acceptable theory in Jewish thought, it also offers great potential for assisting the construction of moral thought.

Firstly, we are commanded by the Torah to remember, protect, and love the stranger since we were strangers. Can this apply to animals? Perhaps we must remember, protect, and love the animals since we were once animals as well.

Secondly, the fact that God created a world that lacked humans for billions of years reminds us that animals have inherent value and are created for their own sake. God does not create without purpose. Ibn Kaspi, the fourteenth century Jewish theologian from Provence, says it best: "In our pride we foolishly imagine that there is no kinship between us and the rest of the animal world . . . It was only after the flood that the consumption of meat became widespread which is tantamount to eating our parent, since it is nearest to our substance" (Deuteronomy 22:6). He explains that we should view animals as our parents, our spiritual ancestors in a sense.

Even further, the Hasidic masters, teach that man is still made up of a Godly soul and an animal soul (*Tanya*). While we have evolved beyond the animal world, we maintain our history and an essence which it is spiritually dangerous to ignore.

I must acknowledge that on a religious level, the veracity of the Creation story is so engrained in my consciousness that it continues to speak to me very deeply. Whereas science suggests that we naturally progress, religion reminds us that we must actively work to bring about progress. But scientifically and logically, evolution must be embraced. Even further, evolution reminds us of our Jewish and human responsibilities.

At the core of Jewish theology is the notion that we are progressing towards the messianic era. The goal of Jewish life is to move society to a more just and holy state. We have been progressing for millions of years and our role is to embrace the nature in which the Divine has placed us and also to transcend nature to further progress in the world.

At a Jewish wedding, we recite a blessing thanking God for creating man ("*yotzer ha-adam*"). This blessing is in the present, not the past, since God continues to create us. James Flynn, the great scientist from New Zealand, has shown that evolution continues as IQ has increased by an average of three points per decade during the twentieth century. In addition to learning more, we continue to find medical cures, expand our technological reach, and solve age-old problems. The Divine hand in partnership with humanity moves society forward. In the twenty-first century, we must be more sophisticated in how we read our sacred texts to guide us toward greater human progress.

Yet while we must discover our origins, Rabbi Abraham Joshua Heschel reminds us that our priority is to discover our destiny:

> Man in search of self-understanding is not motivated by a desire to classify himself zoologically or to find his place within the animal kingdom. His search, his being puzzled at himself is above all an act of dissociation and disengagement from sheer being, animal or otherwise. The search for self-understanding is a search for authenticity of essence, a search for genuineness not to be found in anonymity, commonness, and unremitting connaturally, thus any doctrine that describes man as an animal with a distinguishing attribute tends to obscure the problem which we seek to understand. Man is a peculiar being trying to understand his uniqueness. What he seeks to understand is not his animality but his humanity. He is not in search of his origin; he is in search of his destiny. The way man has come to be what he is illumines neither his immediate situation nor his ultimate destination. The gulf between the human and the nonhuman can be grasped only in human terms. Even the derivation of the human from the nonhuman is a human problem. Thus, pointing to the origin of man throws us back to the question: what do we mean by man, whose origin we try to explore?" (*Who Is Man*, 22).

To actualize our short-lived human experience, we must seek out our origin and our destiny. When we are informed by all wisdom of the world that helps us understood our holy Torah and the meaning of our existence, we can then fulfill our responsibilities most fully. □

CHANUKAH AND THE VALUE
OF GIVING GIFTS

I LOVE TO GIVE AND RECEIVE GIFTS. I ENJOY THE suspense of the unwrapping, the strengthened relationship that can emerge, and the opportunity to provide another with something new that they didn't expect to receive. After all, life is about giving and giving gifts is just another way to fulfill our purpose.

Over the years, however, I've struggled to decide how to approach my annual Chanukah gift buying, and how I can best raise my sensitivities to give better. I wonder how valuable it is to spend so many hours (and hundreds of dollars) shopping for gifts, only to find myself often feeling worse at the end of the day. Further, I'm turned off each year by the parts of our gift culture, such as aggressive competitiveness, that come with the holiday sales. Two of my favorite stores were involved in an alleged riot over $2 waffle irons at a Little Rock Wal-Mart and a pepper-spray attack over discounted Xbox games (not to mention a stun gun attack over a discounted Blu-ray player).

We can seek to repair how we give to others at the holiday time. The root of the Hebrew word for love (*ahava*) is *hav*, which means "to give." When we give to another, we can come to love that individual more. This is why a parent generally loves a child more than the child can love the parent. When we allow others to give to us, we can allow them to love us.

We can release some of our holiday stress and anxiety when we remember that typically the pressure of what gifts we will buy comes from us and not from the receiver of the gifts. And so as receivers, it's important for us to make a gift giver feel good about their giving. Dr. Ellen J. Langer, a Harvard psychology professor, explains that "If I don't let you give me a gift, then I'm not encouraging you to think about me and think about things I like. I am preventing you from experiencing the joy of engaging in all those activities. You do people a disservice by not giving them the gift of giving."

Psychologists say it is often the giver, rather than the recipient, who reaps the greatest gains from a gift and thus are also the most concerned about them. Researchers at Harvard and Stanford, Gino and Flynn, have found that givers are more concerned with giving something costly than receivers are with receiving them. Givers can worry less, and recipients can remind them to be less concerned with big gifts. A 2005 survey, conducted by the Center for a New American Dream, shows that four out of five Americans think the holidays are too materialistic. As receivers, we can remind our loved ones that we do not need or expect expensive gifts.

While embracing a culture of gifts is important there are certain dangers we must be sure to avoid. For example, the Bible looks down upon the desire for gifts: Proverbs (15:27), most poignantly, states, "*Soneh matanot yihyeh* – One who hates gifts will live long." The gift-seeker is at risk for corruption and bribery, developing transactional relationships, and cultivating a personality of entitlement.

There is no such thing as a free lunch, and to expect one is to misunderstand the purpose of our existence, to live a life of service working to repair the world. Rabbi Yaakov Kamenetsky explains that the Torah seeks to prevent us from growing accustomed to effortless profit. When one regularly receives gifts without investing any effort, one begins to expect more and more to receive that which doesn't belong to them.

The Torah also teaches that, ultimately, it is not gifts that build or heal relationships; rather, it is human connection. Before Jacob encounters Esau after a period of estrangement, he sends his brother a large gift consisting of many animals. Esau is willing to rekindle the relationship but he initially turned the gifts down, showing that they were not the reason for his decision. He says, "I have plenty. My brother, let what you have remain yours" (Genesis 33:9). It is not gifts but words that truly heal relationships.

The manner in which we give requires great attention. Marcel Mauss, a twentieth century French sociologist who wrote the classic work on gift exchange, explains that gift economies tend to be marked by three related obligations: the obligation to give, the obligation to accept, and the obligation to reciprocate. Some level of reciprocity can be expected but gift-giving fails when it creates an oppressive sense of obligation, establishes hierarchies, or fosters humiliation or manipulation.

These dangers, however, should not dissuade us from the fact that gift-giving, when done well, can serve to bring us closer together and provide a way for a giver to express additional love. We can all learn to have more sensitivity in how we give and receive. Giving gifts should bring us closer to the receiver and should be done in a way to reinforce the core values that serve as the foundation of our relationships. Givers should consider the needs and wants of receivers, and receivers should be sure to cultivate and express gratitude and not entitlement.

The Sema (*Sefer Meirat Einayim*), the classic commentator on the *Hoshen Mishpat*, actually explains that according to the majority position, "*soneh matanot yichyeh*" does not pertain to a gift intended for the benefit of the giver. When gifts are used to help foster relationships and to further a culture of giving, everyone wins.

In today's economic climate, few can afford to buy gifts the way they once could. We can make our consumption during holiday season more ethical by reducing costs, valuing the spiritual over excessive materialism, engaging in our shopping process respectfully and reconsidering how our giving brings us closer to others. We might also consider making our *tzedakah* contributions (financial gifts to those in need) more integral in the spirit of our holiday giving. We can attach words of gratitude to our gifts that deliberately celebrate our most important relationships. Rather than fight for the last toy on the shelf, we can strive to give better.

After all, Chanukah is ultimately about something greater than gifts. While giving Chanukah *gelt* (chocolates) is an old custom from Europe, giving gifts on Chanukah is relatively new. Professor Jonathan Sarna, the great American Jewish historian at Brandeis University, explains that Jews used to exchange gifts only on Purim, but in the late nineteenth century there was a shift from Purim to Chanukah when Christmas became more magnified. Some explain that Chanukah gift-giving in America really took off in the 1950s when, in a post-Holocaust age, Jews were more concerned with their assimilation in the face of "Christmas envy." At the holiday's core though, for decades we strived to dedicate time to celebrate life's great miracles and to express gratitude for our existence. This surpasses the value of any tangible holiday gift. □

A MORAL CASE FOR BRIT MILAH

B RIT MILAH (JEWISH RITUAL CIRCUMCISION) MAY be uncomfortable to watch, and naturally makes many of us ambivalent in a time of celebration. But is it cruel? Having lived in California, where calls for the outlawing of circumcision have proliferated, I have not heard anyone make the moral case for circumcision. The *Shulhan Aruch* states that "this commandment (*milah*) is greater than (all the) other positive commandments" (*Yoreh Deah* 260). As someone who believes strongly that *mitzvot* have an ethical foundation, I will attempt to make the case for the moral benefit of *brit milah*.

Health

The New York Times reported that the United States Centers for Disease Control and Prevention may consider advocating for circumcision as a tool in the fight against AIDS. It turns out that circumcision can reduce the risk of the transmission of HIV by at least 60 percent. We are talking about millions of lives. This is why some governments (e.g., Uganda and Kenya) started mass circumcision campaigns. Researchers at The Johns Hopkins University have shown that foreskins are more susceptible to sores and have a high concentration of certain types of immune cells that are gateways for the HIV infection. Daniel Halperin, an AIDS expert at the Harvard School of Public Health, found that low circumcision rates correlate with high HIV rates, and vice versa. This is just HIV, not to mention human papillomavirus, chlamydia, cervical cancer, genital herpes, and syphilis, to name a few. These health risks, of course, affect not only an uncircumcised man but his wife as well. Is it fair to avoid giving a boy protection when it is available? It's not only Jewish law to maintain one's health but also Jews should serve as a model for this important health practice.

Sexual Morality

For centuries many have claimed that the removal of the foreskin reduces male sexual pleasure. Maimonides writes:

> As regards circumcision, I think that one of its objects is to limit sexual intercourse, and to weaken the organ of generation as far as possible, and thus cause man to be moderate. This commandment has not been enjoined as a complement to a deficient physical creation, but as a means for perfecting man's moral shortcomings. . . . Circumcision simply counteracts excessive lust; for there is no doubt that circumcision weakens the power of sexual excitement, and sometimes lessens the natural enjoyment (*Guide for the Perplexed* 3:49).

According to Philo, who lived in the first century, the purpose of circumcision is not just to curb lust, but also pride. Many empirical studies have put this into question. Circumcised men may not have less sexual desire or more self-control, but teaching a value of sexual moderation may be one pedagogical goal of this ancient ritual. We have many sexual wrongs in society to be reminded of such as rape, adultery, impropriety, and molestation. Perhaps circumcision can serve as a sacred reminder for men, in our over-sexualized world, to cultivate self-control.

Utilitarian

If an uncircumcised man chooses to have the procedure done later in life, it will be much more painful (even with anesthesia) and dangerous than it would be for a newborn. It is the responsibility of parents to shield their children from unnecessary pain.

Parental Values and Social Acceptance

Parents make health- and aesthetics-related value choices that affect their children's bodies all the time. Should their child be vaccinated, receive orthodontia, get his or her ears pierced? Passing down these values is an important moral relationship parents have with their children. When a parent makes decisions about the bodies of their young children, it can serve as another form of care, a moral necessity for parenting. Not circumcising a Jewish boy may hinder his social acceptance and his chances of finding a Jewish spouse. The overwhelming majority of Jewish women look for a mate who is circumcised. It would be cruel to prevent a man from potentially finding a suitable mate. The Talmud says that a father is obligated to circumcise his son and find him a wife (*Kiddushin* 29a). These two are connected obligations.

Modesty

In the Greek bathhouses, it was reported that men with foreskin felt clothed where as men without foreskin felt naked. Circumcision, according to some, provides an extra layer of nakedness to men requiring them to provide more modesty in covering themselves. In cultures where modesty is a value only prioritized by women, *brit milah* should serve as a reminder that men too must be extremely attentive to developing this moral attribute. We were made just a little bit more naked to ensure our extra cognizance of this virtue.

Unconscious memory

All Jews are commanded to be healers of the world, and thus we need the emotional intelligence of empathy. Many, fortunately, grow up without experiencing any type of physical torment. This is a modern blessing. *Brit milah* can serve as the one early pain experience that remains in unconscious memory, and one seeking to empathize with the pain of another may be able to access it (albeit with some real psychoanalytic work). We give our baby boys one token formative experience, and then we do all we can to protect and shelter the child. This experience helps to ensure that the boy can be a moral agent. However, this reasoning, of course, should not be extended beyond this minor example.

Symbolic Reminder

The Ramban compares the "pruning" of men to the pruning of trees, suggesting that both acts symbolically have the goal of enhancing fertility. This is not an empirical fact but a symbolic point. The Midrash teaches that Adam was born without foreskin but once he sinned in the Garden of Eden, the foreskin grew since he had created the possibility of succumbing to temptations for all men. Removing the foreskin serves as a symbolic reminder that one can live to their ideals resisting temptations. The Kabbalists thus describe circumcision as a *tikkun* for the first sin suggesting that it can serve as a symbolic reminder that we can resist "eating the fruit" and we can and must live by our ideals.

Circumcision, of course, only applies to men. Jewish law is strongly opposed to female genital cutting. Rabbi Samson Raphael Hirsch, explains, albeit as a traditional apologist, that women do not need *milah* because women are naturally more spiritual and religiously committed than men.

> The Torah did not impose these *mitzvot* on women because it did not consider them necessary to be demanded from women . . . God's Torah takes it for granted that our women have greater fervor and more faithful enthusiasm for their God serving calling . . . Thus, at the very origin of the Jewish People, God's foresight did not find it necessary to ensure their bond with Him by giving women some permanent symbol in place of *milah* for men.

Judith Antonelli, a self-proclaimed "radical feminist and religious Jew," explains that:

> Circumcision does something to a boy to bring him up to the level of women. This is indicated by the fact that women are considered in Judaism to be "already circumcised," for one who is uncircumcised may not participate in eating the Pesach sacrifice, and this does not refer to women (Exodus 12:48).

Jews should consider circumcision because it is a holy ritual that Jewish men have performed for thousands of years, even at great risk of persecution. Since Abraham's circumcision at the age of ninety-nine, thousands of year ago (Genesis 17:7), Jews have maintained the holy covenant by circumcising their boys. But even further, circumcision has a solid moral purpose. It should serve as a physical reminder of Jewish responsibility and our sacred task to heal the world as partners with God and that our spiritual and moral endeavors require human effort. The very human organ that is the source of life was chosen to be sanctified by circumcision to teach us that we can use every human desire for a holy purpose. □

A NEW LOOK AT IDOLATRY
AND SLAVE LABOR

IDOLATRY (*AVODAH ZARAH*) IS ONE OF THE GRAVEST
sins in the Torah. In fact, it is one of three sins for
which one must accept death before succumbing
(*Yoma* 82a). But is it merely an ancient relic? As twenty-first century Jews
who have demythologized the world, we simply cannot relate to the worship of trees, rivers, and statues. Nonetheless, today's desire for idolatry is
as strong as ever, clothed deceptively in new forms such as slave labor and
unethical consumption.

Monotheism is inherently inimical to idolatry. The importance of monotheism highlighted in the daily *Shema* declaration is foundational to Jewish
belief. This is primarily a commitment not to believe in or serve any other
god or to make any statues (Exodus 20:3–4). For many, it is also a denial of
multiplicity to the G–d of oneness. While theists and atheists both can act
morally or immorally, all individuals must beware that no absolute object
or value replaces the concept of God. It is my belief that when embraced
properly, a belief in God should inspire more humility. One always knows
that the job of God is occupied.

I would suggest that monotheism and the rejection of idolatry can be
understood not only as a theological, but also a moral, commitment. The
Greek philosophers taught that polytheism leads to moral relativism, since
there are many conflicting bosses. When we embrace one God, on the other
hand, we are guided by the one absolute moral truth and authority.

The great medieval authority, Rabbi Menahem HaMeiri, explains that
an idolater was one who lives a lawless lifestyle. He clarified: "They are polluted in their practices and disgusting in their moral traits . . . but the other
nations, which are law-abiding, and which are free of these disgusting moral
traits and, moreover, punish people with these traits – there is no doubt that
these laws do not apply to them at all" (*Beit HaBehirah*, *Avodah Zarah* 48).
Thus, one's moral life is the barometer for the holy – or for the idolatrous.

Many Jewish sources understood idolatry not to be an intellectual error
but a wrong associated with sexual morality: "The Israelites knew that the

idols were nonentities, and they engaged in idolatry only in order to allow themselves to perform forbidden sexual relations publicly" (*Sanhedrin* 63b). Again the Rabbis teach that the rejection of idolatry is a moral commitment.

Similarly, the prophets constantly compared idolatry to adultery. If one betrays God for another, one is like an adulterer cheating on a spouse. The comparison is not only metaphorical. A desecration of God can be done to God's image. We learn that each human being is created in the image of God – to desecrate a human being is to desecrate God. Immoral activity is also an act of idolatry. Thus, while Romans honored statues of their rulers, Hillel the Elder noted that to wash oneself in the bathhouse was a mitzvah: "All the more so am I required to scrub and wash myself – I, who have been created in God's image and likeness" (Leviticus Rabbah 34:3). A rejection of idolatry can inspire care for physical human needs.

Philosophers have broadened our understanding of modern idolatry in a way we can understand. Emil Fackenheim explains:

> Sinful passion can reach a point at which it becomes an independent power – as it were, an alien god within – a point at which the ordinary relation is reversed and passion no longer belongs to man but man to passion. This is why the rabbis refuse to belittle idolatry by defining it too widely, as indistinguishable from sin in general (*Encounters between Judaism and Modern Philosophy*, 178).

The role of religious life is to become aware of, and take control of this "independent power" that can dominate our capacity for reason and restraint.

Theologian Paul Tillich writes:

> Idolatry is the elevation of a preliminary concern to ultimacy. Something essentially conditioned is taken as unconditional, something essentially partial is boosted to universality, and something essentially finite is given infinite significance; the best example of contemporary idolatry is religious nationalism" (*Systemic Theology* 1:13).

There is only one unconditional, universal, infinite Entity, and when anything concrete or finite is made absolute or infinite, it may be considered an act of idolatry.

Choosing self-interest over the needs of another was considered by the Rabbis to be one form of idolatry. "Anyone who shuts his eye against charity is like one who worships idols, for here it is written, 'Beware that there be not a base thought in thy heart,' etc. ('and your eye will be evil against thy poor brother'), and there it is written, 'Certain base fellows are gone out, as there (the crime is that of) idolatry, so here also [the crime is like that of] idolatry'" (*Ketubbot* 68a). Caught in the traps of insatiability, one can throw off the very moral responsibility that makes us human. The paradigmatic idol, the golden calf, represents this undisciplined pagan behavior combined with materialistic greed.

The *Sefer HaHinuch* links idolatry to consumer spending:

> For we should not attach any item of idol worship to our money or property, in order to gain pleasure from it, and for this reason, the Torah says, "You must not bring an abhorrent thing into your house." And one reason for this commandment is to distance every element of detested idol worship . . . And within the commandment is that one should not attach to his own money, which God graced him with, the money of another which was gained through theft, violence or exploitation, or from any disgusting element, because all of these are included in the elements of idol worship. For man's heart is inclined towards evil, which desires [items paid for by any means] and brings it into the home; and this inclination towards evil is called idol worship (*Sefer HaHinuch*, mitzvah 429).

The Hinuch is explaining that when one merely fulfills a desire for consumption, ignoring the moral duty to consider how it was produced, one worships pleasure over all else. When one worships oneself, it is considered an act of idolatry.

Today, we are aware that as Westerners we benefit from slave-produced products. Consider taking the online slavery footprint survey. You are likely to find that more than twenty slaves produced the food and consumer goods that you use daily. In an age where more than thirty million people live as slaves and millions more work in sweatshops around the world, we must confront this reality. The idol of immediate gratification at the expense of the basic welfare of human beings needs to be smashed. This requires more moral sophistication than an unwieldy hammer.

Today, there is growing transparency in where our food comes from, such as kosher certifications, fair trade stamps, and the ethical kosher seal (Tav HaYosher). There are so many other areas where we do not have access to transparency. Clothes production is a great example. How can we become moral exemplars willing to make significant personal sacrifices in areas where transparency and access to credible reliable information is so difficult?

The Rabbis teach us, "One who sees an idol that has not been destroyed pronounces the blessing, 'Blessed is He who is slow to anger'" (Tosefta, *Berachot* 7:2). Incredible! I would suggest that this wording was chosen because God should be angry at how much evil there is in the world that is unchallenged. Yet God has humbly allowed us to be the ambassadors of truth and the defenders of justice on earth. We can emulate this Divine patience frustrated at an unredeemed world while still feeling a great sense of urgency. May our rejection of idolatry inspire us to live more ethical and holy lives, spreading justice near and far.   □

WASHINGTON DAY: INVOKING THE RELIGIOUS LIBERTY CONUNDRUM

I NVOKING GEORGE WASHINGTON'S FAMOUS LET-ter to the Jews of Newport, R.I., Rabbi Meir Soloveichik of New York's Spanish and Portuguese Synagogue, one of the foremost Orthodox rabbis of his generation, told a congressional committee in the week of Washington Day that requiring health insurance plans to cover contraception threatened "the liberties of conscience" of fellow Americans and "redefined by bureaucratic fiat" the definition of religion itself. He found it appalling that any religious organization – Catholic or not – should be "obligated to provide employees with an insurance policy that facilitates acts violating the organization's religious tenets."

In many ways, it is heartwarming to see an Orthodox rabbi standing up for the religious liberties of his Catholic counterparts. Many of us felt ashamed when many rabbis failed to do this in 2010, when the religious liberty of Muslim-Americans was challenged during the controversy over building a mosque near Ground Zero in New York City. As a minority group that has fought hard for religious equality, and one that rightly takes pride in having received from Washington himself the assurance that religious liberty is an "inherent natural right" that cannot be abridged, we should all feel obliged to testify whenever religious liberties are challenged.

Yet for all that one may sympathize with Catholic institutions coerced into promoting contraceptive services that they consider sinful, Soloveichik's congressional testimony greatly oversimplifies the religious liberty conundrum confronted by those who oversee national health insurance. The guarantee of religious liberty, after all, applies not only to religious organizations, but also to individual citizens. However much Catholic institutions may invoke religious liberty when they deny those they employ access to contraception, it is critical to remember that from the perspective of those employees, the denial reeks of religious coercion.

The analogy to "forcing kosher delis to sell ham," put forward by Bishop William Lori, exemplifies the way the problem is misunderstood. In America (unlike in Israel), people have the right to choose whether they want to sell ham and whether they want to consume it; neither option is proscribed. We all might agree that kosher delis should not be coerced into selling ham, but hopefully we would also all agree that a deli's employees and customers should not be penalized for choosing to consume it.

Similarly, a kosher deli routinely gives its employees a day off on Yom Kippur, a fast day. But the deli would not be within its rights if it provided that benefit to only those employees who fast on Yom Kippur; that would be coercive. Denying insurance claims for contraceptive services represents the same kind of coercion. In First Amendment terms, the contraception issue represents a classic tension between the "no establishment" and "free exercise" clauses of the First Amendment. What Rav Soloveichik understandably saw as a limit upon Catholic institutions' free exercise of their religion, employees of Catholic institutions see, no less understandably, as an attempt to "establish" Catholic doctrine coercively. The Supreme Court generally privileges the "no establishment" clause over the "free exercise" clause in such cases. It certainly does not ignore "no establishment" claims, as Soloveichik does.

Soloveichik, in his testimony, took particular exception to a distinction that the government has drawn between religious employers who hire only members of their own faith and are permitted to conduct their affairs according to church tenets and religious employers who hire members of multiple faiths and are obligated by the government to accommodate them.

"The administration implicitly assumes," he charges, "that those who employ or help others of a different religion are no longer acting in a religious capacity and as such are not entitled to the protection of the First Amendment."

In fact, the government made no such assumption at all. Instead, it reasonably assumes that employers and employees both have First Amendment rights, including the "no establishment" right not to be religiously coerced. Precisely for this reason, chaplains in the military who certainly act in a religious capacity are prohibited from evangelizing those of other faiths, even when their religion otherwise requires them to do so. Where members of different religions dwell together (even when they do so under religious auspices), securing them all the right to the "free exercise" of their faith is much more conducive to social harmony than allowing employers to impose their faith requirements on their employees coercively.

Is there any way of satisfying both the religious strictures of the church and the religious predilections of its employees? If, as in most Western countries, the burden of acquiring health care were placed upon individuals rather than employers being required to provide it, then everyone could choose for himself or herself whether to have a plan with contraceptive benefits. Those with other strong beliefs about health care (such as Christian Scientists) could similarly select plans that accord with their faith. Nobody would be coerced, and everybody could purchase the plan that he or she wants.

To focus on the religious liberties of employers while overlooking those of their employees, and to focus on only the free exercise clause of the First Amendment while ignoring the dangers of coercive religious establishments, is to pervert what Washington meant when he spoke of "liberty of conscience" and to set back the cause of liberty and justice for all.   □

THE ROLE OF JEWISH PRIESTS: A MATTER OF LIFE AND DEATH

JEWISH PRIESTS (KOHANIM) ARE PROHIBITED from attending funerals or encountering the dead (unless it is a close relative). How can the leaders of society neglect one of the most important aspects of community service?

Various explanations have been put forth. The most obvious explanation of this mitzvah is that priests should remain in a state of purity for their holy service, and that impurities come along with death. Ramban explains that it is a practical matter – the Kohanim were simply too busy tending to the sacrificial order to be burdened with the huge tasks of handling matters of death. That they were too busy, of course, does not necessarily mean they were too good. Others explain that God is only served in joy, and death distances one from God. The Kohanim must serve God in a constant state of joy, and thus cannot be involved with death.

However, we have the opportunity to learn the values of humility, empowerment, life, and transparency, and an important moral lesson here as well:

1. Perhaps there is a lesson in empowerment here. All leaders cannot serve the community in every function. There is humility in stepping back at times to empower others in the community to lead.

2. There may be a lesson about the Jewish focus on this world rather than on the World to Come. My esteemed teacher Rabbi Shlomo Riskin, the Chief Rabbi of Efrat, explains:

> The Kohen was the priest-educator during the Biblical and Temple periods. The very first – and unique – commandment concerning him is that he not defile himself by contact with the dead; this is an especially telling limitation when we remember that the primary responsibility of priests of all religions is to aid their adherents to "get to the other world" – that the Bible of ancient Egypt was called the Book of the Dead. In effect the Torah is teaching us that our religious leadership must deal with the living and not the dead: must spend its

time teaching Torah and accessing Jewish experiences, rather than giving eulogies and visiting cemeteries; must be dedicated primarily to this world rather than the world-to-come (*Torah Lights, Emor*, 176).

3. The Torah goes to great lengths to make the wealth of leadership transparent. Perhaps the reason why so many chapters are spent on listing the details of the Temple and the vestments of the priests is to ensure we never become a religion that spends wasteful millions on our houses of worship and holy objects. This is a value that our community has not always been successful at following. Solomon's temple was apparently inlaid with gold, and certainly put his kingdom into debt. Some of the most impressive European synagogues (especially in Germany, pre-Holocaust) were as elaborate as many of the more modern churches. Along with this transparency comes the importance of protecting vulnerable community members from abuse. The priests already had so much power in society as the sole leaders of the Temple. To also handle death and care for the most vulnerable could lead to abuse of that power. Perhaps the community is protecting the vulnerable by distancing the priests from this role. My illustrious teacher, Rabbi Saul Berman, explains that in ancient times, families looked toward the priests to intercede on behalf of the deceased, hoping that they would receive a better place in the afterlife. Here the priests could feel tempted to accept a payoff for intervening. This would be a scandal of the highest order, and the Torah seeks to remove those dealing with divine intervention from such vulnerable situations.

Today, without a Temple, the priests have a very minimal, though unique, role in Jewish life. They are, however, still prohibited from entering cemeteries. This serves as a reminder that each of us must take responsibility – physically, emotionally, and existentially – for death. We may relegate some roles to a priest, but we must all learn not only to take full ownership of our lives, but also of the deaths that occur in our midst. □

RUNAWAY SLAVES IN THE TORAH AND TODAY

WHAT WOULD YOU DO IF AN ESCAPED slave showed up on your doorstep in Canaan in 1400 BCE, or in Richmond in 1810, or in Tel Aviv in 2012? The problem of the runaway slave is both ancient and modern.

Slavery plagued America for more than two centuries, beginning with its evolution in the British colony of Virginia. Many people are unaware that the proponents of slavery – beginning in the 1830s – actually increased their militancy and sought further legal sanctions for human bondage. From 1836–1844, Congress was under the "Gag Rule," which effectively prohibited the discussion of slavery. Southern states routinely intercepted and burned anti-slavery tracts that were sent through the postal system.

The nadir of this movement occurred with passage of the Fugitive Slave Act of 1850, which provided for the return of slaves who escaped from one state into another state or territory. The courts allowed an owner to use "reasonable force" to detain runaways and anyone who tried to help a detained slave escape would be subject to the scrutiny of a federal "grand inquest," a grand jury. Not only were local sheriffs and other officials compelled to cooperate with the apprehension of runaway slaves under penalty of substantial fines, but the law stated that "all good citizens are hereby commanded to aid and assist in the prompt and efficient execution of this law." Thus, all citizens were compelled to support slavery. While the Underground Railroad helped many escaped slaves, runaways were only safe when they reached Canada.

After the Civil War, fought only about 150 years ago, the fugitive slave laws ended along with slavery in America. In contrast, the Jewish tradition has been very progressive, as our holy Torah prohibited this 3,300 years ago!

As we learn in the Torah, if a slave from another town escapes, the Torah forbids the return of the refugee slave to his master (Deuteronomy 23:16). The Torah could have gone in a very different direction, based upon contemporary values. For example, in the ancient law found in the Code of Hammurabi (which was issued before the Torah, about 3,800 years ago in Babylonia), Hammurabi legislated (16–17) that one who hides a refugee slave in his home should be put to death, while one who hands over the slave to his owner should receive a payment.

The Torah, on the other hand, rules that it is forbidden to return a runaway slave. Ramban makes clear that Jewish law does not view the runaway slave as a new slave, but as completely free. We are dealing with a human being, not property, the Torah insists – to return one fleeing for his life would put him at grave danger. The Haamek Davar, Rav Naftali Tzvi Yehuda Berlin (1817–1893), teaches that we must remember that the slave has not just run away from the rigors of slavery, but has chosen asylum specifically to be with you. He is searching for something more in life since he has chosen to run toward you. The Talmud explains that the Torah is dealing specifically with a case of a slave from another country fleeing to the Land of Israel (*Gittin* 45a).

In July 2012, I took a group of our students from the yeshiva in Efrat, Israel, where I was teaching, to Tel Aviv to meet with the African refugees sleeping in the parks. In Israel, great debates have emerged concerning what to do with the 60,000 refugees who have entered Israel since 2006 seeking asylum. Significantly, Israel is the only democratic state with a land connection to Africa, so it is inevitable that a large portion of African refugees would seek to go there. These undocumented migrants cross into Israel either looking for work or fleeing from severe persecution. They are essentially escaping slavery, extreme poverty, or death. The social and economic burdens are immense, and Israel overall is already struggling very nobly with very limited resources. Clearly, Israel cannot be a home for all refugees who wish to come. This is not a fair request of this tiny state already overwhelmed with social and economic issues. Many are pushing for the refugees to be deported, but Jewish law as we have learned is that we may not return a slave to their master. Israel, a nation of refugees itself, must develop a legal process for non-Jewish refugees. Defending the runaway slave is fundamental to our tradition.

Closer to home, today, we are unlikely to encounter literal "runaway slaves." Nevertheless, do we not encounter those who have undergone traumatic experiences? Many have baggage and are running from it. Every day, we try to escape parts of our past that have confined us (failures, pains, losses). When we encounter another, do we return him or her to their master or are we a part of their liberation? How do we embrace those who have just filed for bankruptcy, completed their divorce, or come out of sitting *shiva* for a lost family member? They have been trapped in misery, and when they reach our doorstep, how do we embrace them? In a sense, we are all runaway slaves running out of fear from danger and even our inevitable death. We can never fully understand the emotions attached to one's entrapment; we can merely open our hearts and arms.

According to the Talmud, one may not remind someone of their past (where they have run from) if they have changed their ways, and we may never do anything to block others from their own *teshuva*. This requires humility. In approaching others, we must remember that we do not stand in their shoes and we must not judge them.

In dealing with the Civil War, Abraham Lincoln, fighting against slave owners, said: "My concern is not whether God is on our side; my greatest concern is to be on God's side."

We do not know that the other is wrong. We just know that we must keep our eyes on the prize and do what is right. The Torah's mandate that we may not return a runaway slave still has relevance and far-reaching implications today.   □

THE MITZVAH OF HAKHEL AND A CALL FOR UNIVERSAL EDUCATION

OVER THE YEARS, I HAVE HAD THE OPPORTUnity to teach in classrooms in villages around the world, from Central America to Southeast Asia, and from Africa to the former Soviet Union. One unexpected and saddening phenomenon I have encountered in several penurious countries are the empty classrooms. Many students do not show up or are pulled from school by their families due to intense economic or social pressures. There is an education crisis around the world that is at the root of countless other social and economic problems.

In the Torah portion of *VaYelech*, we learn about the keen Jewish interest in public education, expressed by way of a fascinating communal forum called Hakhel. Every seven years, the king would come out of his palace to educate the public. This was in keeping with the command to "Assemble the people – men, women and children, and the strangers living in your towns, so that they can listen and learn . . ."

According to the medieval commentator R. Abraham Ibn Ezra (Deuteronomy 31:10), this public learning event took place at a time when everyone – even the slave or the stranger – would be able to attend: the beginning of the Sabbatical Year, when working the fields is forbidden in Jewish law (most rabbinic authorities argue that it took place immediately after the Sabbatical Year). This ensured that everyone was able to break from the demands of work and have time for study.

Yet today, too many of the world's children lack the opportunity for intellectual growth. While the number of primary school-age children who do not attend school has been reduced from 105 million in 1990 to 61 million today, the trend has slowed since 2005, and has remained virtually unchanged since 2008. More than half of unschooled children live in sub-Saharan Africa.

A primary reason for this lack of progress is the effect of armed conflict, which prevents 28 million children from going to school, as schools are targeted for attacks, and girls in particular are subjected to physical and sexual abuse. In South Sudan, for example, families often marry their daughters off by age fifteen in order to relieve the crushing economic pressures of recovering from civil war. In Pakistan, numerous girls' schools have been forced to close due to militant attacks on the facilities. Low education levels only heighten the risk of further conflict, as militancy become the only available "career" option for those who lack the training to earn a decent wage.

This should be a call to action.

Jewish law mandates that we not only teach where we can but that we appoint teachers to all of our cities. The *Shulhan Aruch* requires that "Every community is obligated to appoint teachers; a city without a teacher should be put under a ban until the inhabitants appoint one. If they continue to neglect to appoint a teacher, the city should be destroyed for the world exists only through the breath of school children" (*Yoreh Deah* 245:5).

Perhaps we should return to this Sabbatical Year ritual to remind us that we must seriously invest in education, if we wish to move villages and nations out of poverty. Today, only two percent of humanitarian aid goes to education, which will not pull South Sudan or Pakistan out of their crises.

The Talmud teaches that Jerusalem was destroyed "only because they neglected (the education of) school children." Further, "School children may not be made to neglect (their studies) even for the building of the Temple" (*Shabbat* 119b). We must heed this message before yet another generation is lost to ignorance, prejudice, and war.

There are ways to improve education. UNESCO and the EFA Global Monitoring Report note that some policies have proven beneficial in areas where armed conflict has disrupted the educational system, including a shift from humanitarian aid to long-term investment with multi-year commitments and pooled resources to reduce bureaucracy and help the transition to government-run programs. In addition, if donor nations converted six days of military spending to education aid, they could make up the current $16 billion shortfall in education needs for poor nations. While well-planned military campaigns might reduce violence in the short term, in the long term an educational investment in the future of poor nations is a more certain route to peace and prosperity.

In the twenty-first century there is an endemic problem of placing immediate rewards over long-term gains. With education, we cannot afford to delay investing in the future. The Torah reminds us that we must put down our shovels to prioritize public education. We cannot expect struggling villages and nations to address this challenge alone. As Jews who hold the value of education so highly, we must be at the forefront of the policies and financing of global education opportunities.   □

PHYSICAL BOUNDARIES: THE SOCIAL JUSTICE CASE FOR SHOMER NEGIAH

QUESTIONS AROUND THE BOUNDARIES OF physical touch are emerging more and more in American legal and political discourse. When has an employer crossed the line with an employee? When has a teacher crossed the line with a student? Which parts of the human body is the Transportation Security Administration allowed to mandate for touching during a security check? What is the propriety of the New York Police Department's "stop and frisk" policy?

One great problem with touch permitted in the name of security is that it is so easily used to justify violence, especially racial violence. As one *New York Times* editorial explained regarding the NYPD's "stop and frisk" policy, "minority targets are more likely to be slammed against walls or spread-eagled while officers go through their belongings." The injustices of this policing strategy, whose use has been increasing to mostly black and Hispanic youths, needs to be more heavily regulated.

Rambam taught that physical touch is the most base of human experiences, and that we should strive to become intellectual and spiritual beings of the mind and soul. We cannot neglect the importance of our bodies but we must be, and we must see others as more than bodies; the human body is sacred and should be respected. In avoiding intimate touch with non-family members, we are forced to cultivate more meaningful relationships, respecting our fellows' minds as paramount and their bodies as sacred.

Jewish law mandates that intimate touch (kissing, hugging, etc.) be reserved for immediate family (Leviticus 18:6 and 18:19; *Sefer Hamitzvot* 353; *Issurei Biah* 21; *Even HaEzer* 20; *Yoreh Deah* 183). The stricter and more sensitive guidelines that I would propose on the societal level are inspired by, but also transcend, the Jewish legal standards of *shemirat negiah* (the guarding of touch).

Society in the United States is prone to many forms of violence. Intimate touch, from sexual harassment to sexual assault, remains a serious problem. In 2010, the FBI reported 84,767 forcible rapes. However, this did not include male victims or anal and other penetration, which have only been recently added to the count methodology. Thus, the 2010 FBI statistics only recorded three-quarters of the 1,369 rapes recorded by the New York City police, and none of the nearly 1,400 sexual assaults (including rape) recorded by the Chicago police. In addition, since most cases of rape are not reported, even the higher figures are probably significantly off.

Other surveys have confirmed the prevalence of sexual assault in the US. In December 2011, the National Intimate Partner and Sexual Violence Survey reported that:

- one in five women reported that she had been the victim of rape or attempted rape; and
- one in four that she had been beaten by an intimate partner.

This culture extends to the workplace. A telephone poll in 2010 revealed that thirty-one percent of women and seven percent of men had experienced sexual harassment at work.

There is some potential good news: Child abuse cases have decreased by 60 percent between 1992 and 2010. While this decline is controversial, one possible reason for the improvement is the increasing tendency of victims' families to report the abuse, rising from 25 percent in 1992 to 50 percent in 2008. The increase in reporting leads to a decrease in offenses. Thus, in spite of highly publicized cases involving pedophiles, the willingness of people to challenge abusive touching has had an effect.

Other intimate touch remains controversial. The TSA has the responsibility to ensure the security of airline passengers. However, TSA agents have frequently been accused of abusing their authority to touch passengers inappropriately. In December 2011, two octogenarian women charged that the TSA forced them to take off their clothes to examine a back brace and a colostomy bag. The TSA, while officially denying the charges, nevertheless acknowledged that it violated its own guidelines. There are also charges that female passengers have been targeted for body searches in a sexually harassing manner. We must no doubt be kept safe, but we must also be sure to find more ways to avoid boundary-violating touching.

Everyone will have their own personal touch boundaries in their private lives, but not everyone is good at articulating them. For this reason, touch that is not invited should never be issued. I'll often hear folks say, "I'm old enough to be her grandfather," or "I see him every day," or "I don't know if you hug but . . . ," but even innocent touching can alienate others, and we need stronger national and communal boundaries.

Touch, in addition to being a form of connection, can be a power move. In a psychology study, researchers (Willis and Hamm) found that those touched are more likely to be compliant. Participants were asked to sign a petition; 55 percent of those who were not touched lightly by the administrator agreed to sign, while 81 percent of those who were touched did sign. When individuals were asked to fill in a questionnaire, 40 percent of those who were not touched filled it out, whereas 70 percent of those who were touched filled it out. If touch creates intimacy and trust between people, recipients of touch will behave on the basis of that perceived closeness. While this is a beautiful and useful truth, it is also easily manipulated.

Additional studies indicate further that touch is a potent marker of social power. Henley found that those who initiate physical contact with others during daily business tend to be "higher status." Summerhayes and Suchner found that those who touch others are perceived to hold more power in society. Other studies have shown that many men do not know how to interpret casual touch. In 2010, Gueguen found that men very easily misinterpreted a light nonsexual touch on the arm as a sign of sexual interest. Casual touch can escalate to sexual harassment in the workplace, which wreaks havoc on office culture and morale, and destroys marriages and families.

Touch is not merely innocent. It is powerful and consequential. To protect ourselves, we must remain cognizant of the effects, good and bad, of the quotidian and the expected. To protect the vulnerable, we must set stronger guidelines to prevent any unwanted touch in security lines, in frisk searches, in halls of learning and in places of business, no less than in our houses of worship.

By giving more significance to the dignity of the human body, we can raise awareness of other bodily needs (food, shelter, health, etc.) as we recommit to *avodah b'gashmiyut* (serving through the physical).

Stand tall! Honor the one and only body you've been given in life as well as the dignity of others! The principle of *shomer negiah* is not just a religious pious act, it is a Jewish social justice mandate.   □

WE PRAY FOR RAIN: RALLYING FOR WATER JUSTICE

E VERY JEWISH JOKE REVEALS AN INSECURITY. Two men of Chelm went out for a walk, when suddenly it began to rain.

"Quick," said one. "Open your umbrella."

"It won't help," said his friend. "My umbrella is full of holes."

"Then why did you bring it?"

"I didn't think it would rain!"

Jews have always been concerned about (and even prayed for) rain. One of the greatest neuroses we give to our kids is when we teach them to pray for rain but then inform them that the rain we pray for does not fall here.

In the Beit HaMikdash, on Sukkot there was a special joyous ceremony entailing the pouring of water called the Simhat Beit HaShoeva. It was considered a very joyous event and included a lot of singing, dancing, and even juggling.

The Mishnah (*Sukkah* 5:3) teaches that every courtyard in Jerusalem was illuminated from the light of the water-drawing ceremony of the temple: "One who has not seen the rejoicing at the place of the water-drawing has never seen rejoicing in his life" (*Sukkah* 51a–b). The joy of water affected all.

Unfortunately, the simple joy of water does not exist for all today. I recall during my time in Senegal, Africa how polluted all of the village well water was. The lack of clean drinking, bathing, and laundry water was one of the most harmful forces in each community putting each village and each family at increased risk of many fatal diseases.

In fact, about one-sixth of the world's population (more than 1.1 billion people) lack access to safe drinking water, and more than one-third (around 2.6 billion) lack adequate sanitation. This frequently leads to water crisis, where the available potable, unpolluted water within a region is less than that region's demand. These water crises create or exacerbate numerous problems such as droughts and famine, diseases through inadequate sanitation, the sustainability of the planet's flora and fauna, and regional conflict (i.e., "water wars"). With water use doubling every twenty years, and deserts moving north due to global warming, a serious emergency is upon us. While these seem remote, the ongoing drought affecting much of the United States has hurt farmers deeply.

While America has had water problems, Israel is in a deep water crisis. Fortunately, over the last two years, Israel has received more rain than usual. But just prior to that, in recent years, rainfall has been significantly below average (30–35 percent below average), resulting in a severe and worsening water crisis. It is becoming clear that this is not a blip but a trend. Even more troubling, lakes and rivers are drying up. This has even adversely affected the current water quality. Dalia Itzik, a former Israeli Environment Minister, said that 40 percent of water piped into Israel and Palestinian homes is "undrinkable." Israel, comprising desert land, is also surrounded mainly by desert, compounding the regional impact of drought and water crisis.

Water plays a huge role in regional conflict. It will continue to influence future diplomatic discussions between Israel and surrounding countries, especially now that the Jordan River is gradually drying up. This continues a pattern dating from the time that the Philistines sealed the wells that Isaac had dug.

Dr. Uzi Landau, Israel's former Energy and Water Minister, maintained in September 2012 that desalination plants would provide the solution to the nation's chronic water shortage. Currently, these desalination plants produce 300 million cubic meters of drinking water per year, and by 2014 should produce 600 million cubic meters, about half of Israel's water consumption, and by the end of the decade he predicted that nearly all Israelis would be drinking desalinated water.

However, critics point out that Israel had a six-year drought, and increased rainfall in early 2011 would not be enough to make up for this, as there is still a shortfall of about a billion cubic meters of water. The Sea of Galilee and mountain aquifers, the two main sources of water, remain at critically low levels.

Another potential solution is to use recycled water from laundry, dishwashing, and non-toilet bathroom use to water lawns and gardens, wash vehicles, and fill other cleaning functions in place of drinking water. Treated waste water could be used for irrigation, relieving some of the pressure on the water supply.

Traditionally, the crisis of unsafe water was in the diaspora. The Midrash explains "By the rivers of Babylon we sat and wept . . ." (Psalms 137:1). Why did the Jewish people cry by the rivers of Babylon? Rabbi Yohanan said: "The Euphrates (river) killed more of them than the wicked Nebuhadnetzer did. When the Jews lived in the land of Israel, they drank only rainwater, freshwater and spring water. When they were exiled to Babylon, they drank the (polluted) water of the Euphrates, and many of them died" (*Pesikta Rabati*, 28).

At Sukkot and Shemini Atzeret, we return to nature, acknowledging the need for the bare essentials. And we begin to pray for water. This is the water holiday. The Mishnah (*Rosh Hashanah* 1:2) says: "At four junctures [of the year] the world is judged: at Pesach concerning the produce [grain]; at Shavuot concerning the fruit of the tree; at Rosh Hashanah, all people pass before him . . . , and at Sukkot they are judged concerning water."

Water is of such critical importance as most of our planet and most our human bodies consist of water. "Rabbi Shimon Bar Yohai once taught: 'Three things are of equal importance, earth, humans, and rain.' Rabbi Levi ben Hiyyata said: . . . 'to teach that without earth, there is no rain, and without rain, the earth cannot endure, and without either, humans cannot exist" (Genesis Rabbah 13:3).

Further, there is a significant human egalitarian nature to rain.

> A certain non-Jew asked Rabbi Yehoshua: "You have festivals, and we have festivals. We do not rejoice when you do, and you do not rejoice when we do. When do we both rejoice together?"
>
> "When the rain falls," answered Rabbi Yehoshua (Genesis Rabbah 13:6).

The actual prayer for rain occurs after Sukkot, during the lesser-known festival of Shemini Atzeret. During the *Musaf* prayers, the cantor, dressed in a white *kittel* (evoking the solemnity and critical need for water during this season), walks forward for the *Tefilat HaGeshem*, the prayer for rain. In the *Amidah*, from here until Passover, a phrase is added: "*Mashiv ha-ruah u'morid hagashem*" ("Who causes the wind to blow and the rain to fall"). This prayer reinforces the Jewish covenant, where obedience to God's laws is essential for survival. In contrast, ancient Mesopotamian societies, plagued by unpredictable flooding, tyrannical god-kings, and frequent warfare, tended to view their deities as capricious and cruel. In ancient Egypt, the Nile offered a dependable water supply and predictable flooding, but also gave rise to complacency, idolatry, and the worship of material goods. The Jewish model appreciates rain because it is scarce and valuable, and preserves spirituality.

Today, there is a new-found appreciation for water, since we cannot keep doubling our use of water while despoiling and depleting our sources. Is it appropriate for us to build oil pipelines over important freshwater sources, or engage in fracking for natural gas near well water? We must reflect on the concern for water that is present in the holiday of Shemini Atzeret.

In a profoundly mystical Gemara (*Taanit* 2a), we learn of the connection between prayer and rain:

> Rabbi Yohanan said: "The keys to three things were kept in the hand of the Holy One, Blessed be He, and not given over to an intermediary (nature). They are the key to rain, the key to childbirth, and the key to the revival of the dead. The Key of Rain, for It is written, 'The Lord will open unto thee His good treasure, the heaven to give the rain of thy land in its season.' (Deuteronomy 28:12)."

Another Midrash teaches how showing mercy to others who are struggling enables God's mercy to release more rain (Genesis Rabbah 33).

We must think more deeply about how we use our water, donate to villages working on clean water projects, support research, and use the six months as we pray for a rain as an opportunity to get more involved! □

DETERMINISM AND FREEDOM: IS ONE PUNISHED FOR THE MISTAKES OF ONE'S PARENTS?

SCHOLARS HAVE NOTED FOR CENTURIES AN AP-parent biblical contradiction about whether children are punished for the wrongdoing of their parents. On the one hand, Deuteronomy 24:16 says, "Fathers shall not be put to death for their children, nor children put to death for their fathers; each is to die for his own sin," implying that all are judged on their own merits. On the other hand, Exodus 34:7 states, "[God] maintains love to thousands, and forgives wickedness, rebellion and sin. Yet he does not leave the guilty unpunished; he punishes the children and their children for the sin of the fathers to the third and fourth generation," suggesting that children can indeed be punished for the mistakes of their parents.

The Gemara (*Sanhedrin* 27b) gives a clear answer to this question: "It is written, 'He punishes the children for the sins of the fathers'!? That is only when they grasp the deeds of their fathers in their hands." The Rabbis taught that this rule does not operate by metaphysical determinism but rather through human agency. If one chooses to continue the negative path that their parents set them on, then they will be punished for the mistakes their parents made and passed along to them. However, if they choose to break free from their upbringing, then they are virtuous.

Psychologists today believe that parental nurturing plays a significant role in how their children develop, which increases the chance that their children will very likely end up similar to them. While skeptics have tried to discount this while promoting genetics as the sole determinant, research has tended to support the former notion. For example, a study of more than 300 adoptive families demonstrated that there was a significant association between a hostile marital relationship, hostile parenting, and aggressive behavior by adopted toddlers. In addition, the feeling of financial strain was associated with hostile marital relations and aggressive behavior by the adopted toddler. Since the study involved adoptive parents and toddlers, genetics did not play a part in the correlation between antisocial personality traits and hostile marital and parental behavior. Another study largely corroborated these results, showing environmental factors within the family alone accounting for the association between antisocial parental behavior and childhood depression, while indicating that genetic factors were responsible for their child's hyperactivity.

Unfortunately, politics plays a role in this debate. As Professor Eleanor Maccoby, Barbara Kimball Browning Emerita Professor of Psychology at Standford University, states:

> If one does believe . . . that conditions such as poverty, parental conflict, coercive or abusive parenting, dangerous neighborhoods . . . are unimportant for children's welfare, then there's very little point in trying to intervene to change them.

Thanks to the mapping of the human genome, we have been able to locate genes that determine longevity, blood type, and susceptibility to certain diseases, disorders, and disabilities. Research studies have also identified more than fifty locations on the genome associated with obesity. On the other hand, thus far scientists have been unable to predict or develop personalized treatment for obesity, which indicates that we have much to learn in the area of genetic influence on children and how they develop, and what's connected to the psychological and social environment of the family.

Do children grow up to be like their parents? Politically and financially, the answer appears to be mostly yes. A 2005 Gallup poll of teenagers found that 71 percent said that their social and political ideology was about the same as their parents, versus 21 percent who said "more liberal" and 7 percent who said "more conservative." Of course, there can be some generational differences; in the 2012 election, young adults aged 18–29 voted 60–37 percent for Democratic candidate Barack Obama, while their parents voted Democratic at a significantly lower rate. For example, those aged 40–49 voted 48 percent for Obama and 52 percent for Republican Mitt Romney. Financially, a Pew Economic Mobility Report indicated that only about half of Americans earn more than their parents did, with the greatest stagnation in the bottom quintile, where 43 percent raised at this level remain at the bottom as adults. When they grow up, children generally wind up close to their parents' economic level.

As adults, we know where we came from, and in the vast majority of cases we are grateful for the sacrifices our parents or guardians made for us. While our parents, friends, and schools can teach us principles, as we approach adulthood we must make our own decisions. We often reject our parents' advice and make impulsive choices. As we mature, we may realize that our parents knew best, and that we make mistakes. While we are not the clones of our parents, and may choose an independent path, we are their physical creation by virtue of our chromosomes, and their spiritual creation through their nurturing and guidance. As humans, we are constantly seeking autonomy, independence, and authenticity, as we should, but on some level we must also embrace that without reflection and serious transformation, we generally end up quite similar to our parents (for better and worse). May we have the courage and insight to learn from the past and also to truly choose our own destinies.   □

IS HAMAN ALIVE TODAY? PURIM AND HAPPINESS

THE JEWISH HOLIDAY OF PURIM IS A JOYOUS time of celebration. The story of the Book of Esther is familiar: In the 4th century BCE, the Persian King Ahasuerus fell under the influence of his evil prime minister Haman, who resented the Jews for refusing to bow down to him. In revenge, Haman persuaded the King to issue a secret decree to kill all the Jews on the 13th of Adar. Haman made preparations to hang Mordechai the Jew for his refusal to prostrate himself before Haman in submission. Fortunately, Mordechai, who found out about Haman's plot, was in the King's good graces, because he had helped thwart an attempt on the King's life. In addition, Esther the Queen, who kept her Jewish identity a secret, was his cousin and foster daughter. At the risk of her life, Esther came to Ahasuerus and ultimately persuaded him to issue a decree allowing the Jews to defend themselves against their enemies and in addition to put the evil plotter Haman to death. On the 13th of Adar, the Jews triumphed over their would-be killers, and this victory is marked by the celebration of Purim every year on the 14th of Adar. We know this story.

Traditionally, Jews use *groggers* or other noisemakers to drown out the mention of the name Haman during the reading of the Book of Esther (which occurs twice, once on Purim night and again during the day), but it is useful to examine the name of this hateful person. The Gemara (*Hullin* 139b) asks where we see an allusion to Haman's name in the Torah. The answer the sages give is from the Garden of Eden scene in Genesis (3:11): "*Ha-min ha-etz ha-zeh . . .*" – Did you eat from this tree? The word *ha-min* consists of the same three Hebrew letters (*hey, mem, nun*) as Haman.

There is a deep connection between the first human mistake in the Garden of Eden and the life of Haman. Haman was a person, who the sages say had everything: wealth, prestige, and family. He had it all. Yet, Haman could not be happy. As long as Mordechai sat at the gate of the king refusing to bow down to him (Esther 3:2), he could not be happy. At one point Haman even says, "All of this is worthless to me" (5:13). He was only missing one thing and thus everything else – his fortune, his political influence, his large family – lost value and meaning.

When we find ourselves in this mindset, we can never be happy. We may have money, family, friends, and health, yet if we're lacking one thing all the good things are for naught.

This is why Haman's name comes from the tree in the Garden of Eden. Adam had everything one could want: the luxuries of Paradise, a wife, a direct connection to God, literally everything. But he lacked one thing – the experience of eating the fruit. And so he could not be content. This is the essence of Haman: Haman is a historical and literary figure, but even more, Haman represents a concept that is part of the human condition.

Rashi points out that just as Haman's name originates from "*ha-min ha-etz*" – from this tree, so too, he ends up being hanged on a wooden gallows (*etz*) (Esther 7:10). The thing we constantly long for beyond our reach ends up being our downfall.

We protest Haman on Purim because the mitzvah of the day is one of the most difficult of all *mitzvot* in the Torah: the mitzvah to be happy. It sounds easy – get a daiquiri and lie on the beach – but it does not work. Pleasure is one thing, but to achieve true happiness is much more challenging.

We can see this in the modern world. A WIN-Gallup poll asked people from fifty-four countries if they personally were happy, unhappy, or neither. The happiest people were from Colombia, and five of the happiest twelve countries were in Latin America. On the other hand, in the lower half of the happiness list (below even war-torn Afghanistan) were people from Germany, France, the United States, Russian Federation, China, United Kingdom, Hong Kong, and Italy – nations we associate with greater wealth and power. Regionally, people from Latin America were roughly twice as happy as people from the seven wealthiest societies in the world. The futility of Haman remains valid today.

In a related poll, a joint Gallup-Healthways survey of more than half a million Americans found that American Jews were the highest ranking group in terms of "well-being" (emotional/physical health, work environment, healthfulness of behavior), with the very religious netting the highest scores within this group. As we know, religious Jews make many physical and financial sacrifices for their faith, so mere material wealth cannot account for this high level of well-being. Professor David Pelcovitz of Yeshiva University believes that the key to happiness for Jews is "the core ingredients of happiness – family, friends and faith."

In a comment in his work *Ohr HaTzafon*, Rabbi Nosson Tzvi Finkel (the Alter of Slabodka), saw a universal possibility for happiness:

> Every person is surrounded by limitless potential for pleasure and enjoyment. The world and all its details is a source of pleasure. A person's experiences in physical and spiritual areas give him the potential for happiness without end (Vol. III, 84).

While misfortune is never welcome, we can sometimes learn to achieve happiness through such events. Consider a person who undergoes a critical surgical procedure or chemotherapy. This patient is often helped by family and friends who find the right doctor or hospital, drive the patient to and from medical appointments, and help with the recovery and medical expenses and paperwork. This patient, upon recovery, will understand how friends and family enrich us through their love, and he or she may have a rejuvenated appreciation for life and a feeling of happiness.

The Rabbis teach us the key to happiness. One can only be happy when they learn to be *"sameah b'helko"* – happy with one's own lot in life. When we become so grateful for all we have and not focused on all the things we do not have, we can begin to achieve this. To reiterate an earlier point, the Rabbis teach that we should make 100 blessings a day (*Menahot* 42b). These are moments when we step back and reflect upon our good fortune and express gratitude to God for His bounty. Thus we can truly fulfill the mitzvah of the day that we sing in *Havdalah* every Saturday night from the Book of Esther: "*La-Yehudim hayta ora v'simha v'sasson v'ykar*" – For the Jews, there was light, happiness, joy, and honor" (8:16).   □

ROUSSEAU, CIVILIZED MAN, AND HAMETZ IN THE HEART

I T IS GENERALLY VIEWED AS A SUCCESS OF THE Enlightenment that we have cast off what philosopher Jean-Jacques Rousseau called "*homme sauvage*" (the natural, free, wild man) and built up the "*homme civilize*" (the civilized, enlightened, modern man). As Rousseau, who paradoxically opposed much of what the Enlightenment brought about, famously writes in *The Social Contract*: "Man is born free; and everywhere he is in chains. One thinks himself the master of others, and still remains a greater slave than they."

As human beings, we have developed to generally be more self-aware, cultured, and controlled. However, we also have become estranged from our core, free and natural selves, and gotten stuck in a web of complex social conventions and conformist behavioral patterns. This process harms human-to-human and human-to-Divine relationships.

To make matters worse, it has become more difficult to get our hands dirty doing the work that we are here in the world to do, since societal demands and distractions have become so great. Can we recover our original, authentic nature? And if we are not pursuing our purpose naturally, what are we doing?

In *But Your Land Is Beautiful*, the late Alan Paton writes of a character:

> When I shall die, which I certainly intend to do, I will be asked by the Big Judge, "Where are your wounds?" When I say, "I haven't any," I will be asked, "Was there nothing worth fighting for?" And that is a question I do not want to have to answer.

If society is guided by comfortable and conflict-averse decision making, how can we even get our hands dirty in the work? How can we even discover our cause?

We can view this process on a physical and a spiritual plane. Physically, most of us have no idea how to provide for our own food and shelter, instead relying on supermarkets and contractors to do the labor. Historians used to tell a story about an urban government bureaucrat who, when he interviewed a farmer, asked about how many macaroni trees the farmer had. Spiritually, we also have so many diversions, from social media to hundreds of cable television channels and movies on demand, that we forget our spiritual foundations.

There are divergent views on how to arrive at our true natures. Politically, Rousseau believed in pure democracy, where the majority would have unlimited authority, whereas in a modern republic the rights of minorities are protected. In education, Rousseau's argument in *Emile* is that the individual can only discover the authentic true self if he or she is educated in isolation, removed from society. For Jews, by contrast, the education process is all about community and partnership (*hevruta*). We must all do the work to discover ourselves but still remain immersed in society.

As we approach Pesach each year, we begin to search for and remove the *hametz* (leavened foods) from our homes. But is it only from our homes? When Rav Yisrael m'Vizhnitz was walking with his friend, on the way to search for the *hametz*, he stopped and opened his cloak. Uncovering his chest, he said: "You know that the real *hametz* is the *hametz* in the heart – check me here!"

By checking the *hametz* of the heart, we are searching for the spiritual blocks we have accumulated that blind us from our true nature and highest potential. One of the problems is that we must break through a lot of pride to reach a deeper place. This is another Passover message. The first century philosopher Philo asked what we can learn from the nature of *hametz*. He answered that just as leaven is banned because it is "puffed up," so we must guard against the self-righteousness that puffs us up with false pride. Pride and complacency – these are the qualities we must seek to remove from our character. This is the lesson of *hametz*, Passover, and civilized man.

Modernity has led to the caging of the soul and aspects of human potential. We cannot go back in time nor do we wish to. But we must still find avenues to journey in our life enabling deeper insight, discovery, and freedom.   □

WE ARE STILL IN EGYPT:
THE SEDER AWAKENS US
TO SOCIETAL REALITIES

THE PESACH SEDER IS DESIGNED TO BRING about joy, but even more than that its purpose is to remind us of human struggle. Through this moral consciousness, our human conscience is rebooted. *"Ha-lachma anya d'achalu avhatana b'ara d'Mitzrayim. Kol dichfin, yattei va-yechol.* This is the bread of affliction that our ancestors ate in the Land of Egypt. Let all who are hungry come and eat." What kind of gift is "bread of affliction," and why would anyone want it?

Primo Levi, the prominent author and Holocaust survivor, tells the story about his final days in Auschwitz in *If This Is a Man*, in which he writes that the worst days were those after the Nazis left and before the Soviets arrived, when there was no food to be found. Then a man found potatoes and all the survivors began to share the potatoes. At this first opportunity in the concentration camp to share food, the meaning of *lehem oni* became clear: it is through giving from the little bits we have in life that we find our individual and collective liberation. It is through sharing that one is transformed from slave to man.

The *Haggadah* reminds us that we are obligated to view ourselves, today, as if we too are leaving Egypt, as it says (Exodus 13:8): "And you shall tell your son on that day, saying 'It is because of this that Hashem acted on my behalf when I left Egypt.'" Don Isaac Abarbanel (the Abarbanel) had good reason to reflect on this text. He was born into a prominent Jewish family in fifteenth-century Portugal, but then was forced to flee to Spain, after which he was expelled with his fellow Jews in spite of faithful service to the king. He went to Naples, where he was again forced to flee after the French seized the city, and finally found refuge in Venice. In spite of the injustices heaped upon him, the Abarbanel embraced knowledge from around the world along with Torah scholarship, and sought to help his fellow Jews in all lands, including purchasing the freedom of Jewish prisoners in Morocco. His commentary on Exodus 13:8 bears consideration:

Each and every Jew will find him/her self in this exile with political subjection in its own uniqueness as that which happened to our nation collectively in Egypt. For this reason, the Sages said that everyone should see him/her self like he/she left Egypt and this would not be possible without our problems and different distresses. . . . And since God saves us in *galut* (the diaspora) every day therefore it is fitting that each and every person should see themselves as though he left Egypt, that it wasn't only our ancestors that were redeemed in our collective redemption but also us: God redeemed us and takes us out from our different individual afflictions.

This mandate transcends the parameters of collective memory and demands that we attempt to leave our contemporary, spiritual Egypt by seeing those still trapped today. The *Haggadah* is not merely an intellectual exercise; it is, rather, a wakeup call to see the reality of the world around us.

The ancient hardships have endured. It may surprise many to learn that slavery and statelessness are still major problems in the world. In June 2012, then Secretary of State Hillary Clinton estimated that there were as many as 27 million enslaved people worldwide. Meanwhile, the United Nations estimates that there are about 12 million stateless people in the world, who because of their inability to claim citizenship of any country lack any legal protection or social or economic aid. Even in these two areas there is much to do in the world today, and our *Seder* should spur us on to action.

As daunting as these tasks are, we must not become paralyzed by or apathetic to the enormity of the problem, or confuse study with action. Consider this example of what happens when moral commitment serves merely as intellectual exploration:

One of the most ironic examples of goal obsession was the "Good Samaritan" research done by Darley and Batson at Princeton in 1973. In this widely referenced study, a group of theology students was told that they were to go across campus to deliver a sermon on the topic of the Good Samaritan. As part of the research, some of these students were told that they were late and needed to hurry up. Along their route across campus, Darley and Batson had hired an actor to play the role of a victim who was coughing and suffering.

Ninety percent of the "late" students in Princeton Theology Seminary ignored the needs of the suffering person in their haste to get across campus. As the study reports, "Indeed, on several occasions, a seminary student going to give his talk on the parable of the Good Samaritan literally stepped over the victim as he hurried on his way!"

On Pesach night, we should engage in a burst of courage to truly look at the society that entraps so many. The Tibetans are only one of many nationalities yet to find their liberation, tens of thousands of innocents are being slaughtered in the Syrian civil war, and millions are locked away in cells facing daily torture. In every corner of the world, immigrants work from morning to night and still live in poverty, orphans cry themselves to sleep, and widows are left unprotected. There is no shortage of causes to which we should direct our efforts.

It is only by re-entering Egypt that we can access the cries that surround us. Emmanuel Levinas, in writes:

> The trauma I experienced as a slave in the land of Egypt constitutes my humanity itself. This immediately brings me closer to all the problems of the damned on the earth, of all those who are persecuted, as if in my suffering as a slave I prayed in a prayer that was not yet oration, and as if this love of the stranger were already the reply given to me through my heart of flesh. My very uniqueness lies in the responsibility for the other man; I could never pass it off to another person, just as I could never have anyone take my place in death: obedience to the Most-High means precisely this impossibility of shying away; through it, my "self" is unique. To be free is to do only what no one else can do in my place. To obey the Most-High is to be free (*Beyond the Verse: Talmudic Readings and Lectures*, 142).

When the ritual of the *Seder* remains on the level of piety or nostalgia but does not stir the soul to action, it has lost its value. Rav Avraham Yitzhak HaCohen Kook made this point about ritual quite poignantly:

> We can know that our behavior is derived from pure and spiritual motives when our innate sense of what is right become more exalted as a consequence of its religious inspection. If the moral quality of the individual and the public response [to ethical challenges] is diminished by our religious observance then . . . our supposed piety is of no value.

As we take our journey every Pesach back into the depths of Egypt, may we push ourselves to be reawakened to our responsibility to heed the calls of the vulnerable who call out to us in their destitution. As Dr. Martin Luther King, Jr. writes: "The ultimate measure of a man is not where he stands in a moment of comfort and convenience, but where he stands in times of challenge and controversy." □

☐ EDUCATION
AND SOCIAL JUSTICE

THE RIGHT PEOPLE ARE
IN THE ROOM

THERE WERE TIMES WHEN I WAS ONE OF THREE students that would stay awake late enough to hear Rabbi Shlomo Riskin when he would stop by our Beit Midrash at Yeshivat Hamivtar to give a late night class. What I was so profoundly moved by was the fact that Rav Riskin would speak to the three of us as if there were 200 people present. He offered his normal passionate and engaging class since we were the right people in the room.

I learned that an educator must show the full dignity to whoever shows up or whoever is truly in the mood to engage at that moment. Presentation intensity shouldn't be swayed by someone entering the room whether it is one's mentor, supervisor, or a potential donor. We give our best class, presentation, or sermon to all. Those who are present are the right people.

I've been told that Ze'ev Jabotinsky, the twentieth century Zionist leader, once unknowingly accepted a speaking engagement in Russia at the same time as a very prominent leader in the Zionist movement. Only about six people showed up, but he gave his talk and gave his best. It turns out that one of the six in attendance was Menachem Begin, who later became a great Israeli leader and Prime Minister. Begin said that it was that speech by Jabotinsky that solidified his commitment to become active as a Zionist leader. You never know who is in the room.

This point can be made theologically as well. The Jewish people may not have been the perfect people when they received the Torah, but they were the ones who arrived at the mountain. We showed up so God took us seriously.

In my leadership practice, I often feel that I need to be in many places at once. It's easy to feel like one isn't in the right place when one holds multiple, complex commitments. I'm striving to offer those who show up my full presence and my best performance whether or not I hoped for a larger or different attendance. In addition to making this moral commitment to my students, I have the faith that the Ribbono shel Olam has ensured that those who need to learn from me and to teach me are the ones that showed up.

□

JEWISH EDUCATION – TEACHING EMOTIONAL INTELLIGENCE

FOR CENTURIES, THERE HAS BEEN AN ONGOING debate as to where ethics are grounded as universal attributes in the human condition. Immanuel Kant grounded ethics in reason, whereas David Hume looked toward emotions such as sympathy, empathy, and compassion. Today, neuroimaging may offer a new way to resolve this issue.

Brain scans reveal that when participants are engaged in moral reasoning, there is significant activation in areas crucial to emotional processing (a circuit running from the frontal lobes to the limbic system). This supports the argument of researcher Martin Hoffman that the roots of morality are located in empathy. Thus, people learn to follow certain moral principles when they can put themselves in another's place. These findings also bolster the ideas of educational reformer John Dewey, who taught that lessons are best learned by students when taught not via abstract lessons, but through real life events where emotional literacy is acquired.

If we know that emotional development is a key part of moral development, then why is Jewish education so cognitive-based? We teach for text mastery, intellectual reasoning skills, and memorization (all of which are important), but too often leave aside the cultivation of empathy, understanding of shame, actualization of mercy, and control of anger.

Teaching prayer, Torah study, and ritual performance should all embrace a pedagogical approach that is sure to lead to cognitive and emotional development. But even more, it is through volunteerism that the necessary altruistic virtues are cultivated. More than just leaving our students and children in a two-hour *hesed* project to fulfil menial tasks, we must be sure that the right emotional experience is cultivated. Since most of our emotional lives exist beneath the surface of the conscious mind, we must engage in deliberate processing conversations to make sense of our feelings before, during, and after crucial activities. We must ensure that service-learning projects aren't merely about task completion but also that they further the cultivation of compassion and empathy among other emotional virtues.

Rav Kook made the case for how intellect is deficient without emotion and the dangers of neglecting emotional cultivation: "Man cannot live with intellect alone, nor with emotion alone; intellect and emotion must forever be joined together. If he wishes to burst beyond his own level, he will lose his ability to feel, and his flaws and deficiencies will be myriad despite the strength of his intellect. And needless to say, if he sinks into unmitigated emotion, he will fall to the depths of foolishness, which leads to all weakness and sin. Only the quality of equilibrium, which balances intellect with emotion, can deliver him completely" (Gershom Scholem, *Devarim B'Go*, 326–327). Rav Kook emphatically stressed the importance of emotions in education.

As Ecclesiastes teaches, there is "a time to weep and a time to laugh. A time to wail and a time to dance" (3:2–8). To live fully, we must embrace it all.

In his essay, "A Theory of Emotions," Rabbi Soloveitchik made the case for the importance of the totality of emotional experience in religious life:

> Judaism has insisted upon the integrity and wholeness of the table of emotions, leading like a spectrum from joy, sympathy, and humility (the conjunctive feelings) to anger, sadness and anguish (the disjunctive emotions). Absolutization of one feeling at the expense of others, or the granting of unconditioned centrality to certain emotions while denoting others to a peripheral status, may have damaging complications for the religious development of the personality.

While all emotions must be tended to in moral development, the emotional choices we make are crucial. In a lecture on "Morals and Education," Donald Winnicott shows how many religious systems of morality actually harm development. His primary example is the overemphasis on sin and shame over love and trust. Education of the emotions must not only be deliberate, but also carefully measured.

When we properly cultivate compassion, we promote good citizenship. When we give space to reflect upon anger, we teach self-control. When we start conversations about fear and shame, we foster humility and self-aware-ness. When we talk about personal suffering and loss, we inculcate empathy and care. When students are asked to cultivate moral imagination, the most complex emotions can be actualized.

Modern neuroscience teaches us that many moral decisions we make by-pass the prefrontal cortex (the rational brain), creating instinctive patterns of behavior. It is crucial that parents and teachers educate children holisti-cally to produce an ethical personality. These are not mere thought exper-iments. The Greeks used drama to teach emotions, the Jews used real-life experience. We must expose our children to life, "the real world" of poverty, suffering, and struggle, and foster the necessary concomitant emotions of sympathy, empathy, compassion, and love. Through this we can actualize our full service in this world: *"b'chol levavecha"* to man and God.   □

"I AM SEEKING MY BROTHERS": THE LOST JEWISH VIRTUE OF FRIENDSHIP

"**A**ND A MAN FOUND HIM, WHEN HE WAS WAN-dering in the field, and the man asked him, 'What are you seeking?' And he said: 'I am seeking my brothers'" (Genesis 37:15). This story about Joseph strikes me very deeply. As a child who moved to different cities every few years, I con-stantly felt like I was seeking "my brothers." To some degree, we are all wandering in search of our "brothers." Friendship is a challenging virtue to cultivate, even more challenging in our transient times. Yet, in an age that is increasingly interdependent, our culture strangely is moving toward an il-lusion of independence. Cultivating spiritual friendship ensures we remain grounded in the types of human relationships that cultivate virtue.

When I was a campus rabbi at the UCLA Hillel, I realized that as clergy we often speak about outreach, community, and leadership, but rarely about friendship. What is our role in helping emerging adults to cultivate the virtue of friendship?

Barriers to True Friendship Today

Transience is not even the biggest barrier to the cultivation of friendship today. Our Web-based society has weakened the strength of our relationships, and the fast-paced, self-interested nature of these relationships has become more transactional. One can "friend" or "defriend" someone with the click of a finger on Facebook. There are many "friends" created through social networking, but the social bonds are very weak. Web-based friendships may be interesting, entertaining, and enhance social capital but they rarely create strong dependent bonds that foster more moral and spiritually inspired living. Friendship becomes more about the taking than the giving.

Today, we are witnessing increased individualism, decreased institutional affiliation, and more talk about social networks than about relationships. While this helps our emerging micro-communities, it diminishes our traditional communities. True friendship is on the decline. Cornell University sociologists found that adults have only two friends they can discuss "important matters" with – down from three in 1985. Half of those surveyed said they had only one, 4 percent had none. Friendship may still be social but it is less confidential and intimate.

Further, more Americans are living alone. In major U.S. cities, 40 percent of households contain a single occupant. In Manhattan and Washington, D.C., nearly 50 percent of homes consist of one person. Singles are marrying later, divorce is on the rise, and more individuals prefer to live in privacy than within a community. Increasingly, we live alone in a lonely society.

Without deep friendships, we lack adequate self-knowledge and awareness of our blind spots. It can also lead to arrogance, as we become less able to recognize our need for others. To acquire most of our world knowledge, we must rely upon what others have shared with us in order to supplement our own experience. We look to experts for technical knowledge and to friends for subjective knowledge. When we fail to cultivate friendships, we fail to cultivate ourselves.

Friendship on Campus Today

During the day, most students study, work, and exercise leadership through student organizations. Friends are more often social buddies than life partners. They are for "time off" more than for "time on." For many of these students, a friend is less of a rock to rely upon than a partner in finding a social voice and identity. Most students struggle to turn a social buddy into a lasting personal confidante. Of Aristotle's three kinds of friendship – pleasure, utility, and virtue – students tend to understand friendships of virtue the least (*Nicomachean Ethics*, Book VIII). Spiritual leadership may help address this deficiency.

In a friend, we not only find comfort and companionship but also moral accountability. The moral philosopher Alasdair MacIntyre, who frequently references Aristotle and other classical philosophers, explains: "In achieving accountability we will have learned not only how to speak to, but also how to speak for the other. We will, in the home or in the workplace or in other shared activity, have become – in one sense of that word – friends."

I find that friendship on campus is cultivated most deeply in safe spaces created for personal life reflection, intimate sharing, and boundary-breaking and trust-building activities. As a former campus rabbi, I choose not to lead social activities but mission-driven activities, because deeper relationships are cultivated there. When I took student groups on volunteer missions to places like Thailand, Guatemala, Israel, and New Orleans, their hearts are wide open to one another in a way that does not happen at the movies, a basketball game, or a frat party. When we engage in a text study about relationship dilemmas, spiritual yearning, or global poverty, students connect with each other more authentically than they do over their dorm dinners.

There is something to be said for natural socialization, but we should not underestimate the role spiritual leaders can play to bring about friendships. Too often, we focus on building community to the exclusion of creating individual friendships.

This is not to blame teenagers, social media, and the loss of virtue. Rather, the opportunity is upon religious leaders to create meaningful spaces for conversation, sharing, volunteering, and creating mission-driven partnerships. As clergy, teachers, and mentors, perhaps the most important role we can play is to create micro-communities for students to discover friendship in the deepest sense, one that cultivates deeper moral and spiritual commitment and responsibility. Professors, social workers, and college counselors have their role to foster healthy relationships but campus clergy are in the best position to create meaningful spaces for reflection, conversation, and service where students can cultivate relationships committed to the virtues.

The Virtue of Friendship in Jewish Thought

The word for friendship in Aramaic (*chavruta*) means more than just a relationship; it is the primary model of Jewish learning. A *chavruta*, in its truest sense, is a challenger (*bar plugta*), not one who merely supports us, but also challenges us. The Talmud teaches that in religious learning and growth, a friend is even more important than a teacher: "I have learned much from my teachers, but from my friends more than my teachers" (*Taanit* 7a). A friend of virtue can be more connected to our intimate life pursuits more than any teacher can be. Thus, the Rabbis teach that "one is not even to part from one's friend without exchanging words of Torah" (*Berachot* 31a). A friend, on the highest level, is primarily a learning partner, a partner in life.

It is through dialogical care that we engage in the deepest learning. When a relationship no longer merely has an instrumental value but is part of the creation of bonds of truths through mutual self-disclosure, we cultivate intimate relationships. In this shared holy effort, we cultivate solidarity and, in reciprocal transformation, we come to love one another; in the co-construction of values and discovering a shared conception of *eudaimonia* (how best to live), our identities become intertwined.

While friendship has a crucial role in child development, it does not lose its significance in adulthood when virtuous living is most actualized. Maimonides explains that "man requires friends all his lifetime" (*Guide for the Perplexed* 3:49). It is the strong advice of the Rabbis to "acquire for yourself a friend" (*Pirke Avot* 1:6). Like any other moral effort, it does not come naturally but requires deliberation and toil.

My commitment to supporting the cultivation of virtue-based friendships is motivated by Jewish values. To be sure, one clear and important value of friendship is utilitarian; friends help each other in times of distress. Ecclesiastes teaches: "Two are better than one because they have a good reward for their labor. For if they fall, the one will lift up his fellow; but woe to him that is alone when he falls, for he has not another to help him up" (4:9–10). The Bible consistently reminds us to protect the stranger. In friendship, we can move the other, and ourselves, from alienation into a social network and friendship.

Rabbi Joseph B. Soloveitchik valued both a "*haver l'de'agah*, a person in whom one can confide both in times of crisis, when distress strikes, and in times of glory, when one feels happy and content," and a "*haver l'deah*, a friend in whom he or she has absolute trust or faith, a person in whom he or she has absolute trust and faith" (*Family Redeemed* 27–28). A friend is an emotional partner in our high and low journeys. Sometimes friendship is manifest in lifelong commitment. Other times, we can offer moments of the gift of friendship. One is never lonely if they are willing to connect to whomever they encounter. Every moment can be seen as an opportunity for spiritual presence and friendship.

In addition to support, Rabbi Soloveitchik explains (based upon the book of Job) that there is a vital spiritual purpose to friendships:

> Job certainly did not grasp the meaning of friendship. At this phase, even communal and social relations served the purpose of utility and safety. Real friendship is possible only when man rises to the height of an open existence, in which he is capable of prayer and communication. In such living, the personality fulfills itself (*Out of the Whirlwind*, 154).

It is not until Job realizes the importance of opening himself spiritually to others that he truly comes to understand the virtue of friendship: "And the Lord returned the fortunes of Job, when he prayed for his friends; and the Lord gave Job twice as much as he had before" (Job 42:10).

Living a good happy life without deep friendships was unfathomable to the Rabbis. According to one Talmudic story, Honi, the legendary miracle-worker, was depressed from social isolation. He prayed for death that he might be released from his despair. Rava, a great Talmudic sage of the 4th century, then utters tersely that one must choose "either friendship or death" (*Taanit* 23a). The lesson is that we cannot thrive in our life missions without companionship.

When friendship is just about having a good time on a hike or at a movie, it is not impactful nor enduring. But when friendship is about the cultivation of virtue, the opportunity to pursue the good, the exploration of life, and the search for meaning, it is transformative and enduring. As the Rabbis teach: "Any love that is dependent upon a specific cause, when the cause is gone, the love is gone; but if it does not depend on a specific cause, it will never cease" (*Pirke Avot* 5:16). Friendships of pleasure and utility are fun but end as our needs and wants evolve. Friendships of virtue are not whimsical as they are attached to our pursuit of the just, holy, and good.

A friend is more than another who shares our experiences, values, or narratives. To friends, we have special duties that arise from our relationships. To become virtuous citizens committed to moral and religious excellence, life partners are crucial. Religious mentors can play a crucial role in reinforcing these values for emerging adults on campus and strengthening social bonds in an age where they are increasingly threatened.   □

SEX EDUCATION IN ORTHODOX HIGH SCHOOLS

I SAT IN ON A SEX EDUCATION COURSE AT AN Orthodox high school. The class was for seniors, the first one they had been offered on the subject; they were understandably full of questions. I realized, based upon the nature of their questions, how vital this course was.

If you search on the Web for an Orthodox approach to sex education, one of the main responses goes like this: "Education teaches people how to live. If you are educated about sex, you begin to live with sex. This is not a theory. This is fact . . . There is an accepted view within Jewish orthodoxy that sex education should be taught when people are ready to have sex. When adults are ready to get married, they are ready to learn about sex."

This is not a "fact." Do we not teach our students about the ideas of other religions lest they come to follow those faiths? Further, this falsehood does not even have the advantage of being useful. How will students learn about the risks of sexually transmitted diseases, pregnancy, promiscuity, and sex abuse? How will they learn about their anatomy and the menstrual cycle? How will they learn to have mature, sophisticated conversations as adults if their educators censor learning about a vital life reality? The myth that sex education leads to sex must be challenged for the welfare of our children.

The Jewish perspective is that sex in the right context is necessary, good, and holy. Sex education can be taught in a way that maintains and promotes the values of sexual restraint, modesty, and intimacy, while teaching teenagers about the responsibilities, risks, and values that come with an adult sex life. These can help inform other Jewish law related to adultery, *taharat ha-mishpacha* (family purity laws), and *hirhurim* (sexual thoughts).

Orthodox high school students will have sex in marriage or beforehand. Not providing them with a comprehensive education, including sex education, that prepares them for life as observant Jews in the twenty-first century, is irresponsible. A study published in the journal *Pediatrics* found that pregnancy rates are twice as high among teenagers who watch television shows with high sexual content, compared with teens who do not. Given that most modern Orthodox teens are exposed to an entertainment culture that normalizes sex, addressing sexuality is crucial.

Further, avoidance to teach sex education may violate *lifnei iver* (the prohibition against placing a stumbling block before the blind). If we do not include it in our Jewish education, we risk putting our students in harm's way.

Students, if uninformed about the health, moral, and emotional risks that come with sexual activity, may find themselves with herpes, gonorrhea, chlamydia, syphilis, or AIDS; unwanted pregnancy or sexual abuse; and emotional scarring and future resistance to healthy physical intimacy.

We do not want to promote sexual activity in teenagers. However, there are ways to teach this material responsibly to empower students as emerging adults to construct their spiritual and moral guidelines.

We would be naïve to think that some Orthodox students were not already engaged in sexual activity. Nationwide, around 72 percent of high school seniors, and 90 percent of twenty-two-year olds, have had sexual intercourse. The numbers at Orthodox high schools are, of course, much lower, but even students not engaged in sexual activity are thinking about it. Is the classroom not a safe and sacred place to enhance these conversations?

Judaism teaches that there is Torah in everything and that God can be found everywhere. Jewish teachings have much to offer in this realm of thought and experience. Sex education is Torah and should be taught.   □

THE CULTURE OF BULLYING: IT'S NOT JUST KIDS!

ABC NEWS REPORTS THAT CLOSE TO 30 PERCENT of students are either bullies or victims of bullying, and around 160,000 kids stay home from school every day out of fear of being bullied. Up to 10 percent of students either drop out or transfer to another school due to bullying. In the Internet age, cyberbullying has become a significant additional problem. According to research on cyberbullying by the PEW Research Center Internet & American Life Project, 88 percent of students surveyed have witnessed peers being mean or cruel online. This translates to 2.7 million students being bullied by 2.1 million other students, according to 2010 statistics.

But it is not just children. Up to 25 percent of adults experience bullying at work, where criticism focuses on the employee rather than the work. Bullying can also happen when students and teachers bully each other, or in adult social groups and in families. Apparently, the failure to build social and educational communities that cultivate respect for the dignity of the other has an effect that carries over into adulthood.

Bullying has serious consequences for physical and mental health. Among kids, suicide is the third leading cause of death (about 4,400 deaths a year), and for every suicide, there are over 100 suicide attempts. Bullying is heavily correlated with suicide, as more than half of suicides among young people are related to bullying.

Conversely, bullying also influences teen murder: students of all ages who commit homicide are twice as likely as their victims to have been victims of bullying. Among adults, those who are bullied have a higher risk for anxiety, clinical depression, stroke, and myocardial infarction (heart attack).

There has been a surge of interest in bullying with studies on the nature of animal bullying, movies about bullying, campaigns against college hazing, and the research of social inclusion. In addition, there have been efforts to curb bullying in schools. There are comprehensive programs, such as the Olweus Bullying Prevention Program, created by Norwegian professor

Dr. Dan Olweus, that attempt to modify behavior in elementary and junior high schools. However, even a simple approach can sometimes work. In a Middle and High School program in Rochester, Minnesota, intervention has been the key, with the premise that most students do not bully and can become part of the solution. Focusing on a pattern of repeat abuse, the school administration has encouraged students, teachers, parents, and by-standers to report instances of bullying to the school administration, which then quickly acts to stop the bullying. As a result, bullying is cut off before it can become a chronic problem. In the middle school, for example, 76 percent of students had no visits to the principal's office, and 10 percent only had one visit during the school year, allowing the administration to work on the 14 percent who were more likely to engage in bullying.

This program is in accord with the fundamental modern principle of in loco parentis (in place of a parent), in which a school legally takes the place and responsibility of parents when a child is left in their care. Teachers and administrators must be attentive to the emotional harm that happens out-side of the classroom (hallways, recess, lunchroom), but this does not dis-miss the responsibility of parents to take the emotional pulse of their child. Ultimately, chief responsibility falls upon each student who is privy to the interpersonal dynamics firsthand. We must not merely teach our students to cease from bullying. We must teach them to intervene when we witness acts of bullying. "Don't stand by the blood of your fellow!" So much of bullying happens not because of bad intentions but due to group dynamics and social pressures. We must diffuse and attack these group forces. There is no place for threats, put-downs, spreading rumors, and pretending to be someone else.

In Jewish thought, technology is neither good nor bad, as it can be used either way: to heal, build bridges, and to learn, but also to create real dam-age. According to the Jewish laws of *lashon hara* (evil speech), real dam-age can happen through words. At the least, it can hurt another's image or self-esteem and cause emotional pain. At worst, however, it can lead to bodily harm and suicide.

It is very difficult, due to the human tendency to be self-absorbed, to truly value another as much as oneself and to fulfill the rabbinic value that "Your friend's dignity should be as precious to you as your own" (*Pirke Avot* 2:10).

The effect of social intimidation and mockery truly is lethal. "Why is gossip like a three-pronged tongue? Because it kills three people: the person who says it, the person who listens to it, and the person about whom it is said" (*Arachin* 15b). Shaming another is considered a life and death issue.

The Gemara teaches that "Whoever shames his neighbor in public, it is as if he shed his blood" (*Bava Metzia* 58b) since "Life and death are in the hands of the tongue" (Proverbs 18:21). The Rabbis teach again and again that to shame another is akin to murder.

Another form of bullying is through nicknames. Rambam teaches that "It is forbidden to call someone by a name they dislike" (*Deot* 6:8). The Rabbis of the Talmud teach that "One who gives his neighbor a bad name, can never gain pardon" (Jerusalem Talmud, *Bava Kamma* 8:7).

We need a new educational model to address bullying. It cannot simply be with the stick punishing bullying. Rather, it is about educating students about power dynamics as a psychological practice and cultivating meditational practices and group exercises around the awareness of the feelings of others as a spiritual practice.

Whether bullying is emotional, verbal, or physical, and whether it is among adults or children, it can never be tolerated. Bullying does not just happen where we would expect it in schools, prisons, and on playing fields. It happens in the workplace across industries. Most of all, if we wish to address bullying among kids, we must address it among the role models of children. Bullying happens right before our eyes every day in subtle ways. We can model for our children what it means to see the dignity in all people that we encounter. □

CHALLENGES AND OPPORTUNITIES FOR JEWISH SERVICE-LEARNING IN THE 21ST CENTURY

THE JEWISH STORY AND MANDATE ARE BEST epitomized by a biblical passage. Jacob wrestles with God and man, and is then named Israel. This is to say that the Jewish people are named for their key historical and existential experience of having struggled, as humans, with the other and Other. Jacob goes beyond himself in existential warfare – wrestling, struggling – he becomes Israel. Authentic Jewish living is not comfortable, rather its essence is deep struggle and challenge.

When religion fails, it is an opiate to the masses as it merely comforts. When religion excels, it can be one of greatest motivators challenging followers to be their best. One of the challenges today is the desire for too much comfort and pleasure. How do we teach a culture of sacrifice and collective responsibility?

Another core challenge is the nature of truth. In post-modernity, when we can no longer retreat back to absolutism, which end of the skepticism spectrum is embraced: relativism or pluralism? Nothing is true and authentic, or everything is true and authentic?

If we choose pluralism, with our affirmation of others, how can we still stand with full conviction and persuasion for our own self-affirmation?

In our time, we are seeing a return, among all faiths, to particularism, with a transition from monolithic universalism. For example, there are more Jews learning texts today than at any other time before in Jewish history.

In our Jewish cultural return to texts and values, how do we become universalists, or cosmopolitans, through distinctively Jewish hermeneutics?

Similar to empathy, faith is another life lens to see the world. A primary goal of education is to help others cultivate more life lenses so they can see further and to teach them how to take those lenses on and off.

We must put the predicament of being universalists and particularists in historical perspective. Prior to the Enlightenment, Jews were often excluded from social acceptance. Thus in the wake of the Enlightenment, there was a great desire for assimilation once there was access to broader society. The nineteenth century poet Judah Leib Gordon famously recommended: "Be a Jew in the home and a man in the street."

Today in America, there is the opportunity to be a Jew both in the home and in the street. A Jew in America can still be wary of the role of religion in politics and yet bring their unique Jewish voice to the public sphere. As the great twentieth century thinker and activist Rabbi Abraham Joshua Heschel famously argued: "We affirm the principle of separation of church and state. We reject the separation of religion and the human situation."

One of the many reasons why the Jewish people have had such tremendous social impact throughout history has been that we have operated on the periphery of society. We are the paradigmatic outsiders. However, today in America, we are insiders. So we must ask: How can we be insiders but continue to play the social agitator role of outsider?

It is my belief that civil disobedience is one area where we can and must continue to raise our voices to protest wrongs and make our moral voices heard. It is also a way that we ensure that we continue to operate on a grassroots level and not conform through a purely top-down approach.

I taught my students at UCLA that for Judaism to be relevant and to be actualized (to really be lived), it needs to be authentically in the streets, in the hospitals, on Capitol Hill, in the torture room, in the cornfield, in the prison cell. Learning happens in "third spaces" perhaps even more than in institutional spaces.

How does the tradition itself inform the search for twenty-first century social justice? There are a few different camps here:

1. The Tradition is basically irrelevant to current times (too difficult to apply beyond the initial historical context)
2. Literal translation and application
3. The perceived "good" today is what is Jewish (no textual work needs to be done)
4. Extending biblical and Talmudic concepts to the present situation. This is not faith-based but faith-rooted. That is to say that we are not just organizing Jews to do what others do; rather, we are organizing in a distinctly Jewishly way.

I'd contend that this is done through trans-valuation by re-infusing meaning into our Jewish texts, laws, rituals and daily living, and by attuning ourselves to the core moral and spiritual values of the tradition.

Another distinct communal and pedagogical challenge is that there are billions of followers of faith and yet very limited owners of faith.

We cannot engage in religion simply because there is law or custom or community that says to, and we can't disengage simply because we disagree with someone else's interpretation of the meaning of our Jewish acts. Rather each of us can take ownership on our own terms (in conversation with our community but not overtaken by it).

Each Jewish student may feel empowered by the Jewish community in certain ways and extraordinarily alienated in other ways. The challenge is to empower each student to their rightful ownership and to overcome these past alienations to carve their own path.

But authenticity is not just a question about the source of our actions whether a value is rooted in text, tradition, community, or conscience, but also in how the chosen values are lived. One must ask: "Am I living authentically Jewish? Am I acting daily on the convictions that I embrace?"

This requires something that college students allocate little to no time for: reflection. I've worked with them in meditation, spiritual writing, prayer, process groups. Students have interconnected narratives yet they also have fragmented/multiple selves. Reflection helps students to make new connections in their thought and more deliberate choices in their actions.

In addition to the cultivation of the identity and responsibility of the student, the nature of the service (or social justice work) is also crucial. We can no longer wrap peanut butter and jelly sandwiches and drop them on a corner and feel proud of our work. When religious identity and continuity is cultivated on the backs of the vulnerable, we have done a great disservice to all.

It is for this reason that I argue that a Jewish activist identity has to go beyond the important but limited acts of wearing pins, bumper stickers, divisive partisan slogans, club membership, sitting on boards, writing checks, and telling stories from our idealist days. There must be measurable impact on the lives of others.

In our globalized age, we are all interconnected in new ways. Our responsibility changes when we are more aware of each other and of new problems and solutions. We have enough food on the earth to feed everyone. The U.S. wastes 100 billion dollars of food each year, how we can allocate or rethink our distribution of wealth? In a world where 1 billion people live on $1 a day and 2 billion people live on $2 a day, yet 99.9 percent of human genes are the same. How can this be tolerated?

I recall the face of despair of a mother and her baby in a street who approached me in need of twenty more cents to survive. I recall the tear of a farmer I met in a ricefield in Thailand who lived with a family of nine off of $275 a year.

I argue that our Jewish identities are to be socially constructed primarily through addressing the great moral problems of our times on issues such as: HIV, malaria, climate change, environmental justice, homelessness, domestic abuse and domestic workers, and hunger, housing, and access to clean water.

We can ask the power question: What resources do I have access to (intellectual, financial, geographic, political, etc.)? We must not just dream of a healed world but work to make it actual.

So many activists are making it happen today as we are witnessing a new culture of Jewish social entrepreneurship and service with new innovative ideas shaping the Jewish community and the broader world. For example,

Jewish students lead in the Challah for Hunger initiative against hunger in over twenty campuses. Project Sol is an organization of Israelis working on Solar energy projects in Africa. There are many lobbying for domestic worker bill of rights to protest those in servitude working in homes not protected by normal worker law and certainly not enforced. There has been an explosion of the Fair Trade and Environmental Movements.

The Tav Chevrati moves forward in Israel and the Tav HaYosher in New York securing the rights of workers in restaurants. AJWS has been taking the lead in Darfur. Avodah, JFSJ, and Panim are training young Jews to serve.

Curricula must be geared primarily toward Jewish ethics and global justice transformation. College campuses must cultivate armies not just of readers but of doers. Synagogues must see their primary goal as looking not just within the walls of the synagogue but outwards. The academy without faith and religion is like studying anatomy without heart. Faith is about the cultivation of wonder, possibility, and the messianic impulse. It requires serious human toil. Is there a moral component to university experience? Who will insure it happens? □

GADAMER, NOZICK, AND THE SPLITTING OF THE SEA: CHOOSING HOW TO INTERPRET THE WORLD

IN ONE OF THE MOST DRAMATIC SCENES OF VICTOR Hugo's *Les Misérables*, Jean Valjean, a former prisoner who has become beloved mayor of his adopted town, is faced with the challenge of throwing away the life he has built for himself to defend an innocent man. Jean Valjean, standing in the courtroom, asks himself: "Who am I? Can I condemn this man to slavery? Pretend I do not feel his agony. This innocent who bears my face. Who goes to judgment in my place? Who am I?"

Standing before the townspeople, he reveals his true identity, saving the innocent man's life, only to go immediately into hiding. Aware of his freedom, he realizes he must now interpret this difficult situation before him as an opportunity to build up the courage to stand up and do what is true and just.

This is precisely the question that Bnei Yisrael must face between Passover and Shavuot, between redemption and revelation. We have left slavery in Egypt physically and ontologically, experienced the miracles from the hand of God, and we have crossed the sea and seen our enemies drown before our eyes. We now stand redeemed at the edge of the sea. In this crucial moment of identity formation, how will we use our freedom? We are faced with the question that is perhaps the most challenging question of our lives: How do we choose to interpret our lives?

Are we now and forever the victim of Egypt? Are we forsaken and stranded in the desert, and not entitled to more? Or are we the recipients of great miracles beyond anything we could possibly deserve? Are we now responsible in a new way?

Most who left Egypt could still only interpret the world as slaves. This is why we needed forty years in the desert, to transition from a generation trapped in a slave mentality unfit to autonomously lead our own nation, unable to interpret our own realities. And thus immediately after achieving our freedom, we complain, feeling entitled to food and water.

Volunteering on different occasions in the former Soviet Union, numerous Jewish individuals shared with me that they would rather return to Communist Russia, where paychecks were consistent. Everyday expectations, for many, trump freedom.

What would we rather live with – freedom or consistent pleasure?

The twentieth century American philosopher Robert Nozick, in *Anarchy, State, and Utopia*, proposed the thought experiment of a virtual reality machine – if one could have any experience they choose in this machine (and one would forget that they are even hooked up to the machine), Nozick asked, "would one choose to be hooked up" to it? He concluded, perhaps idealistically, that no one in their right mind would choose to be hooked up to this machine, since such happiness is no happiness at all. It is through our free direct engagement and interpretation of our reality, rather than through a mediated experience, that we truly live. We choose to live with reality, knowing that the life situations before us are often not objectively good or bad. We must interpret not illusion but a real world, our real lives.

Must we, then, choose between harsh reality and the ideal? There is something in between. We actually have a machine within each of us that we can turn on and off. It is the machine that we use to interpret the world. Reality does not impose meaning upon us. Rather, we choose to make meaning of our own reality. We choose how we interpret it.

If we wish to look at our closest family members, we can interpret our intimate experiences with them over the years to show how they may be selfish and flawed. But we also may choose to make the case for their depth and goodness. We may decide how we actually choose to view other people.

Similarly, if we wish to view our Jewish tradition as chauvinistic, racist, sexist, and outdated, we will find plenty of sources and proofs to make the case. If we wish to see the Jewish tradition as a collection of some of the most beautiful and powerful moral and spiritual wisdom that has spoken to hearts and souls for ages, we will find plenty to make the case. Because I believe and wish the Torah to be just and God to be good, I choose to interpret texts with charitable interpretations and life events with a lens of faith and devotion. As Hans-Georg Gadamer, the twentieth century philosopher, taught, objective truth does not simply emerge from text. We bring our "prejudices," assumptions, and judgments to the text. All objective human sensory experience passes through the subjective mind to be understood. Do we actively choose our hermeneutic lens and do we defend our tradition? These choices are up to us.

We choose every day, every moment how to interpret the reality before us. This is what the Rabbis are teaching when they say: "*ein adam lomed Torah ela m'makom she'libo hafetz*" (one can only truly learn when the heart is turned on to something). We might say the same about love: One can only truly love another if one actively chooses to love. More important than the realities the world imposes upon us is our response and interpretations of those realities. If we wish to be inspired, we must actually decide that we will open our hearts and allow ourselves to be inspired.

Our inspiration should not arise from allowing others to interpret the world for us. The writers of op-eds and talk show hosts tell us what matters, psychologists tell us what we really feel, friends let us know what we should think, movie critics tell us how to watch movies, and *parsha* emails tell us how we should read the text. We can turn our minds and souls off, since others can think and feel for us. The world seems purely objective, and we just need others to tell us what the real truth is.

Perhaps we do this because on some level, each of us is convinced that we are not smart enough, experienced enough, or competent enough. We feel we must rely upon others to interpret the world for us, as if there actually could be an expert other than ourselves in interpreting our personal realities. When we allow this, or merely react to our life situations without proactively interpreting our life situations, we sacrifice our freedom.

Not everything in life is important, but for those people and things that are important to us, we must actively determine our interpretations. We need to focus on the good in the people and things that we most cherish, even in moments where there is contrary evidence. This is the virtue that the Rabbis call "*ayin tovah*," the good interpretive lens (*Pirke Avot* 5:22).

This is the biggest question that students on campus are addressing. Now that I have my freedom, how will I choose to interpret the world? Do I wish to view the world as my parents have? Do I choose a Jewish lens? Which books, scholars, and ideologies will inform my interpretation of the universe? But this choice is not just the result of a college-age existential crisis. It is a lifelong endeavor of choosing. Each of us can ask, what is my philosophy of interpretation of the world? What is my life hermeneutic?

Politicians see opportunities in crisis. Entrepreneurs see potential ventures in social needs. Optimists see the good amidst ambivalence. How do we as religious Jews interpret the world? What is the life lens that we cultivate? I would propose that when we encounter difficult situations that require courage, the authentic Jewish response is, How do I serve? How do I give? How do I make this situation better?

This is what Hannah Senesh did when she interpreted the risk of the Jews of Hungary being sent to the Nazi death camps as an opportunity to parachute behind enemy lines to attempt their rescue. This is what Rabbi Avi Weiss did on the morning of September 11th when he interpreted the news that others were fleeing from the World Trade Center as an opportunity to take a cab downtown, not uptown. This is what Ruth Messinger does when, as a 71-year old, she hears about a village addressing poverty somewhere in the world and interprets it as an opportunity to travel there to find out how the Jewish community can help.

Right after Bnei Yisrael achieved their freedom and were rescued from the split sea, the Torah tells us that they were strengthened in their faith and sang a reverential song of worship, but only moments later complained for water and for the food of Egypt. In this first opportunity to interpret our free lives, the response, understandable as it was, was one of slaves feeling entitlement, not of free people looking to give.

Each year around Pesach, we have the opportunity to make a *tikkun* (a repair of our first free interpretation). Millions of people every day struggle to make ends meet, to heal a physical or emotional wound, and to overcome despair and sorrow. Miraculously, amidst a difficult world that continues to surprise us and unexpectedly knock us down, the great human spirit perseveres to interpret life situations as opportunities not only to address our infinite personal needs and desires, but also to interpret our life situations as opportunities to serve and to give to others also in need.

Today, and every day, we stand redeemed from Egypt and the split sea amidst new challenges, and must confront this question: "How will I interpret my freedom?"   □

DISHONEST KIRUV: BUILDING RESPONSIBLE JEWISH OUTREACH MOVEMENTS

I SERVED AS A JEWISH OUTREACH PROFESSIONAL for the two years as the Senior Jewish Educator at the UCLA Hillel. I was so fortunate to be able to spend my days talking and learning with students about their life journeys. At its best, Jewish outreach provides a student alienated from Judaism with a warm, inclusive, sophisticated, honest entry point into finding his or her voice and place within the Jewish tradition and community. At its worst, outreach is deceptive, closed, and arrogant. It can be hard to tell the difference, because both types of outreach are done with a smile and a bowl of cholent.

Surveys of the American Orthodox community show the need for, and possible results of, *kiruv* (bringing another closer to the tradition). Of those adults who were raised in an Orthodox home, only 41 percent now identify themselves as Orthodox. On the other hand, 57,000 adults who were raised in a non-Orthodox household identified as Orthodox as adults. Among Jews attending synagogue, only 14–18 percent of those age 45 or older are Orthodox, while the percentage soars to 34 percent among those age 18–34. Since this study, the numbers have increased significantly. The Orthodox outreach movement is working and only growing rapidly.

Orthodox groups engaged in *kiruv* include the National Jewish Outreach Program, with events at 3,700 locations throughout North America (and nearly forty nations); Chabad, with its more than 3,000 emissaries (*shluchim*) in seventy countries; and groups such as Aish HaTorah, J A M, Maimonides, and Ohr Somayach. Of course there are thousands of other professionals (across the ideological spectrum) at Kollels, Hillels, *shuls*, and schools also doing significant outreach work. There are so many responsible and ethical Orthodox outreach professionals in the field that we cannot let those who are more narrow and deceptive ruin the perception of the rest. Outreach professionals are often courageous leaving their comfort zone to engage others in the tradition in inconvenient ways. However, many have been very critical of some *kiruv* tactics, especially among the Haredi, for refusing to acknowledge any opinion but their own and for not answering difficult questions. One critical blog quoted Rabbi Emanuel Rackman's critique of this closed, fundamentalist mindset that can be found:

> A Jew dare not live with absolute certainty, not only because certainty is the hallmark of the fanatic . . . , but also because doubt is good for the human soul, its humility, and consequently its greater potential intimately to discover its creator. (*One Man's Judaism*)

Kiruv, when done immorally, encourages a break from one's family and friends who are not observant, pushes the student to make quick changes in observance, uses Bible codes and flawed philosophical logic with those who cannot detect the difference, uses alcohol to attract students, offers theological certainty, suggests that if one is religious they will be successful in all while dismissing the complexities of all human relationships and struggles, and promises a life of bliss if one merely chooses the true path.

When I was learning at an outreach yeshiva in Jerusalem, there was a sign above my bed that said: "Don't be so open-minded your brain falls out." I was confused why open-minded thinking wouldn't be in sync with sophisticated religious learning. I heard the most repulsive thing on campus when I was in college and have hesitated to even put in writing. I recall a group of us being told by an outreach professional (while being served "a *l'chaim*" – shot of liquor) that "*shiksas* are for practice" (that non-Jews, spoken about derogatorily, are for practice before one ultimately must settle down with a Jew). I was beyond appalled but also confused because this seemed to be a pious Orthodox rabbi giving me advice. While there have been many negative interactions, I am certainly very grateful for the great support that so many outreach organizations provided me during my religious journey.

We must call for an end to these practices. We must not become more concerned with charisma and gimmicks than truth, service, and piety. Are we willing to sell anything just to get five more "unengaged" Jews into the room or to prevent intermarriage? Jewish integrity demands more. Bad *kiruv* claims the ends justify the means (i.e., do whatever it takes to make people more religious). Good outreach sees the individual as an end him or herself acknowledging their *tzelem Elokim* (that they are created in the image of God). Further, Rambam taught that "*ki ha-sechel hu kavod Hashem*" (intellect is the glory of God). To cheapen Torah to gimmicks is an affront to God and to man.

Irresponsible outreach prioritizes and encourages a more insular sense of community and a narrower worldview. This is most troubling on campus when we should be educating young Jews how to be in the world – not to escape from it. I have now encountered students at university who deny evolution, global warming, and the value of secular wisdom due to inappropriate *kiruv* influences.

To be sure, I am an Orthodox rabbi and one of my personal spiritual goals is to help others grow in their observance level. My colleagues and I strive to do that with honesty, intellectual openness, and on the terms that students are interested in. I would like to inspire my Jewish students to be more *frum* (inspired toward deeper religious commitments). But I also want to guide others to where they want to go, not coerce them due to some ulterior motive of mine.

Kiruv and pluralism need not contradict if one adopts a constructivist-contextualist approach. I can embrace the fact that very different responsible choices about one's religious life are valid yet still want others to adopt a position more similar to my own. I respect their past narrative in its proper context and so I must respect their choices yet I also, as a religious educator, hope to partner with them to be inspired to reshape their future narrative not through an invasive imperialism of the soul but rather through a dual liberation. The one doing the *kiruv* should also expect to be *mekaraived* (be brought closer) in the process as well. To me, religious outreach is about engaging in partnered salvation from the world that is to the world that ought to be.

The best outreach involves *hesed*. It is through giving to others, social justice work, service projects, and inviting others to have an impact in the world (all infused with Jewish learning and conversations) where we can empower others to learn and grow in their tradition, as individuals, and as citizens. It is the most honest and effective approach that conveys Judaism is ultimately about service and giving, love and justice.

The more we intentionally try to change young Jews, the more we mess them up. The great fifteenth century kabbalist Meir Ibn Gabbai taught that influencing humans is similar to playing a violin. If you place two violins with their strings facing one another and draw a bow across one string, the same string on the other violin across from it will vibrate as well. So, too, with souls. We do not manipulatively reach out and touch another's soul. Rather we turn our soul on and encounter one another honestly. That is the way Ibn Gabbai teaches we can best achieve a spiritual awakening for ourselves and others. We owe our students the most attractive, powerful, and compelling models of Judaism. But more than that, we owe them honesty, patience, and respect.   □

IS COLLEGE WORKING? THE DECLINE OF THE HUMANITIES

As an educator who has taught students on more than thirty campuses around the country, I see how stressed students are to compete for grades, jobs, and organizational positions. Most students seem more focused on achievement than on their personal life search and intellectual journey. They are, of course, not to blame as a transactional culture has become overwhelming, but we have much to fear for the future of the university and the intellectual culture of our country.

A current study makes us question whether college is actually working to produce the results expected from such an expensive and time-consuming project. Sociologists Richard Arum and Josipa Roksa, in their book *Academically Adrift*, report that 45 percent of college students have not improved their critical thinking and writing skills after two years, and 36 percent still have not improved after four years. What are these students paying so much for?

The cost of a single year in college has soared over the past generation. The College Board estimated that annual tuition and fees are $7,020 for public colleges and $26,273 for private colleges, along with room and board that can add $7,000–$9,000 or more, and expenses for educational materials. Future projections are even grimmer; at the current rate, college tuition will increase to $123,000 (public) and $288,000 (private) for four years by 2034, and Ivy League colleges will then cost $422,000. What is it exactly that students are paying for?

Upon graduation, these students understandably want to pay back their debt and get a start on life. As a January 2012 report released by the Georgetown Center on Education and the Workforce noted, college graduates who majored in the liberal arts earned less than many other majors, as Table 2 indicates.

Major	Unemployment Rate (%)	Annual Earnings ($)
Engineering	7.5	55,000
Computers and Mathematics	8.2	46,000
Health	5.4	43,000
Business	7.4	39,000
Education	5.4	33,000
Humanities (Liberal Arts)	9.4	31,000
Psychology/Social Work	7.3	30,000
Arts	11.1	30,000

Table 2: Recent College Graduate Unemployment
and Average Annual Income (by Major)

It is not surprising that Engineer and Computer/Mathematics majors make more than those whose major was in the Humanities, Psychology/Social Work, or the Arts. However, Business majors, once dominant among the upwardly mobile, now have a much higher unemployment rate than Education majors, so not everything is predictable.

This trend, while apparently accelerating during the Great Recession, has been under way for more than a generation. During the early 1970s, the effect of college overexpansion and a stagnant economy dealt a serious blow to the Humanities, as there were now few academic positions available. From 1970–1982, for example, while the total number of undergraduate degrees increased by 11 percent, the number of degrees granted in the Humanities decreased dramatically:

Major	Decline (%)
History	62
English	57
Philosophy	51
Modern Languages	50

Academic shifting, in addition to affecting our intellectual culture, impacts moral judgment. Studies have shown that college education has a positive influence on moral judgment, but this effect is significantly weaker for business students and is largely absent for accounting students (Cohen, *Journal of Business Ethics*, 2001). There is, of course, great importance to Mathematics and the sciences, but somehow the Humanities have gotten lost in the process.

Fortunately, the Humanities still have an array of champions. Conservative columnist David Brooks, for example, extols a liberal arts education for developing a progressively rare talent for reading and understanding the meaning of a paragraph, adding that it also enables you to write a coherent memo. He urges students to take advantage of the cumulative learning of many civilizations over millennia: ". . . doesn't it make sense to spend some time in the company of these languages – learning to feel different emotions, rehearsing different passions, experiencing different sacred rituals, and learning to see in different ways?"

Harvard Professor Michael J. Sandel takes a different approach. He notes with alarm that America has transformed from a market economy, in which monetary considerations were confined to economic issues, to a "market society," which greatly expands the areas subject to the bottom line of economics. This has highlighted the gap between rich and poor and damaged the possibility of equal access to the political system. As Professor Sandel warns: "We are in the grip of a way of looking at the world and social life and even personal relations that is dominated by economic ways of thinking. That's an impoverished way of looking at the world."

Judaism has much to add to this defense of the Humanities. Rav Aharon Lichtenstein, the great Rosh Yeshiva who also holds a PhD from Harvard in literature, has been a great defender of the Humanities:

The contention that a Torah *hashkafah* (worldview) should sanction scientific studies to the exclusion of the humanities, as only they deal with God's world, blithely ignores man's position as part of that world. To the extent that the humanities focus upon man, they deal not only with a segment of divine creation but with its pinnacle. The dignity of man is not the exclusive legacy of Cicero and Pico della Mirandola. It is a central theme in Jewish thought, past and present. Deeply rooted in Scripture, copiously asserted by Hazal, unequivocally assumed by *rishonim* (medieval rabbis), religious humanism is a primary and persistent mark of a Torah Weltanschauung. Man's inherent dignity and sanctity, so radically asserted through the concept of *tzelem Elokim* (humans created in the image of God); his hegemony and stewardship with respect to nature; concern for his spiritual and physical well-being; faith in his metaphysical freedom and potential – all are cardinal components of traditional Jewish thought . . . How, then can anyone question the value of precisely those fields which are directly concerned with probing humanity? ("Torah and General Culture: Confluence and Conflict," 245).

Rav Aharon reminds us that the study of philosophy, literature, and history can broaden our ethical, spiritual, and religious worldview as committed Jews. If one is going to take loans worth more than $100,000, one should take on the challenge to grow as a human being, not merely as a future worker. Training professionals but failing to teach humanity will destroy the creative fabric of our country.

How we, as adults, spend our leisure time helps to model for our children and students what values and activities they should cherish for their own sake. If we act as though we value money, prestige, and work more than relationships, ideas, and service we can only expect what lessons the next generation will learn from us. If we do not emphasize the importance of personal growth and intellectual search then we should not feel surprised if our children view the primary purpose of university as a way to increase their earning potential.

Maimonides taught that one must "accept the truth from wherever one finds it." As Jews we must have the intrigue and humility to engage the great intellectual traditions that preceded us. The Torah, of course, takes primacy but as Rav Kook taught, we must draw from all truths to "expand the palace of Torah." □

REPETITION AND
THE CULTIVATION OF VIRTUE

REPETITION IS ONE OF THE MOST POWERFUL Jewish tools for the cultivation of wisdom and virtue. We learn this lesson, repeatedly, at the time of year when we finish the reading of the Torah, when we immediately start again from the beginning.

When it comes to the end of the holiday season and our completion of the Torah on Shemini Atzeret-Simchat Torah, the Tur (*Orach Chaim* 699) teaches: "We call it Simchat Torah because on it we complete the Torah. It is appropriate to be joyous when we finish it and we are accustomed to begin Bereishit immediately so that there will be no opportunity for the Satan to accuse us, saying: 'They have already finished it and they do not want to read it again.'" The Satan, our internal voice of opposition, tells us that we have completed our learning and can rest. But following the end of our learning cycle we embrace the communal momentum to continue this cycle once again.

It is not mere repetition but a search for novel insights in Torah study that matters most, as the Mishnah (*Pirke Avot* 5:26) reminds us: "Ben Bag Bag says: 'Turn it [the Torah] over and turn it over and study it because everything is in it. Look into it. Become grey and old over it. Do not move from it because there is no greater measure than it.' Ben He He says: 'According to the trouble [in Torah study] is the reward.'"

Each time we wrestle with the text, we can find new insights that overturn our past understanding, as we see from the Talmud's (*Hagigah* 9b) teaching, "One that repeated a chapter 100 times is not to be compared with one who repeated it 101 times." The Sages taught that Jewish wisdom is attained not primarily through quickness of intellect but through the deepest internalization process, a process that takes hold only with time, patience, and much repetition. Our greatest sages exhibited the virtue of patience in their pedagogical approach (*Eruvin* 54b): "R. Pereda had a pupil whom he taught his lesson 400 times before the latter could master it."

In *The Use of Pleasure*, French philosopher Michel Foucault writes these encouraging words:

> As to those for whom to work hard, to begin and begin again, to attempt and be mistaken, to go back and rework everything from top to bottom, and still find reason to hesitate from one step to the next – as to those, in short, for whom to work in the midst of uncertainty and apprehension is tantamount to failure, all I can say is that clearly we are not from the same planet.

Foucault reminds us that we must have the courage and humility to live with uncertainty and to challenge our previous intellectual structures – not that we should live in perpetual doubt or paralysis, but so that through creative destruction we may build better, stronger, lasting structures of the intellect and spirit.

Of course, we do not merely repeat the public reading of a single passage; we create rituals and habits that broaden us without making them rote. Rambam explains that everything is according to the abundance of a person's actions (*ve'hakol lefi rov ha-maaseh*), that we grow mainly through the quantity of our good deeds rather than through their quality. Excellent performance and pure intentionality are goals, of course, but frequency make virtue sustainable.

Rav Eliyahu Dessler taught (*Michtav MeEliyahu*, Vol. 3, 66), based upon the works of Rabbi Moshe Chaim Luzzato, why some feel the Divine Presence and some do not: "The limitation is with the receiver, since the windows of his heart are polluted . . . the more one cleans them, the more light will enter." We need constant acts of cleaning and refreshing, of rebooting the system, to ensure we can continue to see the world in its deepest and truest ways.

It may not surprise us to think that professional musicians or athletes excel in their craft in large part due to their daily repetition of exercises, or that writers improve their skills by consistently practicing and rewriting. However, our bodies also follow a repetitive pattern known as the circadian rhythm, which cycles about every twenty-four hours: When it gets dark, we tend to get tired and ready for sleep; before we wake, our hormones adjust so that we are alert when we arise. When this rhythm is disrupted, as during long airplane flights, we experience "jet lag." If these disruptions become chronic, the body suffers. Studies have demonstrated that long-term sleep deprivation reduces our cognitive performance and increases our risk for such health problems as hypertension, diabetes, obesity, and cardiovascular disease.

These scientific findings appear to confirm the model of constructive repetitition and practice advocated by teachers and coaches today, and throughout history by poets, philosophers, and rabbis. Aristotle taught: "We are what we repeatedly do. Excellence, then, is not an act, but a habit." Once we are fully committed to repetition and make virtuous practices our habits, they can transform us. This theme was later taken up by the seventeenth century poet John Dryden: "We first make our habits and then our habits make us."

So when we start the Torah anew, we do so with the intention to discover new wisdom in the text and new clarity in our self-understanding as individuals and as a community. On a moral level, we repeat acts of kindness each day, since our work on ourselves and in the world is never complete. On an intellectual and spiritual level we refresh the page, as it were, at least every year, since our work in understanding ourselves, the world, and the Torah is never complete. *Titchadesh!* □

MAKING COLLEGE MORE AFFORDABLE: CALL FOR HIGHER ED. REFORM

I S HIGHER EDUCATION ONLY FOR THE PRIVI-leged? Over the last few decades, between rising tuition costs, the ongoing economic determinism in admissions, and the impossibility of paying off student loans, the answer increasingly seems to be yes. As Americans and as Jews, we believe this state of affairs is neither necessary nor desirable, and our advocacy can help bring positive change on this issue.

Most members of the UCLA community, where I taught and encountered many homeless students, are unaware that hundreds of their classmates are homeless. This is but one example of a prominent university where the problem of student poverty pokes its ugly head. University costs have become crippling for so many, and the excessive predatory loans create long-term debt and significantly diminish the potential for social mobility.

In 2011, accounting for tuition, fees, and room and board, Sarah Lawrence College cost $59,170, NYU was $56,787, and Columbia University (one of my alma maters) was $56,310. These are on the highest end, but there are many private colleges and universities right behind them. In 2010, with these frighteningly high principal and high interest rates, the average debt for students graduating from college is $25,250 – this can take decades to pay off. Even more alarming, outstanding student loan debt reached $1 trillion in 2012, surpassing the total credit card debt in the United States.

This is an issue that President Obama has addressed. In April 2012, he said: "In America, higher education cannot be a luxury. It's an economic imperative that every family must be able to afford."

In 1900, only about 2 percent of eligible adults attended college. Today, about 65 percent enroll in higher education. The biggest boost in college enrollment occurred after World War II, when the GI Bill provided incentives that allowed veterans to go back to school rather than be forced into the workforce. By 1947, nearly half of all those admitted to college were veterans, and nearly half of the 16 million veterans took advantage of the GI bill to attend college courses by the time the program ended in 1956.

Another boon to higher education was low-cost or free tuition. The City University of New York (CUNY) has long provided such an education to hundreds of thousands of students, and many of the leading intellectuals of the immediate pre and post-World War II era earned their degrees at CUNY. In 1976, CUNY initiated a system whereby students who met financial requirements could receive aid from a state-funded Tuition Assistance Program and federal help from Pell Grants and tax credits. These programs continue to enable nearly half of CUNY's students to attend tuition-free. The challenge is to continue to provide quality, low-cost education for hundreds of thousands of students in the face of increasing state and federal pressure to cut programs that benefit education and aid to the poor.

Our society is no longer a trustworthy system of meritocracy, as financial barriers have become too determinative. When students with high test scores from low-income families are compared to students with high test scores from upper-income families, 80 percent of those in the top quarter of the income distribution go on to get college degrees, compared to only 44 percent of those in the bottom quarter. Thomas Edsall, a writer and analyst, writes: "Instead of serving as a springboard to social mobility as it did for the first decades after World War II, college education today is reinforcing class stratification . . ."

The income achievement gap is deepening and must be halted. In the twenty-first century marketplace, a college degree is almost a necessity. The difference in earnings of a high school graduate compared to a college graduate increased in the 1980s from 50 percent to 80 percent. This trend has not changed: In 2007, those with a high school degree annually earned slightly more than $30,000, compared to those with a bachelor's degree earning just less than $60,000. The income gap can be seen even within higher education: The large gap in admissions between competitive colleges and community colleges proves this, with 76 percent of students at competitive colleges coming from families in the top half of the income distribution and 80 percent of students at community colleges coming from low-income families.

At the same time, need-based scholarships and grants, upon which students from low-income homes rely, are becoming more limited. Pell Grant awards have been declining, while tuition costs are increasing at a rate faster than inflation. In 1979–1980, the maximum Pell Grant covered 99 percent of the cost of a community college, 77 percent at a public four-year college, and 36 percent at a private four-year college. By 2010–2011, however, these percentages had dropped to 62 percent, 36 percent, and 15 percent, respectively.

Anthony Carnevale, the co-author of "How Increasing College Access Is Increasing Inequality, and What to Do about It," writes: "The education system is an increasingly powerful mechanism for the intergenerational reproduction of privilege." In addition to significantly increasing income, a college degree works to prevent downward mobility. The trends that indicate rising tuition costs, increased loan burden, and higher earnings for those with advanced degrees must inspire us to solve the challenges of intergenerational mobility. If not, we are heading to a further polarized and unequal society, making it close to impossible to attain the "American Dream."

The disparity of wealth is one of the most significant problems in America today, correlated with the lack of opportunity for educational growth. We must remove barriers to education by increasing government assistance and putting more restrictions on tuition hikes. The model used by CUNY, coupled with a commitment to attract talented professors and a diverse student body, could help rejuvenate higher education. Finally, we must ensure that Congress acts to stave off the "fiscal cliff" of mandated spending cuts and tax increases that, among other debilitating effects on the economy, would further inhibit students from paying tuition or paying off student loans.

In Jewish law and ethics, education and the alleviation of poverty are two of the top Jewish values. We can address and strengthen both by reforming college accessibility. Jewish communities historically demanded money from all for the "*kuppah*" and the "*tamchui*" (funds for the needy), and these funds helped to ensure that all could have food, clothes, burial, and education. In the Talmud, we learn the value of education: "Rav Hamnunah taught: Jerusalem was only destroyed because students were neglected in her," and "Rabbi Shimon ben Lakish said in the name of Rabbi Yehuda Nesiyah: 'The world endures only for the breath of students'" (*Shabbat* 199b). Neglecting education destroys society. We not only help the poor and create a more fair society when we make college more accessible; we also ensure a stronger country with a more competitive advantage, which benefits all of us. Advocate today for change in higher education policy! □

THE CHALLENGE OF DAY SCHOOL AFFORDABILITY: KEEPING OUR EYES ON THE PRIZE

I N RELIGIOUS JEWISH COMMUNITIES, THE AF-fordability of day schools is one of the most discussed social challenges. Supporting vibrant, successful, viable Jewish day schools is no less than supporting the Jewish future – our children are our future, and the values we demonstrate and pass on will determine what they will do with the torch when they are its bearers.

Rising school costs along with a continuing recession have combined to create a crisis in the survival of Jewish day schools. While estimates vary, it is clear that tuition costs have outstripped the ability of many families to pay. One report in 2010 estimated that most Jewish day schools charged about $15,000–$20,000 per student per year, with some charging more than $30,000 year. Among the schools charging the highest tuition is the Milken Community High School in Los Angeles, where the annual tuition is $32,155. In addition, there is an annual security fee of $700, and new students pay a one-time fee of $1,500. This does not count the expected parental contribution toward several fundraising efforts each year, or the flat fee for textbooks. To be sure the school offers a high-quality Jewish education, but how many families can afford to send their children there?

At the other end of the day school spectrum are the elementary and middle schools of Baltimore, which average $8,650 per student annually. While this sounds reasonable, it should be remembered that the average annual gross income of Baltimore families is far less than $50,000. Thus, an Orthodox family that sends three children to day school will spend $25,950 each year in tuition. After taxes and synagogue expenses, Orthodox Baltimore households are using all available funds for day school. The continuing Great Recession has exacerbated this crisis, and scholarship money is not often available. Many families are now at, or past, the point where they can afford to send their children to day school. As Zipora Schorr of Baltimore's Beth Tfiloh Dahan Community School noted: "Those for whom day schools are expendable will opt out unless we find a way to keep them there – this is the biggest crisis to our Jewish future."

In Baltimore, some Orthodox rabbis have begun interpreting *tzedakah* in such a way that half of all disbursements should go to local needs such as day school scholarships. At the same time, some observers have noted additional problems resulting from high tuition – parents working several jobs and thus not being available to spend time with their children; students discouraged from becoming community-serving professionals like teachers and social workers because these careers do not pay enough to support a Jewish family; and families that will fall from the position of contributing to society to being forced to ask for charity.

Fortunately, there may be a more promising future for Jewish day schools. Most proposed solutions fall out into one of the following ten options:

1. Increase philanthropic support to Jewish schools (or offer low-cost loans);
2. Increase state funding of secular subjects within day schools (or move toward the British model of state-funding);
3. Cut down school expenses without cutting quality (raise student-teacher ratio, move to smaller facilities, follow an administrative cost-sharing model, encourage regional benchmark standards, use green technology to cut energy costs, etc.);

4. Increase revenue (rent school space, hold community programs, charge for adult education, establish an alumni database and engage in alumni support drives, encourage current families to contribute to giving programs before graduation, etc.);
5. Restructure how much each family has to pay based upon income (for example, establish a percentage of family income as tuition);
6. Insist upon having only community Jewish schools (which include different Jewish study tracks for students of different backgrounds);
7. Connect Jewish schools nationwide to ensure collaboration and cost-sharing enables all local schools to grow;
8. Give family discounts when volunteers increase involvement and support of the school;
9. Increase enrollment to increase funding; and
10. Explore alternatives to day school (charter schools, public schools, supplemental education programs, etc.).

Families are struggling to meet costs in our recession, and this issue must be addressed more urgently. Furthermore, as Jews, we have major philanthropic responsibilities to address locally, nationally, and globally. A primary purpose of our day school system must be to train our children to fulfill these global moral responsibilities. If the day school system cripples our potential as givers, it has defeated its purpose. If day schools decrease in number and reach, the number of Jewish children who identify with Jewish values such as *tzedakah* and *tikkun olam* will also decrease. This in turn will lead to fewer contributions to the vulnerable and poor in our society, let alone to Jewish day schools. We need to prevent this cascade of problems. For one example of an initiative that is working to tackle this issue, see the Jewish Day School Affordability Knowledge Center, a joint project between the Partnership for Excellence in Jewish Education and the Orthodox Union.

The day school system is potentially the most powerful way of educating, empowering, and activating our Jewish youth base to grow as global Jewish leaders, and is therefore crucial to the future of the Jewish community. We must reprioritize our wealth to ensure that we leverage our personal and communal funds to address the most pressing moral issues of our time. If we do not repair our financially broken day school system, we risk becoming overwhelmed by its burden and becoming less relevant in the cosmic unfolding of human history. Now is the time to change the paradigm. □

THE LOST ART OF SMALL TALK

D URING AIRPLANE TRAVEL, NOT ONLY DO I fail in limiting my consumption of bags of airplane peanuts, I've also never quite mastered the art of how to successfully avoid long conversations with talkative strangers sitting next to me on the plane. Sometimes these conversations can be forced and awkward, but other times, I must admit, these conversations can be pleasant small talk and surprisingly insightful.

The art of small talk is a skill I started to really notice at the World Economic Forum in Davos, Switzerland. There were numerous formal, organized intellectual presentations at the Forum. Former President Bill Clinton challenged world leaders, CEOs, faith leaders, and others gathered at Davos to think about how to maximize the effectiveness of the Forum. I found one of his most eye-opening ideas was his suggestion that the discourse of the formal presentations must also overflow into the halls. The opportunity to work through the great moral and societal problems of our time when such opportunities present themselves – as at Davos, with numerous world leaders and figures in one place – needs to be maximized to its potential. And even at such high-powered events as the World Economic Forum, there is plenty of vitally helpful small talk to be had. It is not only the official and formal events, but also the casual work of the hallways, the small talk between the formal talks, that can a long distance in influencing policy.

In Davos, and also at the White House Chanukah party, I was fortunate to witness interactions between some of the greatest world leaders. I was amazed by the ability of President Obama, and many others, to connect so quickly with strangers through a certain style of small talk.

In these banquet halls, I was frequently reminded of the epic scene of the meeting of Yaakov and Pharaoh which is found in Genesis 47:7–10. With Yaakov – the great theologian – and Pharaoh – the great political leader of the time – one might wonder what these great world leaders of their time would discuss. Theology? World politics? The meaning of life? Fallout from the famine? Nope! Something much more mundane. Rather, *"Vayomer Paro el Yaakov, kama y'mei shnei chayecha?"* Pharaoh (in this great moment) asked Yaakov: "How old are you?" A question which seems much more fit for a chat between kids on a playground than between two figures of immense importance. Why begin such a charged conversation with such a small and insignificant question?

The Ketav V'Kabbalah (Rav Mecklenburg of nineteenth century Germany) suggests that there are two ways we must speak. First, there are times when we use language to communicate specific ideas, wishes, hopes, prayers, and teachings. Second, there are times that we use language simply to serve as the bridge that connects us to another; the substance and content of the conversation are secondary to the goal of connecting and relating.

Rav Mecklenburg refers to the nature of this dialogue between these two giants as "*devarim shel mah b'kach*"; this can loosely be translated as "small talk." He is satisfied with the value and significance of ordinary social discourse and regular human interaction as a valid and legitimate form of conversation for Yaakov and Pharaoh to share. We don't always have to look for great profundity and complexity in every conversation and every relationship. Yaakov and Pharaoh were simply making small talk, and that too is virtuous and valuable as a way to connect.

In general, Jewish law and values teach that we should limit our speech to points of moral and spiritual significance. Our significant relationships should not be based around conversations about the weather, the sports scores, or the celebrity gossip pages, but rather around deeper reflections, feelings, and insights. However, Rav Mecklenburg also teaches that some speech can, and should, prioritize connecting to the other over expressing the content of an idea.

We can see this phenomenon in prayer as well. Sometimes, the goal of praying is to convey the right words and specific messages. Other times, the goal is about the connection between a person and God, and the specific words used are of lesser importance.

The Mishnah, in *Pirke Avot* 6:6, tells us that there are forty-eight tools which can be used to acquire Torah. One of them is "*mi'ut sicha*," traditionally translated as "limiting idle conversation." If we limit our mundane conversations, the Rabbis teach, we will become closer to Torah. I learned an intriguing explanation about this phrase which suggests that the word *mi'ut* not be translated as telling us to limit, but rather that the only type of conversation we should engage in is *mi'ut sicha* or small talk; that this type of talk is healthy and generative. Connecting with others, having human interaction, is an important and integral part of achieving real growth and small talk can be an important method in achieving those goals.

Business people have long known that small talk is an opportunity for marketing. It is also known, making small talk effectively can make you popular, as people respond to those who give them attention. In addition, a series of scholarly studies in 2010 revealed that small talk can boost cognitive ability, especially executive functions. Thus, success can often depend on one's ability to convey simple messages. Nowhere is this more evident than in the case of two Presidents and their fates in the Presidential election of 1932.

Herbert Hoover was regarded as a hands-on businessman who, among other things had run the successful American food relief program during and after World War I, saving millions in Belgium, Russia, and elsewhere in Europe from starvation. This established his reputation as an efficient organizer and helped secure his election to the Presidency in 1928. However, on October 25, 1929, with the stock market already fluctuating wildly, President Hoover issued a statement asserting that the American economy was "on a sound and prosperous basis." After a few dry statements about construction and wages, he concluded with a reference to wheat bushel production, adding that this would "result in a very low carryover at the end of the harvest year." This message, with its uncaring tone and complete disconnect from what was causing a panic, did not resonate with the American people; four days later the stock market crashed, signaling the start of the Great Depression. Hoover's inability to deal with the crisis, or communicate an effective strategy to combat the Depression, led to a dramatic plunge in his popularity, as well as in the confidence of the American people in their government, their country, and themselves.

In contrast, President Franklin D. Roosevelt was a man of enormous personal charisma, who made those interacting with him feel like he truly cared for them and was concerned with their plight. For example, he possessed an amazing ability to remember the names of people he had met only once. When asked how, he claimed that he saw their names on their foreheads. However, a more likely explanation is that he developed a method of remembering people through nicknames; thus, one adviser was "Harry the Hat" Hopkins; even the infamous Soviet leader was "Uncle Joe" Stalin (though he was not called that to his face!). Roosevelt knew how to really engage and connect with people, on both large and small scales – an important criterion for a leader.

Immediately upon taking office, President Roosevelt had to deal with the collapse of the American banking system it, and restore a sense of security and hope to the banking system, as well in the hearts of so many Americans.

He seized upon the method of a direct radio appeal to the American people. His "Fireside Chats" featured a small talk format, in which the President referred to his radio audience as "you," and in which the talk revolved around basic explanations of problems. They were simple and casual, and made the audience – America – feel at ease. Most importantly, they were successful: after his "Chat" on the banking crisis on March 12, 1933, things began to turn around immediately. Americans quickly began making far more deposits instead of withdrawals from banks, and the American banking system was saved. President Roosevelt only made eight of these Fireside Chats during his first term, yet they had an enormous influence on the American public, and undoubtedly contributed much to his unprecedented four successful Presidential campaigns. The American people at large regarded President Roosevelt as a person who cared about them and their well-being; thus, was the social skill of making small talk used to help rescue a nation and its people in the midst of an unprecedented crisis.

Small talk is how we make others feel more comfortable connecting with us. We don't just approach others with big issues, but also value them enough to approach over smaller issues as well.

The Gemara tells us that nobody ever initiated a greeting to Rav Yohanan ben Zakai, since he was always the first to greet them. The Gemara concludes "*v'afilu nochri ba'shuk*," one should even greet an unknown non-Jew in the mall – an encounter of seemingly little consequence in that time. The ability to greet and engage others warmly is at the core of Jewish virtuous living. One need not have a great intellectual master plan for conversation when approaching someone to meet them or greet them. Rather, one can merely seek to offer a smile and a warm connection.

While our intellectual conversations about our grand ideals are crucial to our self-definition, the conversations we have in the hallways and streets can be just as, if not more, important in defining us as both individuals and as a community.

This is not only true locally, but globally as well. Any student of social change who has been watching the revolutions in the Middle East over the last few years in countries including Egypt, Libya, Syria, and Tunisia knows that so much of the great impact and social change emanates not from boardrooms or palaces, but rather from hallways and streets and factories, and even from social media, places where people of all walks of life come together. This power of small talk can bring about deep, transformative connections. We are in an era of heightened small talk that will produce ripple effects around the world, where hundreds of thousands of people can be mobilized to action almost immediately. Repressive governments can no longer rely on media censorship and the use of armed force to be sufficient to oppress their people. The proliferation of social media has greatly weakened their power to do so, as we have seen across the Middle East and elsewhere.

We can also reflect upon moments where we have opportunities for small talk, and thus opportunities to establish relationships, in our lives.

- *Kiddush* at *shul*: A sign of an inclusive community is not just if one is welcomed when they initially enter the building, but if they feel welcomed and cared for when the food comes out. Are elbows thrown? Is one offered a seat? Is this a place for meaningful small talk and connection, or merely a place of rapid consumption?
- With the homeless – whether or not one chooses to give money, food, or other *tzedakah* to those they find in the streets, just interacting with our fellow human brethren who find themselves on the streets can be holy opportunities for smiles and perhaps small talk. When we stop to talk with a homeless individual instead of just passing them by, we are validating their presence and inherent human dignity – we are showing them that we see them, and that we acknowledge that they are just as human as we are.
- In the workplace – so much of the crucial relationship building happens in passing between meetings, at places like the water coolers.
- For family, there are countless ways to use small talk. Ideology and meaning can be constructed at the elaborate Shabbat table – and while doing laundry or washing the dishes. The Rabbis even taught the importance of small talk between spouses before reuniting in intimate ways, offering a chance to reconnect more simply and softly.

Small talk can be fitting at many times in life. Personally, when I think back to my grandmother on her death bed, it was our final small talk rather than some profound statement that connected us even more deeply, even in those last moments of her life.

It is not only in the work of trying to change the world in Davos or Washington that requires change-makers and social activists to engage in small talk. It is also necessary in our intimate and everyday relationships, and in our sacred communal relationships, in what the Austrian-born Jewish philosopher Martin Buber calls "I / Thou" encounters, that offer deep spiritual connections.

May we all merit to make all of our words count: both our words of meaning, and our words of connection.   □

HOW DO WE RELATE TO MORALLY DIFFICULT TEXTS IN THE JEWISH TRADITION?

W E HAVE ALL BECOME FAMILIAR WITH THE tactics of bigots who distort our religious beliefs or make up horrible lies to advance their hatred. Fortunately, most people in our pluralistic society recognize and reject these tactics.

But how would we respond to a skeptic who points to the morally troubling verse, "When . . . the Lord your God delivers them to you and you defeat them, you must utterly doom them to destruction: grant them no terms and give them no quarter" (Deuteronomy 7:1–2)?

Or consider the many admonitions in the Torah to be kind to strangers, and to remember that we were once strangers in the land of Egypt. How do we reconcile this noble idea with these seemingly contradictory commands, "In the towns of the latter peoples, however, which the Lord your God gives you as a heritage, you shall not let a soul remain alive. No, you must proscribe them – the Hittites and the Amorites, the Canaanites and the Perizzites, the Hivites and the Jebusites – as the Lord your God has commanded you" (20:16–17), and "Samuel said to Saul: 'I am the one the Lord sent to anoint you king over His people Israel. Therefore, listen to the Lord's command! . . . Now go attack Amalek, and proscribe all that belongs to him. Spare no one, but kill alike men and women, infants and sucklings, oxen and sheep, camels and asses'" (I Samuel 15:1, 3)?

There are four primary philosophical approaches in relating to difficult texts like these:

First is the "Divine Command Morality" argument; i.e., because God is the source of and determines all morality, there is no contradiction between morality and God's commands. Only the Divine can understand the big moral picture, thus only God has moral reasoning and authority. The problem here is that humans must abandon some of the greatest God-given gifts: moral conscience, reason, and autonomy.

Second is the argument proposed by nineteenth century theologian/philosopher Søren Kierkegaard; i.e., if it appears that there is a contradiction between religion and morality, it is only because God has the power to suspend morality, and we must abandon our human conscience in heroic sacrifice to the Divine command, which supersedes all. This binding of Isaac-type mentality creates the religious personality. The problem here is that one must consciously act against their own moral intuition and that is spiritually and socially dangerous.

Third is the "heretical argument," that there is indeed a contradiction between morality and the religious command, and that we must choose morality as we understand it over religious duty. This individual may be moral but is generally not deemed religious.

Fourth is the "casuistic argument"; i.e., we need both the truths of human morality and of Divine command and that all contradictions can be resolved. Through moral reasoning, we can come to understand and embrace the Divine command. We are never compelled to obey anything immoral if we cultivate our intellectual and spiritual faculties to really understand that, to the well-organized mind, religion and morality can always be reconciled.

This last approach is most compelling, and demanding, for the modern religious person. In working every day to understand our texts, our world, and our hearts and souls, we can best achieve our Jewish mission. Rav Saadia Gaon, the tenth century Jewish philosopher, explains that if we find a contradiction between tradition and reason, then we have made a mistake and we must continue to learn the text over and over and analyze our reason over and over until they are consistent. The text is our starting place, read charitably, but we never neglect our crucial human faculty of moral reasoning.

Rav Kook said it well:

> It is forbidden for religious behavior to compromise a personal, natural, moral sensibility. If it does, our fear of heaven is no longer pure. An indication of its purity is that our nature and moral sense becomes more exalted as a consequence of religious inspiration. But if these opposites occur, then the moral character of the individual or group is dismissed by religious observance, and we have certainly been mistaken in our faith (*Orot HaKodesh* 4e).

We are following the path of Avraham who asked, "Shall the Judge of all the earth not act justly?" (Genesis 18:25), as we continue to challenge all dogmas to achieve the full truth. We should bear in mind that Avraham came from Ur in Mesopotamia, in modern-day Iraq. This region has for millennia been plagued by absolutist god-kings who waged brutal wars on one another. Even when codes of law were created, they often reinforced the extreme powers of the monarch. We should be grateful that we emerged from this land as a people of faith, law, and morality, while acknowledging that we did not always measure up to those ideals. We should remember that the best purpose for studying our sacred texts is not to puzzle over troublesome passages or justify the behavior of another era, but to become motivated to act, today, in the true spirit of *tikkun olam*.   □

☐ HEALTH, ANIMAL WELFARE, AND ETHICAL CONSUMPTION

ETHICAL KASHRUT: BRINGING ANIMAL TREATMENT, WORKERS' CONDITIONS, AND ENVIRONMENTAL ISSUES TO A KOSHER TABLE

THE FIRST ACT OF FOOD CONSUMPTION IN the Bible is also the Torah's first foray into ethics. God instructed Adam and Eve to eat from any tree but the Tree of Knowledge. The human inability to restrain desire led to the possibility of sin. The first human beings ate the forbidden fruit, and the need for ethical standards was born.

Since then, *Halacha* has functioned to make its adherents understand the spiritual potential that food can have in one's life. By legislating various practices, such as making *berachot* (blessings) before and after eating food, distinguishing between dairy and meat meals, separating dishes, and drinking wine and eating bread on holidays, Jewish law highlights the significance of food in life.

In the past ten years, a growing movement has emerged focusing not only on ritual, but also on ethical *kashrut*. This movement emphasizes not only the traditional rules, but also takes into account issues such as animal treatment, workers conditions, and environmental impact, taking its cue from a number of supporting biblical sources:

The Torah prohibits the mistreatment of workers (Leviticus 19:13; Deuteronomy 24:14), as all humans are created *b'tzelem Elokim* (in the image of God). Specific prohibitions include oppressing workers (*lo taashok*) and delaying their payment.

The treatment of animals is also deeply rooted in the Jewish tradition.

Tzaar baalei haim (the mistreatment of animals) is explicitly forbidden by the Torah, and Jewish liturgy is full of praise for God's demonstrated mercy to all creatures. Animals are even given the Sabbath as a day of rest (Exodus 23:12).

Environmental values are found in the many agricultural mitzvot in the Torah, including the Creation story, where God charges humans *l'ovdah ul'shomra* (to work and to guard the earth) (Genesis 2:15).

The Relationship between New Kashrut and Old Kashrut

How do these new "rules" of ethical kashrut relate to the traditional rituals, blessings, and separation of dishes? Many of those who observe *kashrut* believe that the values of ethical *kashrut* may have been the original intention for how religious food consumption was prescribed in the Torah. For others, these values are a positive expansion or evolution from the traditional rules. For still others, the contemporary values of ethical *kashrut* can replace the old, harder-to-understand rituals.

The Torah and other Jewish literature lend support for ethical *kashrut* initiatives. Ramban argues (Leviticus 19:2) that if people consume food that is technically kosher from a ritual perspective but do not embrace the ethics that come along with consumption then they are *naval b'reshut ha-Torah* (despicable with the permission of the Torah). They have broken no formal *kashrut* prohibitions, but their act is shameful, and they have not lived by the moral and ethical intentions of the Torah. Nahmanides is referring to eating in moderation but his value certainly lends to broad extension. Simply put: permissible consumption does not necessarily mean good consumption.

Organizations on the Ground in Israel and America

A number of Jewish groups are working to expand *kashrut* beyond the letter of the law.

Hazon, a Jewish non-profit inspired to create a healthier and more sustainable Jewish community, has spearheaded efforts to promote issues such as environmentalism, spiritual consumption, good animal treatment, and labor concerns. They also host conferences promoting thoughtful food consumption.

Hazon's community supported agriculture (CSA) groups, known as *Tuv Haaretz*, are receiving increased orders from Jewish community members who are interested in the eco-friendly consumption practices of local produce.

Jewish environmental groups such as Canfei Nesharim and COEJL, have argued for eco-kashrut, a framing of the values of *kashrut* around the sustainability of our earth and body.

Another constituency is primarily concerned with the mistreatment of animals. Due to the poor conditions in many factories that mass-produce meat, some consumers support only the strictest vegan products. Others are content with vegetarianism.

A growing movement, however, wishes to continue to consume meat, but only if the animals are treated properly. Small procurers of meat, such as Kol Foods, who are committed to free-range animal living while maintaining their status of glatt kosher (strictest slaughtering standards), are slowly emerging as a force in the contemporary market.

A fast-growing grassroots movement has emerged to secure the rights of the workers that produce and prepare kosher food. In 2004, B'Maagalei Tzedek, an Israeli non-governmental organization, launched the *Tav Chevrati* (the Social Seal) to ensure that workers in restaurants are treated according to the minimum standard required by Israeli law. They have certified more than 350 restaurants in Israel with their seal. About 250 of those restaurants are certified as kosher.

In the United States, a similar project was spearheaded by Uri L'Tzedek, which launched the *Tav HaYosher* (the Ethical Seal) in the spring of 2009. The seal aims to secure workers' rights to fair pay, fair time, and safe working conditions in kosher restaurants. A Conservative Movement initiative, Magen Tzedek, is planning to certify kosher factories which have quality labor practices. Both organizations have argued that the laws of *kashrut* are not to be confused with Jewish ethics but that they can be intertwined in a significant way with our perception of our consumer responsibilities. In short, "ethical" does not redefine "*kashrut*." Rather, it is complementary and distinct.

Self-development or Just Society?

To be sure, a large portion of the Jewish community is not asking these ethical questions. Rather their primary concerns when it comes to food purchases relate to health and finances. But a growing number of Jews, of all denominations and lifestyles, are gaining inspiration from the notion that *kashrut* can help create a society committed to justice.

Some ask why food, among a host of other options, should be at the center of this emerging discourse around ethics. Why not focus on sneakers made in sweatshops or the automotive industry? Proponents of ethical *kashrut* have argued that food must come first for a few reasons:

1. The Jewish community has already demonstrated immense success using money and power to build the kosher certification system. This infrastructure and model can just as easily be used for ethical certification and awareness.
2. As Jews, we have ownership and responsibility over the *kashrut* industry.
3. The laws of *kashrut* have a unique charge to pursue holiness.

Still, some authorities and communities have explicitly rejected ethical *kashrut*. For example, Rabbi Avi Shafran, spokesperson for Agudath Israel, believes that while the ethical treatment of animals and workers may be ideal, the lack thereof has absolutely no consequences for *kashrut*. Speaking metaphorically in response to this issue, Rabbi Shafran has said: "A great poet might opt to not shower, but that bad habit does not necessarily affect the quality of his writing."

I personally believe that Jewish tradition demands more.

Rabbi Yisrael Salantar, the founder of the Mussar movement, once said: "Another person's physical concerns are my spiritual concerns." The physical conditions of the workers that produce meat are at the center of Jewish spiritual and law. The choices of Jewish consumers regarding the treatment of workers, animals, and the earth, had and will continue to have a strong foothold in shaping our understanding of *kashrut* and holiness.

Meant to reflect Jewish values, Kosher food is often unethical

On the morning of May 12, 2008, dozens of federal agents descended on the small town of Postville, Iowa for the largest workplace immigration raid in American history. At the Agriprocessors kosher meatpacking plant, the main employer in Postville, agents arrested nearly 400 undocumented workers, and promptly deported 300 arrestees on false identity charges.

, Besides the implications for the immigration debate (see essay below, "Strangers, Immigrants, and the Eglah Arufah"), the Agriprocessors raid has also impacted America's Orthodox Jewish communities, prompting them to reconsider the human costs of their kosher food products.

Agriprocessors held a near-monopoly in the kosher meat industry, and revelations of worker maltreatment at the plant created shockwaves across the Jewish community. A *shohet*, or kosher meat slaughterer, undergoes years of training and plays a vital community role. Kosher slaughterhouses are assumed to reflect core Jewish values such as honesty and respect for others. Instead, the abuses at Agriprocessors revealed that today, kosher is often not ethical.

As Orthodox Jewish social justice leaders, we at the group Uri L'Tzedek sought to create a system for protecting those with the least among us. Exactly one year after the startling exposure at Agriprocessors, Uri L'Tzedek launched theTav HaYosher, an ethical seal for kosher restaurants. To receive the Tav seal, kosher restaurants and caterers must meet guidelines for fair pay and worker safety based on city, state, and federal law. Compliance officers conduct periodic inspections, and employees can report violations on an anonymous tip line.

This program relies on the carrot rather than the stick. Restaurant owners who have been given the Tav have gained significant business from free advertising, and many people will only buy kosher food with this ethical certification. As a result, the Tav seal is an incentive for restaurant owners to voluntarily uphold the rights of workers.

In addition, the program operates without any government intervention. Synagogues, schools, and other Jewish nonprofits are mobilizing to ensure the rights of kosher restaurant workers, creating even greater incentive for kosher restaurants to receive certification. In 2012, the 100th Tav was awarded to a kosher restaurant in America.

This program does not check workers' immigration status, and in no way reduces the need for governmental policies that curb workplace abuse. Nonetheless, as comprehensive immigration reform continues to stall, undocumented immigrants remain highly vulnerable to the type of abuse once practiced at Agriprocessors. In an age of recession and budget cuts, the Tav HaYosher is one model for activists seeking to ensure fair treatment for all workers, regardless of their documentation status. □

AN OBESITY PROBLEM IN
THE ORTHODOX COMMUNITY?

IT IS BEAUTIFUL HOW MUCH EMPHASIS THERE IS on Shabbat and holiday celebration in American Orthodoxy. However, the celebration of the values of health and exercise are sorely lacking in the community. Parents often do not stress health and exercise for their children, and day schools fall short on creating rigorous health programs. Happily, religious celebration need not compromise our commitment to health.

Obesity is a major problem in the United States, and is a major risk factor for cardiovascular disease, hypertension, and type 2 diabetes. According to the Centers for Disease Control and Prevention, nearly 36 percent of American adults are obese, and the problem is getting worse. As of 2010, every state had at least a 20 percent obesity rate, and twelve had a rate of 30 percent or higher. Even more alarming is that 17 percent of children ages 2–19 are obese, and physicians are now seeing type 2 diabetes (a disease with a normal onset age of 40) in this population. Although today about 7 percent of our population has diabetes (almost all with type 2), the CDC predicts that one in three children born in 2000 will develop diabetes during his or her lifetime – in large part due to obesity.

Although U.S. statistics do not record data based on religion, Israeli data confirm the high risk of obesity in the Orthodox community. The Israel Health Ministry has reported that the ultra-Orthodox (*haredi*) are seven times more likely to be obese than the rest of Israelis. The Ministry noted, "The *haredi* lifestyle focuses on the dinner table . . . At the same time, they don't engage in any physical exercise." Other factors included a lack of practical health education in *haredi* schools and the poverty of many within this community, which leads to consumption of cheaper, simple carbohydrate-based foods (such as potatoes, pasta, rice, and sugar) combined with high-fat meat, rather than more expensive complex carbohydrates and protein-rich foods.

There are many excuses people use to deny the seriousness of this problem, such as the claim that professional athletes are often "obese," using current B M I charts. However, there are relatively few professional athletes among us, so in the overwhelming majority of cases, obesity is a critical risk factor for many diseases. Others do not think they are obese. Researchers at the University of Illinois found that 80 percent of individuals in the normal weight range correctly reported their weight as normal. However, an alarming 58 percent of overweight individuals incorrectly categorized themselves as of a normal weight. In the overweight category, only 10 percent accurately described their body size.

Judaism addresses this issue – the sages even joke about the correlation between religiosity and health. Reish Lakish was in great shape until he became pious and lost his athletic ability, missing his typical leap over the river. Further, the great sage Hillel explains that we must take care of our bodies, since we are created in the image of God (Leviticus Rabbah 34:3). Maimonides went to great lengths to teach the value of health and the importance of taking proper care of our bodies (*Hilchot Deot*).

In addition to sustaining our lives, we must prepare our bodies to serve. Rav Kook suggests (*Orot HaTehiya* 33) that exercise is actually a mitzvah:

> We need a healthy body. We have dealt much in soulfulness; we forgot the holiness of the body. We neglected physical health and strength; we forgot that we have holy flesh no less than holy spirit . . . Our return (*teshuva*) will succeed only if it will be – with all its splendid spirituality – also a physical return, which produces healthy blood, healthy flesh, mighty, solid bodies, a fiery spirit radiating over powerful muscles. . . . The exercise the Jewish youths in the Land of Israel engage in to strengthen their bodies, in order to be powerful children of the nation, enhances the spiritual prowess of the exalted righteous, who engage in mystical unifications of divine names, to increase the accentuation of divine light in the world. And neither revelation of light can stand without the other.

In addition to the aforementioned neglect of exercise and over-consumption of meat and sugars, we should also be more concerned about the Jewish prohibition of *achilah gasah* (over-eating). One Orthodox group, Soveya, has started promoting weight loss through healthier lifestyles. By learning moderation, improving our diets, and taking care of our bodies, we not only fulfill the mitzvah of preserving our lives and caring for our loaned bodies created in the "image of God," we also teach our children the importance of living a balanced, holy lifestyle. □

A SMOKE-FREE WORLD:
A JEWISH BAN ON TOBACCO

W E HAVE BEEN VERY AWARE OF THE ADDIC-
tive nature of nicotine and the serious
health risks of lung cancer (which kills
more Americans than any other cancer), cardiovascular disease, respiratory
illness, and chronic obstructive pulmonary disease (eventually leading to
emphysema). About 20 percent of Americans still smoke, around 450,000
Americans die prematurely every year from smoking, and researchers have
shown that a smoker loses an average of fourteen years of life. Even though
we have over 1,200 Americans dying every day from smoking, for every
death, two more people under the age of twenty-six takes up smoking. One
in five American teens smoke and 80 percent of them will remain addicted
as adults. Cigarettes are also the most frequent cause of fires that lead to
death in homes. And these numbers do not even account for the harm of
second-hand smoke.

In the early seventeenth century, King James I, one of the earliest critics
of tobacco, levied a tax on imported tobacco. Unfortunately, later monarchs
did not continue this policy, and tobacco flourished. History has shown
that cigarettes can never be taxed too much. It has been shown that for
every 10 percent increase in the price of cigarettes, youth smoking has been
reduced by about 7 percent and overall cigarette consumption by about 4
percent. When the Israeli government imposed tax hikes on smoking, the
ultra-Orthodox yeshiva world caused an uproar by opposing the increase,
even though their rabbinic leaders have come out against smoking.

There is an increasing consensus that Jewish law prohibits smoking. This
follows from a Torah commandment to live a healthy life (Deuteronomy
4:15). Even before it was clear that smoking posed great health risks, Rabbi
Moshe Feinstein said that smoking was a prohibition based on Numbers
15:39: "You shall not stray after your heart and after your eyes" (*Iggerot
Moshe, Hoshen Mishpat* 2:76, *Yoreh Deah* 3:35); and that second-hand smoke
is a form of damage upon another (*Hoshen Mishpat* 2:18). Rabbi Aaron
Kotler also made clear in a letter that it is a Torah prohibition to smoke.

In 2006, the centrist Orthodox Jewish law committee of the RCA ruled that smoking tobacco is prohibited by Jewish law. Other Modern Orthodox authorities, including Rabbis Ahron Soloveichik, Aharon Lichtenstein, and Gedalia Dov Schwartz have prohibited smoking. Countless other rabbis have made clear that smoking is prohibited by Jewish law.

In addition, Jewish law does not allow for an alleged right to smoke or to do harm to one's body. Some have suggested that the Jewish concept of "God protects the fools" (Psalms 116:6) should apply to permit smoking. Rabbi Efraim Greenblatt challenges this point: "Who would lie down in the middle of the street and claim 'Hashem protects the fools?!'" He and Rav Chaim David HaLevi suggest that smoking can be considered in the prohibited category of suicide (*Teshuvot Aseh Lecha Rav* 3:18). The *Shulhan Aruch* goes further, arguing that one does not have the right to do as he pleases with his own body if it causes harm (CM 427:10). The Rabbis teach that our bodies are ultimately on loan from our Creator. The Chofetz Chaim writes that if one's doctor tells him that he must stop smoking, he must obey: "How may a slave choose to do as he pleases, if he belongs to his Master?"

The prohibition on smoking does not only apply to individuals, but also to society. Rambam taught that "Concerning any obstruction that is life-threatening, there is a positive commandment to remove it and protect against it and to be exceedingly careful concerning it" (*Hilchot Rotzeiah* 11:4-5). Even though one is obligated to obey one's parents, Rabbi Chaim David HaLevi rules that one is not permitted to provide a cigarette for a parent who requests it (*Teshuvot Aseh Lecha Rav* 6:58, 7:65). Due to the injunction to "not put a stumbling block before the blind" (Leviticus 19:14), one must do everything possible to ensure that others are prevented from accessing the lethal object of a cigarette. Rabbi HaLevi argues that it is a *hillul Hashem* to smoke, since the enlightened world knows how harmful it is, and Jews should not be seen doing foolish things (*Teshuvot Aseh Lecha Rav* 3:18). By this reasoning, it is also a *Kiddush Hashem* (sanctification of God's Name) to be on the front lines of banning cigarettes from society.

Fortunately, more people have realized how harmful smoking is. A poll found that 45 percent of Americans support making cigarettes illegal (and more than 50 percent of Americans between the ages of 18–29). Nevertheless, fully outlawing cigarettes would only lead to the creation of black markets and organized criminal activity. Rather, we must continue to raise the taxes on cigarettes, ban more advertising, and restrict more locations where smoking is permitted. These efforts should especially be directed toward adolescents. It has been estimated that half of the 6,500 new smokers who took up smoking every day in 2010 were younger than 18.

Smokers today should be viewed as "*holim*" (sick individuals) who we must heal. One cannot claim that "freedom and liberty" allows them to increase their burden on the health care system or bring harm to family members, co-workers, and strangers. Creating a more universal health care system is a social justice issue, but so is creating a society that places collective demands on preventive health practices. According to research supported by the National Cancer Institute, smoking reduction and cessation programs saved nearly 800,000 Americans from death by lung cancer from 1975 to 2000. The Centers for Disease Control and Prevention launched a $54 million dollar "scare campaign" based upon new scientific studies showing that the "scarier the message" the more likely to change behavior. We should be scaring people – it's a mitzvah! The tobacco companies invest $10 billion a year in marketing and advertising so we're going to have to fight stronger. We need to redouble our efforts to improve and expand smoking reduction and cessation programs, and to tax and even ban smoking. It is not only a social justice imperative, it is a Torah imperative.   □

THE PROBLEM OF FRUM HEDONISM

I S THERE ANYTHING THAT WE WILL NOT PUT A *hecsher* on? Has pleasure become the guiding religious principle? Many pockets of the American Orthodox community have become so consumed with Jewish law that values and limits on pleasure have been dismissed.

At first glance, the data offers an ambiguous message. For example, a 2008 article estimated that Orthodox Jewish families spent 25–35 percent of their income on activities associated with being Jewish. The Orthodox also had less income than families than other Jews, as a 2005 report from United Jewish Communities noted.

These data appear to reflect continuing trends. Nevertheless, they may not explain what is happening today. What does Orthodox spending on

Jewish experiences mean? Does having an income less than other Jewish families necessarily mean that Orthodox families have not been lured into an American consumerist pattern? Rav Aaron Lichtenstein, in an essay titled "Glatt Kosher Hedonism," talks about the problem of the American Orthodox culture today:

> I mention this point particularly to an American audience. In recent years, one observes on the American scene a terribly disturbing phenomenon: the spread of hedonistic values, but with a kind of glatt-kosher packaging. There was a time when the problem of hedonism for religious Jews didn't often arise, because even if you wanted to have the time of your life, there wasn't very much that you could do. The country clubs were all barred to Jews, there weren't many kosher restaurants, there were no kosher nightclubs, etc. In the last decade or two, a whole culture has developed geared towards frum Jews, where the message is enjoy, enjoy, enjoy, and everything has a hekhsher (kosher certification) and a super-hekhsher. The message is that whatever the gentiles have, we have too. They have trips to the Virgin Islands, we have trips to the Virgin Islands. Consequently, there has been a certain debasement of values, in which people have a concern for the minutiae of Halakha (which, of course, one should be concerned about), but with a complete lack of awareness of the extent to which the underlying message is so totally non-halakhic and anti-halakhic (*By His Light*).

The goal of religious life is to choose the most noble of life paths and to strive to fulfill our highest values during our limited time on this earth. Judaism is certainly not an ascetic religion, but the danger of inappropriate or excessive pleasures has constantly been reinforced. Rabbeinu Bahya Ibn Pakuda, the eleventh century Jewish Spanish philosopher, addressed how pleasure, when over-embraced, can lead to a person's destruction:

> The instinct attracts them to an indulgent lifestyle and a pursuit of wealth, enamoring them of this world's luxury and prominence, until finally they sink in the depths of the sea, forced to face the crush of its waves. The (material) world rules them, stopping up their ears and closing their eyes. There is not one among them who occupies himself with anything but his own pleasure – wherever he can attain it and the opportunity presents itself. [Pleasure] becomes his law and

religion, driving him away from God. As it says, "Your own wickedness will punish you, your own sins will rebuke you. . . ." (Jeremiah
2:19), (*Hovot HaLevavot* 9:2).

While the Jewish legal system includes legal rules and precedent, the
guiding forces in the halachic process are the meta-halachic values. The
Jewish tradition has purpose, meaning, and ethics, and thus the application of the holy law ensures that the intentional values are maintained.
Overemphasizing the strict adherence to law (*ikar ha-din*) at the expense
of going beyond the law (*lifnim m'shurat ha-din*) is oversimplifying religion
and missing the point. Ramban teaches that one can be "*naval b'reshut
ha-Torah*" (a scoundrel with the permission of the Torah) if they only follow
the letter of the law. There is, of course, not one ethic but many that guide
our religious lives. Rabbi Dr. Walter Wurzberger explains the importance
of embracing a pluralism of Jewish ethics that . . .

> . . . manifests itself in the readiness to operate with a number of inde-
> pendent ethical norms and principles such as concern for love, justice,
> truth, and peace. Since they frequently give rise to conflicting obliga-
> tions, it becomes necessary to rely upon intuitive judgments to resolve
> the conflict. There is, however, another dimension to the pluralism of
> Jewish ethics: it is multi-tiered and comprises many strands. It con-
> tains not only objective components such as duties and obligations,
> but also numerous values and ideals possessing only subjective valid-
> ity. Moreover, the pluralistic thrust of Jewish ethics makes it possible
> to recognize the legitimacy of many alternate ethical values and ideals
> (*Ethics of Responsibility*, 5).

It is time to revitalize a values discourse in the American Orthodox community. How do we salvage the community by enhancing our collective
discourse and priorities toward our *raison-d'être*? This is not only the work
of rabbis speaking from the pulpit and educators speaking from the classroom. It is the responsibility of every parent to properly model for their
children how they use their free time and resources, and the duty of every
community member to reinforce during conversation.   □

THE RELIGIOUS VALUE OF REST AND LEISURE

W E ARE IMMERSED IN RESPONSIBILITIES and commitments to work, family, community, society, and the world. I do believe that a primary purpose for human existence is to toil, work, and serve. The value of work is expressed throughout Jewish sources: "Great is work because even Adam did not taste food until he had performed work" (*Avot d'Rebbe Natan*, Chapter 11). But we might ask: is there a religious value to rest and leisure?

Leisure was once a high priority in America. Those who grew up in the period after 1945 experienced a world of increasing leisure time, usually with a husband making the income and a stay-at-home-mom taking care of the home and children. This trend peaked in 1969, when the U.S. Labor Department's American Time Use Survey recorded the most leisure time. Since then, there has been a marked trend toward less leisure time, as the Harris Poll Table indicates:

Year Average Weekly Leisure Time (Hours)

1973 = 26
2007 = 20
2008 = 16

By 2000, ABC News noted that "Not only are Americans working longer hours than at any time since statistics have been kept, but now they are also working longer than anyone else in the industrialized world." Since then, some studies have contended that Americans have more leisure time than ever, or work less than people in industrializing countries. However, these studies often use faulty methodology, such as assuming that today it takes less time to do housework, errands, and other tasks, so therefore there is more leisure time. This ignores the additional tasks that have been added to modern housework as a result of living in larger homes with more devices and furniture, a longer commute, and an obligation to check text messages and emails from work twenty-four hours a day, seven days a week, even on vacation. Indeed, many Americans do not even take their full amount of vacation days (already much fewer than for European workers) annually for fear that they might lose the "competitive edge."

Regardless of the causes of this trend, there is a consensus that working long hours of overtime is deleterious to one's health. Studies based on data from the Centers for Disease Control and Prevention, the American Psychological Association, and peer-reviewed journals reveal that workers with the most overtime had:

- an increased risk for injury, illness, and mortality, along with poorer perceived general health
- higher levels of anxiety, depression, and stress
- greater interference with their responsibility to family and home

Conversely, companies that try to balance work and life reap rewards; their employees demonstrate greater innovation, creativity, and productivity, and make fewer mistakes. In short, physical and psychological health is enhanced by leisure time.

Thus, one might suggest that rest is not only for Shabbat (naturally its highest actualization) but is also an ongoing necessity of great religious value. The great eighteenth century Rabbi Baruch Epstein argued this point:

> And now let us consider, and we can say that for a young man working on Talmudic analysis for five or six hours straight can certainly affect his health . . . and I therefore came upon you at daybreak and told you to go have some tea, and my focus was not the tea but rather the fact that you would have a break . . . And this, too, I believe, that when one rests in order to reach a certain goal, then that rest is as valuable as the goal itself . . . for the goal of the rest is to add strength and power to the actual pursuing of the goal, whether it be learning or good deeds. And this is the very reason why the rabbis have said that that which leads to a mitzvah is as important as the mitzvah itself, for the mitzvah cannot come about without it, and so we consider the mitzvah and that which leads up to it as if it is all one long mitzvah (*Makor Baruch*, part 4).

Rav Epstein taught that rest was not only necessary to prepare to properly fulfill important religious duties (*hechsher mitzvah*), but that it is a mitzvah itself. Some in education today have actually embraced the value of rest and leisure through curricula based on "leisure education." Professor John Dattilo explains:

> Leisure education provides individuals the opportunity to enhance the quality of their lives in leisure; understand opportunities, potentials, and challenges in leisure; understand the impact of leisure on the quality of their lives; and gain knowledge, skills, and appreciation enabling broad leisure skills (*Inclusive Leisure Services*, 211).

From a Jewish perspective, we tend to value mindful rest more than mindless rest. Taking a break does not mean the primary value is to turn off one's own core unique human faculties but the opposite. Mindful rest, where we engage our mind, heart, and soul in different and meaningful ways from the norm, is not only more effective to recharge, it also ensures that our rest helps promote self-actualization. We must never sanction laziness but rather work to elevate all aspects of human experience including our time of leisure.

Maimonides teaches the importance of engaging pleasures that do not just feel good but strengthen us toward our core goals.

> For example: one should try to achieve through his eating, drinking, intercourse, sleeping, waking, movements, and rests – the goal of his body's health, and the goal of having a healthy body should be that one's soul finds its tools whole and ready to engage in wisdom, and to acquire good characteristics and advance in learning and understanding, until the above mentioned final goal is reached. And in the same vein one should not be considering only how pleasurable those actions are – which might cause him to choose only that food and drink which tastes good, and so too with the other physical aspects – but rather one should choose that which will be most helpful and effective, whether pleasurable or not. Or, alternatively, one should always look for that which will give him pleasure according to medicine; for example, if one's appetite is weakened he might need to awaken it with the help of good and spicy foods, or if one's mood is darkened he might need to lighten it through hearing songs or going for walks in the gardens or museums, and sitting amongst beautiful statues, and the like (*Pirke Avot*, Chapter 5 Introduction).

The Torah's promise of Shabbat is a subversive revolution reminding us that as important as work is in our lives, holy rest is in a sense the highest aim. Rest does not merely mean fun, but elevated leisure. Our character can best be assessed by how we choose to use our free time. Does it elevate ourselves and those around us? Does it give us more energy, ideas, and positivity? Do we leave more passionate and committed to our core life goals? Does it broaden our sense of the possible? Does it bring us closer to our loved ones?

The Mirrer Mashgiach (Rav Levovitz) taught that Noah's name comes from *menuhah* (rest), since he was a person concerned with the comfort of the people of his generation. Embracing *menuhah* for ourselves and enabling it for others is an act of emulating the Divine since God created rest and personally enacted it (Genesis 2:2). What is the nature of this rest? The Shabbat *Minchah* prayer describes the Jewish notion of rest in the following way: "A rest of love and magnanimity, a rest of truth and faith, a rest of peace and serenity and tranquility and security, a perfect rest in which You find favor." Rest is about achieving the deepest of virtues when we are relaxed and focused enough to internalize their truths.

We are created to work, to change the world for good. But we must not dismiss the religious and ethical value of rest and leisure for through its responsible actualization, we can truly learn to live fully in emulation of our Creator. □

BUBER, GANDHI, AND RABBAN GAMLIEL: HUMAN DIGNITY OVER ABSOLUTE OWNERSHIP

EVERY YEAR, AROUND NOVEMBER, I LOOK FORward to the holiday season here in America: spending Thanksgiving with my family, the familiar sounds of ubiquitous holiday tunes on the radio, the crispness in the air after the fresh snow. As I reflect on the news, social trends, and the thought of admired leaders in justice and Judaism, the spirit and reality of consumerism gives me pause. Perhaps this feeling of ownership brought out by the holiday season is not the ideal we, as religious people and thinkers, should strive for.

Austrian-born Martin Buber believed in and promoted the idea and reality of Jewish sovereignty in the Land of Israel, although his brand of political Zionism was distinct from most. He opposed the arming of Jewish settlers in Palestine even after they had been attacked, and opposed the creation of a Jewish majority after the Arab boycott. Mohandas Gandhi, on the other hand, was keenly aware of the violence of European colonialism and the resultant poverty afflicting Asia and Africa. He employed a religion-based strategy, Satyagraha ("soul force" or "truth force"), in India as the means to challenge the racist colonial powers and their belief that Western civilization was superior to anything else. Gandhi's followers followed nonviolent civil disobedience, in spite of beatings and shootings, as a way to force the British (and the outside world) to confront the immorality of their colonial rule, and eventually bring independence to India. Buber and Gandhi, born on different continents and representing different religious traditions, each had strong religious conviction that mandated a moral emphasis on political positions; each rejected violence to achieve political goals; and each strove (unsuccessfully) for a bi-national state that would have included their Muslim populations.

Buber and Gandhi differed, importantly, on the question of land ownership rights and how to approach them. In the late 1930s, Gandhi opposed the imposition of a Jewish state in Palestine. While his rationale was not fully stated, it appears that he was concerned that the British would use this issue in order to reestablish their colonial power in the region. He believed that anti-Semitism was a stain on European civilization, and wondered why all Western nations did not welcome Jewish refugees. True to his principles, he would have advocated a nonviolent civil disobedience campaign in Nazi Germany. To Buber, however, the situation went beyond the colonial machinations or racial prejudice of Europe and America – it reflected the threat of imminent annihilation.

In a powerful letter dated February 24, 1939, Buber respectfully, but fiercely, critiqued Gandhi for his deep misunderstanding and opposing of the Jewish struggle for survival, security, and peace: "Jews are being persecuted, robbed, maltreated, tortured, murdered. And you, Mahatma Gandhi, say that their position in the country where they suffer all this is an exact parallel to the position of Indians in South Africa at the time you inaugurated your famous 'Force of Truth' or 'Strength of the Soul' (Satyagraha) campaign." In this letter, explaining why Gandhi misunderstood the Jewish yearning for national sovereignty, Buber made a broader ideological point: "It seems to me that God does not give any one portion of the earth away so that its owner may say, as God does in the Holy Scriptures: 'Mine is the land.' Even to the conqueror who has settled on it, the conquered land is, in my opinion, only loaned – and God waits to see what he will make of it." Buber challenged Gandhi's claim that the land should merely be reserved for the surrounding Arabs, excluding a Jewish presence, and explains that even though the Jews have a right to live on the land, no human has an absolute claim to land ownership. We are all merely temporary residents.

This point – that while we have clear property and land rights, we must at the same time value human dignity and ethics over the pleasures of absolute physical ownership, is expressed time and time again in Jewish thought. One's body is merely a temporary attachment that one must be prepared to separate from, as we see from Rabban Gamliel's actions in this truly humbling Talmudic passage: "It used to be that funeral expenses were harder for the relatives of the deceased than the death itself. This was to the extent that the relatives of the dead would abandon the body and run away from it. Until Rabban Gamliel treated himself disrespectfully, being buried in cotton garments. The people followed him, adopting the practice of being buried in cotton garments" (*Moed Katan* 27b).

Jewish law provides very clear principles for property law, defending one's rights to ownership and rights of consumption. However, a right does not equal a good. We do not spend whatever we wish merely because we can and we do not make eternal claims to ownership. In death, we are taught to remember that we leave our bodies and the garments around them behind. So too, while Israel may be our sacred promised land of dwelling, we do not make eternal claims to absolute ownership. The Yovel (jubilee) year shows that the land is not owned by the Jewish people, but by God. God owns the land and our bodies, and it is blasphemous to claim otherwise.

One of the primary aspirations of religious life is to strive to learn to prioritize our spiritual goals over our physical goals. We have seen how destructive to society it is to fixate on ownership without understanding that we do not have an eternal hold on things. When holiday season comes in, these lessons are important to remember and internalize.　□

PUTTING ETHICS INTO OUR CELEBRATIONS: "JUST SIMCHAS"

J EWISH CELEBRATIONS ARE NOT MERELY ABOUT throwing a party, but transformational events that express our core values. For this reason, Uri L'Tzedek, the Orthodox Social Justice Movement, has launched Just Simchas – to educate, inspire, and empower others to include more social justice into their lifecycle celebrations. Whether one is celebrating the birth of a child, a wedding, or a bar or bat mitzvah, one can now learn how to add more meaning and impact with a "Just Simcha."

When making decisions about the caterer, the food, the venue, the gifts, the invitations, and the apparel among many other decisions, one should inquire about social justice enhancements. One's celebration should attempt to honor the dignity of workers, the sentience of animals, the impact on the environment, the problem of slave labor, and the power of giving.

Just Simchas offers a welcome response to the astounding consumerism that dominates American culture in the holiday season (the months of November and December), almost exclusively for holiday gifts. Consumerism has exploded in the U.S. at all times in the year and in all communities but most especially during holidays.

In contemporary society, property rights and consumerism have been perverted to the status of a cult. The dangerous spirit of Ayn Rand capitalism has taken hold, the political culture has become more elite, and the clamoring for gun ownership and gun rights to protect property has become a religion for some. During the 1980s, credit rules were eased, and credit cards flooded America, leading to a frenzy of consumer spending at shopping malls. (The coining of the term "shopaholic" in 1983 attests to this trend.) Surveys show that, apart from home, work, and school, Americans spent more time in shopping malls than anywhere else. Credit card debt peaked at $976 billion just before the Great Recession in 2008. In April 2012, it stood at $931 billion, nearly $8,000 per household. The period before the December holidays has become particularly associated with rampant consumerism.

Wal-mart, with its emphasis on low prices, has had several notorious episodes illustrating what happens when people value the accumulation of consumer goods over any other value system. In 2008, a crowd gathered outside the Walmart in Valley Stream, New York, long before the 5 AM opening on Black Friday, and police were called for crowd control. Nevertheless, at 4:55 AM the crowd pushed its way in, trampling one worker to death and sending four other people to the hospital with injuries. Even when customers were told about the death and informed of the need to clear the store, many "kept shopping," as one witness said, and were upset only because they had waited on line so long and had not finished shopping. In 2011, the store hours included Thanksgiving evening. In southern California, a woman pepper sprayed about twenty people as videogames were being put out for purchase. A detective stated: "Once the wrapping came off the pallets, there was total pandemonium." A customer noted that people began pulling the plastic off the pallets themselves, and then people began "screaming, pulling and pushing each other, and then the whole area filled up with pepper spray." The next day, in Little Rock, Arkansas, video footage attests that people fought each other over $2 waffle makers.

Tirdad Derakhshani, a reporter who has lived in Iran, Great Britain, and the United States, compared this behavior to the crowd frenzy that has resulted in deaths at European rock concerts and soccer matches, or at the annual hajj to Mecca: "Consumerism, no less than any cult or religion, has the power to level individual difference and independence and render citizens into a homogenous mass. Advertising companies . . . conspire to render the consumer object . . . into a fetish imbued with magical, if not downright divine, powers." Indeed, Black Friday and other specific sale days constitute a ritual of shopping, with set holidays. Derakhshani saw a new principle, that consumerism equals pleasure, superseding the teachings of religion and philosophy. However, since consumerism is its own value, the shopper is never satisfied: "The pursuit of this sort of happiness creates a vicious circle of growing anxiety and dissatisfaction." Spiritual values must offer an antidote to this modern trend.

The amount of money spent, and pressure put on consumers to spend, is enormous. These were the predictions for the 2012 holiday season:

- Americans will spend about $586 billion, an increase of 4 percent since the previous year.
- In 2011, holiday sales represented 19.5 percent of total sales, and in some retail areas it ranged as high as 40 percent of total annual sales.

- On the positive side, it is predicted that retailers will hire about 600,000 workers for the season.
- On the negative side, many retail workers are subject to extreme pressure to work long hours during the holiday season. Despite the long hours, about 1.5 million retail workers remain at or are slightly above the poverty level.
- The average American is expected to spend $854 for gifts, an increase of 32 percent over the previous year. Many Americans will go into debt as a result.

As these statistics display, consumerism can overtake the original meaning of holidays that used to represent a cessation of work and a chance for families to gather together. Today, many workers must leave their family and face verbal and even physical harm from customers and management. Many of these problems persist throughout the year, and they cross religious lines, including in our own community. However, we have a chance to reverse this trend. We can purchase items, but why not purchase Fair Trade *gelt* or greeting cards that support social justice causes? Why not use our Hanukkah observance for *tzedakah*? Why not use a gift as an occasion to teach justice values and raise awareness? Why not expand social justice awareness and impact into our weddings, bar/bat mitzvahs, and other joyous occasions?

. In addition, we can spread the goodness by sharing these ideas with others. With Just Simchas as a resource, we can use our life cycle celebrations as stimuli for our own growth and the growth of *simcha* attendees. We can also make sure that our *simcha* not only avoids harm but further serves as a model for leading and giving. □

THE COST OF A TOMBSTONE: ANOTHER APPROACH

I N PREPARING TO OFFICIATE AT A FUNERAL, I MET the family to make the arrangements and prepare the eulogy. I informed the mourning children that they might consider wearing an old garment at the funeral so that we could rip it before the ceremony ("tear *keriah*") as is traditionally done. The response I received was the first I had ever received of its kind. The son told me that he would not do it. He said that for his father, he would only tear his nicest new garment. His father deserved it. I was very inspired by his unique commitment and how much this ritual meant to him.

There are many meaningful ways to mourn for loved ones; excessive spending on tombstones, however, is not the best Jewish choice.

The Chofetz Chaim taught that more important than saying *Kaddish* for a deceased parent or buying a nice memorial tombstone is doing *hesed*, acts of kindness in their honor (*Ahavat Hesed* 2:15). He suggests that using funds to donate books to a synagogue or establish a loan fund for the poor is more important and useful than purchasing a grand deluxe monument for a cemetery.

While perhaps forty percent of Americans opt for cremation, most still choose burial, which usually involves a tombstone or some other grave marker. While scant data are available for the cost involved, the "average" cost of a headstone or tombstone is often estimated at $1,500 to $2,000. A simple grave marker can cost as little as $200; single or double granite monuments in a Jewish cemetery cost anywhere from just under $1,000 to $4,000, while more elaborate inscribed grave markers cost $7,000 or more and upright headstones reach $10,000 or more.

While lower than the costs incurred by Christians (who often require embalming, rental of a funeral home for several days, etc.), a Jewish funeral in the West tends to follow the lead and can still be very expensive: The average cost of a Jewish funeral can be low ($500–$4,000), medium ($4,000–$6,000, as offered by the Jewish Burial Society or similar groups) or high ($10,000–$15,000), mostly depending on the casket chosen. The purchase of a plot (and additional liner or vault) and the fee for opening and closing the grave adds several hundred to several thousand dollars to the fee.

Around the world, there are differing attitudes toward grave markers. In Asia, Hindus and Buddhists customarily cremate their dead, so there are no tombstones. In the West, many cemeteries have become tourist attractions, where people visit the burial places of famous artists, sculptors, composers, performers, and political figures. Paris's Père Lachaise Cemetery and Vienna's Zentralfriedhof (Central Cemetery) are two that draw many thousands of tourists annually. The Old Jewish Cemetery in Prague, in which notable Czech Jews like the Maharal are buried, draws a steady stream of tourists who tread the narrow passageways. Some object to the commercialism, as you must pay a fee for a ticket to a number of Jewish historical sites and then join with tourists whose attitudes may not be appropriate. Others defend the practice on the grounds that the money raised helps preserve the old Jewish section of Prague. In the United States, people visit Forest Hills to see the graves of Hollywood actors or Woodlawn Cemetery in New York City, among others, to see the elaborately sculpted graves and mausoleums of famous historical figures.

Does an elaborate tombstone, or a cemetery that is a tourist attraction, advance the ideals that our ancestors stood for? Would it not be better for us to use our funds to honor the dead by helping the vulnerable in society or devoting time to bring justice to the world? The *Shelah HaKadosh* taught that one's acts of *hesed* and *tzedakah* can not only salvage a parent from a harsh judgment in the World to Come, but it can move them straight through the gates of the Garden of Eden.

Jewish law forbids speeding up the return of the human body to the earth (through cremation) or slowing it down (through mummification). Rather, we respectfully put the body in the modest shrouds and return it to the Creator through the earth. For many, the grief of the mourning experience is compounded by the stress of the accompanying financial burden. We should be sure to change the precedent from being so prohibitively expensive.

The *Mishnah* teaches that in addition to the behavioral aspects of mourning, there is a significant emotional component arguing that "grief is only of the heart" (*she'ein aninut ela ba-lev*, Sanhedrin 6:8). To fulfill the mitzvah of comforting the mourning (*nihum aveilim*), we should be sure to model modest mourning which focuses more on healing, growth, and kindness and less on grandiose conspicuous consumption to honor the deceased. □

CAGED AND TRAUMATIZED: A CLOSER LOOK AT THE EGG INDUSTRY

FOR YEARS, MY FAVORITE SUNDAY MORNING breakfast was scrambled eggs. Once I learned about what was going on in the egg industry that breakfast lost its innocence, and I found egg alternatives. Do you know where your eggs come from?

In the United States today, close to 300 million hens are suffering inside tiny battery cages that do not allow for any walking or natural movement. A dozen hens can be jammed into a cage that is only 2 feet by 2 feet. The hens are kept in the dark so that they are calmed by the overcrowding and their beaks are sliced off with a searing hot blade to ensure they are less likely to peck a cage-mate to death. The day-old male chicks, worthless to the egg industry, are killed right after birth (usually in a high-speed grinder called a "macerator"). The hens are also killed after only about two years of life when their egg production starts to wane.

To attempt to address this brutal problem of cage size, the egg industry leaders, the United Egg Producers, uniquely joined with the Humane Society to call for better federal standards on hen cages. The improvements would require hens be given a little bit more space (up to 144 square inches each). However this bill (H.R. 3798) would take too many years to be implemented (an eighteen-year transition period) and it wouldn't address the most horrific issues in the industry leaving the hens in inhumanely small and cramped cages and treated cruelly. Many animal welfare advocate groups have called it the "rotten egg bill" and argue that we need more.

We have always known that hens can feel physical pain, but scientists revealed that hens have a very unique capacity for empathy as well. This is a fact the Bible has acknowledged for thousands of years. The Bible has a very special mitzvah to preserve the dignity of hens called *shiluah ha-ken* (Deuteronomy 22:6). On the technical level of this mitzvah, one is commanded to send away the mother bird before taking eggs. The broader value of ensuring compassion for all animals requires that the hens must be provided cage-less free-range treatment, with respect shown for their emotional experience.

The laws of *kashrut* allow for the consumption of regular eggs purchased in any food store without any kosher supervision, but today we must transcend the letter of the law to ensure we are on the forefront of creating a more just world. No egg, produced in today's horrific industry, is fit for consumption.

The Shamayim V'Aretz Institute, which inspires deeper commitments to animal welfare, veganism, health, and the environment, calls upon all members of the Jewish community to act and urge all congressional leaders to demand more humane treatment for hens (and all animals). Further, as a nation committed to justice and holiness, we should all consider changing our diets to only consume food produced ethically.   □

HOW KOSHER IS YOUR MILK?

O N OUR WEDDING DAY, MY WIFE AND I DE-cided that, due to our Jewish convictions, we would no longer drink milk or consume any dairy products. This is a vow we have remained deeply committed to, but we never expected it to become mainstream. Then we found out that one of the greatest Jewish legal authorities in America, Rabbi Hershel Schachter, has made public that he had stopped consuming dairy products due to *kashrut* concerns. I now feel our once-private decision is worthy of a discussion on a broader level.

Jewish law prohibits consuming the milk of a *tereifah* (an animal that is sick or injured, and therefore unkosher) (Exodus 22:30; *Bechorot* 6b; *Hullin* 116b; *Hilchot Shehitah* 10:9; *Shulhan Aruch, Yoreh Deah* 81:1). The Talmud lists eighteen different organic diseases or conditions, and the Rambam has seventy (*Hilchot Shechita* 10:9). However, because the milk we buy in stores today comes from different cows and is all mixed up, as long as we know that the majority of the milk ("*rov*," Exodus 23:2) comes from healthy cows, then we may consider it all kosher without any examination (*Hullin* 11a–12a).

On the other hand, when even a minority (*mi'ut ha-matzui*) of the cows are shown to be frequently sick, then Jewish law requires that we must examine the animals to confirm there is no problem (*Hullin* 11a, 12a; *Bi'ur ha-Gra, Yoreh Deah* 1:4). Dairy production has generally not been considered a problem, and thus the authorities of *kashrut* have been lenient on consumption.

That situation may be changing among some *halachic* authorities. Rabbi Schachter, the leading *rosh yeshiva* at Yeshiva University, is not an animal welfare activist, but he is a halachic adviser to the *kashrut* division of the Orthodox Union and is unwavering in his commitment to the integrity of Jewish law. He believes that today we cannot be sure that more than half of the cows producing milk for mass-market consumption are not injured, sick or have adhesions (growths on the lungs). In an article for Y U Torah Online, Rabbi Michoel Zylberman reported that a rabbi in South Africa observed that 95 percent of cows at dairy farms there have adhesions. Another rabbi observed that, at one dairy farm in America, 80 percent had adhesions.

We do not milk our own cows in our backyards anymore, and most small dairy farms have long been put out of business. Today, it is very likely that unkosher milk is all too often being mixed together with kosher milk at unacceptable levels. As Rabbi J. David Bleich writes in an article on the online site Tradition: "In the modern age, commercial dairies collect milk from, literally, hundreds of cows. Milk from all of these cows is combined, pasteurized and then bottled. Statistically, since a *mi'ut ha-mazui* [a frequently found minority] of dairy cows are indeed *treifot* [not kosher], it is virtually certain that milk bottled in a dairy [farm] contains an admixture of non-kosher milk" (*Contemporary Halachic Problems*, Volume 6, "Is the milk we drink kosher?").

A *tereifah* is an animal that will not live for more than twelve months (*tereifah einah hayah*). If these statistics are accurate, and a substantial portion – if not a majority – of dairy cows qualify as *tereifot*, this means that these animals are so sick that, according to Rabbi Schachter, more than half of them are dying. The fact is, the milk industry is potentially of greater concern for observant Jews than the meat industry, as the slaughtering process requires checking the killed animal's organs for illness, necessitating more care to avoid abuses. Checking for sicknesses and internal adhesions not visible to the eye cannot be done in the dairy industry in the same way, as the animal is milked, not slaughtered.

For those among us who have always attempted to follow *Halacha* to the letter, this matter is worthy of consideration, as it is for anyone who cares for animals and the ethics of how and what we eat. The dairy industry has changed drastically since the original leniencies on drinking milk and consuming other dairy products in America were given decades ago. Consider some of the conditions of the modern dairy farm. Dairy cows are chained by the neck to their stalls and are given electric shocks to ensure that they keep their backs in one position, so that their urine and manure fall in a gutter, and the stalls do not have to be cleaned for each cow individually.

Cows are impregnated yearly, which causes tremendous physical strain on the animal, and, after each birth nine months later, the calves are taken from their mothers immediately. Male calves are then slaughtered for the veal industry, which is even more abusive.

About one-quarter of the animals used to make ground beef are worn-out dairy cattle. These animals are the most likely to be diseased and filled with antibiotic residues. These dairy cows tend to be less healthy than cattle in a large feeding lot due to the stresses of the industrial milk production process. Dairy cows, under optimal conditions, could actually live up to forty years, but they are often just slaughtered at age four due to the decline of their milk output and the strain that results from mistreatment.

Researchers have opened our eyes to very real problems in today's dairy industry. Bovine growth hormone is given to cows to give them unusually large and heavy udders, resulting in increased infection rates, which then lead to the administration of antibiotics. The hormones and antibiotics are in the milk consumed by humans, adding to a possible increased risk of cancer and overexposure to antibiotics.

Cows are hooked up to electronic milking machines several times each day. These machines give off electric shocks and create lesions and mastitis (inflammation of the mammary glands).

In light of all of this, it seems to me that, from a halachic standpoint, let alone an ethical standpoint, it is no longer acceptable to support the dairy industry as it operates today. We must communicate to the industry how we, as Jewish consumers, feel about these abuses and support healthier, more ethical options. In the meantime, we must also consider moving toward almond, soy, rice, and coconut milk alternatives, until the dairy industry cleans up its act. There is no shortage of affordable, healthy, tasty alternatives, so it is relatively easy for us to make the change in accordance with our consciences.

Rav Schachter has taken this legal stringency upon himself. Following his lead, it is time for us all to consider these conditions to determine where we personally fall in this struggle with ethical consumption. The value the Torah seems to be teaching is that treating animals properly is part and parcel of *kashrut*. That leads to the argument that unethical, inhumane practices are not only a violation of the prohibition of *tzaar baalei haim* (inflicting pain on animals) but often result in the production of *treif* milk.

While we wait for the dairy industry to clean up its act, what will happen to those big muscles and strong bones our moms and commercials told us milk will help build? As it turns out, the nutritional information provided to consumers has not always been accurate. Many of us have been misled to believe that milk is the best source of protein, calcium, and vitamin C. The National Dairy Council (NDC) is a marketing arm of Dairy Management Inc., an industry body whose purpose, according to its Web site, is to "drive increased sales of and demand for U.S. dairy products." The NDC naturally does not share the negative public-health consequences. Since the 1950s, educators and governments have allowed the NDC to become the largest distributor of nutritional-education materials in the country. In fact, the health risks of dairy consumption, according to health experts at the Physicians Committee for Responsible Medicine, include osteoporosis, cardiovascular disease, cancer, diabetes, lactose intolerance, and vitamin D toxicity, among others.

Added to all this is the fact that the environmental harm caused by carbon dioxide emissions from today's industrial farms is known to be worse than the pollution caused by our automobiles. Experts estimate that if all Americans ate a vegan diet, that alone would cut greenhouse gas emissions by at least 6 percent. Changing our diets is the most powerful way to help the environment.

While factory farms control most of the dairy industry, there are some smaller dairy farms striving for better. One such innovator I met at a Hazon Food Conference was Albert Straus, who is the president of Straus Family Creamery. This cutting-edge dairy farm north of San Francisco is deeply committed to more sustainable production that is also totally organic, contains no genetically modified organisms (GMO-free), minimally processed, contains no additives, and is certified kosher. They also allow their cows to graze in the fields. But while Strauss products are available at Whole Foods locally, many small farms like this are drowned out by massive commercial producers and the large number of brands available in large supermarkets.

The future lies in the regulation, or lack thereof, by legislators and in the spending patterns of the consumers. One should also remember that organic milk may be healthier because the animals ate organic feed and weren't given synthetic hormones or medications, but that doesn't mean it is cruelty-free. Also, *Chalav Yisrael* (milk produced under kosher supervision) is no different, as much of it also comes from regular commercial farms that merely set aside times to produce supervised milk.

In Jewish law, if an animal is abused, we may not benefit from it. Until we can be totally sure that most cows are not *treif* anymore, we must be stringent on this Jewish law to ensure that we are not consuming the milk of sick and abused cows. The Jewish people need to be at the forefront of reining in the excesses of the industrial farming age.

Next time you stand in the dairy aisle, consider trying a dairy-free month for Jewish law and ethics – and for your health. □

ELEVATING OUR PRAYER: A VEGAN VIEW OF *TEFILLIN*

COULD WE CREATE VEGAN *TEFILLIN*? BY VEGAN *tefillin*, I do not, of course, mean *tefillin* made from corn. That would not fulfill the holy mitzvah. But could we ensure that our Jewish ritual objects, which must come from animals, are obtained in a cruelty-free manner?

Tefillin is a very important mitzvah that originates in the Torah and is mentioned daily in the *Shema* prayer recited twice a day (Deuteronomy 6:4–9). Jews have kept this mitzvah in trying times. There are testimonies of Jews who continued to wear *tefillin* even in the shadow of death during the Holocaust as part of their courageous and determined spiritual struggle. IDF soldiers have donned *tefillin* before going into battle.

Similar to *tefillin*, many *mitzvot* require objects that come from animals, such as the parchment inside *mezuzot*, Torah scrolls made from parchment, and the ram's horn (*shofar*). Embracing these rituals should be the exception to a Jewish vegan's rule of trying not to buy leather and other animal products.

There are, of course, some possible alternatives to buying what is currently on the market to explore. One can try locating a used (but still kosher) pair of *tefillin*, or use a pair received in one's childhood or one passed down through the family so a new pair would not have to be purchased. The number of animals killed for the leather tefillin straps are very minimal, so the emphasis of animal welfare activists would be better placed addressing the factory farming industries that are killing billions of animals each year.

There are some attempts to make non-leather *tefillin*, but wearing those do not fulfill the traditional mitzvah. We are in need of the first kosher and truly cruelty-free *tefillin* produced in the most humane way possible. The *Shulhan Aruch* writes in the laws of *tefillin* that parchment may even be made from a *neveilah*, any animal that either died naturally or was not slaughtered in accordance with Jewish laws. Therefore, it is possible to wear *tefillin* from a cow that lived a long, happy life. We are in search of a farm that will donate hides from cows that lived full lives and died natural deaths. There was one *sofer* (scribe) working to make vegan *tefillin* in Tzfat, Israel, but he found it unsustainable. Perhaps animal shelters for farm animals might be able to supply this need.

Originating in the Torah, humane treatment of animals has been an eternally cherished Jewish value. In the industrial age, where we no longer have cows in our own backyards, a lot of those cherished values have been forgotten as we've assimilated to the mass commercial production of all of our products. We must return to the values of the Torah. When done with compassion, we truly can elevate an animal that has lived a full life. Rabbi Moshe Cordovoro, the sixteenth century Kabbalist, explains well:

> He should not uproot anything which grows, unless it is necessary, nor kill any living thing unless it is necessary . . . to have compassion as much as possible. This is the principle: to have pity on all created things not to hurt them depends on wisdom. Only if it is to elevate them higher and higher, from plant to animal and from animal to human . . . (*Tomer Devora*, Chapter 3).

Rabbi Cordovero explains that we can elevate an animal up to the service of God through our service, but that it must be done with absolute compassion. We cannot be assured today that the leather used for *tefillin* did not come from abused cows slaughtered inhumanely for their meat.

It is worth considering why the Torah intentionally mandated that *tefillin* come from leather. Perhaps we are binding ourselves with animal to fully commit ourselves to serving God and living a moral life. One of the great moral imperatives we have is to reduce suffering for all sentient beings. When we put *tefillin* on each morning, we are reminding ourselves of our life commitment to be merciful to all creatures. As with all moral convictions, ritual helps us to recharge our commitments on a daily basis. *Tefillin* is an animal welfare mitzvah at its core!

Many have suggested that it is impossible not to benefit from animals in some way today. There are animal products and/or the results of animal tests wrapped up in everything from our paints, wallboard, and car tires to the asphalt we drive on. This needs to change, but in the meantime we must live with the current option we're presented in the world while we continue to strive for our ideals. One can still be vegan by refraining from eating animal products while continuing to engage in required ritual use. Now is the time for a paradigm shift to return to the intention of this holy prayer ritual. □

A YOM KIPPUR OF MERCY OR CRUELTY: BRINGING AN END TO KAPOROS

SOME JEWS HAVE A MEDIEVAL CUSTOM TO SACRIfice a chicken before Yom Kippur – "*kaporos*." One grabs the chicken's legs while pinning its wings back and swings it around one's head. These chickens are packed into crates before this procedure and then usually sent to be slaughtered after. Others are often just left in crates to die.

It would be difficult to claim that this practice actually enhances one's moral and spiritual sensitivities in anticipation of the Day of Atonement. In fact, many Jewish legal authorities today agree that this practice is completely inappropriate.

Rabbi Shlomo Aviner, Rosh Yeshiva of Yeshivat Ateret Cohanim in

Jerusalem and prominent Religious Zionist leader, spoke out against this cruel custom: "Since this is not a clear duty but rather a tradition, and in the light of the *kashrut* problems and cruelty to animals . . . it is recommended that one should prefer to conduct the atonement ceremony with money, thus also fulfilling the great mitzvah of helping poor people."

Rabbi David Rosen, former Chief Rabbi of Ireland, writes: "Beyond the objections . . . of the Ramban, Rashba, and the Bet Yosef to the custom of 'kapparot,' and beyond the warnings of rabbinic authorities such as the Chayei Adam, Kaf HaChaim, Aruch HaShulhan and the Mishnah Berurah regarding the halachic infringements involved in using live fowl for this custom, the latter also desecrates the prohibition against '*tzaar baalei haim.*' Those who wish to fulfill this custom can do so fully and indeed in a far more halachically acceptable manner by using money as a substitute."

The primary purpose of the Yamim Noraim (High Holidays) is to connect more deeply with God and to improve ourselves. Taking on a cruel practice and harming an innocent creature has no place in Jewish life. *Tsaar baalei chaim* (the prohibition of harming animals) is a Torah prohibition that requires that we cultivate virtue and that we prevent suffering.

Today, there is a substitute for harming animals. One can allocate money to the poor as an alternative to the sacrifice. Sacrifice ended with the destruction of the Second Temple two thousand years ago, and there is no adequate justification for bringing it back in this context.

During that time of year, we should be cultivating mercy for all those who suffer and not be perpetuating pain on sentient creatures it in the name of piety. Yom Kippur is a time for *teshuva* (growth and change).

The Midrash explains profoundly that *teshuva* was created before the world was created. Rabbi Joesph B. Soloveitchik explains that this demonstrates that free will and the possibility of profound self-transformation exist before nature. We are not determined beings; we are free. When we engage in *teshuva*, we transcend our nature.

In this light, I would suggest that one reason to inflict pain on the animal in this custom is because some believe that the animal soul has won over in them and thus they must transfer their sin onto another animal creature. If we believe that we, on some level, are free, and not determined like an animal, and are spiritually beyond the strict confines of nature, then we need not beat the animal instinct out of us. We consist of nature but we can transcend it. We need not beat the animal inside of us or outside of us to find freedom and improvement.

We need not be afraid to abandon a custom that some have taken on when a higher ethical sensitivity exists. For example, in the mid-twentieth century, observant Jews bought processed foods without *hechsherim* (kosher certification). Today, most observant Jews have committed to purchasing only foods certified as kosher. We abandoned a looser custom since we have more options today. Another example of this is the absence of the customary sheep's or fish's head on the Rosh Hashanah table today. We remain content with carrots and fruit to fulfill the practice of eating certain foods as a good sign (*siman*) for the New Year.

On Yom Kippur, we must have the courage to reflect on our customs and practices to ensure they are promoting life and love and not just tradition for its own sake, without regard for its impact on others. □

TRANSPARENCY IN ANIMAL CRUELTY AND THE HEALTH RISKS OF MEAT CONSUMPTION

A JEW IS EXPECTED TO BE OBSESSED WITH compassion. The Sages taught that being compassionate is a prerequisite to truly being Jewish: "Jews are compassionate children of compassionate ancestors (*rahmanim b'nei rahmanim*) and one who is not compassionate cannot truly be a descendant of our father Abraham" (*Beitzah* 32b).

The *Shulhan Aruch* teaches that "It is forbidden, according to the law of the Torah, to inflict pain upon any living creature. On the contrary, it is our duty to relieve the pain of any creature." One of the greatest violations of this sacred covenant of compassion is found today in the treatment of animals on mass production farms. Secret video footage of the abuse of cows at a California slaughterhouse in 2008 led to the largest beef recall in American history, and did a great service for the health of Americans. Instead of acknowledging this or improving conditions, however, local governing bodies are pushing for less transparency on how those animals are treated and for barring those involved in animal welfare work from even working at these institutions. The cattle industry and the corporate group American Legislative Exchange Council (ALEC) have sponsored or written many of these bills. For example, in California, the absurdly mis-named "Animal and Ecological Terrorism Act" would impose a fine upon anyone who did not turn over evidence taken secretly (including video) at a slaughterhouse to law enforcement authorities within 24 to 48 hours. Similar laws have been proposed in Nebraska and Tennessee, while in Arkansas, Indiana, and Pennsylvania, proposed laws would outlaw making a video at any agricultural operation.

In other words, these laws would criminalize the act of documenting something already classified as a crime. As Matt Dominguez, from the Humane Society said: "Instead of working to prevent future abuses, the factory farms want to silence them. What they really want is for the whistle to be blown on the whistle-blower." These perverse, shameless bills must be rejected. Just a basic survey of the videos that have been released have shown how farm workers are punching and kicking pigs, tossing baby pig-lets into the air, caging hens alongside rotting bird corpses, burning and snapping off chick beaks, stomping and throwing turkeys against a wall, and burning the ankles of horses with chemicals.

I believe that most Americans continue to support these companies be-cause they just do not know what's happening behind the scenes. Rather than actively or passively covering up these atrocities, we must demand transparency. Our elected and agency officials should know that we want animals to be treated humanely, and that those who exhibit such cruelty to animals should be brought to justice.

In addition, meat consumption is connected to serious health risks, as attested by reports that are constantly released. Harvard and National Cancer Institute researchers have added to data showing the link between meat consumption and premature death. One must wonder if based upon the biblical obligation to guard our health (Deuteronomy 4:15), we must inquire as to whether it is now forbidden to consume meat on the grounds of health alone, not to mention ethics.

Meat was already dangerous for human consumption even prior to the injection of antibiotics into the animals. Red meat consumption has been linked to higher levels of cancer and cardiovascular disease (heart disease, stroke, and atherosclerosis). A landmark 2009 study, the National Institutes of Health-AARP Diet and Health Study, examined more than half a mil-lion men and women ages 50–71 years over a ten-year period. Results show conclusively that daily consumption of red meat resulted in a higher risk of overall mortality as well as mortality due to cardiovascular disease and cancer, with higher consumption of red meat correlated with higher risk of earlier death. People with the highest consumption of red meat had the following risk:

- Increased overall mortality: 31 percent for men; 36 percent for women
- Increased cancer mortality: 22 percent for men; 20 percent for women
- Increased cardiovascular disease mortality: 27 percent for men; 50 percent for women

As if this were not enough reason to reduce red meat consumption, researchers from the Harvard School of Public Health have now found that there is also an increased risk of type 2 (adult-onset) diabetes. Eating one hot dog a day (50 gram of processed meat), for example, produced a 51 percent increase in risk for diabetes. This can further exacerbate risk factors for early death, such as hypertension, high total cholesterol, bad cholesterol, and triglycerides, which are associated with red meat consumption.

Unfortunately, the new tempting in-vitro meat (lab created!) may have serious health concerns as well. However, there are plenty of bean, nut, grain, and vegetable alternatives to meat where one can attain all of the necessary protein, iron, and vitamins and nutrients needed for a balanced diet. These options have the added benefit of reducing your risk for early death. For example, researchers from the Harvard School of Public Health reported that replacing one serving of red meat with nuts could reduce mortality risk by 19 percent.

To fulfill our life missions as happy and effective individuals, we must proactively embrace the healthiest of lifestyles. Rabbi Samson Raphael Hirsch explains this mitzvah:

> Limiting our presumption against our own body, God's word calls to us: "Do not commit suicide!" "Do not injure yourself!" "Do not ruin yourself!" "Do not weaken yourself!" "Preserve yourself!" . . . You may not . . . in any way weaken your health or shorten your life. Only if the body is healthy is it an efficient instrument for the spirit's activity. . . . Therefore you should avoid everything which might possibly injure your health. . . . And the law asks you to be even more circumspect in avoiding danger to life and limb than in the avoidance of other transgressions.

The prohibition of eating meat with milk may be an attempt to reduce our meat intake. My revered teacher, Rabbi Shlomo Riskin, the Chief Rabbi of Efrat, explains that "The dietary laws are intended to teach us compassion and lead us gently to vegetarianism."

Preserving one's health is one of the highest commandments in Jewish law. If one's health is in jeopardy, one must eat forbidden foods, violate Shabbat, and even eat on Yom Kippur (*Pesahim* 25a). Perhaps the reason God originally created humans to be immortal, according to the Torah, is linked to the mandate for humans to live off a vegetarian diet. The concession after the flood permitting the consumption of meat is, in the modern world, linked to shorter life spans.

Good tasting protein alternatives are now easily available. There is very little sacrifice to becoming vegan, vegetarian, or to merely reducing one's meat intake. If not for moral reasons, do it for health.

Anyone can do a "meatless Monday," but maybe try a "meatless month!" Perhaps it won't be as challenging as you expect. For the health reasons pulling us toward reducing our meat intake, it's worth a shot. □

□ SUPPORTING THE ALIENATED

DO WE PRIORITIZE
THE VULNERABLE IN JUSTICE?

I N JEWISH LAW, WE ARE TOLD THAT IT IS UNJUST
to be biased and be swayed by poverty, to favor the
case of the poor over the rich in a dispute. Within
the realm of a formal court's judgment this is crucial (Exodus 23:3, 6).
However, does this notion still apply today, where the disparity of wealth
between the poor and the rich has become so large that the poor often can
no longer properly advocate for themselves?

This notion of equality before the law is mostly a fallacy today in
America, since the poor have such a serious disadvantage in the courtroom.
The *New York Times* reported that more than 90 percent of criminal cases
are never tried before a jury; most people charged with crimes just plead
guilty, forfeiting their constitutional rights. The prosecution usually promises to give a deal to those who plead guilty and go all-out against anyone
who tries to go to trial. It is simply cheaper to plead guilty than to try to
pay for legal counsel.

Every individual should have the same fair opportunity before the law,
because we must be committed to truth and justice. But this is not the reality today. Even if it were true, Judaism teaches that we must go over and
above the law (*lifnim m'shurat ha-din*) to support those more vulnerable
(*Bava Metzia* 83a). Furthermore, we learn that God created and destroyed
many worlds that were built upon the foundation of *din* (judgment), and
then God finally created this world built upon *rahamim* (mercy) (Rashi
to Genesis 1:1). Our world can't exist on pure judgment, rather, as fallible
beings we rely upon the grace, empathy, and kindness of God and man.

We must be moved toward mercy for those who are suffering, and this must affect how we build society. President Obama explained the importance of empathy in jurisprudence when choosing Supreme Court justices: "I will seek someone who understands that justice isn't about some abstract legal theory or footnote in a casebook; it is also about how our laws affect the daily realities of people's lives. I view the quality of empathy, of understanding and identifying with people's hopes and struggles as an essential ingredient for arriving at just decisions and outcomes." Law is not only about principle, it is also about life.

This is all the more true outside of the courtroom. Within the realm of Jewish grassroots activism, we learn that our primary responsibility is not equality, but to prioritize our support for the vulnerable.

Numerous Jewish teachings remind us that our primary responsibility is to protect and prioritize the most vulnerable individuals and parties: "God takes the side of the aggrieved and the victim" (Ecclesiastes 3:15). When there is conflict, God simply cannot withhold support for the one suffering.

Rav Ahron Soloveichik writes: "A Jew should always identify with the cause of defending the aggrieved, whosoever the aggrieved may be, just as the concept of *tzedek* is to be applied uniformly to all humans regardless of race or creed" (*Logic of the Heart, Logic of the Mind*, 67).

This is what it means to be Jewish, to prioritize the suffering in conflict.

This point is made time and time again by the Rabbis. The Talmud, based on the verse "Justice, justice, you shall pursue" (Deuteronomy 16:20), teaches that the disadvantaged should be given preference when all else is equal. The Rambam teaches that even if the disadvantaged arrive later than other people, they should be given precedence (*Sanhedrin* 21:6, *Shulhan Aruch, Hoshen Mishpat* 15:2).

Thus, in a court of law, all parties are ideally treated equally, as we are guided by the Jewish value of *din*. Today, however, justice does not prevail. Further, in activism we must favor the vulnerable, since we are guided by the Jewish value of *hesed*. In life, we must learn to balance all of our values: love, justice, mercy, etc. In justice, we do not just choose one guiding principle: As Isaiah Berlin teaches, moral life consists of embracing a plurality of values.

We must always be absolutely committed to the truth and be sure that our justice system is fair for all parties. Yet we also, as changemakers, have a special and holy role to give voice to the voiceless and to support the unsupported in society. This is the role of Jewish activism. The Rabbis teach that "Even if a righteous person attacks a wicked person, God still sides with the victim" (*Yalkut Shimoni*). All people deserve our love and care but we must follow the path of God and make our allegiances clear: with the destitute, oppressed, alienated, and suffering.   □

FIGHTING FOR THE INNOCENT

W E ALL AGREE THAT A STABLE SOCIETY must have a strong, punitive justice system that maintains order and security. One flaw in every justice system, however, is the perpetual possibility of mistakenly punishing the innocent. Unfortunately, in our justice system, this happens too often.

There are six primary reasons for wrongful convictions:

1. Eyewitness misidentification: Eyewitness testimony is notoriously unreliable. It is difficult to recall exactly the circumstances of any situation, especially one that catches a person by surprise. For example, do you remember the exact wording of every interaction you had yesterday? As time goes by, it becomes even more difficult to recall what happened.

2. "Snitch" testimony: Witnesses, usually those already in prison, come forward claiming to have heard the suspect confess in order to get favorable treatment on their own cases.

3. Police and prosecutorial misconduct: Examples of this include crime labs claiming that they had test results when no tests were actually performed, and prosecutors and police hiding evidence pointing to another suspect. Unfortunately, these occurrences, if discovered, happen long after the trial, and those who commit such obstructions of justice are rarely punished.

4. False confessions: Authorities are often eager to close a case and thus put pressure on those accused to admit to a crime they did not commit. The accused, scared and feeling overwhelmed by the odds against them, admit to the crime, figuring that they will be punished anyways and that this will result in a less harsh sentencing. An example of this is the case of the Central Park Five, in which four of the five then-teenagers confessed to raping and

killing a woman in Central Park, and only years later were proved innocent through DNA testing.

5. Poor defense counsel: Lawyers can, and often do, make many mistakes when defending a client. This is especially true in the case of public defenders, who receive enormous caseloads and are so overburdened that it is impossible to do a thorough job on each case.

6. Junk science: This applies both to methods that are not really science when empirically tested, and to legitimate science performed poorly. Poor evidence, later disproved with stronger science, has led to too many incarcerations.

How many prisoners in the American justice system are actually innocent? While it is impossible to truly know, over the past decades, experts have offered varying percentages: Samuel R. Gross and Barbara O'Brien estimated "at least 2.3 percent"; Jon B. Gould and Richard A. Leo put it at 3 to 5 percent; James S. Liebman et al. place their estimate at 7 percent; and the newest estimate, by John Roman et al, places its estimate at 5 percent, except for sexual assault, for which the wrongful conviction rate may be as high as 15 percent!

Jewish law strongly upholds the principle that the innocent should not be punished. When God reveals to Abraham his plan to destroy Sodom and Gomorrah (Genesis 18:17–33), Abraham challenges God: "Will you also destroy the righteous with the wicked?" When God offers to spare the cities if there are fifty righteous people, Abraham solicits for forgiveness if there is a number slightly lower; eventually, God decides that if there are even ten righteous people, he would spare the cities. Thus, from the time of Abraham it was important that punishment should be reserved for the guilty, and the innocent should be spared, even, sometimes, to the extent that it may mean letting the guilty go unpunished.

Today, there are those who are dedicated to ensuring that the innocent do not languish in jail. The National Registry of Exonerations, a joint project of the University of Michigan Law School and the Center on Wrongful Convictions at Northwestern University School of Law, in less than a year of investigating data, has recorded the occurrence 1,040 exonerations since 1989. The Registry helps highlight the need to scrutinize convictions (especially in states with the most exonerations, such as Illinois and Texas) to make sure that they were honestly obtained and that the defendants had sufficient and competent defense.

The Innocence Project, founded by Barry C. Scheck and Peter J. Neufeld of Yeshiva University's Benjamin N. Cardozo School of Law in 1992, is a group that uses the relatively new science of DNA testing to establish the innocence of many prisoners. The staff of lawyers and Cardozo clinic students, and allies in many states, has thus far exonerated 301 prisoners, who had served an average of nearly fourteen years (and eighteen of whom had been on death row), using DNA evidence. One wonders what may have happened to so many other innocent prisoners had such technology been available earlier.

One case illustrates the great value of the Innocence Project for American society. In 1974, James Bain was convicted of raping a nine-year old boy in Florida. The primary evidence at the time revolved around the blood type of the semen on the victim's underwear. The jury believed the prosecution's claim that Bain's blood type was AB, even though the blood sample was group B. Once DNA evidence became available, Bain tried five times to get the Circuit Court to examine his case, but was rejected each time. Finally, after the Innocence Project became involved, DNA evidence was examined, and confirmed that Bain was not the rapist. James Bain was exonerated and released on December 17, 2009, after serving thirty-five years for a crime he did not commit.

The case of the *Central Park Five*, the subject of a 2012 documentary by Ken Burns, illustrates the continuing difficulty of former prisoners even after they have been exonerated. In 1989, a young white investment banker was found unconscious after having been raped in Central Park. The police quickly focused on five black or Latino mid-teen boys who had been in the park. After each of the accused underwent 14 to 30 excruciating hours of intense interrogation, each of the boys either confessed, or said that others had been involved in the rape. Apart from that, there was no physical or DNA evidence that linked the boys to the rape, and the victim had no memory of the crime. Ed Koch, then the Mayor of the City of New York, as well as law enforcement officials and the media engaged in a campaign of vilification against the five, and they were quickly convicted and jailed. After their release, their conviction was vacated in 2002, as a serial rapist who eventually committed three more rapes and a murder eventually confessed to the crime, and his DNA matched the 1989 rape. As a result, in 2003 the Central Park Five filed a $250 million suit against the city officials responsible for violating their civil rights. Far from seeking a settlement, New York City has challenged the suit, and even filed suit against Ken Burns and the others involved in the making of the documentary to surrender all the notes and video not shown in the documentary. To this day, the New York Police Department stands by its 2003 review which concluded that the police did nothing wrong in their handling of the case.

We need a justice system, and we need to punish those who disobey the law, but we must ensure that the rights of the innocent are protected. If a prisoner is found to be innocent, that prisoner should be set free and given compensation. Earl Warren (1891–1974), who served as a District Attorney, Governor of California, and Chief Justice of the Supreme Court of the United States, was well aware of the often coercive methods by which law enforcement obtained confessions and convictions, and how careful scrutiny needed to be applied to ensure that only the guilty were convicted and incarcerated. As he said: "Life and liberty can be as much endangered from illegal methods used to convict those thought to be criminals as from the actual criminals themselves."

There are more than fifty Innocence Projects in the United States, under the umbrella of a network called the Innocence Network, and they can use our help. This is nothing short of the championing of justice over injustice, and as a community, we must support their work.   □

RELIGIOUS FREEDOM
AND SHARIA LAW

DURING A TRIP TO PARIS, WHEN A MUSLIM cab driver picked me up, I noticed a slight discomfort came over me. I realized, at that moment, that American religious fanatics had succeeded at convincing me to be afraid. Religion, at its best, furthers deep value formation and creates bridges and connections whereas religion at its worst is destructive and spreads fear throughout society. There is a growing religious fanaticism, with diverse manifestations, that seeks to promote fear of the other and that fear almost inevitability leads to hate. This fear and hate is unfortunately not absent from major segments of the Jewish communal discourse.

There is a conspiracy theory in circulation that Muslim leaders are attempting to replace American law with Sharia (Islamic law). This fear has escalated to a level where as many as thirteen states are considering or have passed bills that would formally prohibit the application of Sharia. In Oklahoma, 70 percent of the electorate approved this amendment to the state's Constitution: "The [Oklahoma] courts . . . when exercising their judicial authority . . . shall not consider international laws or Sharia Law."

The Orthodox Union has spoken out against this discrimination, as has the Anti Defamation League. National director of the ADL Abe Foxman has written, "The anti-Sharia bills are more than a matter of unnecessary public policy. These measures are, at their core, predicated on prejudice and ignorance. They constitute a form of camouflaged bigotry that enables their proponents to advance the idea that finds fault with the Muslim faith and paints all Muslim Americans as foreigners and anti-American crusaders."

David Yerushalmi, an Orthodox lawyer in Brooklyn, has made it his mission to show that Sharia sanctions militant jihadism, arguing that "because jihad necessarily advocates violence and the destruction of our representative, constitution-based government, the advocacy of jihad by a Sharia authority presents a real and present danger."

To be sure, I am personally very concerned about many messages coming out of the Islamic community. I'm also concerned about how Sharia is being applied in extreme and dangerous ways around the world. There are radicals who choose a fundamentalist approach to Islamic jurisprudence. This is happening in parts of Iran and Saudia Arabia, and in radical groups like the Taliban, but discrimination is not the appropriate response.

Maimonides made it clear not only that Islam is not an idolatrous faith, but rather that the Jewish people can learn a lot from Muslim thought (*Maachalot* 11:7). In addition to learning from our Muslim brethren, we should commit to supporting their autonomy.

Furthermore, the banning of Islamic law is a violation of the First Amendment right to free exercise of religion and of the establishment clause, by giving pre-eminence to one religion over another. All Americans should be afraid of the implications of this movement upon their own personal liberties.

Jewish, Christian, and Muslim legal tribunals have operated in the U.S., presiding over matters of religious ritual and internal disputes, in cooperation with the government courts for over half a century. Certain cases, due to their religious nature, are not able to be brought before the secular courts due to the separation of religion and state. If religious communities can't have their own private jurisdiction, where are they supposed to deal with their most pressing day-to-day issues? Banning religious arbitration leaves them without options.

We should never forget the real threat of terrorism motivated by Muslim fundamentalists, but as free-thinking American Jews, we must learn to distinguish between real threats and false fear tactics.

What a powerful message it would send for the committed Jewish community, which has no lack of tension with the Muslim community, to commit to serve as defenders of religious freedom for all. It is precisely at a time of freedom such as now that we must safeguard these freedoms for all people. The biblical imperative, "U'vaharta ba-haim," that we must choose life is a direct mandate for expanding freedom and liberty to all. Now is the time to defend those under attack. We must do it for ourselves, for the sake of others, and to honor our core Jewish values.

Now more than ever, we need to challenge the conspiracy theories and ensure that we raise our moral voices to promote the freedom that we are so blessed with for all. It is not only religious communities that should feel concerned for religious freedom. Government and business should be disturbed since fear mongering destroys communal trust and the basic fabric of our society which hurts all. We all flourish in a culture of hope and collaboration not a culture of fear and isolation.

We cannot allow religion based on fear and hate to overcome a religion of love. Rabbi Shlomo Carlebach once said: "If God had given me two hearts, I could use one for hating and the other one for love. But since I was given only one heart, I have only room for love." □

THE JEWISH PERCEPTION OF TATTOOS: A FAIR PREJUDICE?

I SPOKE WITH YOUNG FORMER GANG MEMBERS undergoing tattoo removal at Homeboy Industries, a job-training site in Los Angeles that provides hope, training, and support to formerly gang-involved and previously incarcerated men and women. Their tattoos serve as serious barriers to employment and acceptance into mainstream society. A Harris Poll taken in 2008 estimated that 14 percent of Americans now have tattoos and the Pew Research Center shows that a whopping 26 percent of those between 18–25 have at least one tattoo. Is the typical Jewish perception toward these individuals with body art fair?

Personally, I would never consider getting a tattoo. I found myself dismayed by another's choice to scar his or her body with a lifelong design. However, many of those with tattoos are often more scarred socially than physically.

There is some perception by many Jews with tattoos that they are outcasts and that they can never even be buried in a Jewish cemetery. To be sure, the Torah does prohibit tattoos, called *k'tovet kaaka*: "You shall not make gashes in your flesh for the dead, or incise any marks on yourselves: I am the Lord" (Leviticus 19:28). But this was a concern for idolatrous lettering and most modern tattoos are not a biblical, but only a later rabbinic, prohibition (*Tosafot, Gittin* 20b).

The Mishnah (*Makkot* 3:6) suggests that the prohibition is the writing of the name of a deity on one's skin, and Maimonides writes: "This was a custom among the pagans who marked themselves for idolatry" (*Laws of Idolatry* 12:11). Aaron Demsky, a professor at Bar Ilan University, even suggests that non-idolatrous tattooing may have been permitted in biblical times. Certainly if a tattoo was forced upon someone (as was done in the Holocaust and still happens in many gangs and during certain medical procedures), there would be no prohibition at all (*Shulhan Aruch, Yoreh Deah* 180:2). Also, some Jewish legal authorities permit cosmetic tattooing when done for one's self-respect (*kavod ha-briot*). Further, while there is a prohibition against getting a tattoo, there is no obligation to remove already-inscribed tattoos. There is no mention by Rambam or in the *Shulhan Aruch* of a requirement of tattoo removal. The laser removal process is very expensive and painful, and it takes a long time. One cannot be blamed for not choosing this option.

Tattoos should be discouraged today, because the Jewish tradition holds that we were created in the image of God and that our bodies are on loan for this life of service. Therefore, we must take care to protect them. However, there is also a prohibition to block someone's attempt to repent and grow (*teshuva*). Rambam writes: "Repentance atones for all sins, even someone who was wicked all his days and repents at the end; we don't remind him of any part of his wicked past" (*Laws of Repentance* 1:3).

Many Jews today believe that they cannot be observant Jews or be buried in a Jewish cemetery because of a tattoo they got years earlier. This is not true.

Even more tragic is the struggle those who were lured into gangs, drugs, and tattooing have in trying to rebuild their lives. They do not have to open their mouths – the stereotypes that come with a tattoo speak a million words. The tattoo may be an indication about the past. But it is not an indication of the future.

We can all strive to be more inclusive and less judgmental of those who are tattooed. As I learned at Homeboy Industries, this scar on the skin often represents a scar on the soul. Who are we to further deepen that pain?   □

ESTABLISHING COMMUNITY MEDICINE BANKS AROUND THE WORLD

D ID YOU KNOW THAT ABOUT 30,000 INDIVID- uals die every day from curable diseases? Some evils are entirely dreadful because they are not preventable; there is little we can do in the face of a hurricane or tsunami. But it is even more tragic when we ignore preventable human suffering.

In Buenos Aires, Argentina, I took my UCLA Hillel students to volunteer at the Refuot community medicine bank, funded by the Fundación Tzedaká. Since 1999, Refuot has distributed around 580,000 medicines to more than 12,000 Jews and non-Jews through seventy Jewish centers in Argentina. I left the medicine bank inspired by their heroic work and yet deeply troubled by how much more work there is to do to improve medicine access worldwide.

One story among thousands is that of Juan Granovsky. He was born in 1937, and worked for decades in a fumigation and disinfection company. He receives about $90 a month in retirement benefits, but it is not enough to cover the cost of the medicines he now needs. He suffers from diabetes, high cholesterol and blood pressure, and has had six heart bypass operations. Granovsky typifies the patient who would have no access to medication without the help of the medicine bank. Where would Juan turn if the medicine bank wasn't here for him?

Usually these needed medicines are donated from pharmaceutical laboratories, but if someone is in need of another medicine, the medicine bank purchases it after searching for the best drug prices on the market. The Argentinean government covers some HIV and cancer treatments, but the community medicine bank is needed to treat patients with other diseases such as Parkinson's, Crohn's, and diabetes that the government is not equipped to address. All medicines are packaged and then sent to hospitals and health professionals, where they are dispensed to patients.

The idea that we are responsible to ensure that others have access to medicines is not a new one. The great Talmudic sage Rav Huna set the model for the importance of granting others access to the drugs they need. "Whenever he discovered some [new] medicine he would fill a water jug with it and suspend it above the doorstep and proclaim, 'Whosoever desires it let him come and take of it'" (*Taanit* 20b). Rav Huna understood the loss of human dignity felt when an individual is unable to meet personal health needs and those of loved ones. Further a society based on intellectual, moral, and spiritual values cannot thrive if all must be consumed with their basic physical survival needs.

Rabbi Eliezer Waldenberg, the great twentieth century Jewish legal authority, taught that Jewish law demands that every community must play a crucial role in granting access to medicine: "When poor people are ill and who cannot afford medical expenses, the community sends them a doctor to visit them, and the medicine is paid for by the communal fund" (*Tzitz Eliezer* 5:4).

The most strategic way to address sickness is by improving exercise, nutrition, lifestyle, and preventive care. But where health counseling, governmental funding, and education are unavailable or insufficient, medicines are especially crucial. We should consider helping to financially support Refuot, establishing more amazing community medicine banks, and advocating pharmaceutical companies to donate more medicines to those in need worldwide.

Pharmaceutical companies must do more to provide universal access and government must provide tax incentives that help companies to do so. Most importantly, like Refuot, we all can and must support local and foreign organizations ensuring the just distribution of drugs to those who need them.

There are few situations in life as terrifying as a life-threatening disease without access to the necessary medicines. How can we let innocent individuals die around the world when a pill that costs less than one cent to produce can save their lives? God commands us to take care of the poor, the starving and the sick and with 30,000 dying every day of curable diseases we don't have much time to delay.   □

JEWISH SOCIAL JUSTICE IN POST-APARTHEID SOUTH AFRICA?

As a scholar-in-residence in Cape Town in 2012, I was full of curiosity. What would an Orthodox Social Justice movement look like in post-apartheid South Africa? What unique opportunities does the Jewish community have to address the racial and economic dynamics that still plague the region?

Similar to the Civil Rights movement, Jews were overrepresented in the struggle against apartheid. Many distinguished themselves in the struggle against apartheid, including:

- Helen Suzman, the lone Progressive Party representative in Parliament for years, who constantly denounced apartheid. Opponents frequently told her to "Go back to Moscow" or even "Go back to Israel," to which she retorted: "It is not my questions that embarrass South Africa; it is your answers."

- Colin Jankelowitz, an eminent lawyer, who defended many African National Congress (ANC) members in the 1950s and 1960s, including ANC leader Govan Mbeki in a trial in Port Elizabeth.

- Joe Slovo was a long-time colleague of Nelson Mandela in the ANC and the South African Communist Party. Governmental repression forced him and his wife, Ruth First, into exile, where she was assassinated by a parcel bomb. Slovo is said to have his family roots in the Soloveitchik dynasty.

However, most Jewish establishments and Jews remained primarily focused on internal Jewish communal issues rather than addressing the apartheid and it really was not until 1985 that the rabbinate as a whole condemned apartheid. Of course, in 1990, the Jewish community supported President DeKlerk's dismantling of apartheid, the negotiation process, and the first democratic elections in 1994. Many Jews in Cape Town have shared their shame with me of this part of their history.

There are about 70,000–75,000 Jews in South Africa today, a population that is declining. There is significant wealth and infrastructure in the community and we found multiple domestic workers in just about every home we visited. I wondered what it would be like to open conversations and learning about our societal obligations to alleviate poverty, suffering, and oppression of all people in our midst.

I was fortunate to have been invited to teach at numerous local synagogues, schools, and organizations. The first comment I received after a class I gave on labor rights and business ethics was: "You should have come twenty-five years ago!" The next comment was: "We have never heard these Jewish teachings." To be sure, there have been great rabbis in South Africa, but similar to the trend in the United States, the focus of the observant communities has continued to minimize the importance of social justice, civic engagement, and collective responsibility.

Jewish communities around the world are missing opportunities to show moral leadership on crucial local and national issues because rabbinic leadership is often focused on maintaining ritual commitment and not in inspiring public leadership, ethics, and social responsibility. In Cape Town, a city much safer than Johannesburg, Ohr Somayach and Chabad are growing as they promote strict ritual observance, while the Modern Orthodox leadership and community remains very small.

I cannot help but wonder how much greater of a role the Jewish people could have had in preventing the harms of apartheid had they still viewed themselves as minorities and not merely as "whites" or if they viewed fighting injustice and oppression as a Torah mandate. How can we ensure that religious leaders around the world charge their communities beyond their comfort zones to intervene at the most morally precarious times?

It is always easier to critique from the outside. Most religious Jews in America, after all, were pretty removed from the civil rights movement in the 1960s. The situation in South Africa was perilous, as the entire nation was stained with apartheid, not just a region.

While South Africa was part of the British Empire during World War II, many Afrikaners (the Dutch Boers) sympathized with the Nazis, which created an atmosphere of fear. In the post-1945 era, the Cold War began to dominate the political field. In South Africa, anti-communism was enjoined with support of colonialism and apartheid. South Africa legislation institutionalized apartheid, especially after 1948: laws banned marriage or extra-marital sex between races, defined people by race, forced blacks and other races to live in separate areas (Bantustans), required blacks to carry identification (the Pass Laws), and jailed nonwhite people if they were found outside their assigned place of residence. The Communist Suppression Act of 1950 deemed any activity that opposed apartheid to be communist, and thus all opposition was banned.

The South African government maximized its propaganda as well, backed up with wealth and military might. It raised fears that the end of apartheid would lead to a bloodbath of communism and tribal war, enlisting the help of Zulu Chief Buthelezi against the ANC, most of whose members (including Mandela) were members of the Xhosa tribe. For years, many Western nations were reluctant to criticize South Africa for Cold War considerations. To many in the Jewish community, especially after 1967, opposition to apartheid meant an alliance with communists and anti-colonial forces who in turn were increasingly antagonistic toward Israel. The "lesser of two evils" predominated.

One legal career illustrates this philosophy. Percy Yutar, the son of Lithuanian immigrants, became a lawyer, but due to discrimination had to slowly move up the legal ladder until he eventually became a prosecutor in the Transvaal. When Nelson Mandela was seized in the government raid on ANC headquarters, Yutar was appointed as the prosecutor for the 1964 Rivonia trial, which resulted in the convictions and lifetime prison terms for Nelson Mandela and other ANC leaders for crimes against the apartheid state. Yutar was an enthusiastic prosecutor, calling Mandela and others communist stooges. In retrospect, many see his vigorous prosecution as a way to establish his credentials as a loyal South African, as opposed to several of Mandela's codefendants who were Jewish (notably, Denis Goldberg).

After twenty-seven years in prison, Nelson Mandela became the President and national hero. In spite of the brutal repression he had endured, Mandela chose not to extract revenge from his political foes. His Truth and Reconciliation Commission, which allowed apartheid agents to confess their crimes in exchange for amnesty, exemplified his approach. In his book, *Long Walk to Freedom*, reflecting on South Africa's Jewish community, he writes about the Jews: "I have found Jews to be more broad-minded than most whites on issues of race and politics, perhaps because they themselves have historically been victims of prejudice." While he acknowledges communists and anti-colonialists as allies, and does not agree with policies of the current Israeli government, Mandela expressed support for the existence of a secure Israel in 1990. In 1995, as President, he invited his former legal nemesis Yutar to lunch. To his credit, Yutar acknowledged his past error and praised Mandela.

In South Africa, we were too late to act, but now is the time to deal with global problems. The Torah calls upon us to transform our religious fervor into social activism, standing tall and proud with the oppressed, wherever they may be.

If we are a community of prayer, then we must ensure our prayer works as a subversive force that inspires us to change society. "Prayer is meaningless unless it is subversive, unless it seeks to overthrow and to ruin the pyramids of callousness, hatred, opportunism, falsehoods. The liturgical movement must become a revolutionary movement, seeking to overthrow the forces that continue to destroy the promise, the hope, the vision" (Heschel, *On Prayer, Moral Grandeur and Spiritual Audacity*, 257–267).

Today, South Africa is plagued with violence, H IV, and poverty. For example, the South African Department of Health Study estimated that in 2010, among pregnant women age 15–49 years, more than 30 percent had H IV. While this level has reached a plateau (the government was slow to acknowledge the situation), this remains an enormous problem. Preliminary results from a U N ICE F report indicate that more than half of South Africa's children live in poverty, and a quarter (five million) have H IV. Fully two-thirds of all child deaths could be prevented with improved primary care. South Africa has the highest rate of violence against women of any nation in the world not at war where a woman is raped every twenty-six seconds and one in four men abuses his wife.

Two decades ago, de Klerk partnered with then-African National Congress leader Nelson Mandela to end the notorious system of racial separation known as apartheid. De Klerk said in an interview held about twenty years later: "Fact is that in South Africa, transition is taking its time. I'm convinced it's a solid democracy and it will remain so, but it's not a healthy democracy . . . It is practical policies which have failed to bring a better life to the masses, which led to the enrichment only of the few, also amongst the new black elite. The middle class is growing fast, but somehow or another, the quality of service delivery had deteriorated substantially. Education has actually moved some steps backwards." Unemployment remains very high, with a rate of 50 percent among blacks between ages 18 and 34.

The Jewish community in South Africa must play a crucial role to address the local suffering. More than 80 percent of the South African Jewish community consider themselves Orthodox, an astounding number. This religious community has a tremendous opportunity to create a real *Kiddush Hashem* as the globe continues to watch how the South African drama evolves in the coming years. There are partners in Israel and the United States to help support the South African Jewish leadership in this struggle.

□

SURVIVORS GUILT AFTER THE FLOOD: SHAME AND HEALING

THE FLOOD HAS ENDED. THE WATERS HAVE dried up. The survivors completed their *aveilut* (year of mourning) for all those who passed and leave the ark to attempt to rebuild the world. Noah, the captain and leader, exits and – what does he do? He gets drunk. In fact, he gets so drunk that his sons find him unclothed in his tent. Cham enters the tent, looks at his father naked and then tells his brothers, Shem and Yafet, who walk in backwards, without looking, and virtuously cover their father with a blanket.

From a psychological perspective, how do we understand these different reactions to catastrophe and its aftermath?

Noah is a survivor; having witnessed the destruction of all he knew, he has profound survivor's guilt. He is broken, so he drinks, and his sons react differently to his moment of vulnerability. Cham is able to see his father's pain and so he is willing to look upon the results of that pain. Shem and Yafet, on the other hand, are unable to accept seeing their father in this condition, so they refuse to. Cham is a model for us, as he is courageous enough to see his father as he truly is at that moment – pained, ashamed, and naked. Where he goes wrong is in telling his brothers about it. He fails to help, yet sometimes we may hurt someone less by staring at her scar than by looking away.

At some point, we must realize that our parents are fallible and flawed, like all humans. We must also come to realize this about all of our role models, friends, and family members. We cannot hold close ones or heroes up as perfect; if we do, we inevitably become disappointed when we discover their imperfections, and risk becoming cruel and hurting them because we have been unwilling to see their humanity and vulnerability from the start, treating them as liars, as if they had broken promises they never made, falsely presenting themselves as perfect when in fact we were the only ones who thought them so.

This is what happens to Noah: With the flood and the destruction of the entire world, he finally discovers that the world was not a perfect place. Unlike his brothers, Cham follows this path and sees the imperfections in his father and is able to face this loss of innocence and the harsh truth that his father is, in the end, human. It takes courage to deal with this loss with equanimity, as it amounts to a loss of security. Furthermore, in looking upon his father's nakedness, Cham showed that he was trying to to understand the trauma that must have led to this turn of events. Shem and Yafet may be more "modest" than Cham, but in covering Noah and avoiding looking at him, they show they prefer to avoid understanding their fellow's trauma, hide from the truth, and cover up that which they cannot deal with.

At the end of this story, Cham is cursed by his father. I would suggest that he is not cursed metaphysically but practically and psychologically, in that he must now live with the pain of seeing the nakedness of his father and the cruelty of the world that led to it. The blindfold has been taken off.

Rabbi Daniel Reifman suggests that Noah gets naked because he believes he is like Adam (the first person who lived in the Garden of Eden without clothes), and that he is the new first man of the world. Cham's recognition of his nudity reminds him that he cannot (and humanity can never) return to that state of pure spiritual bliss or a life without feeling shame.

People often exploit another's vulnerability in order to shame them. In Franz Kafka's "Hunger Artist," a man starves himself and locks himself in a cage. Others pay to walk by and stare, getting pleasure from observing him. Kafka teaches that a sick part of human nature causes us to enjoy, on some level, seeing the abasement of others. Similarly, the press or gossip often takes private information and makes it public, exposing someone's shame and transferring ownership of an individual's image to the public. A contemporary scholar on the emotion of shame, Gershen Kaufman, writes: "Shame is the most disturbing experience individuals ever have about themselves; no other emotion feels more deeply disturbing because in the moment of shame the self feels wounded from within." As a result, shame can isolate the individual. Legal scholar Martha Nussbaum writes: "Shame involves the realization that one is weak and inadequate in some ways in which one expects oneself to be adequate. Its reflex is to hide from the eyes of those who will see one's deficiency, to cover it up." One example of shame is being seen when we do not know we are being observed. We may sing in the shower, and not know that someone outside can hear us, and then we discover that we were heard. We may have been comfortable with our singing alone, but ashamed that we were not in control of who heard us.

Shame should be distinguished from guilt. The root of the word "shame" is actually thought to derive from a word meaning "to cover." Covering oneself, literally or figuratively, is a natural expression of shame. Distinguishing between shame and guilt, researchers Fossum and Mason write in *Facing Shame* that "While guilt is a painful feeling of regret and responsibility for one's actions, shame is a painful feeling about oneself as a person." Shame is so painful because it's not external; rather it's about one's core personhood, the value of one's self.

Aaron Hass, an academic at California State University, writes: "An even more insidious and self-destructive element than guilt has also been observed in survivors of the Holocaust. One can balance guilt with restitution. Shame, however, results in a certain withdrawal, in a belief that one is not worth consideration. For the survivor who experiences shame, there is a further disbarment from humanity."

In shame, people feel exposed in their pain. We must learn to look while we simultaneously honor. If the Rabbis teach that to shame another is akin to murder, then to honor the vulnerable is to save a life.

To be sure, Jewish law demands the right to privacy. Rabbi Norman Lamm explains this well: "Unauthorized disclosure, whether the original information was received by complete consent or by illegal intrusion, whether ethically or unethically, remains prohibited by the Halakha." He continues: "The Halakha insists upon the responsibility of each individual not to put himself into a position where he can pry into his neighbor's personal domain, and this responsibility can be enforced by the courts . . . the Halakha comprises more than civil law; it includes a sublime moral code. And its legal limit on voyeurism is matched by its ethical curb on the citizen's potential exhibitionism. It regards privacy not only as a legal right but also as a moral duty. We are bidden to protect our own privacy from the eyes and ears of our neighbors."

The right to privacy is always honored, yet some realities that were meant to be private can become exposed to us. When the pain of another becomes revealed to us, we cannot hide from it. We can only look, support, and honor the dignity of the other.

Shem and Yafet teach us that there are some things we do not look at. Cham teaches us that it is precisely some of these same things that we must look at. They teach us that we must cover the vulnerable; he teaches us that we must first look at them and recognize their humanity and their trauma.

In addition to becoming more sensitive about how we talk about others' vulnerabilities, we should become more willing to share our vulnerabilities with those we care about. If we, like Noah, do not, they will inevitably become exposed at times and ways we do not want.

The Rabbis teach that the flood occurred because the generation no longer had any shame for their theft or promiscuity: "There is always hope for the man who is capable of being ashamed" (*Nedarim* 20a). And that shame should not only be socially induced but also come from our conscience and awareness of God's presence: "There is a great difference between the man who feels shame in his soul and the man who is ashamed only before his fellow man" (*Taanit* 15a).

A story is told of Rav Yisrael Salanter. On Shabbat, Rabbi Yisrael was stuck in Kovno. The whole town offered to house him, but he decided to stay with a childless baker, as that way he would not take another's food portion on Shabbat. This baker, while observant, was no scholar. As he welcomed the honored rabbi into his house, he exclaimed to his wife: "The challahs are not covered! Why must I always remind you to cover the challahs?" The embarrassed wife, recognizing the rabbi, began to weep as she quickly covered the challahs. When the baker asked Rav Yisrael to honor them by reciting the Kiddush, the rabbi inquired: "Can you tell me why we cover the challahs?" "I know that answer," the baker replied. "Even a small child knows that. If at the table there are a variety of foods, then we say the first blessing over the bread, and then we do not have to make another blessing. However, on Shabbat night, the first blessing must be over the wine. We must not shame the challah, as it expects the first blessing, so we must cover it over until we have blessed the wine." Rav Salanter gave the baker a sharp rebuke. "Why do you not hear what your mouth speaks?" he asked. "Do you not think that our Jewish tradition understands that a challah has no feelings and cannot be embarrassed? You must understand that our laws seek to sensitize us to the human feelings: our friends, our neighbors, and – above all – our wives!"

Here, once again, is a primary purpose of Jewish ritual – to teach us over and over the sensitivity of the human emotions and the value of *kavod ha-briot* (honoring others). May we have the courage to see the true vulnerability of those we love and the sensitivity to cover them, honor them, and share ourselves with them as well. In this way, we rebuild the world and the human spirit after the flood. □

☐ PRESSING POLITICAL ISSUES IN OUR TIME

IS THE TORAH POLITICAL?
THOUGHTS ON THE NATURE
OF LANGUAGE

ONE OF THE MOST COMMON AND POLARIZ-
ing debates in America today is about the
relationship between religion and politics.
To what extent should church and state be separate? Should our religious
values and principles influence the way we participate in civil society, and
should our texts and laws inform how we vote? These questions assume that
religion and politics are completely separate entities, a notion this essay will
challenge. Is it, perhaps, that the Torah not only addresses the political but
is itself fundamentally political?

The Language of the Torah

The Rabbis of the Talmud explain that the Torah was not revealed in a perfect Divine language but in an imperfect human language, so that it could
properly be understood (*dibrah Torah k'lashon b'nei adam*), (*Sanhedrin* 64b;
Yerushalmi Shabbat 19:2). For the Rabbis, the origin of the Torah is Divine,
but when revealed in the language of humans it enters the same subjective
mind and world as ordinary language. This invariably renders perfect interpretation or textual consistency impossible. This is not a hermeneutical
problem unique to Torah. Rather, we understand in modernity that our
mystical insights and psychological depth can never adequately be captured
in language. Human experience is more profound than human language.
Our primary grasp of the Divine, albeit elusive, is experiential and beyond

the capacity of language. Rav Shimshon Raphael Hirsch explains the importance of this concept "*dibrah Torah k'lashon b'nei adam*":

> Jewish scholarship has never regarded the Bible as a textbook for physical or even abstract doctrines. In its view, the main emphasis of the Bible is always on the ethical and social structure and development of life on earth; that is, on the observance of laws through which the momentous events of our nation's history are converted from abstract truths into concrete convictions. That is why Jewish scholarship regards the Bible as speaking consistently in "human language"; the Bible does not describe things in terms of objective truths known only to God, but in terms of human understanding, which is, after all, the basis for human language and expression. (*Collected Writings* Vol. 7, p. 57)
>
> A politician knows how to speak to a crowd and engage each different faction with his message. Come and see how the voice went forth to all of Israel, to each and every one in keeping with his particular capacity to the elderly in keeping with their capacity, to young men in keeping with their capacity, to the little ones in keeping with their capacity, and to the women in keeping with their capacity. As it is said: "Moses spoke and God answered him with 'a voice that he would have been able to withstand" (Exodus Rabbah 5:9).

God is the ultimate master of language and can speak to each individual's particular language.

Baruch Spinoza argued that the Torah was political and thus it no longer had authority once the Jews lost political sovereignty. This is not the Jewish approach and we must rediscover what it means to be a religious-political people again both in the homeland and diaspora.

The Torah was given to be interpreted, to spread debate and argument over interpretation. The Rabbis, as the great interpreters of the Torah, created factions. Textual interpretation became a politically charged process. Perhaps, given the fragmented nature of the Jewish people in the twenty-first century, today's rabbinic establishments are more political than they have ever been.

While the Torah is holy and elevated, the Rabbis teach that the language of the Torah is regular human language. Thus, a philosophy of language that is true for secular language can also be true for religious language. So we may ask, what is the relationship between language and politics?

What Is Politics?

In the narrowest sense, politics is concerned with government, but in the broader sense, politics refers to power dynamics in social relationships. When humans interact, their various interests interact. Individuals attempt to influence one another so that their wants and needs will be met. This can be achieved through force, coercion, persuasion, request, or various other means. These power dynamics can be found not only in government but in academia, business, the non-profit world, and everyday social life. Rather than always being "dirty and corrupt," politics is an inevitable part of our everyday lives. It is not bad that life is political but merely the inevitable nature of existence in a world of complexity.

The Nature of Language: Is Language Political?

Scholars in linguistic anthropology, applied linguistics, and sociolinguistics have maintained that language is political. John E. Joseph has added that language and politics are dependent upon one another. Joseph states: "It is evident that the state is a creation of nature, and that man is by nature a political animal" (*Language and Politics*, 2). Joseph believes that language originated from the expression of human needs and the desire to create friends and allies to achieve one's goals. In addition, the birth of language was also the birth of politics:

1. languages themselves are constructed out of practices of speech and writing, and the beliefs (or "ideologies") of those doing the speaking and writing; 2. my language is shaped by who it is that I am speaking to, and by how my relationship with them will be affected by what I say; 3. the politics of identity shapes how we interpret what people say to us, so much so as to be a prime factor in our deciding on the truth value of their utterances.

Joseph explains that politics occurs wherever there is an unequal distribution of power and where human behaviors are altered by the present power dynamics. He suggests that we use language to navigate our social existence within a political world, based on these five dimensions of relationship between language and politics:

- The politics of different ways of speaking
- The politics of talking to others
- The politics of what "the language" is

- The politics of which language to speak
- The politics of policing the language

Joseph argues that language is inherently political, as it is linked to identity, standardization, nationhood, and propaganda. Even if a speaker or writer has no political motivations per se, the utterance is still capable of being received as having political intent or meaning. When we observe applied linguistics, we can see the socio-political manifestations of language.

Jean-Louis Dessalles, a French scholar of the evolution of language, also argues that the birth of language was due to the needs of political coalitions.

> We humans speak because change profoundly modified the social organization of our ancestors. In order to survive and procreate, they found themselves needing to form coalitions of a considerable size. Language then appeared as a means for individuals to display their value as members of a coalition (*Why We Talk: The Evolutionary Origins of Language*, 331–332).

Stephen May explains that for too long, linguistics "has been preoccupied with idealist, abstracted approaches to the study of language . . . in isolation from the social and political conditions in which it is used." This neglect of historic and political factors has also afflicted the field of sociolinguistics, "despite its emphasis on the social, and of many discussions of LP [language policy] as well" (Language, Ideological Debates *Language, Ideological Debates*, 255).

In a hermeneutical act, we choose how we interpret the world, an experience, a person, or a text. This is a willed experience. Since all language is communicative, even a passive observer changes the observed. All language affects a listener and demands an interpretation. Language thus affects society as a whole through the construction of new realities.

Ludwig Wittgenstein, in his earlier years, believed that language had a purely analytical and logical nature. But his views evolved and he later argued that language was always embedded and can only be understood in relation to its context. John Austin and John Searle write of "speech acts," since language cannot be understood outside of its context. Language is not eternally true but contextual.

Friedrich Nietzsche and Michel Foucault teach that we must be a part of a process of genealogy, or analysis, to uncover the historical relationship between knowledge, truth, and power. While truth and knowledge are often presented as being of a universal and eternal nature, they are actually produced through the struggles within and between institutions and disciplines of thought. Foucault explains that we gain "power-knowledge" when we make sense of ourselves and become subjects through the acquisition of knowledge. No individual or group holds power; power is a complex flow between different groups and relationships throughout society. This dynamic set of relations change with circumstances and time. Foucault, based upon Nietzsche, explains that "the will to power" is the notion that our social rules, discourses, sets of meaning, and truths do not merely emerge naturally but are produced to support particular groups and causes. All truth is political, since it is formed through power struggles.

Whereas Martin Heidegger critiques "modernity" for forgetting the importance of being, post-modern philosophers have argued that it is language that has been forgotten. "Language" does not refer to English, Spanish, Hebrew, etc., but to the system of differences. The way we think and speak is conditioned by the particular "language" in which we dwell, the pattern of distinctions and connections that makes up our particular human experience. Language is neither objective nor commonly understood, but is subjective and tied to context and experience. In post-modernity, one is aware of the deconstructiveness of all systems of meaning and truth (i.e., the ability to understand language and truth in its context and system of power). Jacques Derrida is concerned with temporality and the effects of time on language, arguing that language is tied up in nets of identities and difference. Language can never describe the transcendental moves related to presence or absence since they are atemporal and outside the bounds of language, and anything outside of language we cannot speak about. Relational dynamics are the constitutive character of language.

In the structuralist tradition of linguistics, thinkers such as Ferdinand de Sassure and Roman Jakobson point out that language is only intelligible as part of an overarching structure. Words are signifiers that do not intrinsically point to the idea or thing being signified but are arbitrary signs that only make sense given the entire web of language.

Still another modern thinker, Noam Chomsky, teaches that there is a "Universal Grammar," the set of innate principles that serve as a foundation for all languages. However, some have misunderstood this to mean that languages are natural objects born out of mind. Chomsky meant this for the linguistic knowledge of individuals, but he has denied that it holds true for languages in general. Rather, languages are historical constructs born out of a political process.

The limitations of language can be exploited. The Sapir-Whorf hypothesis proposes that the language we speak affects the way we think. Edward Sapir describes language as an "art," and the power to shape language belongs to those most adept at foreseeing which forms will meet with approval. Psychologist Steven Pinker argues that people's thoughts are determined by the categories available by their language. Further, Quentin Skinner teaches that the human capacity is limited by our language capacity, as our language constrains our thoughts.

The Choices of "Correct Language"

Who chooses if Ebonics is correct, or if Yiddish is appropriate? Who decides if a new word makes it into the dictionary and how it becomes defined?

Erving Goffman, in "The Presentation of Self in Everyday Life," discusses how everyday social interactions, including spoken dialogues, are "theatrical performances" used to negotiate various stigmas. These "theatrical performances" of language often have direct effects on policy, enabling one faction to win.

All language has political implications. Race was not important ideologically in the 1700s, but within 300 years the discourse had turned to the idea that blacks were born to be slaves. This, of course, has had long-lasting political implications.

Aristotle argues that "man is by nature a political animal" (*Politics* I, 2). Rambam, following the reasoning of Aristotle, teaches that man is naturally a political and social being who seeks to form factions, classes, and communities (*Guide for the Perplexed* 2:40). All of our acts, not only our language, are political! Who determines which word choices are "politically correct" and which are not? It is not insignificant when we choose (or reject) language that our society tells us is not "politically correct." Whether one refers to an individual as an "illegal alien" or a "domestic worker" is a political choice that represents very different values.

Two examples can illustrate how politics affects language. Russia, from the time of ancient Rus and its communal village land (the "*mir*," which also means "peace") through the Soviet period, has been a collective society. Even today, translators find it almost impossible to adequately express the word "privacy" in Russian. On the other hand, in the United States, where individualism has often been promoted over any obligation toward social welfare, Social Security, which used to be called (accurately) an old-age pensions system, is now referred to as an "entitlement," which gives the false impression that it is a handout that an austere government has every right to cut.

George Orwell, in his seminal essay "Politics and the English Language," critiques the political use of language that seeks to conceal and not express meaning. He explains that we must learn to speak more clearly since this "is a necessary step toward political regeneration." Aware that all language is political, he admits: "Look back through this essay and for certain you will find that I have again and again committed the very faults I am protesting against." We all make word choices that conceal rather than merely express.

The Divine Engaged in "Politics"

That God is referred to in masculine in the Torah has been described as a political choice. Words inevitably have values based upon their historical usage and current connotation.

If a nation is necessarily political, then when God names and designates a nation, is God creating a political faction? Further, since the choice of an audience is a political decision, is the Torah a message only for the Jews, or for the world? Is God the ultimate Divine politician trying to persuade constituents to abandon other candidates and vote exclusively for Him? The Jewish people, through our holy scriptures, are broken up into coalitions, separations, and given unique designations. To deny the political nature to our tradition is to neglect the significance of those Divine value choices.

But Isn't There an Apolitical Torah Somewhere?

The Torah primarily addresses issues of this world and so its essence is political. To be sure, there is a spiritual and transcendental aspect to Torah as well that should not be overlooked. There are spiritual values that enable human transcendence from earthly concerns and God does, of course, have the capacity to use apolitical language. This is the primordial language that was used to create worlds. Human language, however, is a self-interested construct.

Perhaps only the rare apolitical use of human language exists within a space of love where one truly transcends oneself for another. Here, an other-interested language rather than a self-interested language is used, but this must be a very deep love-act. Ethics, justice, and politics are reserved for the public sphere since society is the primary concern of Torah. But love and care are uniquely reserved for intimate relationships. In a relationship of intimate love and care, language can have transcendental moments beyond the laden dimension of politics. This is an important part of the great miracle of human love.

Conclusion

What are the political implications of embracing language and all religion as political? The implication is that we transition from false notions of politics as solely partisan (e.g., Republican or Democrat, for or against a proposal or piece of legislation). We confuse ourselves and deceive others when we claim we are apolitical because we do not reveal our political party. Rather, as humans, our word choices engage a political process of conveying a meaning that attempts to connect with and persuade others. Even altruistic words and actions are persuasive, since politics is not only about intent, but impact. By embracing the Torah and God as a political act, we not only learn how to hold ourselves accountable for our language, we also raise the bar on the significance of our word choices. Where there is human difference, there is a need to clarify intentions. Where there is human want, there is a need to fulfill desires. Where there is human interaction, there are the politics of collaboration and competition, solidarity and combat, understanding and confusion. Onkeles claims that it is language that makes a being uniquely human. Embracing the reality that language has a political nature should inspire humility. We can remember our human limitations and how our language is self-interested and value-driven.

The Chofetz Chaim suggests that we must become so careful with our language that we perhaps should not even comment on whether we like the color of an object we observe, since we may offend a listener who owns something with this color. All language affects others within a complex web of meaning. May we learn to use this capacity wisely in our complex world.

The Torah not only must address the most pressing political issues of our time, the Torah itself is political. When we embrace the Torah's political choices, we can respond to contemporary political issues with more Jewish integrity. ▢

GUN CONTROL VS. GUN RIGHTS

URING A CLASS AT A MODERN ORTHODOX synagogue in New York City on the topic of halachic approaches to weapons, I asked the group of twenty-five people (most between 50–65 years old) how many of them owned guns. I expected one or two hands to emerge, but was astonished to find that about 50–60 percent admitted to having a gun at home. Shortly after, I learned that there is an Orthodox organization now training Orthodox Jews to use guns and to bring them to synagogue as a form of "protection." If the religious Jewish community in America has joined the consumers of guns then we must also enter into the national gun discourse.

Our Jewish perspective on the controversial issue of gun control and gun rights cannot be based only on the interpretation of the Second Amendment. Rather we must explore the sources to understand our responsibilities as Jewish Americans.

There is clearly a case to make for gun rights in Jewish law. To start, one is not culpable for killing a pursuer (*rodef*) who has intent to kill (Exodus 22:1). Some halachic authorities go further and say that the homeowner is obligated to kill the pursuer (Rambam, *Hilchot Rotzeah V'Shmirat Ha-Nefesh*, 10:11). The right to self-defense is a Jewish priority.

However, Rambam is not the only Jewish consideration on this issue. Halacha also requires that we consider practical consequences to ensure that we protect the dignity of human life. We must consider the facts of our current society. Access to weapons makes it easier to fulfill crimes of passion, suicides, and tragic accidents in the home. In 2005, for example, over 30,000 people died as a result of a firearm in the United States; suicides accounted for 55 percent of this total, while accidental gun deaths accounted for 3 percent. Many deaths could be prevented if access to a gun wasn't made so easy.

Advocates for gun control are not suggesting that we abolish the rights of gun ownership. They are merely suggesting that more precautions be put in place such as safety mechanisms, no-gun zones, a ban on big-volume magazines that allow for so many bullets to be released at once, and the enforcement of stronger background checks.

I believe this is the responsible position that Jewish law supports. With certain protections, we can work to prevent events like the January 2011 shooting of Congresswoman Giffords, the 1999 Columbine High School massacre, and countless homicides, suicides, and accidents that occur in America each year.

We know that Jewish law requires that we make our home and our property safe (even for intruders): "If you build a new house, you shall make a fence for your roof, so that you will not place blood in your house if one falls from it" (Deuteronomy 22:8). Rambam extends this to other unsafe things that one owns, such as a swimming pool or a tall stairway (*Hilchot Rotzeach* 11:1–5). A gun certainly falls into this category.

While we must address the societal demand for weapons, Jewish law reminds us that the supply of weapons is also something we must deal with. "You shall not curse the deaf, and you shall not place a stumbling block (i.e., something dangerous) before the blind; you shall fear your Gd – I am the Lord" (Leviticus 19:14). The *Shulhan Aruch* explains that we must actively seek out and destroy dangerous things in society: "And for every stumbling block that is a danger to someone's life, there is a positive commandment to remove it and to destroy it from among us and to take good caution; as it says: 'You shall guard your lives' (Deuteronomy 4:9). And if you don't remove the stumbling block that brings danger you have neglected a positive mitzvah" (*Hoshen Mishpat* 427:8). In the hands of people who are mentally unfit or untrained, guns are "stumbling blocks"; they become tools for violence against others and self-inflicted violence. Using these laws and explanations, I believe Jewish law requires us to ensure the safe supply of weapons.

Rabbi J. David Bleich, Rosh Kollel at Yeshiva University, took a firm stance: "Jewish law recognizes that indiscriminate sale of weapons cannot fail to endanger the public. The daily newspaper confirms this deep-seated distrust far more often than is necessary. As the bearers of an ageless moral code, Jews ought to be in the vanguard of those seeking to impress upon our legislators that handguns are indeed 'stumbling blocks' which must not fall into the hands of the 'blind.' Criminals do commit crimes, and it is precisely because 'morally blind' criminals are disposed to crime that Judaism teaches that it is forbidden to provide them with the tools of their trade."

The *midrash* condemns a land filled with weaponry (Genesis Rabbah 21:13). The Rabbis, commenting on the words, "God placed at the East of the Garden of Eden the Cherubim and the flaming sword," teach that, "At the East of the Garden of Eden at the very spot where stood the Cherubim with the flaming sword – there hell (Gehinnom) was created."

The Mishnah describes weapons as "shameful" things to be seen with (*Shabbat* 63a). One should be embarrassed to own a weapon, even in the case when they must.

The issue of guns is not only a domestic political issue. It is also an issue of foreign policy. Who are America and Israel morally responsible to prevent from having dangerous weapons? The Gemarah says that it is forbidden to sell weapons to any idolater and some rabbis went so far as to say that it is forbidden to sell them even weapons of defense (*Avodah Zarah* 15b). We must review American and Israeli arms-policies to ensure that we are living up to our responsibilities. Then we can truly heed the cry of the prophets, to ensure that "Nation shall not lift sword against another nation and we should no longer know war" (Michah 4:3).

In District of Columbia v. Heller, the monumental Supreme Court decision which struck down a DC ban on handguns, the logic of original intent was implemented. While the vote ended in a 5-to-4 victory for gun rights, it was oddly 9-to-0 in a victory of original intent interpretation over consequentialist interpretation. Our job as Jews is more complicated. While we are concerned with the intention of law, we are also concerned with the consequences of law. We must assess whether having fewer guns in the world leads to more death, and then we must follow our holy Torah to "choose life."

This is a complex issue that evokes strong feelings. I do not imagine I will convince Jews like those I spoke to at the New York City synagogue to sell their weapons. However, I hope that Jews will, keeping with their religious responsibility, enter the political discourse and work to make society safer while keeping the essence of the Second Amendment intact.   □

KWAME APPIAH, JEWISH EMPIRICISM, AND THE GUNS DEBATE

P HILOSOPHERS HAVE LONG DEBATED HOW knowledge is acquired. Empiricists believe in the primacy of our senses for determining human knowledge. Rationalists believe that many of our most important ideas and knowledge can be attained by methods independent of our senses and experiences, such as by intuition and deduction.

One strict empiricist was Thomas Reid (1710–1796), a Scottish philosopher whose philosophy brought him in conflict with Enlightenment philosophers such as David Hume, another Scottish philosopher of the same time period. Reid believed that our senses inevitably lead us to valid beliefs. Any belief that is contradictory to this "common sense" is false, given that common sense beliefs must be in accord with each other. He explains that every significant discovery is achieved through "patient observation, by accurate experiments, or by conclusions drawn by strict reasoning from observations and experiments, and such discoveries have always tended to refute, but not to confirm, the theories and hypotheses which ingenious men had invented" (*Essays on the Intellectual Power of Man*, 367–368).

This debate has led to fascinating, if sometimes confusing, dialogues. However, can empiricism offer practical ways to improve society today? Kwame Appiah, a philosopher at Princeton University who was raised and has studied and lectured all over the world, is one who seeks to know how fundamental progress can be achieved through translating philosophical thought into action. He has published widely in many areas of philosophy, and is keenly interested in how philosophical theory affects political thought and action.

Employing his extraordinary multi-cultural education, Appiah proposes in his lecture series Experiments in Ethics that we must have empirical backing for our philosophical theories. He explains:

Nothing is more usual than for writers, even, on moral, political, or physical subjects, to distinguish between reason and experience, and to suppose, that these species of argumentation are entirely different from each other. The former are taken for the mere result of our intellectual faculties, which, by considering a priori the nature of things . . . establish particular principles of science and philosophy. The latter are supposed to be derived entirely from sense and observation, by which we learn what has actually resulted from the operation of particular objects . . .

But notwithstanding that this distinction be thus universally received, both in the active and speculative scenes of life, I shall not scruple to pronounce, that it is, at bottom, erroneous, at least, superficial . . . It is experience which is ultimately the foundation of our inference and conclusion (*Experiments in Ethics*, 10).

Appiah goes beyond the mere philosophical argument to urge an active pursuit of justice:

Morality is practical. In the end it is about what to do and what to feel; how to respond to our own and the world's demands. And to apply norms, we must understand the empirical contexts in which we are applying them. No one denies that applying norms, you will need to know what, as an empirical matter, the effects of what you do will be on others, as an empirical matter, the effects of what you do will be on others (*Experiments in Ethics*, 22).

Jewish thinkers have also examined this issue. Rambam explains the importance of the quest for truth and how we must alter our positions in line with new observations. Significantly, he noted that Aristotle had been accepted over the old beliefs of Jewish sages on an astronomical question: "It is quite right that our Sages have abandoned their own theory: for speculative matters every one treats according to the results of his own study, and everyone accepts that which appears to him established by proof" (*Guide for the Perplexed* 2:8).

Rambam further explains: "Similarly it is not proper to abandon matters of reason that have already been verified by proofs . . . A man should never cast his reason behind him, for the eyes are set in front, not in back . . ." (*Letter on Astrology*).

Rav Moshe Feinstein, the twentieth century Jewish legal authority, explained that many aspects of Jewish law can be affected by contemporary science: "We thus see that unless we are compelled otherwise, we should assume that matters that are dependent on nature should be based on the assessment of the Rabbis of every given time" (*Even Ha-Ezer*, 2:3). On many matters we must apply contemporary research to apply timeless values in the real world. Other times, we break beyond the academies to the populace to "go out and see" (*puk hazi*) what is being done.

The Rabbis had the humility to acknowledge new findings and the importance of legal evolution:

> "Six things heal the sick"– and the Talmud explains each one. You must first of all know that the healing practices that we do now is not the same as the healing practices that the earlier authorities practiced. And there were certain matters that the earlier authorities knew regarding properties of foods that we do not know now. And nowadays we cannot rely on those [early] healing practices, because we do not know how to perform the practice effectively . . . (*Responsa of the Geonim*, Harkavi, 394).

In the 1950s, Israeli Chief Rabbi Yitzhak HaLevi Herzog lamented that, as science progressed and added to our knowledge, "we bury our heads in the sand" when science comes in contact with the Torah: "It is imperative that we cultivate from within our holy *yeshivot* – from the geniuses among them – people to be men of science of every field, and thus we will not be dependent on others regarding matters of physiology, chemistry, electricity, and all matters that touch upon our holy Torah."

For example, there is currently a debate concerning various gun control provisions, including a restoration of the assault weapons and high-capacity magazine ban that had been in place from 1994 to 2004. Consider the following facts from contemporary researchers:

- 15 of the 25 worst mass shootings during the past half century occurred in the United States
- 5 of the 11 deadliest shootings in America occurred from 2007 onward [after the Assault Weapons Ban was allowed to expire]
- States with the strictest gun control laws have the fewest deaths by firearms

- The assassin who shot Representative Gabrielle Giffords fired 31 shots in 15 seconds due to his large magazine clip (33 rounds). Only when he stopped to reload was he subdued. Had he not had access to the large clip, he would have had to reload much earlier, and more people would have survived.
- All 26 victims of the December 2012 Newtown, CT, mass killings were killed by a semi-automatic rifle with a high-capacity magazine.

In contrast, gun control opponents have flooded the Internet with claims that gun control does not work, but offer vague denunciations of old computer games, exhortations to arm even more citizens, and offer no explanation for why high-capacity magazines are necessary for hunting or target practice. There are moral truths that do not require empirical investigation to be verified, and every law of course cannot simply be overturned based upon new scientific findings. However, much of the application of those moral truths requires empirical tests to ensure they achieve the moral goal. For example, Jewish law wishes to save innocent life. In the debate between gun control and gun rights, the data clearly demonstrate why increased gun control will achieve this goal. Jewish law seeks to balance the value of self-defense with the value of saving life. The statistics help us to identify what Jewish law must endorse. A more complete explanation of the Jewish approach to gun rights and gun control is needed.

This is just one example. If we truly care about honoring our core Jewish values then we must ensure our principles have the correct impact. To do so, we must embrace not only the descriptive but also the prescriptive, not only the "is" but also the "ought." Rather than getting caught up in stubborn ideologies or partisan politics we must have the humility and courage to embrace empirical research and apply evidence within our argumentation.

There are countless Jewish moral dilemmas posed in the twenty-first century that require constant reassessment of contemporary research and the facts on the ground. Empirical research must be applied, in the most pressing way, to end-of-life issues and other pressing moral dilemmas. The Torah is actualized when our timeless Jewish values are kept alive and relevant by acknowledging and wrestling with new realities in the most intellectually honest and critical ways. □

WHY SHOULD WE CARE ABOUT THE RELIGIOUS VIEWS OF OUR CANDIDATES?

URING THE PRESIDENTIAL RACE OF 2012, once again the role of religion in politics re-emerged as a common tension that cannot be dismissed. American Jews have often feared bringing religion into the political discourse out of fear of anti-Semitism, but this concern has hopefully lessened since Senator Joseph Lieberman was a serious Vice Presidential candidate while being open about his traditional Jewish practices and perspectives. In our commitment to build a just society, we have an imperative to ask questions about the religious views of our politicians.

A current study in the *International Journal for the Psychology of Religion* found that there is no difference between the ethical behavior of religious believers and nonbelievers; rather, the key difference was the type of, and approach to, religious belief. For example, they found that those who believed in a loving, compassionate god were more likely to cheat than those who believed in an angry, punitive one. Religious beliefs matter in moral decision-making.

I would propose that we use a positive, rather than a negative, test for analyzing the religious beliefs of our leaders. Rather than not voting for someone who is not a part of our religious sect or who does not hold our particular ideology, we must vote for someone, regardless of their sect, who holds the core values that we cherish most. Religious values should be critically considered just as we consider good judgment and policy experience. By taking an affirmative approach, we can work to remove religion as a source of divisiveness and strive to include it as a source of inspiration, direction, and unity.

The full range of Christian American life was represented in 2012's crop of candidates. Bachmann is an Evangelical Lutheran, Perry is a Methodist, Herman Cain and Ron Paul are Baptists, Newt Gingrich is (now) a Catholic, and Mitt Romney and Jon Huntsman are Mormons. General national acceptance of this diversity is a significant change from the days when people wouldn't vote for Kennedy, the first Catholic President, because of his religion. Even four years ago, forty percent of voters said that they would not vote for a Mormon president and Romney was a serious candidate.

The differences between the ideologies of politicians matter. We learn that our forefathers had very different relationships with God (our prayer liturgy differentiates between *Elokei Avraham*, *Elokei Yitzhak*, and *Elokei Yaakov*), and those relationships produced very different types of ethical personalities.

Republican presidential candidate Rick Perry held an all-day Christian prayer event where he "called on Jesus to bless and guide the nation's military and political leaders and those who cannot see the light in the midst of all the darkness." He later shared a thought, "In every person's heart, in every person's soul, there is a hole that could be filled by the Lord Jesus Christ." In a conversation about his faith, he referred to evolution as "a theory out there." To what extent should Perry's public pronouncements of faith over science and the promotion of his own faith legitimately affect our judgment of his fitness as a politician one way or another?

Michele Bachmann, another former aspirant for nomination as the Republican Party's candidate for President, was asked what she meant when she said that the Bible necessitates that she be submissive to her husband, and the crowd booed the question. For many, probing about the specifics of religious beliefs and practices seems to be strangely taboo. We, as a country, should be able to hold a sophisticated discourse about religion without descending into bigotry.

Ignoring the religious views of our politicians only impoverishes the conversation. Our choices of leadership are made with more nuances if we allow theology a place at the table and it can help ensure more honest and passionate deliberation. When we debate politics, we cannot check our moral and spiritual convictions at the door, nor can we expect politicians to do so.

For my part, I want to know that those leading our country feel humble before the Divine, see God in all people on the planet, value spiritual transcendence over personal materialistic gain, and believe that at the end of their lives they will be held accountable for their actions. I also want to know how their particular beliefs influence their economic and social policies.

I remain confident that religion is one of the most important forces in the world and that religion still offers more hope for a healed world than any other institution in existence today. Religious adherents in America, at their worst, perpetuate dogmatic ignorance, religious absolutism, intolerance, and social exclusivism. But at its best, religion unites, challenges, and inspires.

While the great economic superpowers of the world are only a few hundred years old, Islam, for example, is 1,500 years old; Christianity, 2,000; and Judaism, 4,000. All ancient faiths of the world offer wisdom that economics and politics can't provide on their own.

Religion, at its best, shapes our community of shared responsibility. The Talmud teaches that one must pray only where there are windows (*Berachot* 31a). Our religious lives must connect to the outside world – religion fails when it is reserved merely for the sanctuary. So we must not only publicly advocate for the value of religion but for good religion that furthers love, tolerance, and service.

What are some Jewish questions that we ask of our politicians? When we ignore the religious beliefs, practices, and communities of our leaders, we abandon our hope in the possibility of uniting our diverse country while honoring the distinct differences among us and of intertwining the wisdom of our ancestors with the wisdom of our founding fathers.

It matters to me how the President of the United States makes decisions. I want to know how a politician explains theodicy and conceptualizes the problem of evil. I want to know whether they believe God is an activist or pacifist, and what they believe about the source and limits of human freedom and responsibility. I want to know how each candidate interprets and is guided by the Scriptures on issues of reward and punishment.

There are questions we should all be grappling with: Are we a "Christian nation?" Can an observant Jew or committed Muslim or absolute atheist lead this country? How do particular religious values impact political policy?

Sociologists Paul Froese and Christopher Bader found that 95 percent of Americans believe in God but the god that is believed in varies greatly. About 28 percent believe in an authoritative god, who is engaged in the world but is judgmental, whereas about 22 percent believe in an engaged but benevolent god. About 24 percent believe in a "distant" god that is removed from the day-to-day happenings of the world, while 21 percent believe in a god that keeps close track of every misstep and sin.

A 2010 Gallup Poll shows that the number of Americans who believe that religion "can answer all or most of today's problems" fell from 82 percent to 58 percent, and that religion "is old-fashioned and out of date" leaped from 7 percent to 28 percent. If this is true, then these folks have a lot of fair questions to ask politicians who are guided by different religious values. The various ways that Americans view God can have real-world practical implications, thus it is important for us to probe into the theology of our candidates since this knowledge may be deeply telling of their likely behavior in office. After all, when religion works, it penetrates the mind, body, and soul. These are the very faculties that are employed when a President decides whether our country is going to war, whether welfare should be granted, whether the death penalty should be allowed, and what values are prioritized in our national marketplace of ideas. □

PURIM: THE IMPORTANCE OF DEMOCRACY

I N 2011, LIBYAN DICTATOR MUAMMAR el-Qaddafi's troops were marching toward Benghazi, the unofficial capital of the Libyan rebels. Qaddafi was calling the rebels "rats," and a 10,000-person massacre seemed inevitable. But on Purim itself, in Libya (historically part of the Persian Empire), NATO made the decision to intervene, saving the pro-democracy rebels. "*Nahafoch hu*" – the opposite of the tyrant's plan occurred. Fortunately, Purim has been a bad time for tyrants in modern as well as ancient times.

Yet strangely there are still some rabbis that question whether democracy is the best alternative to tyranny. Rabbi Elyakim Levanon of Elon Moreh in Israel said: "Rabbis aren't bound by democracy's restrictions." He stated that the democratic process "distorts reality," because it creates a false middle ground of compromise. To Rabbi Levanon, this is why rabbis are committed to the uncompromising "absolute truth" of Torah, and are not committed to democracy.

In the Book of Esther, we learn that the lives of tens of thousands of Jews were at risk in the Persian Empire because the whims of King Ahasuerus and his minister Haman almost led to our destruction. What we learn from the Megillah is the danger of unchecked power, as in any system of absolute dictatorship the welfare of the masses is subject to the whims of one person.

A dictatorship may appear to work out on occasion. Ahasuerus's predecessor, Cyrus the Great, was a virtuous leader for his time, allowing the Jews to return to Israel, among other displaced peoples who were returned to their lands. However, because the Persian emperor was considered the prime deity, allegiance to the capable Cyrus was then transferred to his successor, the capricious Ahasuerus. Together with the malicious Haman, Ahasuerus emerges in the Purim story as an unchecked power that almost led to our destruction. In the long run, dictatorship never works, because the masses are subject to the whims of a few. There is no good alternative to a responsible democracy.

Contrary to Rabbi Levanon's model – that we cannot support democracy since we must only be committed to an "absolute truth" – is the Talmudic model, which demonstrates a discourse of argument, diversity, and collaboration.

In the democratic process of the Talmud, the Rabbis held a very strong belief in the value of dissenting opinions. The *Mishnah* asks, "Why do we mention an individual view along with the majority (accepted position) unnecessarily?" One answer is, "That if a first person says, 'so I have a tradition,' a second will say to him, 'You (first person) heard it as the opinion of so-and-so (an earlier third person)'" (*Eduyot* 1:6). The position will be eliminated based upon his historical dismissal. However, there is another reason given: "That a court may approve an individual view and rely on him" (1:5). The first explanation suggests that we preserve minority positions to set a precedent for their complete rejection in the future. However, the other opinion suggests that we preserve minority positions in order that future generations can be aware of them and rely on them. The latter opinion suggests a Talmudic democratic process, as the majority position is chosen but the minority position is still of great value.

Still another Talmudic position suggests that the unaccepted minority position is also true: "These positions and those positions are (both) the words of the living God" (*Eruvin* 13b). Yet even more than valuing truth, the Rabbis value peace. In a cosmic battle between shalom (peace) and *emet* (truth), peace struck truth down to the earth (*Genesis Rabbah*). The Rabbis teach via metaphor that the value of peace usually trumps the value of truth.

Rav Kook explains that a society of peace is only possible when the foundation is one of argument. Moses was the greatest leader, yet even he did not rule alone; he appointed a Council of seventy that evolved into the Sanhedrin – with its spirit of argumentation, representatives from every city, and local as well as national councils – which was eventually instrumental for the Talmud. There is an ethos of democracy and representative government underlying the foundations of Talmud. While dictators can carry out massacres on a whim, the Jewish idea is that one execution in seventy years evinces a "bloody court." Only where there is collective engagement in policy can there be a strong enough foundation for the good and just society.   □

MAJORITARIANISM, ECONOMIC INEQUALITY, AND REPUBLICANISM

D EMOCRACY HAS DEEP ROOTS; HOWEVER, the modern secular version of democracy has some liabilities. One primary danger is majoritarianism, where all decisions are made by the majority, regardless of its effect on people. Thus, in a majoritarian system, major laws can pass even if only 51 percent support a law and 49 percent strenuously object, without regard for whose rights may be infringed. Minorities (such as the Tamils in Sri Lanka, the Catholics in Northern Ireland, and the secularists and Christians in Egypt) would be particularly vulnerable in this type of system.

The political scientist Arendt Lijphart offers a blistering critique of majoritarianism. He distrusts "straightforward majority rule in which both majority and minority would simply promise to behave moderately," adding: "This is a primitive solution to ethnic tensions and extremism, and it is naïve to expect minorities condemned to permanent opposition to remain loyal, moderate, and constructive."

Instead, Lijphart advocates for "consociationalism" to provide universal participation within a society. In heterogeneous societies, it is essential for 1) power to be shared, and 2) group autonomy: "Power sharing denotes the participation of representatives of all significant communal groups in political decision making, especially at the executive level; group autonomy means that these groups have authority to run their own internal affairs, especially in the areas of education and culture." These two core principles comprise "consociational" democracy. The Talmudic system, as we have seen, shows respect for minority opinions through procedural legitimacy (legal respect) and through treasuring minority opinions (attitudinal respect), and is not merely dismissive. Conversely, democracy today runs a risk of majoritarianism.

It might be a stretch to say the Talmudic model is consociational. However, the Talmud definitely takes steps away from majoritarianism and toward consociationalism. The idea of procedural legitimacy, with "participation of representatives of all significant communal groups," is hinted at in the Talmud's requirement to include minority opinions. This inclusion ensures that majorities cannot simply ignore minorities forever. Second, the idea of representation by one's "own community" is suggested in the Sanhedrin's inclusion of a representative from each community. The point is that good intentions are not enough; to believe that intentions are sufficient is "naïve." Rather, respect for minorities must be institutionalized (albeit in their own way) in consociationalism and the Talmud.

To be sure, the Torah demands that we reject perversions of justice even within a democracy: "Do not be a follower of the majority for evil; and do not respond to a grievance by yielding to the majority to pervert (the law)" (Exodus 23:2). We must engage in civil disobedience when society goes astray; however, society ultimately must have procedural legitimacy and the rule of law, as espoused by Max Weber's secular concept of rational legal authority. In a commentary on the previous biblical verse, the Rabbis promote some level of conformity to the majority (where the majority rules by procedural legitimacy): "Follow the majority! If the majority rules 'impure,' it is impure; if the majority rules 'pure,' it is pure" (Midrash Psalms 12). Civil disobedience, on the other hand, is a protest against the seemingly unfair and arbitrary measures that lack procedural legitimacy. Civil disobedience has deep Jewish roots from Abraham protesting God's decision to destroy Sodom to the Civil Rights and Soviet Jewry movements.

On an individual level, freedom is attained through spiritual means (*Pirke Avot* 6:2), but on a collective level, freedom is attained through political compromise. While the personal religious realm is one of ideals, the public political realm is one of pragmatics, where the perfect is the enemy of the good. Pragmatism and compromise are necessary to ensure that things get done. The Midrash teaches that there is the heavenly Jerusalem (an ideal of ideals) and the earthly Jerusalem (embedded in messy difficult discussions). Being a modern Jew requires that we balance our most idealistic commitments with the need to create change in a complex, ambiguous world.

We must always remain committed to procedural legitimacy, because the ideals we hold must be enacted in a valid manner, with complications and compromise.

Democracy is not perfect, but it is the best model we have for navigating a messy human society in modern times. The right to live with freedom is rooted in the Torah itself: "Thou shall proclaim liberty throughout the land to all the inhabitants thereof" (Leviticus 25:10). This passage concerns the *Yovel* laws (jubilee year). However, while democracy ensures that everyone has equal civil and political rights, it makes no assurance for economic rights, and economic inequality results. Thus, everyone can vote and run for office, but they are not constitutionally guaranteed an economic livelihood to support their families. To ensure such a guarantee, something else is needed: government health care, soup kitchens, and other social services. The Torah has this unity: "liberty" refers not only to political liberty, but also to economic liberty from landlessness and indebtedness.

Columbia University Professor Alfred Stepan, a leading political scientist on democratization, has contrasted "democratic transition" with "democratic consolidation." Democratic transition involves the replacement of dictatorship with a polity that fulfills all formal characteristics of democracy ("free and contested elections"). But after democratic transition, democratic consolidation is still necessary to ensure that democracies are "the only game in town." Once democratic consolidation has occurred, "the behavior of the newly elected government that has emerged from the democratic transition is no longer dominated by the problem of how to avoid democratic breakdown."

Professor Stepan lists "economic society" as one necessary supporting condition for democratic consolidation: "Modern consolidated democracies require a set of sociopolitically crafted and accepted norms, institutions and regulations – what we call 'economic society' – that mediate between the state and the market." He goes on to say that "even the best of markets experience 'market failures' that must be corrected if the market is to function well. No less an advocate of the 'invisible hand' than Adam Smith acknowledged that the state is necessary to perform certain functions."

Professor Stepan then quotes Smith's assertion that government has "the duty of protecting, as far as possible, every member of society from the injustice or oppression of every other member of it, or the duty of establishing an exact administration of justice." Here we see Professor Stepan echoing the Torah's double meaning of "proclaiming freedom." For example, the creation of a permanent and hereditary slave underclass inhibits democratic consolidation, even if some slaves might achieve a skilled job, or if selective emancipation is possible. While freedom in its formal characteristics might refer only to political liberties, freedom can only be "consolidated" with economic liberties (or "economic society") as well. The Yovel laws can count as part of the governmental consolidation of economic society, in that they "protect . . . every member of society from injustice."

From a Jewish perspective, we know that even more than granting rights, the Torah gives us obligations. Maintaining a free and just society is not easy and requires the effort of all. In addition, even when the democracy is not in a Jewish state, we are called upon to support the government: "Seek the peace of the city to which I have exiled you and pray for it to God, for through its peace will you have peace" (Jeremiah 29:7). Furthermore, the state protects us: Rabbi Hanina, the deputy Cohen Gadol, says, "Pray for the welfare of the government, because if people did not fear it, a person would swallow one's fellow alive" (*Pirke Avot* 3:2). This is why we are bound by the laws of the land via Shmuel's mandate of "*dina d'malchuta dina*," the law of the country is law (*Bava Kamma* 113a).

This is another important critique of democracy: republicanism. It is not enough for everyone to vote for policies that specifically benefit them. There must also be some spirit of patriotism and community, as in John F. Kennedy's "Ask not *what your country* can do for you – ask what you can do for your country." The great Harvard Professor John Rawls taught the "Veil of Ignorance," in which a hypothetical citizenry votes on the laws in their society, *without* knowing where they will be in society – rich, poor, strong, weak, etc. This forces people to consider the general good instead of their own specific interests. Along these lines, Adam Smith cites the government's "duty of erecting and maintaining certain public works and public institutions which it can never be in the interest of any individual, or small number of individuals, to erect and maintain; because the profit could never repay the expense to any individual or small number of individuals, though it may frequently do much more than repay it to a great society."

When Adam Smith writes of the government's duty to erect public works, institutions, and other laws that would never be in the interest (or ability) of a single individual, he also is asking something of the government and its citizens. He is asking for the government and the people to not only vote by considering their individual interests, but to research the issues, become informed citizens, and do what is best for the polity. As the institution of *Yovel* did in ancient times, so we should do today. While Judaism does have a notion of representation (*shaliah adam k'moto*), the appointee is still expected to be knowledgeable and accountable.

Unlike Smith, some capitalist economists such as Milton Friedman have criticized democracy on the grounds of efficiency. They claim that voters are irrational and unknowledgeable, and make the government and country less efficient through their voting patterns. This criticism dates back to the earliest democracies. In *The Republic*, Plato critiques democracy through the narration of Socrates, as "a charming form of government, full of variety and disorder, and dispensing a sort of equality to equals and unequaled alike." A more recent criticism is that democracy does not provide adequate political stability, since power shifts so frequently. More cynical critics claim that democracy is merely an illusory façade masking an elite oligarchy.

On a more positive note, one of the greatest endorsements of democracy is exercising our freedom to vote at all possible opportunities. Rabbi Moshe Feinstein, in a letter written in 1984, explains that all American Jews must vote, since we must express our *hakarat hatov* (gratitude) to the leaders of the great nation we reside in. Rabbi Shmuel Kaminetsky dismissed those who doubt the impact of their individual vote, noting that recent elections have been decided by just a few hundred votes. "Therefore, I urge all members of our community to fulfill their obligation to vote for those who strengthen our nation – whether materially or spiritually."

Rabbi Ahron Solveitchik goes further in explaining our commitments to rights and obligations to ensure that we pursue justice for all in society:

> While contemporary civil law has evolved from the Torah (from the *mishpatim*, in which humanity is in the "image of God"), the Torah maintains a core distinction from civil law: whereas modern jurisprudence is completely and exclusively grounded in human rights, Torah jurisprudence is additionally founded upon the pillar of duties. In terms of human rights, *tzedek* and *mishpat* are used together (Psalms 89:15). Thus, we do not inflict an injury on others because it would violate their human rights. Their rights come first, and from this comes our duty to not harm others. This is a universal duty: When one delves into the *halakha*, one can readily see that the Torah does not make a distinction between Jews and non-Jews within the realm of *mishpat* and *tzedek*. . . . A Jew should always identify with the cause of defending the aggrieved, whatsoever the aggrieved may be, just as the concept of *tzedek* is to be applied uniformly to all humans regardless of race or creed.

To reiterate, democracy today is far from perfect. The three main challenges addressed here are majoritarianism, economic inequality, and republicanism. The Talmudic tradition helps to alleviate these problems and should be looked to for its wisdom on these matters. The first critique, majoritarianism (mob rule), is addressed by the Talmudic respect for minority opinions and the Torah requirement for procedural legitimacy. The second critique, economic inequality, is addressed by the Torah's recognition that liberty has political and economic elements. The third critique, republicanism, is addressed by the Torah's sense of duties in addition to rights.

Rabbi Joseph B. Soloveitchik explains that all people are equally a part of redeeming the world in what he uniquely coined "Judaic democracy." He points out that we all can serve God in our own way: "Every person possesses something unique, by virtue which he differs from the thou, making him or her irreplaceable and indispensable – the inner worth of a one-timely, unique, never-to-be-duplicated existence, which can and must serve God by self-involvement in the drama of redemption on all levels."

Thus, the core value of collective freedom is Judaic democracy, which compels us to grant all individuals equal opportunity to create change in society. While communism, notorious for restricting individual opportunity, did not succeed, there are still many other government models that are antithetical to the spirit of Judaic democracy. On Purim, as we reflect upon the dangers and pains the Jewish people have undergone over centuries while living in totalitarian regimes, let us remember that hundreds of millions of people are still not free today – and that they may have an opportunity to expand their freedoms. Concomitant to our search for personal spiritual liberation, we must advocate for the physical freedom of all others. What is at stake in our activism to bring freedom to all people around the world is nothing less than the dignity of humanity.

The world has undergone tremendous changes since the Arab Spring of 2011. Among the countries with revolutionary fervor causing instability and turmoil were Egypt, Tunisia, Libya, Yemen, and Syria. The year 2011 may actually have been one of the great revolutionary years in modern history. Political commentators have reached back to the 1848 revolutions to draw comparisons, and *Time* named "The Protester" the person of the year 2011. Major protests occurred not only in the Arab World, but also in parts of Europe, North America, Asia, and Africa. No one could have expected that global governments would have changed in the ways they have. There is an opportunity for Jews today to unequivocally call for the freedom of all people and the abolition of totalitarian regimes. Living in a democracy requires all of us to engage in collective matters and to educate ourselves on most pressing contemporary issues beyond our parochial sphere. Further, we can look to our core Jewish values to educate us on the moral values needed in every democracy to value every person in addition to the system itself.

On Purim, as we learn about the dangers of tyranny, may we learn to convert our gratitude for living in modern democracy into action that helps to make others free. □

THE AMERICAN JEWISH VOTE: NOT ALL ABOUT ISRAEL

W HETHER OR NOT A CANDIDATE FOR PUB-lic office supports the state of Israel is important to American Jews, but it is not the only issue we care about.

Indeed, in 2012 it was apparent that all major Presidential candidates were pro-Israel, so American Jewish voters were able to concentrate on voting for the candidate who best embodies the principles of the Torah and the American republic.

While Jewish law does not mandate that we support one party or another, there is an imperative to vote. The positions of Rabbi Moshe Feinstein and Rabbi Shmuel Kaminetsky on the importance of American Jews voting for their leaders are presented in the previous essay.

As American Jews, we have many commitments. We must support the welfare and security of the Jewish people. We must also use our vote to promote peace and protect the vulnerable in greater society. Ignoring American domestic policy decisions impoverishes our choices and is irresponsible.

Our choices of leadership are made with greater nuance if we allow all of our concerns as American Jews a place at the table, and this will help ensure more honest and passionate deliberation. We cannot check our moral and spiritual convictions at the door of the voting booth.

American presidents have supported Israel from its inception. While we may have disagreed with these Presidents on individual issues, each has given significant aid, validity, and support in times of need. While we cannot assume this support will always be there and must always offer our unequivocal support to Israel, polls offer encouragement that the American commitment to Israel remains solid.

A Gallup poll in 2012 shows that Americans are more pro-Israel today than they've been in over twenty years. An overwhelming majority favor the strongest American support for the Jewish democratic state. Consequently, any presidential candidate will almost certainly be pro-Israel. Thus, I believe that one's primary responsibility in an upcoming election is to vote for what is best for the American people and for what promotes national and global justice.

The most pressing need to address is those suffering right before our eyes. The great twentieth century halachic authority, Rav Shlomo Zalman Auerbach, taught:

> In relation to the obligation to pay the costs of saving the life of a sick person who is in danger of dying: From the straightforward reading of *Sanhedrin* 73a, we see that one is obligated to do everything to save him, and if not, one transgresses the negative commandment: "Do not stand idly by the blood of your neighbor" (*Minhat Shlomo*, Volume 2, 86:4).

The Jewish people have moved beyond the *shtetl*, where we just relied upon righteous individuals to help those in need. Today, we know that we need government, non-profits, and individuals – in a word, the whole social system – to be engaged in relieving the poor and sick from their suffering.

This is the paramount priority we must remember when voting: Which candidate best supports the mission of the Jewish people to defend the vulnerable? Who will most effectively stop genocides, get millions of Americans back to work, reform education, and reduce crime? Which candidate throws off the responsibility of helping the poor, relegating it to the assumption that wealthy individuals will supply the need?

In an era where Americans give only one percent of income to charitable causes, we cannot naively hope for the grace of individuals. Ensuring the welfare of the vulnerable must be supported and enforced.

Our faith must inform how we vote. As Rabbi Abraham Joshua Heschel argued, "We affirm the principle of separation of church and state. We reject the separation of religion and the human situation." In the end, the core message of the Bible is that the Jewish people are created to be ambassadors of justice and defenders of the vulnerable. May the Jewish voice emerge in election year to transcend our self-interest and ring loudly as a call to protect the vulnerable.   □

WHAT IS FAIR TAXATION?

I F ONE LISTENED ONLY TO THE AVALANCHE OF political ads during the 2012 election campaign, one might believe that Americans were being crushed under the heaviest federal tax burden ever, and that raising taxes on the wealthy (the "job creators") was tantamount to national economic suicide. This view, bolstered by much of the record $4–6 billion raised for the Presidential and Congressional campaigns, was heavily supported by a small group of billionaires, perhaps topped by casino magnate Sheldon Adelson, who reportedly made contributions of a record $150 million himself. In total, billions of dollars were spent by people who claimed that they were forced to spend too much in federal taxes.

In reality, Americans today have the lowest federal tax burden since 1950. Historically, in the 1950s and early 1960s the economy was very healthy, and the top income tax bracket paid around 90 percent. When tax rates were dramatically reduced for the wealthiest Americans, as in the 1920s and over the last decade and a half, brief prosperity resulted, followed by a catastrophic economic crash and the greatest inequality in wealth between the very rich and the rest of the population.

The Jewish tradition has much to say about fairness in taxation, and consistently endorses the principle that those who benefit the most from society have the greatest obligation to pay for the support of the community. For example, Deuteronomy 15:4 states: "And there shall be no needy among you." In addition, farmers were instructed to go over their fields and vineyards only once, and not to reap the corners of their fields: "Leave them for the poor and the foreigner" (Leviticus 19:9–10). According to the Mishnah, the community was expected to support a communal kitchen, burial society, and other needed infrastructure (*Peah* 8:7). Later, more defined funds presided over by prominent members of the community were set up to deal with the poor. In order to achieve this, citizens were taxed in proportion to their ability to pay. Thus, Jewish law has consistently upheld the idea that a fair taxation is necessary for the maintenance of the community.

We can see this trend in the 1979–2005 period, which was especially unique for its lower taxes on the wealthy. Congressional Budget Office data indicate that among Americans:

- The top one-hundredth of one percent had an income growth of 384 percent, while their tax burden decreased by 11.4 percent.
- Median income increased by 12 percent, and the tax burden for the middle quintile decreased by only 4.4 percent.

In addition, from 2000–2007, the top 0.1 percent of American earners saw a 94 percent increase in income, compared with a 4 percent increase in income for the bottom 90 percent of earners. As former Secretary of Labor Robert Reich observed, citing 2011 data, poverty – especially among the young – is on the rise, and there are deliberate efforts to create even greater economic inequality:

- 21 percent of American school-aged children lived in poor households, a 4 percent increase since 2007.
- Nearly one out of every four children lived in a family that had difficulty obtaining a sufficient food supply at some point during the year.
- In spite of this, about 60 percent of all cuts in the proposed 2011 Republican budget targeted child food, nutrition, school programs, food stamps, and Medicaid.

In the past, this trend toward lower taxes for the wealthy and greater inequality of wealth led to a pattern of booms and busts. The worst economic downturn occurred after one such period, culminating in the stock market crash in 1929 and the ensuing Great Depression. The second worst economic downturn came at the end of George W. Bush's second term in 2007, also following a period of tax cuts for the rich and great economic inequality. During his Presidency, the stock market lost about 25 percent of its value, and the NASDAQ lost nearly half its value. In contrast, President Bill Clinton, who raised income taxes for the highest earners, presided over a booming stock market, with the Dow Jones average climbing more than 7,000 points over his two terms. Thus, raising taxes on the wealthy appears to aid economic growth, while cutting taxes for the rich only exacerbates income inequality and encourages reckless financial schemes that can lead to deep economic recession.

The year 2012 offered stark evidence of how lowering taxes for the wealthy tends to increase economic inequality. In one three-month period in 2012, ExxonMobil's profits were $16 billion, the highest ever recorded by an American corporation. In spite of this, the oil industry will receive an average of more than $15 billion of subsidies annually from the federal government. On the other hand, most Americans continued to struggle. For example, the greatest number of jobs created was in retail sales, where the average annual salary was less than $21,000. In addition, the number of those unemployed, working part-time but trying in vain to get full-time work, and those who gave up looking for work reached more than 23 million. In a callous gesture, the extended benefits period (the last twenty weeks) of unemployment insurance was cut off due to congressional failure to renew the program, throwing millions of people off unemployment benefits. If Congress fails to act, an additional two million Americans will lose their unemployment benefits.

The 2012 Presidential election campaign offered Americans the opportunity to choose whether to continue the Bush tax policy or return to Clinton-era policy of a slight increase on the tax rate of income above $250,000. Republican Presidential nominee Mitt Romney stated that he paid a 14 percent rate on his income tax in the one year for which he released his returns. However, his effective tax rate was around 10 percent – far less than the rate most middle class Americans pay. In November 2012, the American people voted to re-elect President Barack Obama, thus voting to raise taxes on the wealthy. As Americans, as Jews, and as activists for justice, we must continue to press Congress to carry out this policy.   □

ARE TAXES FAIR, GOOD, OR JEWISH? A DEFENSE OF PROGRESSIVE TAXATION

T HE WHOLE NATION WAS INTENSELY DEBAT-
ing what constitutes a fair system of taxation.
It is very peculiar that there are American Jews
today who adhere to the Tea Party mantra that all government is bad, that
taxes should always be reduced, and that a flat tax should be embraced.
While Jewish law cannot be applied to the U.S. tax system to advocate for
an individual policy, it is clear that Jewish values support taxation to achieve
a just society. A flat (regressive) tax system will harm the middle and lower
classes, so we are obliged to embrace a progressive system.

Jewish Law and Thought on Taxation

Jewish law is unequivocal about the obligation to obey the law and pay
taxes (*Bava Kamma* 113a; *Nedarim* 28a; *Bava Batra* 54b–55a; *Gittin* 10b).
The principle of *dina d'malchuta dina* explicitly includes tax money (*Bava
Kamma* 113a; *Hilchot Malveh ve-Loveh* 27:1), and tax evasion is prohibited
by Jewish law (*Hilchot Gezelah ve-Avedah* 5:11). As tax evasion is also a fel-
ony according to secular law, and evokes harsh criticism from the public,
Jewish law also describes it as a "*hillul Hashem*". Additionally, one cannot
pay cash for a service where it is known that the receiver will not pay taxes
on it since the consumer is enabling the wrong. Finally, Jewish law is clear
that it is legitimate and important for the government to collect funds for
collective benefit as long as there is a transparent system in place, and the
tax collecting individual is not dishonest or arbitrary (*Bava Kamma* 113b;
Gezeilah V'Aveida 5:11). As Rav Moshe Feinstein explains, Americans live
in a legitimate and just society that can be trusted ("*medina shel hesed*").
We benefit from the public goods supported by the collective to create the
possibility for a good life for each individual. At the very least, we must pay

what we are required to but ultimately we must do more and advocate for a just taxation system.

The Gemara explains that our public financial matters as Jews are the paradigmatic opportunities for creating a *Kiddush Hashem* or *hillul Hashem*, a consecration or desecration of God's name (*Yoma* 86a). While there is one flat tax (*mahatzit ha-shekel*), this is not regressive, as some advocate today, and it is an anomaly in any case. This was an important statement that all citizens have a responsibility to build and support their government and that it is not only the responsibility of the wealthy. Yet the potential harm that would be caused by today's proposals for a flat (more regressive) tax structure would be immense, and is not sanctioned in Jewish tradition. The other required contributions in Jewish law are proportionate to one's wealth (*terumot, maasrot, matnot aniyim*, etc.). The rich take more responsibility in society so that we can create a more equitable society. This is the Jewish way.

Historically, the Rabbis themselves have imposed taxes to sustain local infrastructure. Jewish law embraces different categories for local, city, and national taxes: *hilchot shecheinim* (rights of neighbors), *ben ha-ir* (obligations of the citizen), and *din ha-melech* (rights of the king). There are different types of taxes and different levels of obligation based upon utility of public goods and personal wealth. For example, "Rav Nahman bar Rav Hisda levied a poll tax on the Rabbis . . . Rav Papa levied an impost for the digging of a new well on orphans . . . Rav Yehuda said: 'All must contribute to the building of doors in the town gates, even orphans'" (*Bava Batra* 8a). All citizens have a responsibility to pay taxes, but the level of responsibility varies.

The Rashba, the great thirteenth century Spanish Talmudist, taught that tax should not be collected from each person equally; rather, one's responsibility in paying taxes is proportional to one's wealth (*Responsa Rashba* 3:381). Dr. Aaron Levine, the late business ethics scholar, discussing the position of the Rashba in *Welfare Programs and Jewish Law*, explains: "If we assume that the rationale behind [the Rashba's] call for a wealth tax is the ability-to-pay principle, the use of a progressive income tax would serve as a good substitute equity guidepost for the charity levy in modern times." We are all blessed with various levels of financial stability and our public responsibility is proportionate to our abilities.

Discussing the Rashba, Dr. Meir Tamari, Director of The Center for Business Ethics and Social Responsibility in Jerusalem, and author of *With All Your Possessions*, writes: "He points out that the poor are unable to contribute a pro rata share. This is the pattern that is repeated in many different countries and periods: a basic premise that justice demands is that each one contribute according to his benefit (from the system supported through tax); considerations of righteousness, however, demanded that the rich contribute a greater proportion of the communal budget." In theory, one should only pay for what they benefit from, but Jewish law took a turn from individualism toward righteousness. Rabbi Eliezer Waldenberg, the great twentieth century Jewish legal authority, embraces a progressive tax model as necessary to meet the needs of society (*Tzitz Eliezer* 2:22).

The Jewish tradition understands dual financial duties as it distinguishes between taxation and charity. According to Jewish law, one must give a minimum of 10 percent (Deuteronomy 14:22; *Tosafot Taanit* 9a), and a maximum of 20 percent of one's income to charitable causes (*Ketubbot* 50a), unless one could comfortably exceed this limit (*Shulhan Aruch, Yoreh Deah* 249:1). One might conclude that tax money paid to the government could be considered one's charitable contributions, but Jewish law rejects this (259:6). Rabbi Moshe Aleppo, in the early twentieth century, rules that tax payments due to "an obligation from the king" must not be conflated with one's *tzedakah* (*Divrei Moshe, Yoreh Deah* 19). Further, Rabbi Moshe Feinstein writes: "We never find that the law is that since the government takes money you are exempt from charity" (*Iggrot Moshe, Yoreh Deah* 1:143). Tax payments fulfill an enforced requirement to sustain a society reciprocally based on a collective commitment. *Tzedakah*, on the other hand, is an unenforced obligation to support those who have not been adequately assisted by the collective system. The two cannot be equated.

These obligations pertain both to a Jewish and non-Jewish government and its contributors. "The Rabbis taught: We support the non-Jewish poor with the Jewish poor, visit their sick with the Jewish sick, and bury their dead with the Jewish dead out of the way of peace" (*Gittin* 61a). Rabbi Ovadia Yosef, the late leading Israeli halachic authority, teaches that "even from our own charity we are obligated to support the non-Jews" (*Yabia Omer* 7, *Orach Chaim* 22). We cannot only contribute to our family, friends, and fellow Jew. Being a part of a nation-state requires that we support the larger system that sustains us.

The Jewish voice must be a voice advocating for the needs of a more just society, since God designated us as to be a "*mamlechet kohanim v'goy kadosh*," a kingdom of priests and a holy nation (Exodus 19:6). We as a nation are to be advocates for the just and the good ensuring that "the good life" is accessible to all. How can we argue that taxes should be lower when we know that Americans, on average, donate only about 1 percent of their income to charity? Who will ensure that the education system is maintained and improved, that the elderly have care, that the sick are provided for, and that the country is defended? Some suggest that charity should replace government to take care of those in need, but private funds cannot possibly meet the needs of the 45 million Americans dependent on food stamps, the 15 million who are unemployed, or the 50 million who lack health insurance. It is simply not the Jewish way to naively hope that millionaires will all of a sudden become exceedingly charitable.

In addition to the problem that most citizens are not actualizing their charitable potential, many dodge their tax commitments as well. Dr. Tamari explains: "Contrariwise, it seems that it is possible to attribute the growth of an underground economy in the United States (which has the lowest tax rates in the Western world) to the 'loopholes' used by the wealthy to pay little if any tax." The Torah does not embrace some modern secular notions of liberty that claim our freedom is infringed by asking the wealthy to take more responsibility. Rather it is the opposite: taxes support the operating environment that enables individuals to earn their high salaries and live in freedom. It is incumbent upon us to reduce the disparity in net pay of American citizens, to lessen the economic divisions between different members of society and bridge the gap between the "haves" and "have nots." The alternative is the perpetuation of social forces that block social mobility and this is antithetical to Jewish values.

Poverty in America and Barriers to Social Mobility

In addition to ensuring that tax money is distributed wisely and fairly, we must be sure it is collected in the fairest manner. Flat taxes are regressive. For example, if everyone paid a flat rate of 30 percent, the teacher earning $50,000 per year would be left with $35,000, while the principal being paid $150,000 would be left with $105,000. They would both pay the same tax rate, but the teacher would have a heavier tax burden, and would be much less likely to be able to pay for housing, food, transportation, and other basic living expenses after taxes.

Even when we don't have a technical obligation to give of our own, the tradition teaches us to embrace the path of compassion. Rashbam explains "'And I will hear them because I am compassionate': Even if, according to the law you have the object and you have no obligation to return it except to go beyond the letter of the law, one might think that I [God] will not hear his cry, but I will because I am compassionate and merciful" (commentary on Exodus 22:26). At times, the value of being compassionate and creating the just society must outweigh the value of the right to private property ownership.

The prophets teach us that the paradigmatic wicked society is one that collective neglects its poor. "Behold, this was the iniquity of your sister Sodom: pride, fullness of bread, and careless ease was in her and in her daughters; neither did she strengthen the hand of the poor and needy" (Isaiah 16:49). Further, the Rabbis teach that one who embraces private ownership at the expense of the poor living by a principle of "Mine is mine, and yours is yours" is like the paradigmatic evil Sodomite (*Pirke Avot* 5:10). A model of capitalism that allows for significant wealth accumulation but does not also enforce levels of wealth redistribution is not a model Judaism can promote. Economic equality and caring for the poor are Jewish values to be defended, and Jews should be on the front line advocating for ethical taxation.

The rich are getting richer and the poor are getting poorer in America. From 1981 to 2010, the income share of the bottom 90 percent fell from 65 to 52 percent while the income of the top 10 percent rose from 35 to 48 percent. Further, the top 1 percent of earners now takes home more than 18 percent of national income – a startling increase from 1973, when the rich's share of income was only 7.7 percent. The richest 5 percent are making 37 percent of consumer purchases. Since the late 1970s, the middle and lower classes have been progressively weakened. Robert B. Reich, the American political economist, argues that the economy won't recover until we revive the middle class.

The government must intervene to ensure that the "American dream" is still attainable for all and that social mobility is a reality. Social mobility is a sign not only of a just society but also of a dynamic economy indicating that one of the most important tenets of capitalism is being met: a merito-cratic system where smart and bold people have a better chance of achieving success regardless of whether they start out rich or poor. But social mobility is on a rapid decline in the U.S. today. Since the 1980s, the very rich do very well while the typical American makes little-to-no gains. The average American is losing incentive to work harder. Only the rich can get rich while others find their social mobility blocked even if they do everything right as they are caught in a poverty trap. Even when poor individuals seek to upgrade their skills through years of work experience or by going back to school, they cannot keep themselves afloat while trying to advance.

So who is to blame? Charles Karelis, a philosophy professor at George Washington University, explains that we cannot blame the poor or the rich for today's crisis of poverty in America. Rather, our traditional way of thinking of economics just does not apply to the poor. When one is poor, one's economic worldview is shaped by deprivation, and one sees the world around oneself not in terms of goods to be consumed but as problems to be alleviated. Karelis explains that when in poverty, one no longer prioritizes addressing the need for goods since they are fully consumed by the need to address major problems such as survival. Economists considering the purchasing of goods and the health of the economic system too often neglect that the poor don't fit into their models. If one cannot afford to pay their credit card bills, rent, day care, car insurance, or even for food, yet one still works multiple jobs – then there is a huge disincentive to work at all.

We need to treat poverty as its own problem within economics and have specific solutions to address it systemically making everyone stronger. Too often economics remains on the theoretical level aimed at the achievement of "pareto-optimum." A pareto-optimum is a situation where it is impossible to make one person better-off without making some other person worse-off. But today, we can find economic solutions that are win-win creating a stronger, safer, and more just society for all.

Several studies have shown the United States to be less mobile than comparable nations. Markus Jantti, an economist at a Swedish university, found that 42 percent of American men raised in the bottom fifth of incomes stay there as adults. Meanwhile, just 8 percent of American men at the bottom rose to the top fifth. How can America be understood as classless if 65 percent born in the bottom fifth stay in the bottom two-fifths (Economic Mobility Project of the Pew Charitable Trusts)? Our country is not only less equal but also less mobile!

The late Harvard moral philosopher John Rawls argued for the redistribution of wealth as a moral imperative. Rawls explains in "A Theory of Justice" his thought experiment of the veil of ignorance: "No one knows his place in society, his class position or social status; nor does he know his fortune in the distribution of natural assets and abilities, his intelligence and strength, and the like." To ensure social mobility, Rawls argues for inheritance taxes on the basis that a completely unregulated transfer of wealth from parent to child would result in the entrenchment of wealth in some segments of society while others would be blocked from mobility. As wealth continues to amass in the family from generation to generation, the problem of wealth disparity increases.

Poverty is not, as some have described, a lack of motivation. Rather the problem is that our system no longer enables one in poverty to climb out. And we cannot rely upon some naïve notion of charity that values free will and the cultivation of virtue through giving over the needs of the poor. Spoken nobly, this is one of the great philosophies only the rich can embrace. Virtue in the rich cannot take priority over the survival needs of the most poor in our midst. Enhancing social mobility is not only a moral imperative – it is also an economic need. The Organization for Economic Co-Operation and Development (OECD) notes: "First, less mobile societies are more likely to waste or misallocate human skills and talents. Second, lack of equal opportunity may affect the motivation, effort and, ultimately, the productivity of citizens, with adverse effects on the overall efficiency and the growth potential of the economy."

Creating more social mobility will not only allow for a more just state and a stronger economy but perhaps also for a happier society. While ethics, of course, are not determined solely by what makes people happy, it should be noted that a new study has shown that people are happier in countries with more progressive taxation, because they are more satisfied with basic government services, such as quality of health care and education. Among the world's developed nations, the United States taxes its citizens at one of the lowest rates, as a percentage of GDP. According to Citizens for Tax Justice, the bottom 20 percent of income earners are paying around 21 percent of their income in taxes while the tax rate for the 400 richest Americans was only 18 percent.

The Jewish Mandate

Jewish law is opposed to the radical laissez-faire economic policies that many advocate today.

The obligation to help the poor is of utmost importance in the Jewish tradition, and this is achieved most successfully in a sophisticated collective system of government and not-for-profit agencies. Taxes in the United States are collected on three levels – federal, state, and local – comprising taxes on property, income, sales, imports, estates, and gifts. These taxes ensure that we can achieve our collective goals to improve our education system, provide quality health care, defend our country, and protect our environment. A progressive tax structure ensures the proper distribution of money, helps protect the poor in society, and ensures a more stable income stream for the government in times of recession. It is our responsibility to ensure that the most vulnerable in society are protected and that our nation is strong. Progressive taxation is a crucial part of the solution especially in a country that taxes as little as the American government does in comparison to other countries around the world.

Without a more fair tax system, who will ensure the old, sick, poor, and unfortunate are cared for? Jews must continue to take leadership in advocating for progressive taxation.   □

HURRICANE SANDY, FEMA, AND THE NEED FOR BIG GOVERNMENT

THE RABBIS TEACH (*TAANIT* 11A) THAT "AT A time when the community is suffering, no one should say, 'I will go home, eat, drink, and be at peace with myself.'" To effectively aid those who are suffering, we need the cooperation and collaboration of each and every individual. We need strong individuals, effective non-profits, and committed states. However, we also need to recognize the most powerful collective body available to address the suffering. In our society, the mechanism that represents the people is the government, and it must be effective. Government does not always have to be big to be effective, but oftentimes it does, especially when responding to disasters on a large scale.

Hurricane Sandy, which struck the east coast in October 2012, was the largest Atlantic hurricane on record and the second-costliest, behind only Hurricane Katrina. At least 253 people were killed and an estimated $65.6 billion was lost due to damage and business interruption. For weeks, many in this, the wealthiest country in the world, were suddenly lacking the basic necessities of life, such as shelter, heat, power, and water. The most dramatic damage occurred in southern New Jersey and the New York City metropolitan area. In New Jersey, the historic Seaside Heights roller coaster was carried out into the Atlantic Ocean, where its tangled ruins remain today. Videos of the famous Jersey shore area revealed miles of destroyed board-walks and beaches that had virtually disappeared, along with hundreds of demolished houses and boats. To the north, nearly 100 people died within a 65-mile radius of New York City as a result of Hurricane Sandy. Manhattan had never before flooded, but Hurricane Sandy's waters were nearly four feet higher than the city's ten-foot walls. Scores were killed in their homes on the coasts of Staten Island and Queens. Some ignored mandatory or-ders to evacuate, others were elderly and infirm, but all were victimized by a flood surge that filled houses with water within minutes, allowing no escape. Others were killed by falling branches and trees. Millions of people were without power, and received little-to-no information from their util-ity companies about when power might be restored. The catastrophe was reminiscent of Hurricane Katrina in 2005, and many feared a repeat of the government's feeble response to that storm might occur again.

This time, fortunately the Federal Emergency Management Agency (FEMA) was ready to act. Within three days, FEMA had deployed about 2,300 disaster-relief personnel across several states; provided shelter to more than 10,000 people; rescued some 700 people; and delivered around 700,000 gallons of water and 1.5 million meals to others in need. Perversely, many in the House of Representatives propose that we slash the agency's funding by up to 40 percent, arguing that disaster relief should be han-dled by the states and private sector, not the federal government. The ar-gument typically goes that the federal government is overly bureaucratic and slow to act while states can be nimble, understand the needs of the localities and their constituents better, and thus should be charged with more responsibility.

The federal government must have the capacity to swiftly respond when it comes to disaster relief. Of course, as past mistakes reveal, a bigger FEMA does not necessarily mean a better FEMA, nor enhanced relief ability. The agency spent nearly $900 million on prefabricated homes in New Orleans after Katrina, but then was prevented by its own regulations to put them to use. People were getting sick because the contractors used too much form-aldehyde in the construction of the houses and the fumes were intoxicating. Rather than providing housings for thousands who had lost their homes, they rotted in storage lots. In spite of this, FEMA can only be effective if it is allowed to be a large agency. When the national government can address disasters effectively, it saves everyone money, including the states and the private sector, which limits the damage caused when roads and power lines are not repaired quickly and people cannot return home and rebuild. One thinker wrote in Slate.com: "But that requires financing by an entity capable of rapidly financing expensive projects – i.e., the federal government . . . and (slashing federal disaster aid) is the height of penny-wise, pound-foolish thinking."

When Hurricane Sandy hit, New Jersey Governor Chris Christie, who had previously expressed his contempt for government and whose policies led to the dismissal of tens of thousands of government workers, met with President Obama and with FEMA. Governor Christie said: "The federal government's response has been great. I was on the phone at midnight . . . with the president, personally; he has expedited the designation of New Jersey as a major disaster area." He later added: "The folks at FEMA . . . have been excellent." New York Governor Andrew Cuomo and Christie alone estimated the losses of just their two states at nearly $78 billion. California representative Donna Edwards noted that, with global warming looming, the challenge is great, and the need for response greater: ". . . the importance of investing in this infrastructure now so that we don't make it more vulnerable later on needs to be high on the priority list, because the damage to us in terms of our long-term economy and competitiveness is really huge."

Our nation has confronted emergencies before, and the federal government has often been the ultimate solution when the private sector failed. During the Great Depression, the stock market failed, thousands of private banks failed, private charities failed, and when President Franklin D. Roosevelt took office in March 1933, the nation was on the precipice of total failure. President Roosevelt closed all the banks for four days, and then announced that the federal government would guarantee bank deposits through the Federal Deposit Insurance Corporation. The result was that the banking system (and currency) was saved, the economy had a chance to recover, as the American people had a renewed confidence in their government and its roles and abilities in helping people. The private sector had no plan; government was the solution.

A profound *midrash* (*Bava Batra* 10a) teaches about how humans are not in control over nature.

> He [Rabbi Yehuda] used to say: "Ten strong things were created in the world: A mountain is strong, but iron cuts through it. Iron is strong, but fire can make it bubble. Fire is strong, but water puts it out. Water is strong, but clouds contain it. Clouds are strong, but the wind can

scatter them. Breath is strong, but the body holds it in. The body is strong, but fear breaks it. Fear is strong, but wine dissipates it effects. Wine is strong, but sleep overcomes its power. Death is stronger than all of them. But *tzedakah* saves from death, as it is written, 'And *tzedakah* saves from death.'" (Proverbs 10:2)

When nature, death, or other forces overcome us, the best thing we can do is fight back with *tzedakah* (with love, kindness, and charitable giving). We must all do our part as individuals and we need strong non-profits and state-level responses, but we must also unite to support a stronger federal government that is best equipped to address crises wherever and whenever they strike. This is the essence of America: to be united in both our times of need and times of hopes, our traumas and our triumphs.   □

TORTURE, WAR, AND BIN LADEN: A JEWISH PERSPECTIVE

FOR THOSE OF US FAR REMOVED FROM THE TORture cell and battlefield, it is all too easy to be misinformed about intelligence gathering and its efficacy and morality. But to maintain our national integrity, we must gain clarity on this crucial moral and political issue. Torture is ineffective, illegal and immoral, and it makes us less safe. It must be stopped at all levels.

The Bush Administration argued that torture – or in the words of its officials – "enhanced interrogation techniques," was an effective weapon in the war on terrorism. One year after the anniversary of the killing of Osama bin Laden, Jose Rodriguez, the former chief of the CIA's Counter-Terrorism Center during the Bush Administration, wrote a book, *Hard Measures: How Aggressive CIA Actions after 9/11 Saved American Lives*, about why he believes the use of torture by the United States enabled the capture of Bin Laden. However, countless intelligence experts have agreed that torture is not an effective technique for attaining reliable information.

Senator John McCain, who was himself tortured as a prisoner during the Vietnam War, has openly challenged this: "It was not torture, or cruel, inhuman and degrading treatment of detainees that got us the major leads that ultimately enabled our intelligence community to find Osama bin Laden." Reuters reports that a Senate Intelligence Committee report is expected to corroborate Senator McCain's statement. In regards to the "enhanced techniques," Committee Chair Senator Dianne Feinstein said: "Nothing justifies the kind of procedures that were used."

Torture is ineffective and is known to produce faulty and false confessions. Further, the use of torture in the U.S. makes us less safe and more vulnerable, as it can inspire our enemies to commit acts of terror and use torture against our soldiers overseas. Does anyone believe that the Abu Ghraib scandal, in which photographs of American guards torturing and humiliating Iraqi men became public, made Americans safer? Why does Rodriguez, who had torture tapes destroyed supposedly to "protect" the identity of the interrogators, feel so secure in his justifications that he is going around the country and on television revealing his identity while promoting his book?

On January 22, 2009, President Obama issued an Executive Order to end torture, reaffirming that torture is illegal, a point already made by Congress in signing the U.S. Convention Against Torture and Other Cruel, Inhuman or Degrading Treatment or Punishment. This document defines torture as "any act by which severe pain or suffering, whether physical or mental, is intentionally inflicted on a person for such purposes as obtaining from him or a third person information."

Torture inflicts the cruelest punishments, crossing all boundaries of human dignity. It is degrading to all – the perpetrator, victim, and citizens who allow it – and is a violation against God, as humans created in the "Image of God" are broken on the deepest level.

Uri L'Tzedek has launched a prison reform campaign in the Jewish community, and we stand with the National Religious Campaign Against Torture (NRCAT) in solidarity with other faith leaders across the country united against any use of torture. As American faith leaders, we understand that the role of the prophetic tradition is to remind us of our absolute moral duties to honor the sacredness of human dignity.

The use of torture is against Jewish law and Jewish values. To be sure, according to Jewish law, one is permitted to defend oneself by killing an attacker if one's life is threatened (Mishneh Torah, *Hilchot Rotzeah* 1:6). Judaism does not oppose self-defense. But a captured prisoner is no longer in the category of attacker (*rodef*), and therefore, extreme measures of what would otherwise be called self-defense may not be inflicted upon a captured individual. We do not inflict cruel pain upon one individual in the hopes that we may help others. One is obligated to save the lives of others (Leviticus 19:16), but one may not do so in reckless, painful, and immoral ways contrary to the value of the mitzvah (obligation) itself. Jewish law is committed to the ethics of just war – and torture crosses the line. Judaism also teaches that humiliating another is like killing him, and that "pain is worse than death."

Rabbi Aryeh Klapper, a leading Jewish thinker in Boston, writes that "endorsing torture fundamentally desecrates God's Name. The role of Judaism is to raise moral standards in the world, not to legitimate a lowest moral common denominator." This is what torture has become, the lowest activity a human or government can engage in. It is the abuse of a helpless, trapped prisoner without quality results. It has been used by tyrannical governments throughout time, and has no place in a twenty-first century democracy committed to human rights.

Nietzsche writes: "Whoever fights monsters should see to it that in the process he does not become a monster. And if you gaze long enough into an abyss, the abyss will gaze back into you." We must fight evil in the world with full force, but we must be sure to never lose our souls in the process.

□

RELIGIOUS FREEDOM: SHOULD THE TEN COMMANDMENTS BE PROMOTED IN PUBLIC?

ONE OF THE GREAT DEBATES IN AMERICA today is over the role of religion in the public sphere. To what extent is the United States government embracing religion? Are we "one nation under God?" Most concretely, should religious teachings such as the Ten Commandments be allowed on the walls of courthouses and classrooms?

The question of separation between church and state has long been an important one in America. In Virginia, the Church of England was the established church, and in Massachusetts, it was the (Puritan) Congregationalist Church. In England, this split contributed to a bloody civil war. In the colonies, there was a move to eliminate the concept of an established church. In 1763, for example, Virginia patriot Patrick Henry argued in the "Parson's Cause" that parishioners should not have to pay so much to support the established church. While he technically lost the case, Henry persuaded the jurors to award each parson one penny in damages, thus weakening the established church's hold.

Another Virginian, Thomas Jefferson, played a pivotal role in clarifying the separation of church and state. As author of the Declaration of Independence, Jefferson avoided any Christian terminology, and referred to "Divine Providence" rather than a Christian "God." While he opposed the Constitution, Jefferson did contribute to the push for a Bill of Rights to be added to the Constitution, and the First Amendment begins with an explicit rejection of an established church: "Congress shall make no law respecting an establishment of religion, or prohibiting the free exercise thereof . . ." When he became President, Jefferson emphatically endorsed this separation in a letter to the Danbury Baptist Association in 1802:

> I contemplate with sovereign reverence that act of the whole American people which declared that their legislature should "make no law respecting an establishment of religion, or prohibiting the free exercise thereof," thus building a wall of separation between Church and State.

In the twentieth century, many church-state issues have gone to the Supreme Court. During the 1950s and 1960s, the Warren Court tended to have a Jeffersonian view in overturning religious practices in the public sphere. More recently, a more conservative federal judiciary has tended to allow these practices, and a number of Republican politicians have espoused the idea that the United States is (or should be) a Christian nation. In 2006, the Supreme Court made conflicting split decisions, striking down the posting of the Ten Commandments in Kentucky courthouses, but allowing it on the grounds of the Texas Capitol, both by 5–4 decisions. Proponents of the public posting of the Commandments argue that it is needed to avoid moral decadence and that God cannot be removed from our culture. But is it true that posting this declaration helps to put God in society and raise our moral commitments?

Religion should be in the public square, but in a way that celebrates diversity and, most importantly, in a way that actually works to further our collective goals. Religious values should be modeled for others to emulate, not jammed down people's souls. Those seeking spiritual homes might be more receptive to growth and change if religious leaders were less forceful with their ideologies. Rather than creating a culture of plaques, we need a culture of action. Values should be lived, not hung on walls.

Further, the celebration of the Ten Commandments is the celebration of one religion's expression. Christianity may be the most practiced religion in America, but we must be sure to preserve pluralism and prevent the marginalization of minorities. Indeed, there is evidence that America is less Christian than before, and that there is more "mobility" in religion than we suppose. Consider the following:

- While 76 percent of Americans identified as Christian in 2008, this is a decrease from 86 percent in 1990. During the same period, those indicating no religion rose to around 15 percent.
- In 2009, Gallup poll data revealed that only about 45 percent of American Christians (Protestants and Catholics) attended church regularly.
- 2007 Pew Forum on Religion and Public Life data shows that 44 percent of adults have changed (or dropped) the religious affiliation of their birth.

We should take this into account, and acknowledge that the Ten Commandments require serious theological commitments in addition to moral obligations. In addition to maintaining a pluralism of values, we must strengthen religious pluralism. While the Commandments do appear in the Torah twice, Rambam (responsa 263) opposes the practice of standing in synagogue for the reading of the Ten Commandments, since one might come to think that these teachings are more important than all of the other values in the Torah; Rav Ovadia Yosef (*Yehaveh Daat Responsa* 1:29) accepts this position. Christianity may prioritize these ten, but Judaism is much broader in its commitments. Our religious values cannot adequately be expressed through statues of the Ten Commandments.

Judaism is a religion of debate, argument, and discussion, not dogma. Putting up statements about commandments flies in the face of celebrating a lived tradition. This is why it was originally prohibited to write down the Oral Torah. It should be spoken about and lived, not put onto the library shelf and archived.

The Ten Commandments debate should not be viewed as a debate between the religious and the secular. Rather, the truly religious should value
religious expression that works, values the dignity of human difference, and
celebrates learning and discourse over the posting of plaques.   □

JEWISH VALUES: FASTING IN OPPOSITION TO SOLITARY CONFINEMENT

O N JUNE 8, 2012, I FASTED AS AN INDIVIDUAL
in solidarity with tens of thousands of
American individuals in solitary confine-
ment. I also fasted in solidarity with hundreds of faith leaders across the
country calling for an end of solitary confinement.

The day following the fast was a historic day, as the Senate held its first-
ever Congressional hearing on solitary confinement. Leaders from Uri
L'Tzedek, RHR-NA, the National Religious Campaign Against Torture,
and other clergy around the country fasted for twenty-three hours prior to
the hearing to draw attention to the physical and emotional harm caused
by prolonged solitary confinement.

The fast symbolized the twenty-three hours prisoners spend in solitary
confinement cells daily. This was as an important opportunity to advocate
on behalf of the tens of thousands of individuals languishing in solitary
confinement across the country.

We have seen in prisoner hunger strikes in California, Virginia, and
across the country that prisoners are refusing food as one of the few means
they have to protest their conditions in solitary confinement.

U.S. Senator Dick Durbin, the Senate's Majority Whip, chaired this first-
ever hearing on the human rights, fiscal, and public safety consequences
of solitary confinement in U.S. prisons, jails, and detention centers, which
explored the detrimental psychological and psychiatric impact on inmates
during and after their imprisonment, the exorbitant costs of running solitary housing units, the moral human rights issues surrounding the use of

isolation, and some of the successful state reforms that have taken place.

The United States is a world leader in its use of prolonged solitary confinement. This extreme treatment had been used sparingly for more than 150 years. However, after a federal supermax facility to hold inmates exclusively for solitary confinement opened in 1983 in Marion, Illinois, the number of state facilities mirrored the exploding prison population over the next generation. There are now forty-four state-run supermax prisons, and at least 80,000 people in the U.S. criminal justice system are kept in solitary confinement on any given day, with some serving for years, even decades.

From 1995 to 2000, the growth rate of these segregation units significantly surpassed the prison growth rate overall: 40 percent compared with 28 percent. While authorities claim that this is necessary due to the presence of gangs and other violent offenders, the reality is that the United States has decided to quadruple its prison population (now the largest in the world), while not providing adequate funding. Thus, throwing prisoners in solitary confinement for even minor violations is now the norm.

Solitary confinement has a tremendously adverse effect on health. For example, a 2006 study found that up to 64 percent of prisoners in solitary confinement were mentally ill. Clinicians have even created a term for those affected by this confinement: Special Housing Unit (SHU) syndrome. Some of the symptoms include:

- Insomnia and paranoia
- Uncontrollable feelings of rage and fear
- Distortions of time and perception
- Increased risk of suicide

University of California at Santa Cruz Psychology Professor Craig Haney studied 100 solitary confinement inmates at a California supermax, and found that 90 percent experienced "irrational anger," thirty times the rate found in Americans who are not in prison. A high percentage of the inmates also experienced lethargy, depression and despair to the point where they were unable to initiate any activity. Since the United Nations Convention against Torture defines torture as an intentional act that causes "severe pain or suffering, whether physical or mental," then surely solitary confinement is torture.

We use a hunger strike because it is a time-honored tradition among those seeking redress for social injustice. Over the past century in Asia, for example, the hunger strike has been used by Mohandas Gandhi (India),

Benazir Bhutto (Pakistan), and Aung Suu Kyi (Myanmar) to protest religious warfare and the suppression of civil liberties. In the United State, Cesar Chavez was noted for his hunger strikes to promote labor and civil rights for Latinos in the Southwest. In addition, it is not well known that Alice Paul and her group of militant suffragists, the National Woman's Party, engaged in a hunger strike after being jailed for picketing in front of the White House in 1917–1918 in an effort to get President Wilson to support a federal woman suffrage amendment. In addition to enduring force-feeding, many were put in solitary confinement, and Paul had the added torture of having a flashlight shined in her face every hour of the day. In spite of opposition from moderate suffragists and those who saw picketing during wartime as unpatriotic, Paul and her organization witnessed the passage of the Nineteenth Amendment giving women the right to vote by Congress a year later, and its eventual ratification in 1920.

Jewish values are opposed to the abuse of prisoners and to the practice of solitary confinement. The Rabbis teach us that one important way to inspire mercy from above is to take fasts upon ourselves. We do so with trepidation and caution to remember the frailty of the human condition and to stand in solidarity with all who are suffering. □

SHOULD CHILDREN BE IN SOLITARY CONFINEMENT?

IN 1840, CHARLES DICKENS VISITED A PRISON IN Philadelphia and wrote: "I hold this slow and daily tampering with the mysteries of the brain, to be immeasurably worse than any torture of the body."

Upon feeling pain from the news that undocumented workers are sometimes placed in solitary confinement, I was further dismayed and saddened to learn that prisons in America are also putting children in solitary confinement.

It is estimated that there are between 20,000 and 80,000 people in America stripped of their humanity in solitary confinement on any given day – immigrants, children, and even those with mental illnesses who are all put in solitary. As CNN reports, "The 17–year old drew his suicide note in strips of wet toilet paper on the floor of his jail cell – a concrete box where he was being held in isolation. 'I'm sorry 1 4 3 fam,' Kirk Gunderson wrote. Code for 'I love you, family.'" This teenager then tied a prison blanket to a smoke detector grate and hanged himself.

"Growing Up Locked Down," a joint Human Rights Watch/American Civil Liberties Union report, noted that in 2011, more than 95,000 minors (younger than 18 years old) were held in prisons and jails. While it is difficult to generalize how many of these children were held in solitary confinement, 2012 data compiled for the report from the New York City Department of Corrections shows the following:

- More than 14 percent of youth offenders were held in solitary confinement at one time, with the average period in solitary at the Rikers Island detention facility being 43 days
- Nearly half the adolescent detainees at Rikers Island have been diagnosed with mental health problems, yet adolescents in solitary confinement are routinely denied all services and treatment that might help their mental health status

The report details the harsh conditions that many youths face in solitary confinement, including no visitors, including family members; no access to reading materials or writing implements, nor any chance to attend classes or programming; and exercise limited to a small outside metal cage, in solitude, a few times each week. Thus, solitary confinement means 22 hours or more each day of cramped isolation, usually locked behind a solid steel door. If they are lucky, these young prisoners may have a cell with a window, or an occasional book such as the Bible. Many adolescents treated this way respond by showing signs of extreme stress, from having hallucinations or losing touch with reality to cutting themselves and attempting suicide, as well as a deterioration of their physical health from a lack of exercise.

Why has this happened? Until the 1980s, young offenders were not thrown in with the adult prison population and did not experience the same harsh treatment. However, since the 1980s, in a wave of legislation that more than tripled the U.S. prison population, most America states have instituted laws that prosecute minors as adults for many crimes, with an enormous rise in long prison sentences and periods of solitary confinement.

There remains a concerted lack of appreciation that minors have special needs and possibilities for rehabilitation.

The joint report notes that solitary confinement can do permanent damage to the mental and physical health of teenagers:

> Experts assert that young people are psychologically unable to handle solitary confinement with the resilience of an adult. And, because they are still developing, traumatic experiences like solitary confinement may have a profound effect on their chance to rehabilitate and grow. Solitary confinement can exacerbate, or make more likely, short and long-term mental health problems. The most common deprivation that accompanies solitary confinement, denial of physical exercise, is physically harmful to adolescents' health and well-being.

Many scientific studies have confirmed what every parent and teacher knows: teenagers often act in an impulsive, risky manner.

Millions of American teenagers have been diagnosed with attention-deficit/hyperactivity disorder (ADHD) and associated mood and anxiety disorders and other mental health problems. This, of course, does not exclude harmful behavior but provides us more context. These conditions result in an abnormal pursuit of stimulation and extremely impulsive behavior, without regard for consequences. Consider these mental health findings:

- Teenagers with ADHD have approximately four times as many driving accidents and three times as many tickets for speeding violations as teenagers who had not been diagnosed with ADHD
- In one study, more than half of the teenagers diagnosed with ADHD contracted a sexually transmitted disease
- Teenagers diagnosed with ADHD are far more likely to use recreational drugs and abuse alcohol, have a gambling problem, and have unstable personal relationships than their peers

There are scientific explanations for this type of abnormal adolescent behavior, and for why adults usually exhibit them less. Along with obvious physical changes that take place in teenagers' bodies, there are very important changes that occur in the adolescent brain. We now know that this is because the adolescent brain is not fully developed, especially in the frontal lobe, which governs cognitive processing (e.g., the ability to organize thoughts and plans). In particular, the dorsolateral prefrontal cortex, which controls impulsive behavior and allows a person to consider the consequences of actions, does not fully develop until our mid-twenties. Many psychiatrists now understand that an adolescent with this developing brain may be particularly impressionable at this age, and the stress of solitary confinement may do permanent mental health damage, whereas a more rehabilitative regimen may improve the adolescent's mental health and produce a well-adjusted adult, one who can contribute to society.

The anonymous voices of teenagers in solitary confinement speak to us through the joint report:

- "The anger and hurt gets so intense that you suspect everyone and trust no one and when someone does something nice for you, you don't understand it."
- "I cut myself. I started doing it because it is the only release of my pain. I'd see the blood and I'd be happy . . . I did it with staples, not razors. When I see the blood and it makes me want to keep going. I showed the officers and they didn't do anything . . ."
- "We didn't do anything wrong to be put in isolation. They say it's to protect us but I think it puts us in more danger . . . [H]ow could we be charged as men but be separated from men. It makes no sense."
- "There is nothing to do so you start talking to yourself and getting lost in your own little world. It is crushing. You get depressed and wonder if it is even worth living."

Human rights organizations consider solitary confinement for minors, as well as the denial of visits or access to services, to be violations of international law. They point out that youthful offenders could be housed in separate facilities in which rehabilitation could be stressed through reinforcement of positive behaviors, and that solitary confinement should never be used on these prisoners. The joint report cited above offers key recommendations that include banning solitary confinement for minors; segregating minors from adults in jails and prisons; strictly limiting, regulating and monitoring these policies and practices; and finally, for the United States to ratify international treaties that protect minors from inhumane treatment. We must act resolutely to ensure that our age is not remembered as a time when thousands of teenagers were routinely treated in such a cruel manner by our own government. We must stand up together and call for these policies to come to an end with all due haste.

I have argued adamantly that Judaism is opposed to solitary confinement and so are other faiths. This is why the NRCAT (National Religious Campaign Against Torture) came out strongly in support of SB 61, a bill that would limit the harmful practice of solitary confinement of youth in the juvenile justice system in California.

Momentum to halt the use of prolonged solitary confinement in U.S. prisons continues to build nationally, with the first-ever Congressional Hearing on the use of prolonged solitary confinement convened in 2012 by Senator Dick Durbin (IL). Following the hearing, in February 2013, the Federal Bureau of Prisons committed to the first-ever independent and comprehensive assessment of its use of prolonged solitary confinement in U.S. federal prisons.

SB 61 sets standards for the use of solitary confinement at state and county juvenile correctional facilities. Among the provisions of SB 61, the bill would:

- Define solitary confinement as the involuntary placement in a room or cell in isolation from persons other than staff and attorneys.
- Provide that solitary confinement shall only be used when a minor poses an immediate and substantial risk of harm to others or the security of the facility, and all other less restrictive options have been exhausted.
- Provide that a minor or ward shall only be held in solitary confinement for the minimum time necessary to address the safety risk.
- Provide additional restrictions on the use of solitary confinement for minors with suicidal or self-harming behavior.
- Provide that clinical staff shall review minors or wards regularly to ensure that their physical and mental health is not endangered.
- Empower existing county juvenile justice commissions to report on the use of solitary confinement in juvenile facilities.

In a moment when the use of prolonged solitary confinement of youth is under increasing scrutiny around the country, SB 61 presents California with a critical opportunity to lead the way nationally in increasing access to rehabilitation and reducing harm for our young people. I would urge all to support SB 61 and to speak out against solitary confinement around the nation. ▢

IS OUR LABOR SYSTEM BROKEN?
A JEWISH CALL FOR MINIMUM
WAGE INCREASES

L ESSENING THE GAP BETWEEN THE RICH AND THE
poor is one of the most crucial moral issues to
address in America today. Much of the problem
has to do with fair wages. Some progress has been made. At the beginning
of 2012, eight states raised their minimum wage, yet the federal wage floor
for most workers today remains at $7.25 an hour. The integrity of our labor
system is broken and we must respond.

This is not a particularly new problem. The national minimum wage
began during the Great Depression and Congress has adjusted the rate
sporadically, but has not indexed it to price changes, often resulting in decreasing value in constant dollars.

The Fair Labor Standards Act, passed during the New Deal, established
a minimum hourly wage of 25 cents in October 1938. Afterward, it was
raised intermittently, reaching its highest value in constant dollars in 1968,
at the peak of the "Great Society" of President Lyndon Johnson. Afterward,
the minimum wage stagnated, although in 1989, during the Presidency of
Republican George H. W. Bush, the minimum wage was raised with bipartisan support, passing the House by 382–37 and the Senate by 89–8. Today,
politics has trumped justice.

The issue has become too muddied with partisanship. There was no increase from September 1997 until July 2007, at which point the minimum
wage had fallen 22 percent in constant dollars while corporate profits had
increased by 50 percent (*Time Magazine*, July 24, 2009). Even then, the wage
was only raised in three increments, rising from $5.85 in July 2007 to its cur-
rent level of $7.25 by July 2009. Some have noted that the decline in value of
the minimum wage has coincided with the decline of the American middle
class, as previously the minimum wage offered some families the chance to
climb into the middle class, but now the gap is too wide.

Some argue that raising the cost of labor will hurt workers, since employers can hire fewer workers. At times, this may be true, but many have shown why this is false. Speaking on this issue, Nobel Prize-winning economist Robert Solow stated that ". . . the evidence of job loss is weak. And the fact that the evidence is weak suggests that the impact on jobs is small."

Indeed, minimum wage workers tend to work in industries that cannot be outsourced or eliminated (e.g., the fast food industry), so it is unlikely that a rise in minimum wage would reduce these jobs. One significant study looking at the food industry found that raising the minimum wage did not lower employment, and dozens of studies have confirmed these conclusions. For example, a study looking at airport employees found that not only did higher wages not lead to lower employment, but that it led to a reduced employee turnover.

We must consider not only the microeconomics but also the macroeconomics. There is evidence to suggest that when low-wage workers have more spending-power, this will create jobs and create more demand for labor. For example, in 2006 the Economic Policy Institute estimated that raising the minimum wage from $6.55 to $7.25 would increase consumer spending by $5.5 billion, thereby supporting the economy.

Economists suggest that most often, higher labor costs are transferred to consumers in higher prices and to a smaller profit margin, but not to a reduced employee size, since a certain number of employees are needed to function properly.

At the end of the day, minimum wage reform is still not enough. Even if we raise the rates, it will not be enough to push low-wage earning families above the poverty line. We should embrace a living wage to achieve that, but we also need an accumulation of small wins to improve lives: raising the minimum wage is a moral imperative. The 2010 U.S. Census laid out the extent of poverty in graphic detail:

- Nearly 47 million people live in poverty (15 percent), the highest number recorded. Of these, more than 20 million lived in extreme poverty (i.e., an income less than half the poverty level)
- Among children, 22 percent live in poverty
- More than 17 million households (14.5 percent) are food insecure, the highest number ever recorded in the United States
- 50 million people lack medical insurance, which will become more critical if the Supreme Court declares the Affordable Care Act unconstitutional

There are many national attempts to raise the minimum wage in motion. For example, proposals that New York State's current minimum wage of $7.25 an hour, which is lower than that of eighteen states and the District of Columbia, be raised to $8.50. This increase, sponsored by the New York Assembly Speaker Sheldon Silver, would put higher wages into the pockets of more than 880,000 workers, and this would go right back into the economy. Mr. Silver said: "When you work full-time at the minimum wage, you are poor in New York. You're not making enough to get by. We want to have people able to support their families, plain and simple."

Raising the minimum wage helps poor families move out of poverty, spurs job creation, and stimulates economic growth and thus it is our Jewish obligation to lead this fight for justice. Rema teaches that when one is involved in a communal issue of public monies one must engage (act and vote) "*l'shem shamayim*" (for the sake of heaven; i.e., for the right reasons not based on self interest) (*Hoshen Mishpat* 163:1). It is crucial that Jews fall out on the right side of this national debate as advocates for systemic change for the poor.

Raising the minimum wage is actually a mitzvah. Rambam says that ensuring others have work that can sustain them is the highest rung of the hierarchy on how to give *tzedakah* (*Matnot Aniyim*, 10:7). In Judaism, *tzedakah* does not mean charity but justice. We rectify social wrongs and fulfill our obligations through the giving of *tzedakah*. By raising the minimum wage, we are enabling others who work to move out of deeper poverty. Rambam is dealing here with private voluntary giving; this value is all the more true when being applied to a system of legislation, as the mission of the Jewish people is to perpetuate our most precious values of the good and the just into broader society. Our messianic dream is the creation of a society where Torah values are actualized in the world to create a more just and holy civilization.

The Rabbis already limited the wealth of owners selling essential food to help the poor through the laws of "*onaah*." The owner could not keep more than one-sixth profit in order that others could be sustained as well (*Bava Batra* 90a; *Hoshen Mishpat* 231:20). For the Rabbis, the value of maintaining an orderly just society where the needs of all can be met trumps the full autonomy of owners to maximize their profits to no end.

The primary wage responsibilities fall upon employers. Rabbeinu Yonah, the thirteenth century Spanish rabbi, taught:

> Be careful not to afflict a living creature, whether animal or fowl, and even more so not to afflict a human being, who is created in God's

image. If you want to hire workers and you find that they are poor, they should become like poor members of your household. You should not disgrace them, for you shall command them respectfully, and should pay their salaries (*Sefer HaYirah*).

Rabbeinu Yonah is teaching that when we hire a worker and find that they are still poor after we pay them, then we must treat them as "members of our households" (*b'nei beitecha*). If we choose to become an employer then we must take responsibility to ensure our workers do not live in poverty.

The minimum wage, in its current state, is a collective violation of the biblical prohibition of *oshek* (worker oppression), as workers remain poor while they work to their full capacity (Leviticus 19:15). The previous verse tells us that we must not be enablers of social wrongs (*lifnei iver*) linking the two responsibilities of fair wages and Jewish activism. Now is the time for a collective Jewish intervention to ensure that those who work can live.

Today, one working in New York City on the current minimum wage of $7.25 an hour will have a gross annual income between $12,000–$14,500, based on a 35- to 40-hour work week, after which Federal and state income tax, Social Security, and other taxes are deducted. These workers, often working multiple jobs, beg for food, pile on debt, and take handouts. It is evil to argue that one working all day every day should live in poverty. There is no theory that trumps the imperative for basic justice in a nation with record corporate profits. As Barbara Ehrenreich, who once described her vain attempt to survive on a wage (above the minimum) in *Nickel and Dimed*, wrote in 2007: "There is no moral justification for a minimum wage lower than a living wage. And given the experience of the . . . states that have raised their minimum wages, there isn't even an amoral economic justification."

Today, we can act to create change! We must make our Jewish voices heard in Congress at this crucial time where legislators are deciding whether or not to raise the minimum wage. Uri L'Tzedek and partners now have over 400 clergy members calling for a rise in the minimum wage in New York. Has your rabbi signed on? Have you signed on? □

DAMAGE BY WATCHING:
DOMESTIC DRONES AND PRIVACY

JEREMY BENTHAM, A LEADING EIGHTEENTH CEN-
tury utilitarian thinker, advocated the panopticon
prison, where convicts would be placed under con-
stant surveillance by a central control station. The most notable critique of
the panopticon prison model came from philosopher Michel Foucault, who
viewed it as integral model for a "disciplinary society."

What Bentham did not acknowledge is that constant surveillance is a
form of torture and that shame and loss of dignity go along with constantly
being seen and observed.

Fortunately, Bentham's misguided effort to rehabilitate criminals by
keeping them under 24-hour surveillance did not take hold, and today even
most zoos provide some privacy for their animals. Not so long ago, people
scoffed at the depiction in George Orwell's late novel *1984* of cameras observing an individual's every movement and word, even within their own homes.

Today, however, for a generation that regularly sees police helicopters
hovering over urban neighborhoods and millions of surveillance cameras
in stores and other public places, we may now stand at a point where the
government's ability to spy on us even at home becomes a reality. Would
you like to be filmed and recorded by a government machine while taking
a shower, undergoing a medical examination, or doing other sensitive activities during which you would expect privacy?

Drones, sometimes called unmanned aerial vehicles (UAVs), are re-
motely controlled electronic devices that can observe activity while remaining undetected. Large surveillance devices, including spy satellites, can
already provide remarkably clear photographs of ground targets, although
they cannot see inside houses or hear speech and other sounds. Remote-
controlled drones, which look like small planes or helicopters (and can be
operated by people nearby or on the other side of the world), now have
the capacity to identify individual humans and are capable of intercepting
electronic communication. They have grown progressively smaller; some
drones now have wingspans as wide as 10 feet, while drones that operate for

an hour or two and can be launched by an individual on the ground have wingspans as narrow as 6.5 inches.

Federal authorities are seeking to license thousands of domestic surveillance drones to be launched as soon as 2015. Legal experts are suggesting that our privacy will be called into question on an unparalleled scale. To this point twenty-four civil liberties and privacy organizations have submitted a formal petition to the U.S. Customs and Border Protection demanding that the agency cease the flights of all Predator drones along the borders until clear legal guidelines have been established.

The case for using drones is easy to make. They can make society safer by providing better perspective and evidence, which means more harm may be avoided. Even so, just as with wiretaps and other surveillance methods, the use of drones for specific missions must be carefully regulated by the legal apparatus.

Even with court and other regulations, domestic drone use has an enormous potential for abuse. Consider the already frightening capabilities of drones:

- The ARGUS wide-area surveillance system of drones can monitor all moving people and objects in an area nearly 39 square miles wide. When coupled with the "Persistics" system, it can simultaneously track literally thousands of "targets" and their activities.
- Drones are inexpensive, encouraging their proliferation. While police helicopters can cost $500,000–$3 million apiece and are expensive to fly and maintain, drones may eventually cost as little as $100 each. Since there is little expense involved, there is a greater incentive to use drones more often, whether or not there is a critical need. In addition, some drones are small enough to hover just outside windows or other spaces that a noisy helicopter could never risk.
- Drones for private use are already available, and they are inexpensive. The Parrot AR.Drone 2.0, for example, sells for about $300, and features cameras that face forward and downward and can be controlled and viewed in real time via an iPad. Drones can already be equipped with tear gas and rubber bullets, and manufacturers are requesting authorization to build them. How long before someone manages to equip these machines with a weapon or bomb that could be detonated with no risk (and hardly any expense) to the terrorist?
- A 2012 law passed by Congress authorized the Department of Homeland Security to offer grants to local law enforcement authorities

so they could purchase drones. On the state level, legislation to authorize domestic drones has been introduced in 35 states, and is still active in 30 states. Legislation has passed at least the committee stage in eight states.

- There are estimates that by 2020, 30,000 domestic drones may be in use.

There is a further danger that drones will continue the infamous legacy of weapons developed for war crossing over into civilian society. Many people remember the Thompson submachine gun as the weapon of choice for gangsters (and in response, law enforcement) during the Prohibition era, but few remember that it was developed during World War I for military use. Similarly, the Vietnam War-era AR-15 semi-automatic rifle and its variants have become the weapons of choice in mass shootings in Newtown, Aurora, and other places. We must always use caution when introducing military devices into society, and consider who might eventually get their hands on that technology.

No one's civil liberties need to be violated if drone surveillance is done properly. Additionally, drones can save government money — the technology is relatively inexpensive compared to employing more police officers or building more vehicles. Criminals can be under surveillance more effortlessly.

But our goal as a society isn't safety alone. We are also deeply concerned with privacy, dignity, and freedom. There would be great losses to becoming a "surveillance society" where every word and movement is tracked, recorded, and scrutinized.

There have been important developments around the country to regulate the use of drones. Many limits should be placed upon the use of drones. A Rhode Island bill, for example, would prevent drones from carrying weapons, limit the time a drone could be used against an individual, notify those targeted that they had been subject to surveillance, and provide legal redress for anyone who had been subjected to illegal surveillance by a drone. Seattle returned the two drones it had purchased without using them after its mayor decided to prohibit their use. A bill has been introduced in Congress to forbid the use of drones without a warrant. Public opinion may also turn against aggressive use of domestic drones. A Gallup poll released in March 2013 revealed that 79 percent of Americans oppose the use of drones to assassinate American terrorists living in this country. There should be audits and oversight to be sure that the surveillance procedures are not abused.

There are two relevant Jewish prohibitions here: *hezek re'iah* (visual surveillance – damage by watching) and *hezek shemiyah* (aural surveillance – damage by listening). While there is no physical contact, they are still considered damage for which one is legally liable. Rabbi Norman Lamm wrote back in 1967: "Unauthorized disclosure, whether the original information was received by complete consent or by illegal intrusion, whether ethically or unethically, remains prohibited by the *halakha*."

Israeli Supreme Court Justice and Talmudic scholar Menachem Elon, of blessed memory, was vocal about this issue and argued in 1994 that "The protection of privacy in Jewish law goes beyond prohibiting the observation of another's activities. There is a legal duty to prevent the possibility of observation that would infringe another's privacy; the mere existence of such a possibility inhibits the freedom of an individual to act as he wishes in his home or courtyard."

I hope you'll join me to ensure that drones are not used in such a fashion by signing the petition to the deputy commissioner of the United States Bureau of Customs and Border Protection sponsored by the Electronic Privacy Information Center, that calls on the government to suspend the use of drones until rules are established protecting the public's right to privacy. Write to your Senators and Representative to see where they stand on pending legislation on drone use and keep track of your state's legislation.

There are already industry groups and manufacturers lobbying to promote the indiscriminate use of drones. It is critical that we all raise our voices to see that this emerging technology does not become a monstrous violation of privacy. We must make sure society and technology can help us do that. But this must be heavily regulated with strong checks and balances. Using drone technology runs the risk of losing all personal privacy and puts civil society, no less than the individual, at risk. □

WHAT TO DO WITH GUANTÁNAMO BAY? THOUGHTS ON ISOLATION AND TERROR

THE LUBAVITCHER REBBE TAUGHT "YOU SEE, if there is one place on earth that is most un-Godly, it is prison. In prison a person is stripped of that which makes him uniquely human: his freedom. For this reason there is no punishment of jail in Jewish law." This is even truer when one never experienced a fair trial yet is subject to isolation and torture.

The Guantánamo Bay prison (sometimes abbreviated as GTMO and known as "Gitmo") has been in operation since shortly after the September 11, 2001 terrorist attacks. While at first people believed that the prison, which is located in the Guantánamo Bay Naval Base in Cuba, would be filled with dangerous terrorists awaiting trial, the increasingly evident reality is that it houses people stuck in a legal loophole that allows them to be held indefinitely without being charged with a crime, under conditions that the International Red Cross has characterized as "tantamount to torture." Even the United States government admits that 92 percent of the prisoners never fought for al-Qaeda, and that 86 percent were turned over as a result of corrupt and generous bounty offers made by members of the American military to villagers in Afghanistan and Pakistan.

Statistics compiled by the American Civil Liberties Union reveal an alarming abuse of rights and freedoms, with the overwhelming majority of prisoners not being a threat to national security:

- 532 prisoners were released under the Bush administration, and 72 under the Obama administration; of 166 prisoners remaining, 86 were cleared for release in 2009
- Of 21 children imprisoned at Guantánamo, the youngest was 13; Yasser Talal Al Zahrani was imprisoned at 16 and became the youngest apparent suicide at age 21
- The oldest prisoner was 98 years old
- More than 200 FBI agents have reported that Guantánamo prisoners

were abused; in addition, at least 26 prisoners were initially tortured at secret overseas jails and then shipped to Guantánamo

Here are three examples showing how there is not even a pretense of legal procedures at Guantánamo.

1. Lakhdar Boumediene, a Bosnian citizen who lived and worked there for the Red Crescent, was arrested but found innocent of being an al-Qaeda operative. After his acquittal, acting on the word of an unnamed informant who was judged even then to be unreliable, the Americans kidnapped Boumediene and transported him to Guantánamo, where he was imprisoned for more than seven years. He was beaten, kept in uncomfortable positions for hours at a time, exposed to extreme temperatures, and deprived of sleep. He went on a hunger strike and was force-fed for two years. After a Supreme Court challenge, a federal court found there was no evidence to hold him, and he was finally released in 2008. He now lives in France with his family.

2. The *Road to Guantánamo* is a 2006 British docudrama that tells the story of three British citizens who were in Pakistan at the beginning of the war in Afghanistan. They were swept up by the Allied forces and sent to Guantánamo, where they were held without charges and under brutal conditions for two years before finally being released.

3. The lack of accountability and due legal procedure has even extended to American citizens. James Yee, a West Point graduate whose grandparents came to America from China in the 1920s and later converted to Islam, became a Muslim Army chaplain and volunteered to serve in the Guantánamo prison. On September 10, 2003, when returning to America on leave, he was detained and then arrested, held for 76 days in solitary confinement, and then publicly accused of and charged with a battery of moral and political offenses that included being an al-Qaeda agent and a "Chinese Taliban." It took Captain Yee until March 19, 2004 to receive a dismissal of his court martial charges, and until April 14, 2004 to successfully appeal and remove the charges from his record. Even so, as he writes in *For God and Country: Faith and Patriotism Under Fire*, "Since my case was dismissed, nobody has taken responsibility for what happened to me. Nobody has explained what went wrong or why." He was not even asked to leave the service. After he left voluntarily, Captain Yee did not receive the items taken from him when he was arrested, and later learned that he was still under surveillance.

The continuing history of the infamous Gitmo, the longest operating wartime prison in the history of the United States, is a story of political pandering. With enough evidence to warrant a trial for barely two dozen prisoners, President Obama signed an executive order to close the prison in 2009, but congressional opposition has prevented the President from sending any prisoners to American prisons or courts for trial. Even though the Government Accountability Office concluded that transferring these prisoners could be done safely (and 500 terrorism suspects have been tried in federal courts since September 2001), Congressional intransigence continues. Typical of the intensely paranoid rhetoric is the statement from Senator Lindsey Graham of South Carolina, who warned against any attempt to "bring these crazy bastards that want to kill us all to the United States." Congress passed legislation in 2009 that prevented the President from bringing any of these prisoners to the United States for trial, or even send them to other countries. Two of the original forty-eight prisoners stuck in a legal no-man's land (no evidence against, but for other reasons cannot be released) have already died in prison. President Obama has decided that no prisoner will be sent to "unsettled" areas such as Yemen, but the United States has also not allowed arrangements for prisoners to go to other countries until the situation becomes settled. Thus, they are subject to indefinite imprisonment without charges.

Meanwhile, the horrors of Guantánamo continue, and in the spring of 2013, Guantánamo detainees went on a hunger strike to protest conditions and the detention center's continued existence. Dozens of the 166 prisoners continued to be held despite having been cleared for release. We must continue our efforts to close Guantánamo.

Marine Corps General John Kelly, the head of U.S. military forces in Latin America, said the Guantánamo prisoners had begun the hunger strike because "they had great optimism that Guantánamo would be closed. They were devastated apparently ... when the president backed off, at least (that's) their perception, of closing the facility."

Lawyers for the Center for Constitutional Rights (CCR) who represent the detainees said that the detainees have decided to hunger strike because of "the crushing reality that after eleven years in indefinite detention, there is no end in sight to their suffering."

There are various ways to take action, and not remain silent in the face of this ongoing tragedy.

Participate in Witness Against Torture fasts and vigils. Write to Congress about closing Guantánamo.

We cannot be silent in the face of this ongoing tragedy.   □

IMMIGRATION REFORM:
A JEWISH IMPERATIVE

BIPARTISAN GROUP OF EIGHT U.S. SENATORS announced a new immigration reform effort. The next day, President Barack Obama gave a speech outlining his own plan for immigration reform. We hope these comprehensive efforts help resolve the continuing confusion over this issue. In just the first half of 2012, hundreds of bills and resolutions, often contradictory and misguided, were adopted by 41 state legislatures addressing immigration. Anti-immigrant extremists around the country are moving to amend the 14th Amendment to the Constitution's guarantee of citizenship to anyone born in the United States, recognizing only those born of citizens. This would affect the 350,000 children born in the United States each year to at least one undocumented immigrant parent. With an estimated 11.5–12 million undocumented immigrants living in the United States today – facing deportation regardless of how long they have been here – change in our country is long overdue.

Contrary to popular perception, President Obama stepped up the detention of undocumented immigrants during his first term. In 2011, U.S. Immigration and Customs Enforcement removed nearly 400,000 undocumented immigrants from the country, and nearly 55 percent were convicted of felonies or misdemeanors; in 2012, I C E detained 410,000 undocumented immigrants. However, on January 29, 2013, President Obama acknowledged that this situation should not continue. He proposed a legal procedure by which undocumented Americans could register and, once passing a background check, gain provisional legal status, and eventually permanent resident status and citizenship. The one potential hold-up is border security issues: Republican leaders may insist that the borders be absolutely secure before implementing the policy, while the President wants to implement the procedure earlier.

Oddly, this is occurring at a time when immigration to the U.S. is decreasing. The Pew Hispanic Center announced in April 2012 that the net migration from Mexico to the United States has stopped and possibly even reversed. They note that from 2005 to 2010, about 1.4 million Mexicans immigrated to the United States while the same number of Mexican immigrants and their U.S.-born children moved from the United States to Mexico. Asians, not Latinos, are now actually the largest group of new arrivals in the United States.

While there is mostly speculation on the effect of undocumented Americans on employment, it has been shown that over 50 percent of them pay taxes. As with other Americans, they pay sales tax.In addition, in 2007 they and their employers were responsible for an estimated $11.2 billion in Social Security and $2.6 billion in Medicare contributions, in addition to other taxes and unemployment insurance payments. Since these workers use fake identification to obtain work, they can never receive unemployment insurance, Social Security, or Medicare, so they actually pay into our system without receiving benefits from it. In 2006, when Texas conducted the first comprehensive economic review of the impact of undocumented Americans, it was discovered that while these Americans produced $1.58 billion of revenue, they only received $1.16 billion in state services, so Texas made $462 million in profit from undocumented Texans.

Critics of immigration reform have used outlandish and false statements to justify their positions, echoing the bigotry against Italian and Jewish immigrants a century ago. Arizona Governor Jan Brewer said this in 2010: "The majority of the illegal trespassers that are coming into the state of Arizona are under the direction and control of organized drug cartels and they are bringing drugs in." On January 29, 2013, the influential conservative radio pundit Rush Limbaugh made this outrageous statement concerning Hispanic immigrants: "I've seen . . . research data which says that a vast majority of arriving immigrants today come here because they believe that government is the source of prosperity, and that's what they support."

No one has ever presented credible evidence to back either of these false claims. Most of these undocumented immigrants are from Mexico (59 percent, 6.8 million) who are fleeing poverty back home, yet most still live in poverty and insecurity here. About 3 million live in California and about 2 million in Texas, close to the border. Their life in the homeland they are fleeing is one of pain and sorrow and they must leave behind their families and all they know to try to survive. Their stories are tragic; at "My Immigration Story," you can read their stories of anxiety over coming to the United States at an early age, but still subject to being deported to a country they never knew; of trying to comply with, and work within, the legal framework but being stymied by decades of bureaucratic foot-dragging; of relatives separated by a border, of loved ones' burial places that cannot be visited.

In the Torah, there is a positive commandment to love the foreigner in our midst (Deuteronomy 10:18), and a negative commandment against oppressing or perverting justice for them in any way (Exodus 22:20, Deuteronomy 24:17). The Rabbis elaborated on this prohibition: "You shall not wrong or oppress the stranger, for you were strangers in the land of Egypt. You shall not wrong with words, and you shall not oppress financially" (*Mechilta d'Rabbi Yishmael, Mishpatim*). We not only owe them basic human rights; we also have specific religious obligations to go above and beyond to protect them from harm. We should be grateful that America is a desired home for those fleeing dire straits and be proud of what we have to offer.

Significant numbers of Jews immigrated (and continue to immigrate) to the United States without documentation. We also needed a safe refuge like many others fleeing poverty and persecution today. Our responsibility to the vulnerable immigrant (and heroic journeyer) requires that we honor the image of God in all people. Perhaps Emmanuel Levinas, the French Talmudist and Jewish philosopher, said it best: "The respect for the stranger and the sanctification of the name of the Eternal are strangely equivalent" (*Nine Talmudic Readings*: "Toward the Other," 27).

Now is the time to hear the eternal calls of our religious traditions and of human conscience to ensure the dignity of all humans by providing a pathway to citizenship for undocumented immigrants currently in the United States. We are long overdue but sure to prevail, since our commitment is steadfast and justice is on our side. □

STRANGERS, IMMIGRANTS, AND THE *EGLAH ARUFAH*

Responsibility to the Stranger

THE JEWISH TRADITION PLACES A STRONG emphasis on our duties towards the stranger. The Rabbis returned repeatedly to the injunction "You shall not wrong or oppress a stranger, [for you know the feelings of the stranger,] for you were strangers in the land of Egypt" (Exodus 22:20). Rabbi Samson Raphael Hirsch elaborated on this teaching, explaining that there are no preconditions for receiving basic rights other than being human:

> "You shall not wrong or oppress a stranger, for you were strangers in the land of Egypt."
>
> Here it says simply and absolutely, "for you were strangers," your whole misfortune in Egypt was that you were strangers there. As such, according to the views of other nations, you had no right to be there, had no claim to rights of settlement, home, or property. Accordingly, you had no rights in appeal against unfair or unjust treatment. As aliens you were without any rights in Egypt, out of that grew all of your bondage and oppression, your slavery and wretchedness. Therefore beware, so runs the warning, from making rights in your own State conditional on anything other than on that simple humanity which every human being as such bears within. With any limitation in these human rights, the gate is opened to the whole horror of Egyptian mishandling of human beings" (Commentary on Exodus 22:20).

Rabbi Hirsch went further, noting the central role of the treatment of strangers to a just society:

> Twenty-four times, whenever, and in every case, where the Torah lays down the law concerning rights of persons and things, the "stranger in

the land" is placed under the special protection of the law. The degree of justice in a land is measured, not so much by the rights accorded to the native-born inhabitants, to the rich, or people who have, at any rate, representatives or connections that look after their interests, but by what justice is meted out to the completely unprotected "stranger." The absolute equality in the eyes of the law between the native and the foreigner forms the very basic foundation of Jewish jurisdiction (Commentary on Exodus 1:14).

Sodom, the paradigmatic evil society, is said to have been cruel to guests: "They issued a proclamation in Sodom saying, 'Everyone who strengthens the hand of the poor and the needy and the stranger with a loaf of bread shall be burnt by fire'" (*Pirke D'Rabbi Eliezer* 25). The main crime of Sodom was that they did not sustain the needs of the stranger passing through their midst.

We are all Strangers . . .

We learn that the stranger is not just the other. We are all strangers. "The land shall not be sold in perpetuity, for the land is mine; for you are foreigners and temporary dwellers with Me" (Leviticus 25:23). Not only were the Jewish people considered strangers; before God, all humans are like strangers: "For we are like foreigners before You, and like temporary dwellers, as were all of our forefathers – our days on earth are like a shadow, and there is no hope" (I Chronicles 29:15). Further, we learn in the book of Psalms, "Hear my prayer, God, give ear to my outcry, be not mute to my tears; for I am a foreigner with You, a temporary dweller like all my forefathers" (39:13).

There is a striking Midrash about how being human means there is no place on Earth that we do not belong:

> "God gathered the dust [of the first human] from the four corners of the world – red, black, white, and green. Red is the blood, black is the innards, and green for the body. Why from the four corners of the earth? So that if one comes from the east to the west and arrives at the end of his life as he nears departing from the world, it will not be said to him: "This land is not the dust of your body, it is of mine. Go back to where you were created." Rather, every place that a person walks, from there he was created and from there he will return" (*Yalkut Shimoni*, Genesis 1:13).

To Feel Like a Stranger

Abraham was the first Jewish hero, willing to journey beyond his home for a higher purpose: "The Lord said to Abraham: 'Go forth from your native land and from your father's house to the land that I will show you'" (Genesis 12:1). Rabbi Joseph Soloveitchik explains the nature of the unique heroism of the stranger:

> Bondage to man excludes Divine friendship. The beloved must tear down all the social and political barriers that fence in the individual and imprison his initiative and liberty. The charismatic person is anarchic, liberty-loving; he frees himself from all the fixed formulas and rhythms of an urbanized civilization and joins a fluid, careless, roving nomad society. An ancient Egyptian document describes the nomads as follows: "Here is the miserable stranger . . . He does not dwell in the same spot; his feet are always wandering. From times of Horus he battles, he does not conquer, and is not conquered" (Buber, *Moses*, 25). The stranger is indomitable; he may lose a battle, yet had never lost a war. He will never reconcile with political subjection. Roaming, wandering, he will escape persecution and oppression. When the need arises, the nomad stands up and fights for his freedom and many a time proves superior in battle to the settled king. Abraham's heroism on the battlefield is the best illustration (*The Emergence of Ethical Man*, 153).

The Rabbis teach, "He who has not made good in one place and fails to move and try his luck in some other place has only himself to complain about" (*Bava Metzsia* 75b). We should be slow to judge harshly those who leave all they have known to make a better life for themselves and their families, even though we cannot condone breaking the law. "Do not judge your fellow human until you stand in his place" (*Pirke Avot* 2:4).

These words should resonate with us, as we consider the case of undocumented immigrants trying to make their way to and in the United States.

Immigration in America: The Historical Record

At its best, America has recognized that we are all strangers, and has prided itself on being a "Nation of Immigrants." Our country has prospered as a gathering point for those who dared to leave their settled environments, and who became strangers in a new land to search for liberty and opportunity. In the 1630s, more than 20,000 Puritans left their native England to join the new Massachusetts Bay Colony. After a century of religious persecution from English monarchs, the Puritans welcomed a unique and unprecedented feature of the Massachusetts Charter: the absence of outside control from England. This allowed New England colonists to break with their old lifestyles, and to combine monarchical rule with representative government, forming the basis for American democracy.

After America gained independence, immigrants continued to make profound contributions toward the country's economy. One might even say that America was made by immigrants. Charles Hirschman, a sociologist at the University of Washington, expounds on the benefits of immigration:

> During the middle decades of the nineteenth century, immigrants from Germany and Scandinavia played a major role in settling the frontier. Irish immigrants worked as laborers in cities and were the major source of labor in the construction of transportation networks, including canals, railroads, and roads . . . immigrants have also played an important role in the transition to an urban industrial economy in the late nineteenth and early twentieth centuries. Immigrant workers have always been overrepresented in skilled trades, mining, and as peddlers, merchants, and laborers in urban areas."

The Shameful History of American Xenophobia

Unfortunately, despite the many contributions of immigrants to American society, they have time and again encountered irrational hostility from existing citizens. Before German immigrants played a key role in settling the American frontier, they were derided by Benjamin Franklin, who regarded them as strangers because they spoke German instead of English: "Why should the *Palatine Boors* be suffered to swarm into our settlements and by herding together establish their Language and Manners to the Exclusion of ours?" Irish Catholic and Jewish immigrants encountered hostility from Protestant "nativists" because of religious differences. One nativist party advocated exclusionary policies against Irish immigrants, in order "to resist the insidious policy of the Church of Rome and all other foreign influence."

In 1924, nativists helped pass an Immigration Act that made Jewish immigration to America almost impossible. During hearings on the Act, religious Jewish neighborhoods of the Lower East Side were cited as a primary example of "failed" immigration. The shameful historical legacy of this act is that Jewish refugees fleeing Hitler were barred entry to the United States. We can only imagine how different things might be today if the American government had heeded the Yalkut Shimoni's maxim that "every place that a person walks, from there he was created and from there she will return."

Immigration in America Today

In the current age of globalization, we have opened our borders to international trade and finance, but restricted the entry of immigrants to the United States, especially from Latin America. Between 1970–2000, international financial investment has doubled as a percentage of U.S. output, and merchandise exports have nearly tripled. During this same period, the number of undocumented immigrants increased from fewer than 1 million to 8 million.

Immigration has positive and negative effects on the economy. On the one hand, immigrants have expanded the wealth of the typical American. James Smith of the Rand Institute estimates that immigrants have increased total American output by $10 billion a year. On the other hand, immigration can drive down wages, especially for manual workers. Pia M. Orrenius and Madeline Zavodny, two researchers at the Federal Reserve, found that annual wages of low-skilled workers dropped 2.3 percent due to immigration. While immigrants use social services, they also pay taxes. Multiple studies have found that immigration actually creates jobs for Americans.

Regardless of the economic effects of economic immigrants, we should recognize that their presence in the United States is a natural consequence of globalization. As John Hansen explains in a Council on Foreign Relations report, rising economic immigration is directly related to globalization:

> During the past twenty years, Mexico has experienced several severe economic contractions, with emigration from the country spiking in the aftermath of each downturn. In terms of the economic benefits, this is exactly when one would want workers to move – when their labor productivity in the United States is highest relative to their labor productivity at home ("The Economic Logic of Illegal Immigration," 15–16).

If we want to experience the benefits of globalization, we must also be will-ing to accept the entry of immigrants seeking economic opportunity. Yet American immigration policy allows no way for these economic migrants to enter the country legally, as Hansen explains: "Long queues for U.S. green cards mean there is little way for legal permanent immigration to respond to such changes in international economic conditions." Because economic migration to the United States is closely connected to interna-tional trade and investment flows, restrictive government policies have failed to stop immigration from Latin America. All these policies have done is force economic immigrants to accept an undocumented status, to enter into situations of vulnerability, and, at times, to face mortal danger.

Immigration Raids: Destroying Communities

Immigration raids are a prime example of the dangers faced by undocu-mented immigrants. Since 2005, federal authorities have conducted large-scale raids of worksites suspected of employing undocumented immigrants. Tens of thousands of undocumented immigrants have been arrested as a result of these raids. These immigrants were not gangsters or criminals; they generally had no prior criminal history, and many had lived peace-ably in the country for years. However, because immigration raids have occurred across the country, without warning, they have created a sense of fear among the entire immigrant population.

Sociologist Saskia Sassen has referred to long-term undocumented residents as "unauthorized yet recognized": "Undocumented immigrants' daily practices in their community – raising a family, schooling children, holding a job – over time can earn them citizenship claims in just about all developed countries, including the United States. There are dimensions of citizenship, such as strong community ties and participation in civic activities, that are enacted informally through these practices" (*Territory, Authority, Rights*, 294). The spate of immigration raids has undermined this informal contract, sending a message that even if immigrants make years of contributions to the community, their good standing can disappear in a moment.

This message, in turn, undermines community, and for evidence we need not look too far from home. In 2008, federal authorities conducted an immi-gration raid on the Agriprocessors meat processing plant in Iowa. The raid served an important purpose, as employees in the plant reported shocking stories of workplace abuse. But this abuse would have been reported sooner if workers had not feared deportation. Further, the raid caused untold damage to the Postville community, where the plant was based. Overnight, businesses closed down and hundreds of homes were abandoned. Many undocumented residents of Postville, who had lived in the town for years, fled in fear of capture, and were replaced by temporary workers who were less invested in the community; years later, Postville has yet to fully recover from the loss. The story of Postville has been repeated in towns and establishments across the nation. Undocumented immigrants who are recognized as productive members of the community – parents, talented scholars, and civic activists – are finding their community status erased after one encounter with police, and American society is the poorer for it.

Death at the Border: Operation Gatekeeper

The most notorious American immigration policy is Operation Gatekeeper, enacted in 1994 by the Clinton Administration. This ongoing policy has deployed troops, border fences, and surveillance near major population centers in an effort to deter economic migrants from crossing the U.S.-Mexico border. The policy has failed to slow immigration. Between 2000–2008, the estimated undocumented population increased from 8 million to 12 million, but by forcing economic migrants to take more dangerous routes, Operation Gatekeeper has had tragic consequences. Between 1994 and 2009, at least 3,861 immigrants have lost their lives attempting to enter the United States from Mexico. While immigrant deaths occurred before Operation Gatekeeper, the Center for Immigrant Research has noted a marked increase in the number of deaths since 1994.

Some immigration opponents claim that high U.S.-Mexico border surveillance is needed for national security. While we must ensure terrorists do not enter our country, mass migration from Latin America has historically not been a security risk. The Foreign Military Studies Office stated in 2002 that although there is frequent smuggling from Mexico, "no apparent link exists between the international smugglers and any terrorist organization." In fact, the Office identified America's northern neighbor, Canada, as a more likely base for terrorists to sneak in. We can prevent terrorist infiltration by working together with the Mexican government, just as we work with the Canadian government. There is no need for policies that place immigrants seeking economic opportunity in life-threatening situations.

The immigrant exists in a liminal space similar to what French psycho-analyst Jacques Lacan called the *nebenmensch*, the other who is both differ-ent and similar. The immigrant is the post-modern hero who transcends boundaries, defying categorization or clear belonging or labeling, calling upon others to respond to her social ambiguity. What should be the Jewish response to the vulnerability of undocumented immigrants? I suggest that it should incorporate the ethos of the *eglah arufah*.

Eglah Arufah and Collective Responsibility

In some fashion, this ritual can be revived. Modeled off of the *eglah arufah* ceremony, in February 2012, the Israeli Tzohar Association of Rabbis gath-ered to pray alongside the highway, on the spot where a female soldier was killed in a hit-and-run. The Torah's case of the *eglah arufah* involves a corpse that is discovered between two settlements when no one knows who the murderer is. The priests and the elders of the nearest towns lead a unique ceremony and declare, "Our hands have not spilled this blood" (Deuteronomy 21:7).

The fifteenth century Portuguese Jewish philosopher Abravanel explains that the goal of the ritual is to jolt the residents from their normal routines to respond and take responsibility for the heinous crime that occurred. When murder occurs, life cannot go on as usual, as Israeli Bible scholar and educator, Nechama Leibowitz, describes:

> We see then that responsibility for an evil act does not fall only on the perpetrator and not just on the abettor. The crime does not only involve cooperation, but also negligence, omission, and inattention. One who sits in his quiet corner and ignores the rest of society and its corrupt ways and "with dualists do not mingle" (Proverbs 24:21) and guards his soul with every safeguard – and sees oppression and theft and robbery but does not arise and does not move and does not struggle and does not protest – he also cannot say, "Our hands have not spilled this blood."

The Gemara says that the leaders are responsible, since they failed to pro-vide this wanderer with food and escort (*Sotah* 38b). The sixteenth century Jewish thinker, the Maharal of Prague, explains that the poor wanderer was hungry and was killed while trying to steal food. Even though the victim died while committing an illegal act, the leaders who failed to feed him are responsible. Even though the town's leaders did not do any direct harm, they are held responsible for the death.

Just as the wanderer who was commemorated through the *eglah arufah* broke the law, so too undocumented immigrants today break the law. Nevertheless, the leaders who turn a blind eye to their needs are responsible for their suffering. In the case in Deuteronomy, the individual was guilty of theft, a sin condemned very strongly by Jewish law. Rav Ahron Soloveichik writes: "We assume that the person was starving and attempted an armed robbery in order to obtain food" (*Logic of the Heart Logic of the Mind*, 175). This is all the more true with someone crossing international borders without documentation which is not an act condemned by Jewish law, and although we are bound by the law of the land, there is no reason why we should take less responsibility than in the case of the *eglah arufah*.

The idea that leaders are accountable for their generation is prevalent in Jewish thought:

> As long as one is but an ordinary scholar, he has no concern with the congregation and is not punished [for its lapses], but as soon as he is appointed head and dons the cloak [of leadership], he must no longer say: "I live for my own benefit, I care not about the congregation," but the whole burden of the community is on his shoulders. If he sees a man causing suffering to another, or transgressing, and does not prevent him, then he is held punishable (Exodus Rabbah 27:9).

Once we accept the role of moral leadership, we are truly accountable for our community. But the Rabbis teach us that societal accountability is not granted solely to those who have been granted formal authority, but to all those of learning. "If a person of learning participates in public affairs and serves as judge or arbiter, he gives stability to the land . . . But if he sits in his home and says to himself, 'What have the affairs of society to do with me? . . . Why should I trouble myself with the people's voices of protest? Let my soul dwell in peace!' – if he does this, he overthrows the world" (*Midrash Tanhuma, Mishpatim* 2). Responsibility does not just apply to the scholar. The Rabbis confirm that this responsibility is upon all of us. "Everyone who can protest the sin of his household and does not, is responsible for the people of his household; for the people of his city, he is responsible for the people of his city; for the whole world, he is responsible for the whole world" (*Shabbat* 54b). There are many different ways to take responsibility and to fulfill the commandment, "You shall not stand idly by the blood of your neighbor!" (Leviticus 19:16). The world continues to exist because humans are responsible agents. When we give up our ability to hear the voices of protest and the cry of the sufferer, we bring the world to ruin.

In modern times, Rabbi Abraham Joshua Heschel explains it well in his 1971 "A Prayer for Peace": "O Lord, we confess our sins; we are ashamed of the inadequacy of our anguish, of how faint and slight is our mercy. We are a generation that has lost its capacity for outrage. We must continue to remind ourselves that in a free society all are involved in what some are doing. Some are guilty, all are responsible." We are not culpable for the deaths and the abuses of the immigrants in our country, but we are certainly responsible to change the situation.

The mitzvah of *eglah arufah* today must go beyond *leviyat orhim* (a few symbolic courtesy steps to walk our guests out from our homes). Most of us cannot relate to the fear that undocumented workers feel in America today. We have undocumented residents dying alongside the Mexican border, being detained by the U.S. Immigration and Customs Enforcement, and waiting in vain for adequate health care. More than 200 individuals die each year trying to cross the Mexico-United States border, and many of the survivors are sexually assaulted or abused on the way. The blood of these *gerim* (strangers) within our midst may be on all our hands.

In the spirit of the elders of the community who would "speak up and say: 'Our hands have not spilled this blood,'" we should work to ensure that that undocumented immigrants are treated fairly in our communities, restaurants and neighborhoods. Now is the time for the American Jewish community to speak up, and address the plight of strangers in our midst. Then, even if others are complicit in the neglect and marginalization of undocumented immigrants, we will at least be able to say, "Our hands have not spilled this blood."　□

CONTEMPORARY POLITICS: OATHS MADE IN VAIN

T HE POWER OF SPEECH IS ONE OF THE MOST amazing human faculties: The great Bible commentator Onkelos (on Genesis 2:7) goes so far as to suggest that this is the defining feature of being human. How we use our speech ultimately determines what we are about.

In business, it's often said that one should "under-promise and over-deliver." This is the opposite approach typically offered in politics, which is to over-promise (and, unfortunately, under-deliver). Politicians and aspiring officeholders often make commitments that are impossible to meet.

In Jewish law, a false commitment is called a *shevuat shav* (a vain oath). There are four kinds of vain oaths:

- An oath to something which is obviously true
- An oath to something which is obviously false
- An oath to transgress a commandment
- An oath to do the impossible

It's the fourth category, an oath to do the impossible, that has become very common today.

Words truly matter and we must discern, when we either make a promise or consider another's promise, what is at least sincere versus what is a *shevuat shav*. It is not only politicians but all of us who can learn from this lesson.

Business marketing, especially in the stock market, has a particularly bad reputation for *shevuat shav*. We can go back to the times of Charles Dickens who in his novel *Nicholas Nickleby* (published between 1838 and 1839) describes in Chapter 2 a joint stock scam in which wealthy businessmen tout the initial offering of stock (to draw unwitting victims to invest) while simultaneously planning to get out with a huge profit before the stock crashes. In the twentieth century, there were more incredible promises. Carlo "Charles" Ponzi, after several small-time swindles, came upon what became known as the "Ponzi scheme," attracting investors with the promise of outrageously high returns in an unrealistically short amount of time. In reality, he used the incoming money to pay off the original investors, while taking a good deal of the money for himself. After about a year of this, he was arrested and spent the next twelve years in jail. Incredibly, many criminals have repeated this scam and found willing victims, most infamously in the Bernie Madoff scandal.

While business promises can ruin people financially, political promises during political crises can cost lives and influence policies for decades. When President Woodrow Wilson called for war against Germany in 1917, he made impossible promises: "The world must be made safe for democracy. Its peace must be planted upon the tested foundations of political liberty. We have no selfish ends to serve. We desire no conquest, no dominion." He later released his Fourteen Points for a just peace, and sailed to Paris twice to press his case. Unfortunately, the United States had as its allies the most oppressive government in the world, Russia (still headed by a tsar and responsible for countless pogroms that killed many Jews and drove millions more to America and other countries), and the two largest colonial powers, Great Britain and France. While the tsar was soon overthrown, neither Great Britain nor France wanted to part with its colonies after the war, making a mockery of President Wilson's lofty Fourteen Points. French Premier Georges Clemenceau, known as "the Tiger," sarcastically remarked that "God has Ten Commandments. Wilson has Fourteen." In America, the popular entertainer Eddie Cantor drew tremendous laughter at the Ziegfeld Follies when he made fun of Wilson's trips to Paris: "Presidents may come and Presidents may go, but Wilson does both!" The public derision contributed to a lengthy period of isolation throughout the next two decades, and delayed the American reaction to the later rise of fascism in Europe.

In recent times, the Bush administration made absurdly optimistic predictions about the Iraq War. Asked in February of 2003 how long the Iraq war would last, Defense Secretary Donald Rumsfeld said: "It could last six days, six weeks. I doubt six months." In March, Vice President Dick Cheney added: "Weeks rather than months." The war lasted eight years and cost about $800 billion, with thousands of casualties, and undoubtedly contributed to Democrat Barack Obama's two presidential election victories.

Economic crises have also contributed to over-the-top promises. Republican Herbert Hoover was considered an expert in business when he ran for President in 1928, claiming that unemployment was "widely disappearing": "We in America today are nearer to the final triumph over poverty than ever before in the history of any land." In October 1929, in response to instability on Wall Street, Hoover said: "The fundamental business of the country . . . is on a sound and prosperous basis." Four days later, the stock market crashed, precipitating the Great Depression. In spite of this, Hoover continued to insist that things would work themselves out. Throughout 1930, he maintained that business had turned the corner and that the worst of unemployment would be over, comments that were adapted by the media to "Prosperity is just around the corner." As the Depression worsened, the promise quickly became a joke, with particular jabs from popular composers. In his Pulitzer prize-winning 1931 musical, *Of Thee I Sing*, George Gershwin wrote a satirical song, "Posterity Is Just Around the Corner." Even the usually upbeat Irving Berlin, who lost a fortune in the Wall Street crash, turned a cynical eye to the President in his 1932 musical *Face the Music*: "Mr. Herbert Hoover says that now's the time to buy, so let's have another cup of coffee, and let's have another piece of pie!" In the meantime, people died of malnutrition and an entire generation suffered psychologically from the fear that their savings might disappear at any moment. Ultimately, the Democratic candidate won each of the next five presidential races.

Needless to say, Americans do not have a monopoly on false political promises. Tens of millions of people have died in wars in which their leaders promised centuries of glory, and their only legacy was the destruction of their own countries as well as other lands. During the Cold War, there was no world war but there were many economic disasters caused by false promises. In the "Great Leap Forward" of 1958–1960, Mao Zedong promised to jump-start Chinese industry and agriculture in an effort to beat both the Americans and the Soviets, with whom he had grown progressively more hostile. Small communes were set up throughout the countryside, and 600,000 "backyard furnaces" were set up to make steel. However, these tiny furnaces proved useless, as they could not generate temperatures high enough to make high-grade steel, and they sucked up so many agricultural and industrial resources that mass starvation resulted. The "Great Leap Forward," in retrospect, proved to be the "Great Collapse," with a terrifying number of needless Chinese dead. It took China years to recover.

Sometimes a promise can seem ambitious in one era and ridiculous in another. Democratic President John F. Kennedy, in a speech to Congress in May 1961, pledged to land a man on the moon before the decade was out. This notion fit in with American youthful idealism as well as with the bipartisan ethos present in government during the Cold War, and the technology was in the works. In July 1969, the United States landed the first man on the moon during the presidency of Republican Richard Nixon. On the other hand, during the Republican presidential primary campaign in 2012, Newt Gingrich said that if he were elected, there would be a manned moon base in operation by 2020. However, most scientists immediately scoffed at the possibility and others saw this as a self-serving attempt by the candidate to appeal to the Florida space industry, questioning how a candidate who proposed cutting the budget could justify tens of billions of dollars of additional expenditures. Gingrich was soon out of the campaign.

Today's political promises and their lack of fulfillment are not as catastrophic as in the past, but there are some that deserve attention. In 2008, candidate Barack Obama promised to close the Guantánamo Bay prison in Cuba, to add 5 million new jobs in clean energy enterprises, to end foreclosures, and to keep unemployment under 8 percent with a stimulus plan. While President Obama has faced unprecedented opposition (including hundreds of filibusters from the Republicans in the Senate) that pushes for incredibly high tax breaks for the wealthy, cuts for poverty programs, and ludicrous claims that these will create rather than destroy the job market, many critics argue that Obama has not done enough to counter the opposition. For example, while the unemployment rate fell to 7.6 percent in March 2013, it was mostly the result of 500,000 people dropping out of the work force. Today, the labor participation rate is 63.3 percent, the lowest since 1979. This cannot be seen as a promise fulfilled, and should not be permitted as the "new normal."

There are those who maintain that you have to make impossible promises in order to get elected or stay in business. However, we should always ask whether a promise is at least plausible or whether it deserves to be denounced as a *shevuat shav*. An informed market and an informed electorate, with real accountability for those who keep and fail to keep their promises, are the way forward for a just and prosperous society. The Torah teaches us not to publicly set false expectations for personal gain. We should take this lesson to heart in our personal lives and raise the bar in our public discourse.

□

☐ ADDRESSING SCANDALS AND SOCIAL WRONGS

THE BODIES EXHIBIT
AND THE JEWISH VALUE
OF HONORING THE BODY

OULD YOU IMAGINE ARRIVING AT A MUSEUM and seeing one of your loved ones who passed away on display for others' amusement? The Body Worlds exhibitions are among the world's most popular touring attraction, having been visited by more than 32 million people. A knock-off exhibit opened in 2005 and there have been serious allegations that the bodies displayed in this Bodies Exhibit were stolen or otherwise unethically obtained in China. In addition to the very problematic origins of the bodies, the use of human bodies for public entertainment or "education," which could be achieved through multiple other means such as an animated 3D exhibit, is inappropriate and must be condemned.

Thomas Hibbs, a professor of ethics at Baylor University, compared these immoral and spiritually dangerous exhibits to pornography, as they reduce the human subject to "the manipulation of body parts stripped of any larger human significance." We must not allow our children to attend these exhibits on field trips, and the exhibits should be banned worldwide.

In 2008, the organization behind the exhibits, acknowledged these concerns when they posted the following disclaimer on their website:

> This exhibit displays human remains of Chinese citizens or residents which were originally received by the Chinese Bureau of Police. The Chinese Bureau of Police may receive bodies from Chinese prisons. Premier (the organizers of the exhibit) cannot independently verify

that the human remains you are viewing are not those of persons who were incarcerated in Chinese prisons.

Then New York Attorney General [later Governor] Andrew Cuomo has said, "The grim reality is that Premier Exhibitions has profited from displaying the remains of individuals who may have been tortured and executed in China." In addition to this tremendous injustice of the unknown origins of the bodies, staring at human remains is an unacceptable form of public entertainment. Some of the corpses are set up so it appears as if they are playing poker or conducting an orchestra. What does it say about our society that there is a desire to gawk at corpses arranged in such a demeaning way? While there is a valid discussion about when cadavers may be used for medical research and advanced education, using corpses for public entertainment is a step too far.

Judaism teaches that the body was created in God's image and is therefore *kadosh* (holy). It is to be treated with respect at all times; dead bodies are not to be left unattended, and funerals are to follow death as quickly as possible.

According to Jewish law, the return of the body to the earth can neither be slowed down nor sped up and thus both cremation and mummification are forbidden. The body should naturally lie in the earth. The moral paradigm is set forth by no less than the Divine who buries Moses after his passing.

Tending to the needs of the deceased is considered the greatest *hesed* since the favor can never be returned. The value of human life is of the highest importance in Judaism and it supersedes almost all other values. To parade the vehicle of life around like crude art is fundamentally against our values.

While the soul has a higher Jewish value than the body, there is still tremendous value given to the honor of the dead's body (*kavod ha-met*). Even when one is hypothetically hanged as capital punishment, the body is taken down immediately so the public cannot stare at it (Deuteronomy 21:22–23). This is the source for the biblical mitzvah of *halvayat ha-met*, or escorting the deceased to burial (*Sanhedrin* 46b). The mitzvah of honoring the dead is given such prime importance by the Rabbis that it supersedes Torah study (*Ketuvot* 17a).

Directly relevant to our case, the Rabbis teach that one who sees a corpse and chooses not to conform it to burial is mocking that person and is like one "who mocks the deprived" (*lo'eg la'rash*; Proverbs 17:5), and blasphemes God (*Berachot* 18a).

There is, no doubt, great existential value in pondering death and recalling the frailty of our humanity; however, we need not stare death literally in the face to reach this spiritual goal. It's possible to gain insight into our mortality without compromising the body of another human being. The exhibit calls upon others to "Celebrate the human form" through their display of corpses, but as Jews we must speak out to ensure that celebrations of life honor the Divine and the bodies that God has given us on loan.   □

GAMBLING: MORE THAN A FUN GAME OF CARDS?

ANYONE WHO HAS HELD A LOTTERY TICKET knows the thrill of taking a gamble. Personally, I recall the emotional intensity of the poker games in the basement of my friend's house as a child. With money on the table, even as a twelve-year old, this friendly get together was no longer a game. Five years later, I recall passing through an Atlantic City casino on a family trip shocked to see it full of yarmulke-wearing Jews. I wondered if gambling was an acceptable Jewish sport.

The Justice Department reversed its position on the 1961 Wire Act saying that it applied to sports betting but not online gambling. This change will give states the ability to legally operate more online gambling and will inevitably inspire an explosion of Internet gambling across the nation. Casino advocates suggest that increasing access and funding to the gaming industry will provide more jobs and entertainment. Is every job worth filling? Clearly, we should not support prostitution simply because it employs more people.

About $5 billion is spent on gambling in the U.S. every year. Those who are addicted to gambling can accrue tens to hundreds of thousands of dollars in debt, leading to bankruptcy, and/or poverty, which in turn often lead to prostitution or theft. Further, neglecting to cultivate impulse control can lead to many other types of legal and moral mistakes. Gambling, at its worst, can lead to the most significant dangers. A study found that 17 percent of suicidal patients in Australia had gambling problems.

Many enjoy a casual game of poker with some friends. However, others have taken the game too far, to the point where gambling destroys them and their families. One need not be diagnosed as a "clinical pathological gambling addict" to know there is a problem. Gambling addictions can be manifest in many ways including certain careers where one is constantly playing the stocks with too much risk.

Statistics show that those with compulsive gambling problems are more likely to harm family members through domestic and child abuse. Further, children raised in a home with parental gambling problems are at significantly higher risk of suffering from depression, behavior problems, and substance abuse.

From a religious perspective, we are told to live by reason and faith (not luck of the dice) and that our *parnassah* (sustenance) should be attained through work.

The Rabbis state that there are two types of gamblers that are untrustworthy and therefore not valid witnesses in a Jewish court of law. These are the dice-player and, according to one opinion, the man who bets on pigeon-racing (*Rosh Hashanah* 1:8; *Sanhedrin* 3:3).

The Rabbis argue whether gambling constitutes thievery (*Eruvin* 82). Rabbi Yehuda argues that "*asmachta kanya*," i.e., gambling is not theft. Since both parties who gamble are aware that they might lose their money, and they accept the terms of the game; the winner legally acquires the money from the loser. The Sages, on the other hand, argue that "*asmachta lo kanya*" – earning money through gambling, where the bettors believe they will win and the loser surrenders his money halfheartedly, does not constitute a proper legal acquisition. The Rabbis thus suggest that earning money through gambling is considered theft.

Tosafot follows the position of Rabbi Yehuda that gambling is not theft, but argues that significant gambling would be forbidden. Rambam, however, is more stringent and argues that gambling is indeed theft (via rabbinic decree). Rabbi Yitzhak Ben Sheshet (Rivash) argues that even if gambling is not strictly forbidden by Jewish law, it is nevertheless a "*davar mechu'ar*" – a disgusting activity.

While it may technically be permitted, according to some, to play cards, bet on horses, and participate in a raffle in a social manner (*Havot Yair* 61; *Arik Responsa*, ii, no. 65), when it's taken to its extreme it should be condemned. Rav Ahron Soloveichik suggested that one has violated the Torah by being addicted to anything. A person shouldn't run after the lusts of this world and sell oneself to them. We should seek activities of leisure that add meaning to our lives and benefit to others. One may justify an occasional casual, low-stakes game of cards to connect with friends, but gambling as a consistent high-stakes activity is forbidden at most and deeply frowned upon at least.

Our core Jewish values are most relevant not only when we work but also when we play. What games we play and how we play them when we're "off" serves as one of the greatest indicators of our true character.   □

JEWISH LAW ON TEXTING WHILE DRIVING

THE ORTHODOX COMMUNITY HAS BEEN IN A panic about the news that observant teenagers are texting on Shabbat. However, we must address a much greater life-and-death concern.

The National Transportation Safety Board has issued a sweeping recommendation to ban the use of mobile phones while driving. Even though distracted drivers cause thousands of accidents each year – about 3,000 documented highway fatalities, not to mention the hundreds of thousands of injuries – a writer in the *Washington Post* proclaims that you will have to tear her cell phone from "her cold, driving hands." How is it that one in five drivers still texts while driving? Texting while driving is currently illegal in thirty-five states – we have fifteen to go! Thousands of lives are at stake.

Actually, according to Jewish law, if a driver were to kill another while texting, it would be, at the least, unintentional murder, and, at worst, an "act approaching the intentional" (*Hilchot Rotzeach* 6:4). The moral battlefield exists in the unintentional realm. We are responsible to set up our lives so that caution deters us from making mistakes that cause great harm to others.

My esteemed mentor and colleague Rabbi Yosef Kanefsky argues: "To cause the death of another through an act of gross negligence – albeit unintentionally and without any premeditation – is categorized as a 'great sin,' one which legally approaches intentional murder." He continues, "It is self-evident that our system demands that we not drive while distracted by our cell phone, lest we, God forbid, inadvertently injure or kill someone."

The Torah explains: "If you build a new house, you shall make a fence for your roof, so that you will not place blood in your house if one falls from it" (Deuteronomy 22:8). Commentators explain that we are obligated to be extremely proactive to ensure that all of our property is only used in ways that avoid any possible harm to another.

A *New York Times* article suggested that "drivers using a phone are four times as likely to cause a crash as other drivers," and that certain cell phone use makes one as unfit to drive as one with a blood alcohol level of .08 percent, a state of intoxication.

I used to text while driving, until I became aware of the results of distraction. It can be really hard to stop, but we must! We must be terrified by the consequences.

Commit to never again text while you drive. Commit not to read or learn Torah on your iPhone while you are driving! Do it to save a life. Do it to save your own life. Do it because it is Jewish law! □

THE CHALLENGE OF OFFERING MORAL REBUKE IN THE WORKPLACE

AT WORK, WE CONSISTENTLY OFFER POSITIVE reinforcement and constructive feedback to others to improve the quality of our collective efforts. From a Jewish perspective, we are not only concerned with the efficacy of our work but also the ethics of the workplace. In addition to personal accountability, all Jewish workers have a sacred duty to be a moral presence as well.

There is actually a biblical commandment to offer rebuke (*tocheha*): "You shall not hate your brother in your heart; you shall reprove your fellow and do not bear a sin because of him" (Leviticus 19:17). The verse teaches that we offer reproof for two reasons: that our resentments do not lead to hate, and that wrongs are not carried out for which we too would be responsible.

Rather than speaking *lashon hara* and *rechilut* (speaking negatively about another and spreading gossip), we are to confront the individual directly. We care about the moral and spiritual welfare of others; thus, it is vital that we give feedback when we see others going astray.

According to one position, this mitzvah only applies when we think the other will be receptive to hearing the reproof. If not, it is considered counterproductive. "Just as there is a mitzvah for a person to say words of rebuke that will be accepted, so too there is a mitzvah for a person not to say words of rebuke that will not be accepted" (*Yevamot* 65b). It's only a mitzvah if one suspects the other has the integrity and emotional intelligence to truly see their blind spot and correct the wrong. The goal with rebuke, according to this position, is not just to express righteous indignation, but to create change and stop a wrong or abuse occurring before our eyes.

Rabbi Zeira, however, taught that one should offer rebuke whether or not one believes it will be accepted (*Shabbat* 55a). We simply cannot stand idle while others do wrong in our midst. Regardless of whether our voice will be heard, we cannot remain indifferent. As Rabbi Abraham Joshua Heschel taught: "We are a generation that has lost its capacity for outrage. We must continue to remind ourselves that in a free society all are involved in what some are doing. Some are guilty, all are responsible." Thus, we must express outrage at wrongs. The Rabbis teach: "Everyone who can protest a wrong in one's midst and does not, is responsible for those people. For the people of his city, one is responsible for the people of the city. For the whole world, one is responsible for the whole world" (*Shabbat* 54b). If we don't speak up, our own moral integrity is in jeopardy as a bystander. The Rabbis teach *shtika k'hodaah*, when we stay silent we are considered to be in agreement. According to this position, we don't need to correct the wrong but we cannot stand idly by.

The obligation to give *tocheha* is not a simple command. The rabbis teach that no one today is on the spiritual level to engage in rebuke properly as few are self aware and humble enough to give *tocheha* properly and few are humble enough to properly hear and accept it (Sifra, *Kedoshim*). For this reason, *Sefer Hassidim* suggests that we can only really give rebuke to one that we feel love for. Clearly, we have to carefully check our motives before challenging another's conduct.

Of course, any feedback should be given gently, in private, at the right time and in the appropriate environment. Most importantly, we should be sure not to shame another when challenging them. This is a very difficult skill to learn.

There is a very important place for rebuke in the workplace, to ensure we have a moral influence upon co-workers and to establish clear ethical workplace boundaries. We cannot live in a world where wrongs are ignored, nor can we work in environments where there is indifference toward the welfare of others. Abuses must be addressed. Some acts require whistle-blowing when they reach a level of harm or illegality. Other acts require rebuke or constructive feedback.

We cannot do this alone, and should create an open work culture where feedback is acceptable and encouraged when boundaries are crossed. We must learn the art and ethics of critique in order that we can build a stronger society committed to truth, human dignity, and transparency. We can start by checking our own practices, taking our own self-accounting, and inviting others to approach us if we ourselves ever cross boundaries. □

AMIA AND MINORITY INSECURITY: HOW DO WE ATTACK CORRUPTION?

W HEN IN ARGENTINA WITH MY STUDENTS in March 2012, we visited AMIA, the Jewish community center of Buenos Aires, that was bombed in 1994, leaving 85 dead and hundreds injured. It was heart-wrenching to hear the personal stories only a few days after the attack at the Jewish school in Toulouse.

It is crucial when minorities are attacked anywhere in the world that everything possible is done to help them feel safe and that the justice system makes clear that these attacks are never tolerated. Because there was no justice in Argentina (no one went to jail), the community still feels very vulnerable and insecure. When minorities are attacked, due to anti-Semitism, homophobia, Islamophobia, etc., it is not only an attack upon individuals but upon the whole group, making all feel vulnerable. We cannot only speak up when it is our own people and sites attacked. Hate and violence must be condemned wherever it pokes its head.

According to 2010, FBI statistics on 8,208 hate crime victims, 48 percent were victimized due to race, 19 percent due to religion, and 19 percent due to sexual orientation. In racial bias, 70 percent of victims were black; in religious bias, 67 percent of victims were Jews, and nearly 13 percent were Muslims (a rising figure); in sexual-orientation crimes, nearly all victims were homosexuals and lesbians.

Corruption is more difficult to quantify. Transparency International monitors perceived corruption on a worldwide basis (with 0 as most corrupt and 10 as least corrupt), and the results may surprise you. According to its *Corruption Perceptions Index 2011*, the United States only ranks 24th (7.1 score), behind most of Western Europe, Japan, Barbados, Qatar, and Chile. Israel fares worse, at 36th (5.8 score), behind Uruguay, the United Arab Emirates, and Botswana. However, both are significantly less corrupt than Argentina, which is in a twelve-way tie for 100th place with its dismal 3.0 score.

While we cannot state that there is a direct correlation between a government's level of corruption and its ability or willingness to combat hate crimes, it is probable that a more corrupt society will not successfully prosecute these crimes. For example, no one has ever been convicted of the AMIA attack, and the Argentinean government has come under scrutiny for incompetence and corruption in mishandling the investigation. While this is discouraging, our disillusionment with politics cannot lead us to disengage. We must continue to attack corruption proactively. Governments that allow for corruption, intolerance, and injustice must be challenged. We can tolerate political difference, but we cannot tolerate scandals and corruptions.

In Argentina, I spoke with Rabbi Ernesto Yattah, a community leader working to address governmental corruption. Others told me that almost everyone cheats on their taxes, pays bribes, and accepts the corruption, and just lives with it. Rabbi Yattah is calling upon Jews to reverse this cycle. He told me that first we must understand corruptology (how corruption permeates society) so we can address it systemically. The word "corrupt," from the Latin *corruptus* (meaning "abused" or "destroyed"), connotes something that is "utterly broken." It is a critical defect in any society.

According to what Rabbi Yattah called "the politics of inclusion," corrupt politicians make society more corrupt so that they alone are not blamed. For example, they often ensure that the police force is corrupt, operating through bribes. When corruption is systemic, everyone just throws their arms in their air, enabling corrupt politicians to benefit from the inertia. When we attack the peripheral manifestations of corruption, we are attacking the base as well.

Combating is rarely easy or risk-free. According to "the politics of reflection," one standing up to corruption has to be willing to face countercharges that he or she is also corrupt. When you fight corruption, the established force will come back at you with ten times the strength. Nevertheless, we know that corruption can be overcome. The Book of Genesis (6:12), for example, describes a world before the flood where "everyone on earth was corrupt." In a post-flood world, order was achieved.

Today, no problem can be ignored or relegated to others who face corruption in remote areas as the world is now too interconnected to live with the veil of isolation. Just as an economic crisis in Asia or South America affects Europe, so too, hatred anywhere in the world is a threat to all. Corruption is a force that creates insecurity, fear, and a foundation for injustice. We cannot look away from it. Thus, the role of the Jew in the public square is to be a voice of conscience, challenging those who shatter social trust, and in support of all victims of injustice.   □

THE BIBLE AND THE LOS ANGELES RIOTS: ROLE OF RELIGION IN THE PUBLIC SPHERE?

I N THE TWENTY-FIRST CENTURY, THERE IS ONE primary role for religion in the public sphere: Radical Spiritual Intervention.

Riots occur when people within a community become so enraged at authority that they unleash their fury. This often overflows into an indiscriminate attack on anyone in the rioters' path. It takes enormous courage to face this uncontrolled violence. As Fidel Lopez, an innocent victim, was being viciously beaten, cut, and burnt in the streets during the Los Angeles riots, Reverend Bennie Newton entered the dangerous streets waving a Bible in the air, warning the attackers: "Kill him, and you have to kill me, too." Risking his life, the holy reverend saved the innocent victim's life as the attackers backed away.

Local, state, and even national authorities can also be guilty of rioting against their own people. During the height of the civil rights struggle in

1963, nonviolent demonstrators were beaten, sprayed with fire hoses strong enough to strip bark from trees and break ribs, and bitten by attack dogs; some were even murdered. In spite of this, Dr. Martin Luther King, Jr., fellow members of the Southern Christian Leadership Conference, and allied clergy (including Rabbi Abraham Joshua Heschel) risked their lives in staying with the movement.

One little-known episode is worth relating. On May 5, 1963, two days after the notorious use of fire hoses and attack dogs at the orders of the notorious sheriff "Bull" Connor, Birmingham civil rights demonstrators, accompanied by their clergy, came out of church dressed in their Sunday clothes. They knelt and prayed in front of the same firemen who had earlier sprayed and injured dozens of demonstrators. While the exact details have been debated, it is apparent that the moral force of the clergy and those praying had an effect on the firemen, who refused to turn their hoses on. There was no violence that day.

Religious leadership has a unique role: to carry the Bible into the streets and to protect the vulnerable. This is what Moses did when he risked his life three times to save others under attack (Exodus 2). There are complicated questions about how religious values can legitimately be appropriated in political discourse, but there is nothing complex about the role of religion in stopping brutal violence. When a woman is being raped, a homeless man beaten in the streets, a child molested, an animal abused, one must grab a Bible and enter the scene. It is not for everyone, as it may be dangerous. But there is no place where the voice of God is more necessary.   □

BOOK BURNING:
PRELUDE TO PERSECUTION

I N JULY 2012, THE BIBLE SOCIETY IN ISRAEL [Messianic Jews] sent Christian Bibles to all 120 Members of the Knesset. In response, one Member of Knesset, Michael Ben-Ari, publicly cut his up and threw it in the trash. In December 2001, a teacher in Beit Shemesh led his students in burning a copy of a Hebrew translation of the New Testament that had been given to a student by missionaries. In another episode in 2008, kids burnt hundreds of copies of the New Testaments sent by missionaries, arguing it was a commandment to do so.

While the insensitivity of particular groups of missionaries needs to be addressed seriously, this situation should be handled by the police, and book burning is never appropriate. Those who argue that Christianity is idolatry, and that therefore that it is a mitzvah to destroy copies of the New Testament, are in error. While it is prohibited for Jews to practice Christianity according to Jewish law, it is not "idolatry," and even if another book embraced idolatrous ideas, no one worships the actual book. Even further, destroying things unnecessarily violates the Torah prohibition of *baal tashhit* (Deuteronomy 20:19–20; *Hilchot Melachim* 6:10).

Books should never be burned, as they represent learning. As Knesset Speaker Reuven Rivlin declared in opposing the action of MK Ben-Ari: "I condemn any disrespect of holy texts of any religion . . . Every holy book is important to its believers." Book burning has a terrible history connected with anti-Semitism, censorship, small-mindedness, and oppression. Rambam's books were burnt, as were Rav Moshe Feinstein's. Torah scrolls have destructively been burnt for centuries; these are shameful moments in Jewish history. They are part of a disgraceful tradition of infamous acts, such as the Nazi book burnings, the burning of the books and burying of scholars under China's Qin Dynasty, the burning of the Library of Baghdad, the destruction of the Aztec codices, and the destruction of the Sarajevo National Library.

America has had its share of book burnings. In 1836, the Quaker abolitionists Angelina and Sarah Grimké, who came from the South, wrote an anti-slavery tract, *Appeal to the Christian Women of the Southern States,* which was filled with religious references. When copies reached Charleston, the postmaster seized all the copies and publicly burned them. This increasingly fanatical defense of slavery fueled the secessionist movement – South Carolina was the first state to secede and the state where the Civil War started, with the attack on Fort Sumter in 1861.

In 1953, Wisconsin Senator Joseph McCarthy dispatched his aides Roy Cohn and David Schine to search U.S. Information Service Libraries in Europe and Asia in a paranoid quest to find Communist influence in the United States government. As a result, several "subversive" books from these libraries were literally burned to symbolize that the State Department had been purged of the alleged influence of communism.

This helped spur the banning of books and blacklisting of scholars and performers for a decade, in addition to promoting the mindset that led to the Vietnam War.

In a similar way, the Quran burning in the United States in 2010 was extremely disturbing. This practice insults the core religious faith and humanity of nearly two billion people worldwide. In addition, it carries a warning. In Heinrich Heine's 1821 play, "Almansor" (a Moor, a Spanish Muslim), commenting on Christians who publicly burned the Quran, says that this burning is but a "prelude," and adds: "Where men burn books, they will in the end burn people."

Holy books are sacred even when we disagree with them or with their advocates. We should not only respect other religions and people of other faiths; we should seek to learn from them. While we, as Jews, are committed to being firmly rooted in the Torah, we still must have the humility to open our minds and hearts to the teachings of other faiths.

The Mishnah (*Pirke Avot* 5:17) teaches: "Every dispute which is for the sake of Heaven in the end will be permanently established. And every dispute which is not for the sake of Heaven in the end will not be permanently established." When religious people are arguing with good intentions to pursue the truth, they should be listened to. The Rambam taught that we should "accept the truth from wherever it is found."

The Maharal taught (*Baer HaGolah*, chapter 7):

> It is proper, out of love of reason and knowledge, that you do not [summarily] reject anything that opposes your own idea, especially so if [your adversary] does not intend merely to provoke you, but rather to declare his beliefs . . . And even if such beliefs are opposed to your own faith and religion, do not say to him, "Speak not and keep your words." Because if so, there will be no clarification of religion. Just the opposite, tell him to speak his mind and all that he wants to say so that he will not be able to claim that you silenced him. Anyone who prevents another from speaking only reveals the weakness of his own religion, and not as many think, that by avoiding discussion about religion you strengthen it. This is not so! Rather, the denial of one who opposes your religion is the negation and weakening of that religion . . . For the proper way to attain truth is to hear [others'] arguments which they hold sincerely, not out of a desire to provoke you. Thus it is wrong simply to reject an opponent's ideas; instead, draw him close to you and delve into his words.

We should also remember that attempts to repress other religious beliefs that we disagree with frequently backfire, and that these religious factions grow even stronger as a result. A poignant Midrash teaches: "Do not be so quick to destroy the altars of non-Jews lest you be forced to rebuild them with your hands" (*Midrash Tannaim Devarim Mechilta* 4). The Roman Empire, through brutal episodic efforts at suppression, only strengthened the faith of Jews and Christians; similarly, the Roman Catholic Church, through the Inquisition, torture, and executions, only strengthened the faith of Jews and, during the later Reformation, the faith of Protestants. On the most self-interested and pragmatic level, we must never be destructive to other religious factions because those people will come to hate us and may seek to harm us (*mi'shum eivah*). Rather the Halacha is that we must pursue the ways of peace (*darchei shalom*) in all that we do.

We must draw closer to others with different theologies, to be respectful and to learn. The last thing that should ever happen is public desecration of the works of another faith. The great majority of Jews and Israelis believe this, and no attention should be paid toward the extremists acting against Jewish values. We must speak out against others who shows intolerance to others and who shame their sacred texts in acts of spite. We can heal the world together when we see decency and dignity in all people, showing respect to their theologies even when we disagree with them.

Even when we are provoked and our tolerance is tested, we must rise above. The Torah's "ways are ways of pleasantness and all its paths are peace" (Proverbs 3:17). □

THE ASSAULT ON RABBI ROSENBERG: IGNORING SEX ABUSE

RABBI NUCHEM ROSENBERG IS A REFRESHINGLY bold advocate against child sexual abuse which occurs in the ultra-Orthodox world. He works within his own Satmar Hasidic and other communities across the ultra-Orthodox spectrum, publicizing claims of sexual abuse and providing victims with the strength and support to speak out about what was done to them. This brave and courageous man was a victim himself – of an attack in which chemicals were thrown in his face with the intent to harm or kill him. Thankfully, Rabbi Rosenberg survived the attack, and recovered.

It seems highly unlikely that it was just a coincidence that this attack occurred in the same week as the conviction of Nechemya Weberman. Mr. Weberman is, or perhaps was, a leading Satmar community member and unlicensed therapist who was "found guilty of repeatedly sexually abusing a girl who came to him for counseling."

Sadly, when it comes to sexual abuse, many insular communities, such as the ultra-Orthodox, prefer to cover up such heinous crimes, shielding the perpetrators and attempting to silence the victims. Of course, this is exactly the opposite of how such situations should be handled; those who are guilty of such abuses should be exposed and condemned, and their victims should receive the unconditional support of their communities.

If a religious community prefers to knowingly hide sex offenders in its midst, and suppress efforts by victims and their advocates to come forward with the truth, then the secular authorities becomes the best hope of dealing with this grave problem. There have long been attempts within ultra-Orthodoxy to cover up incidences and perpetrators of abuse, and it is past time for justice to fully be done. Unfortunately, sexual abuse can be found in every type of community in the world, but responsible communities are outspoken and active in punishing those guilty and supporting those wronged. These are the types of behavior only too rarely exhibited in the ultra-Orthodox world today by brave people like Rabbi Rosenberg, who learned the hard way what happens when a person confronts powerful forces aligned against justice.

It is bad enough when one of the three cardinal sins of Judaism, sexual immorality (the other two being murder and idol worship), is so flagrantly violated. Now, rather than being applauded for their efforts, those who fight against this abuse find themselves being victimized in different ways. Sadly, the Talmud teaches that there is only one thing equal to these three cardinal sins, and that is *sinat chinam* – warrantless hatred – which, when it occurred between Jews in ancient times, is seen in *Yoma* 9b as one of the main reasons for the destruction of the Second Temple.

This is not the first case of this kind to come to light in an ultra-Orthodox community. On July 11, 2011, in a separate Hasidic community in Brooklyn, eight-year old Leiby Kletzky was abducted, drugged, and suffocated to death by Levi Aron, another member of the same community; pieces of

Kletzky's dismembered body were found by the police in Aron's freezer and a nearby trash bin. In spite of their having been "all sorts of rumors about" Aron, the community was in shock that "one of their own" had committed the murder. Poor Leiby paid the price for his community members' failure to act on their suspicions.

Whereas rumors about Aron had floated about for years, the New York Police Department acted with considerably greater speed: Within 36 hours of Kletzky's disappearance, Aron was identified as the kidnapper, tracked down, and arrested. He confessed on the spot to Kletzky's murder. There have been times in Jewish history when Jews had good reason to distrust or even fear secular legal, judicial, and police authorities. But this was America in the year 2012; there were no Cossacks coming to attack us, or K G B agents coming to arrest us. We can trust in, and should cooperate with, the police and local authorities. Indeed, when there is greater cooperation between police forces and various communities, the more trust they build between each other, and the effectiveness of policing increases as well.

The allegations that were raised in 2012 of past sexual abuse against Yeshiva University (confirmed by the university's chancellor and former president) serve as yet another example of an individual religious community's, this time among the Modern Orthodox, inability to police itself effectively. The statement by Yeshiva's current president, and the spirit behind it, is impressive and important, but it is only the beginning of the sea change we must see in our communities.

May we, as American Jews, do all we can to eradicate abuse in our communities, and may we make clear to all that Judaism is against all abuse, is in favor of attacking this ill with all fervor; and sees those who commit or cover up such as crimes as going against the laws and spirit of the Torah. May Rabbi Rosenberg continue his fight for justice with success and in peace; and may he find many to join him in his holy quest. □

□ GREAT LEADERS
IN OUR TIME

THE KAPISHNITZER REBBE
AND THE STEIPLER RAV:
LOVING FAMILY THROUGH
ACTS OF KINDNESS

I N THE JEWISH TRADITION, LOVE IS CONSIDERED
to be more of an action than an emotion. Rabbi
Joseph B. Soloveitchik writes:

The Bible spoke of the commandment to love one's neighbor (Leviticus
19:18). However, in Talmudic literature, emphasis was placed not only
upon sentiment, but upon action, which is motivated by sentiment.
The *Hoshen Mishpat*, the Jewish code of civil law, analyzes not human
emotions but actual human relations. The problem of *Hoshen Mishpat*
is not what one feels toward the other, but how he acts toward him
(*Family Redeemed*, 40).

Former British Chief Rabbi Jonathan Sacks in *To Heal a Fractured World*
makes the same point in explaining the importance of performing acts
of loving kindness. He notes that *hesed* usually means "kindness," but it
may also be translated as "love" expressed through deed, in a covenantal
bond. Through this covenant, there is mutual respect for the integrity
and freedom of the other in acts of *hesed*, which do have a deep emotional
component:

Hesed exists only in virtue of emotion, empathy, and sympathy, feel-
ing-with and feeling-for. We act with kindness because we know what
it feels like to be in need of kindness . . . Societies are only human

and humanizing when they are a community of communities built on face-to-face encounters – covenantal relationships.

Rabbi Sacks agrees with philosopher Emmanuel Levinas who writes that the image of a "face" is a key to what makes us human:

> Society is faceless; *hesed* is a relationship of face to face. The Pentateuch repeatedly emphasizes that we cannot see God face to face. It follows that we can only see God in the face of another" (*To Heal a Fractured World*, 45–55).

Of course, we see the face of another most in those closest to us – our families. There is a powerful story about the Kapishnitzer Rebbe about the importance of taking care of family. A prominent businessman from the community who worked in Manhattan asked to see the Rebbe about an opportunity to give *tzedakah*. He stressed that he would go to the Rebbe in Brooklyn to discuss the matter. Instead, the Rebbe said that he would go to the man's office, for he had an important message to deliver.

When he arrived, the man barred any interruption, cutting off all phone calls and leaving customers waiting. He invited the Rebbe into his office. There, the Rebbe detailed the dire financial situation of a family with many children. The breadwinner had lost his job, his health was suffering, and financial pressures were crushing the family's spirits. Something needed to be done immediately. The businessman immediately offered to write out a $1,000 check for the unfortunate man, but wondered why the Rebbe had to deliver the message in person. The story concludes: "Pen poised above his checkbook, the man asked, 'For whom is the check?' The Rebbe stared at the floor for a few long moments, then answered, 'For your brother.'"

Tzedakah does not, of course, have to be in the form of money. The Steipler, Rav Rabbi Yaakov Yisrael Kanievsky, who endured abject poverty, harassment in the Russian army because he insisted on observing his religion, and who eventually went deaf, was extraordinary for his combination of wisdom and common sense, was widely sought after for advice. A young man once visited the Steipler Rav and complained bitterly, "I don't know which way to turn. My home is in constant chaos. I come home every Friday afternoon before Shabbat and the dishes are still in the sink, there are diapers everywhere, and the floor is not even swept. My wife is just not getting things done. I can't live like this anymore." The Steipler Rav looked at the young man with incredulity and said: "You don't know where to turn? I'll tell you. Turn to the nearest closet and take out a broom. Has it occurred to you that you can help!"

There is plenty of work to do in the broader Jewish community and around the world, but we should be sure that in the process of doing that holy work we never forget the needs of our family. My great teacher Rabbi Avi Weiss likes to tell a story about how he was unable to pick up his visiting parents at the airport. He kept saying, "I love you. I just can't pick you up at the airport." His parents finally replied: "Avrami, stop loving us so much and just pick us up at the airport." There is great value to love as an emotion, but Judaism reminds us that that love is ultimately manifest in action, not feeling.   □

RABBI DAVID HARTMAN: A TRANSFORMATIVE FORCE AND A UNIQUE LEGACY

I N FEBRUARY 2013, WE LOST A *GADOL* (A GREAT leader). The world was blessed for more than eighty years (1931–2013) with the presence of a hero of Torah, a progressive force for good, a religious pluralist, and an astounding teacher of ethics and spirituality. Rabbi David Hartman was my teacher and the rebbe of thousands around the world. His reach extended from secular Israelis to religious Israelis, from Reform through Orthodox, from the young to the elderly, from the homeland to the diaspora. He was a rabbi's rabbi, a philosopher for philosophers, and a teacher for teachers.

David Hartman was born to a *haredi* family in Brooklyn, New York, and studied in several *haredi* yeshivas. However, he soon became dissatisfied with these yeshivas: "My decision to leave Lakewood for Yeshiva University was motivated largely by dissatisfaction with the intellectual insularity I had come to associate with the ultra-Orthodox yeshiva world" (*The God Who Hates Lies*, 19). He was later ordained as a rabbi at Yeshiva University in New York. He then earned a master's degree in philosophy from a Roman Catholic institution, Fordham University, and taught for years in the United States and Canada.

Two existential threats to Israel played a pivotal role in Rabbi Hartman's life. The Six-Day War of 1967 motivated him to later move with his family to Israel (make *aliyah*) in 1971, and then the 1973 Yom Kippur War spurred him to found the Shalom Hartman Institute in Jerusalem in 1976. For more than twenty years, he was Professor of Jewish Thought at the Hebrew University of Jerusalem, and he also was a guest lecturer at the University of California, Berkeley. In addition, he served as an adviser to Israel's education minister from 1977–1984, and provided advice to several prime ministers.

While his credentials were impressive, his ideas were superior. He was the founder of a new Jewish movement which combined traditional religious law (Halacha) with liberal views and a pluralistic approach to the study of Judaism. His chief areas of concern included the lack of resolution on *agunot* issues, the conversion crisis, Zionist land-fundamentalists, and women's issues in Jewish law. At his Institute, he could finally realize his aspirations:

> I founded an institution to house this unfolding endeavor. It was at the Shalom Hartman Institute that I was able to find and collect people with great minds and great honesty, uninterested in hiding in a verbal, metaphysical religion disconnected from their daily experience of life. There I have been provided with the moral nourishment of a living dialogue with people who have intellectual courage and respect for alternative ways of life and thinking. Many seem to find it a refuge of intellectual freedom; no one is attacked or criticized for thinking in new ways. The institute became my spiritual home, in which I met fellow truth seekers who were able to live with uncertainty and doubt (*The God Who Hates Lies*, 23).

Throughout, he stressed that religion should not stress what is "forbidden," but rather "loving kindness." He was rewarded with the loyalty of many students, as he noted in an interview in 2011: "A lot of young people come to me and say, 'If not for you, I wouldn't be religious.'"

When I was learning in yeshiva in Efrat, I would go up in the evenings to the Hartman Institute to learn directly from Rav Hartman. I always left touched and perhaps even startled by his intensity and how much passion he brought to his Torah explanations, Jewish legal analysis, and critique of society. It was all wrapped in one. He could move from Rabbi Akiva to Ben-Gurion to Simone de Beauvoir seamlessly. He encouraged us to push for more and better from ourselves, from our learning, and from society. I recall how he inspired me to continue on to rabbinical school. He believed rabbis have a crucial role to play. He writes:

> I soon realized that the main religious issue facing Judaism in the modern world was not the authority of *halakha*. The role of the rabbi in America today is not to be an authority figure or a judge. What are missing are not answers but questions! The rabbi has to instill a desire to ask questions, to be bothered by Judaism, to feel that Judaism is important enough to want to ask about it (*A Heart with Many Rooms*, 213).

He was not a pseudo-Zionist who yelled out slogans and stats he did not understand; rather, he was the most authentic type of Zionist: a dreamer. He believed that Zionism was about cultivating a constant longing for a better Jewish democratic state and a holier and more just world. He inspired his students to dream. He writes in *Israelis and the Jewish Tradition* that we should move away from the spiritually dangerous approach of interconnecting the modern state of Israel with messianism and should ground this new national relationship in Torah and ethical responsibility:

> Today we have an opportunity to reestablish the normative moment of Sinai, rather than the Exodus story, as the primary framework for evaluating the significance of Jewish history. To be religiously significant, a historical event does not have to be situated between the moment of the Exodus and the coming of the Messiah. It can be significant by encouraging us to discover new depths in the foundational moment of Israel's election as a covenantal people. I respond religiously to the establishment of the state of Israel from a Sinai-covenantal model for the following reasons. In reestablishing the Jewish nation in its ancient homeland, Jews have taken responsibility for all aspects of social life. The divine call to become a holy nation committed to implementing the letter and spirit of the Torah must influence our economic, political, and religious institutions. Through the establishment of the state of Israel, we are called upon to demonstrate the moral and spiritual power of the Torah to respond to the challenges of daily life.

He further elaborated that one should not succumb to the lure of ultra-nationalism in *A Living Covenant*:

> I give preference to the *midrashim* that imply that the covenant was
> made in the desert to teach the community that Judaism as a way of
> life was not exclusively a function of political sovereignty. We were
> born as a people within the desert in order to understand that the land
> must always be perceived as an instrumental and never as an absolute
> value. The memory that the covenant was made in the desert prevents
> us from falling victim to the idolatry of state power.

Having sovereignty and dwelling in the state of Israel is not an end in itself.
Rav Hartman taught: "The prophets taught us that the state has only in-
strumental value for the purpose of embodying the covenantal demands of
Judaism" (*A Heart of Many Rooms*, 264).

In Rabbi Hartman's last work, he fleshes out more of his dream for the
Jewish state.

> I affirm Martin Buber's deep assessment that the kibbutz was an ex-
> periment that did not fail. The aspiration to build an egalitarian soci-
> ety with an emphasis on social justice, with a health system in which
> no human being would be deprived of decent care, with schooling,
> through the university level, that is affordable for the majority, in con-
> trast to the astronomical cost of an equivalent combined Jewish and
> general education in the diaspora – these achievements are inspiring
> to many Jews who relate to its mission as being "a light of nations"
> (Isaiah 42:6). In a very deep and significant way, Israel is the public
> face of the Jewish people. If the world seeks to understand who the
> Jews are, they point to the Jewish state as in some way mediating for
> them a profounder understanding of the Jewish soul (*The God Who
> Hates Lies*, 180–181).

Most influenced intellectually by Maimonides and by his teacher, Rav
Soloveitchik, Rav Hartman grounded Jewish ethics in the religious philosophy of Imitatio Dei.

> When Maimonides describes morality as an imitation of God's ac-
> tions, he is describing a morality which has its roots in an intellectual
> understanding of God. The ground of this morality is neither specific
> rules nor principles but, rather, the actions of God as they are manifest
> in nature. The key difference between the morality of the multitude
> and the morality of the religious philosopher is that the former is

rule-dominated and based in the juridical authority of God, the latter, an imitation of the God of Creation. Knowledge of God based on the study of nature reveals loving kindness, righteousness, and judgment as constant features of being. The constancy of God's *hesed*, reflected in being, guides the religious philosopher to act with *hesed* toward men even though they have no claim on him.

Rav Hartman believed that reason and ethics (not simple faith and obedience) were the essence of Jewish living. He explains beautifully the Midrash Sifra that it is a principle of faith in the Jewish tradition that God liberated the Jews in an exodus from Egypt (*yetziat Mitzrayim*). However, the rabbis go on to explain that the obligation is not primarily a requirement of belief but of action. The one who truly believes in the miraculous exodus is honest in weights and measures. The one who acts ethically in business has embraced the deepest meaning of this theological value. The truth is not a historical fact merely to be noted, but is rather a value that must transform our character.

He taught, and modeled, that we must cultivate the emotional intelligence and ethical sensitivity to respond to the true needs of the other.

Tzedakah involves empathy – listening and sharing in the pain of the person in need irrespective of one's ability to solve or ameliorate the problematic condition at hand. *Tzedakah* is not only measured by concrete, efficacious action but also by the subjective response of empathy when action is impossible. *Tzedakah* not only involves [the mitzvah of] *Give to him readily* ("*naton titen*" – Deuteronomy 15:10), but also the one, *Do not harden your heart* (15:7). The subjective component of the norm, of *tzedakah*, is expressed in the empathy and openness of one's heart to the person in need irrespective of the feasibility of effective action.

Empathy, however, did not imply an intellectual laxity, or acquiescence to whatever one was taught. Rav Hartman believed that students of Torah should feel empowered to ask hard questions and challenge authority.

> The empowerment of people to take part in the discussion, to feel intellectually free to become engaged and argue with the tradition, must take precedence over issues of authority and obedience if Jewish education is to renew the discussion that has defined Judaism for the past two thousand years. The paradoxical dialectic of this system is to create the student who is at once totally claimed and totally free (*A Heart of Many Rooms*, 122).

He was firm in his absolute commitment to Halacha and believed that we should observe Jewish law with joy.

Serious Christian thinkers are perplexed by the notion of joy in Halacha. . . . Halacha appears to mitigate against the experience of joy. The expression "yoke of the commandments" frequently used in halachic writings conveys the idea that *mitzvot* (commandments) are a heavy weight pressing hard upon a person. This attitude of "pharisaic legalism" with its submissive obedience to the letter of the law hardly seems conducive to joy, an experience normally associated with feelings of ease and spontaneity.

Yet to Rabbi Hartman, Halacha was innovative, not static:

> What we need to learn from the past is not so much how previous generations solved particular problems, or the particular forms of their halakhic frameworks, but rather the underlying spirit and teleology that infuses Halakha. It is not only to legal norms that we owe our allegiance, but also to the values and the human character that these attempt to realize (*A Heart of Many Rooms*, 243).

While one should embrace an intellectually critical Judaism, Rav Hartman taught that it should never be devoid of passion. He writes in "Morality and the Passionate Love for God" in *Torah and Philosophic Quest* (91):

> To describe the goal of the individual excellence in Maimonides' thought as "intellectual virtue" is to miss the passionate love characterizing the religious philosopher's relationship to the object of his knowledge. To Maimonides, the importance of philosophy is that it enables one to become a passionate lover of God. The intoxicated lover of God represents the philosopher who strives to eliminate any distraction from the joy of intellectual love of God. In Maimonides' description of the lover's yearning for solitude one can sense the terrible emptiness the lover feels upon being separated from his beloved. Mostly this is achieved in solitude and isolation. Hence every excellent man stays frequently in solitude and does not meet anyone unless it is necessary.
>
> *Because he has set his passionate desire upon Me, therefore I will rescue him; I will set him on high because he has known My name* (Psalm 91:14). You know the difference between the terms "one who loves [*ohev*]" and "one who loves passionately [*hoshek*]"; an excess of love [*mahabbah*], so

that no thought remains – that is directed toward a thing other than the beloved, is passionate love [*ishq*] (*Guide*, III 51).

Rav Hartman was a prophetic figure ahead of his time who felt the conflicting emotions of one deeply wrestling with society but also transcending it. He writes of the prophet:

> The aspiring prophet must transcend this egocentric dependency on society, so that his assumption of political leadership will not be grounded in the longing for power. The disdain for the community, then, is the condition of the prophet during his ascent, i.e., when he is struggling to transcend the political leader's dependency on the community. . . . Disdain for the community characterized the prophet during his ascent; in exact contrast, love for the community becomes his characteristic quality during his descent.

His Torah was grounded in pluralism. It was a social and pragmatic pluralism (a deep respect and even reverence for the other) but also an epistemic pluralism (embracing the multiplicity and complexity of Divine and human truth).

> The radical particularization of history eliminates the need for faith communities to regard one another as rivals. Competition between faith traditions arises when universality is ascribed to particular historical revelations. When revelation is understood as the concretization of the universal, then "whose truth is the truth?" becomes the paramount religious question, and pluralism becomes a vacuous religious ideal. If, however, revelation can be separated from the chain of universality, and if a community of faith can regain an appreciation of the particularity of the divine-human encounter, then pluralism can become a meaningful part of biblical faith experiences" (*A Heart of Many Rooms*, 165).

In 2009, Rabbi Hartman delivered a short lecture, "The Rise of Extremism and the Decline of Reason," in which he strongly condemned the increasing tendency of extremists within the Orthodox community who equated "the more extreme, the more right wing" with being a "holy Jew." In lamenting the decline of reason, he noted: "The less intelligible things are these days, the more attractive they have become." Finally, he warned of the dismal future if this trend continued: "The deepest challenge to Judaism is that we have given up on the belief in the rational capacity of human beings to build a decent life. We've given up on reason, the greatest treasure that human beings have."

Today, there are many who engage in polemics, who vilify anyone with a contrary opinion. Rabbi Hartman, with his openness and pluralism, offers a welcome contrast. While he was a committed Zionist who had answered the call of Israel when it was threatened, he favored diplomacy with the Palestinians, and anonymously helped support educational courses that supported peace and social justice in Israel.

On a personal level, Rabbi Hartman taught me to have a profound respect for my students and congregants. He had a unique ability to identify the problem of religious relevance in the modern world, and an equally effective solution, as these two excerpts illustrate:

> Like many rabbis, I noted in most of my congregants – indeed, in most of the Jewish people at large – a deep estrangement from the religious framework of the Torah. Jewish tradition was not deemed worthy of serious attention; it was not, in William James's words, a live option. I realized then that my task was not to proselytize, but to counter indifference by cultivating an awareness of Jewish tradition as a theological and cultural option that commands attention, that cannot easily be dismissed. My years in the rabbinate taught me pedagogical empathy: a teacher must begin at the place of the students, listen before speaking, hear and share in the deep estrangement of Jews from their tradition – to enter that estrangement and to try to understand the roots of modern Jewish alienation (*From Defender to Critic*, xii).

Rav Hartman did not make it easier for us. Rather he raised the bar that we must constantly be choosing and re-choosing our way of life.

> My own variation on the synthesis of tradition and modernity is not a philosophy meant to serve as the platform for a new movement or institution, but a process of living experience among individuals and communities that chose to adopt its angle of vision. It is a process that demands constant introspection and renewal and cannot be branded or co-opted by any formal or official frame of reference. It stands

separate from all expressions of institutionalized Judaism, because it
never knows what new forces it will absorb as it moves into the future"
(*From Defender to Critic*, xviii–xix).

Rabbi Hartman was recognized internationally for his work. He received
honorary doctorates from Yale University and the Hebrew Union College,
and awards such as the Guardian of Jerusalem Prize (2001), the Samuel
Rothberg Prize for Jewish Education (from the Hebrew University, 2004),
and the Liebhaber Prize for Religious Tolerance (2012).

Rabbi Hartman is well-represented in print and on video. The Shalom
Hartman Institute has published many of his books. On video, there are
several lengthy radio interviews featuring Rabbi Hartman. YouTube has
nearly forty videos featuring Rabbi Hartman, along with many more from
the Hartman Institute and from his children, Dr. Tova Hartman and Rabbi
Dr. Donniel Hartman. Among the provocative titles are "Why Judaism
Survived;" videos on religion after the Holocaust; a video of the lectures
and discussions for his eightieth birthday tribute; and a significant lecture
(quoted above), "The Rise of Extremism and the Decline of Reason."

Rav Hartman will be missed. He has left children, grandchildren,
great-grandchildren, students, books, an institution, and a legacy that will
live on for many generations to come. May we honor the Rebbe's memory
through our increased commitment to making the Torah relevant as a rigorous force for love, kindness, and peace.   □

THE POPE AND JEWISH COMMUNAL PROFESSIONALS: THE NEED FOR TERM LIMITS

I HAVE BEEN INVOLVED WITH MANY INSTITUTIONS
where someone clearly overstayed his or her welcome in a certain position. That person should have
retired, transitioned, or resigned years (maybe even decades) earlier, but
found ways to maneuver such that he or she could stick around, with the

majority of folks involved in the organization becoming deeply resentful and the organization itself having its growth stunted.

Pope Benedict XVI resigned in 2013, marking the first papal resignation in hundreds of years (and then only because there was more than one Pope at the time), he was nearly 86. When Pope Benedict was elected in 2005, he was the oldest Pope elected since 1730. Pope Benedict has had a pacemaker for years, and had a routine operation to replace its batteries. While religions often stress tradition, it must also be noted that, although people now live longer due to advances in medical care and knowledge of healthier living, there are also medical conditions that can greatly inhibit the ability of an elderly person to perform the full-time duties of a religious spiritual or communal leader.

After announcing that he was leaving the Jewish Funders Network, Mark Charendoff argued that there should be term limits for Jewish professionals. He offers a number of benefits:

- Avoid falling "into a rut, into a certain way of doing things, of thinking, of acting, after being in any job for too long."
- We can "move those years of experience and expertise into another agency."
- "It is sometimes hard to feel that accountability if there is no longer any danger of being held accountable."
- They make room for new executives to "recruit new senior lay leadership, opening up space on boards that may not have seen enough diversity in background or in thinking."
- Open opportunities for middle management to grow into higher positions. "And we may find more opportunities for women to fill what have traditionally been male dominated roles."
- "We'll save money. CEO salaries rise over the course of their tenure and well they should."

American political history has many such examples of leaders who held on to the reins of power too long. Republican Representative Joe Cannon served forty-six years in the House of Representatives from 1873–1923, including a stint as Speaker of the House from 1903–1911. As Speaker, he earned the nickname "Czar Cannon" because of his dictatorial manner and opposition to every progressive measure, even resisting the formidable efforts of President Theodore Roosevelt. He was finally overthrown as

Speaker by a coalition that included members of his own party. So much necessary legislation was needlessly held up due to his destructive authority.

The Senate in the twenty-first century further illustrates the case for term limits. Republican Mitch McConnell, who entered the Senate in 1985, has been the Minority Leader since 2007. As of September 2012, Republicans in the Senate had filibustered 375 bills during the Obama Presidency, far and away a record. In December 2012, Senator McConnell achieved the dubious distinction of becoming the first Senator to filibuster his own bill; he proposed a vote on raising the debt ceiling, but then blocked it when the Democrats did not object to the vote. On the other side, Democratic Senator Harry Reid, who has served since 1987, has been the Senate Majority Leader since 2007. Senator Reid has acceded to most of this obstruction by not pushing for a revision of the filibuster rules, and as a result everything in Congress is stalled, including the Farm Bill that regulates foreign aid and food stamps in addition to agricultural policies.

The American public bears some of the responsibility for this. A January 2013 Gallup poll reported that three-fourths of Americans favor term limits, although they also re-elected at least 90 percent of congressional incumbents in 2012. (Part of this may be due to gerrymandering, which has made most congressional district races noncompetitive). Americans have always backed term limits in theory, although no term limit legislation has ever passed both houses of Congress. The one national term limit, under the 22nd Amendment which was ratified in 1951, limits a President to two terms in office (and no more than ten years in the event of taking over the Presidency before running for the presidency). Oddly, this amendment passed as a reaction to the four-term administration of perhaps the most popular president in history, Franklin D. Roosevelt.

There are those who point out that term and tenure limits do not always make sense. For example, when President Franklin D. Roosevelt was frustrated by the "nine old men" of the Supreme Court who had declared so many New Deal laws unconstitutional, he tried to enact legislation that would force the retirement of elderly judges. However, as critics pointed out, the oldest justice on the Court in 1937 was 81-year old Louis Brandeis, perhaps the most progressive justice. Nevertheless, as our population ages, and as the prevalence of debilitating conditions such as Alzheimer's, Parkinson's, stroke, and complications from cardiovascular and other diseases increases among the elderly, lifetime tenure can impede the workings of an organization. In addition to health concerns, term limits are compelling due to the corrosiveness of entrenched power, best summarized by Lord Acton, who in 1887 wrote, with reference to the Catholic Church: "Power tends to corrupt, and absolute power corrupts absolutely."

We would be wise to consider policies that limit the terms of our religious as well as political leaders. When our institutions do not provide term limits, leaders might assume the wisdom and humility to transition themselves for the welfare of the organization and broader community just as Moses actively brought Joshua into leadership to prepare the community for the next stages of their journey (Deuteronomy 31:7–8). Succession planning honors the community but it can also honor one's own legacy, coloring one's memory with the virtues of humility and selflessness.   □

IS ALL OF JEWISH LEADERSHIP WORK HOLY? THE NOTION OF META-HOLINESS

WE OFTEN THINK OF CLERGY, SCROLLS, and the synagogue as the realm of the holy. But is the work of all Jewish communal leadership holy? What does it even mean to do holy work?

In searching for a compelling Jewish notion for the holy, we can review many different approaches.

1. Coming Close to the Other: For Hassidim and Kabbalists, many Rabbis were known as HaKadosh (the holy one), since they achieved a spiritual and cognitive level closest to the Divine (as compared to other approaches of holiness dealing with the behavioral realm). For some, holiness means anything having to do with God; holiness is about embracing the Other. Levinas took this vertical theology and made it horizontal (embracing the Other includes in its deepest sense embracing the other). Levinas writes: "Holiness represents the moment at which, in the human . . . the concern for the other breaches concern for the self."

2. Separatism and Asceticism: For Ramban and Rashi, holiness is more individualistic, concerned with separatism and asceticism. For Ramban,

attaining holiness is about going beyond the letter of the law (*naval b'reshut ha-Torah*) and avoiding excess (*she-ni'hiyeh perushim min ha-mutarot*). For many, this is about purity, and for others it is about ethics. The Rabbis of the Talmud teach that to be holy is to be *poresh me'ha-arayot*, one who abstains from prohibited sexual acts. Holiness as asceticism goes further. The Vilna Gaon was the exemplar of the concept of *pat b'melah tochal*, that one should subsist on bread and salt. The ultimate asceticism is to separate from the nations of the world (Leviticus 20:26: "You shall be holy to Me, for I, the Lord, am holy, and I have set you apart from other peoples to be Mine"). The Jewish people are considered holy since they have a unique mission.

3. Communal Ethics: Holiness is about community. Jewish law requires a *minyan* to say *Kaddish* and *Kedushah* and other prayers concerned with holiness. It is not only about giving to others, but also to seeing value and utility in all others (all in the community have a purpose and a way to contribute to building holy community of shared values through partnership). Moses tells the people: "*v'l'hiyotchah am kadosh l'Hashem Elokechah*," that we be a holy nation to the Lord (Deuteronomy 26:19). There is an individual ethic as well, of course, of "*Kedoshim t'hiyu*," you shall be holy (Leviticus 19:2) is a mandate that each individual should collectively be a holy nation through the emulation of the ways of God.

4. The Good for its own sake: Many have claimed that the Land of Israel is holy, and thus the Jews must fully own and possess it. Professor Moshe Halbertal has made the opposite claim, arguing that because the land is holy, it is God's and no person or group of people can ever fully take ownership of it. Halbertal has argued that the holy is that which cannot be instrumentalized (i.e., used for political gain); rather, the holy is good for its own sake, not to achieve some other benefit. For example, Jewish law says that one cannot pass through a synagogue because it is a faster route, a short cut. The holy is an end in itself, not an instrument for gain. Holiness does not simply exist in the world, rather an act that brings holiness into the world is a creative act. One makes a *hillul* (desecration) when emptying the value from the valuable and one makes a *kiddush* (sanctification) when filling a void with that which is true and good.

Of course, none of these models are mutually exclusive. We may or may not buy into them and we could favor portions of these approaches. But as Jewish leaders, we play a role in "meta-holiness" (by providing the space for the synthesis of different approaches of holiness). Whether one is a rabbi, educator, director, philanthropist, academic, social worker, or volunteer, when one holds and nurtures the system that enables other individuals and the community to actualize its holiness potential, the leader actualizes a role of meta-holiness. Of course, there must be transparency and accountability when dealing with possible abuses of the holy, especially for those who influence and control our eco-system of meta-holiness. While we should strive to live as individuals along the holy path, and should join and contribute to holy communities, we can also play a role of actualizing meta-holiness, providing sacred space for others to think, grow, and have impact. This is perhaps the pinnacle of holiness when we embrace the humility to create a space for creative holy expressions. ☐

☐ ISRAEL AND SOCIAL JUSTICE

ZIONISM: THE GREAT JEWISH ETHICAL PROJECT

I RECALL THE TIME WHEN, LIVING IN ISRAEL, I stood with more than 100,000 Israelis as a link in a human chain. Our purpose that day in the desert was to spread a message of hope, peace, and solidarity. For me and my Jewish identity, this event was particularly formative. For too long, the focus by the religious community has been on the land and we are overdue to solidify the real Jewish priority.

"The people demand social justice!" chanted hundreds of thousands of Israelis in the streets during the tent movement of the summer of 2011. I was inspired by the demonstrations spread throughout the country, from Tel Aviv and Haifa down to Beit Shemesh and Eilat. I was inspired to learn that after a devastating earthquake in Haiti, the Israeli medical relief team was first on the scene. I was inspired by the new wave of Israeli Jewish social justice organizations such as Bema'aglei Tzedek, MiMizrach Shemesh, Yahel, Zika, B'Tzedek, Kolot, Atzum, Atid Bamidbar, Elul, Bina, and Hillel.

I am a Religious Zionist. For me, Zionism is the great Jewish ethical project to create a just state guided by Jewish values. Zionism is not fulfilled merely through achieving sovereignty but through building a society of ideals that transcends its own borders and bottom line. The Midrash refers to Jerusalem as *Ir Tzedek*, city of righteousness, since the city should ideally serve as *ohr la-goyim*, a light to other nations. When we do not meet the mark, I feel pained.

Many see the Israeli social justice movement as an attempt to uphold the values of Religious Zionism. Rabbi Yuval Cherlow, the head of a yeshiva in Raanana, explains his decision to join the tent social justice movement calling for more affordable living for all Israelis:

> The question of our existence as a society of justice and morality is the most important thing. I'm putting things mildly. There is the possibility that this movement will turn us into a more just society. There is nothing more important in religious terms . . . Secondly, this gives us a chance to break down the dichotomy . . . between the political right and the economic right. That's why I think it is important to be part of the attempt to turn this protest into a movement for making amends.

I am inspired by Israel's Declaration of Independence, which states that Israel "will foster the development of the country for the benefit of all its inhabitants; it will be based on freedom, justice and peace as envisaged by the prophets of Israel; it will ensure complete equality of social and political rights to all its inhabitants irrespective of religion, race or sex; it will guarantee freedom of religion, conscience, language, education and culture . . ."

Only in our own land can Jews fully actualize, in such a sustainable and systemic way, the Jewish values of *tzedakah*, *mishpat*, *rahamim*, and *hesed* (righteousness, justice, mercy, and kindness). We are more responsible when we have a homeland. We are watched and we have no excuses. We control the country's destiny.

Maimonides explains that the purpose of Jewish law is to perfect the body and the soul. In Platonic parlance, by "well-being of the body," he means the creation of the just state; by "well-being of the soul," he means intellectual perfection. However, he goes on to explain that the primary purpose of Jewish law and our main priority must be to create the just state, "because the well-being of the soul can only be obtained after that of the body has been secured" (*Guide for the Perplexed* 3:27).

Our responsibility is to intertwine our *tikkun medinah* (healing of state) with our *tikkun olam* (healing of world). Thus, it is our responsibility as Zionists to further internal moral and spiritual progress within the country and to ensure that Israel is giving this example beyond its borders.

Religious Zionism, in many ways, is broken as factions fall into various forms of extremism. It is time that the foundation of Religious Zionism be social justice and the model just state. While the country has a long way to go to create the model state or model citizen that can inspire the world, we should be proud of how much progress we have made since 1948 and be excited about how much more important work we have to do together.

As an American Jew, I feel a responsibility to bring our culture of tolerance, diversity, and civic engagement to Israel to strengthen the commitments there.   □

BECOMING BUILDERS
OF JERUSALEM:
THE MODEL JUST SOCIETY

I N 2012, I WAS HONORED TO DELIVER THE CAPE Town, South Africa, community-wide keynote address for Yom Yerushalayim – Jerusalem Day. Hundreds gathered together in a powerful celebration of the liberation of Jerusalem on the 28th of Iyar in the year 1967. I was reminded of the power of Jerusalem to unite the Jewish people.

Rav Avraham Yitzhak HaCohen Kook taught that Zionism is the secular aspect of statehood but that Jerusalem is the soul of that movement, and they build off of one another. Jerusalem is a center of the world. In 2010 and 2011, Jerusalem welcomed about 3.5 million tourists a year. Students flock, journalists are in abundance – the whole world is watching Jerusalem.

Even though Jerusalem does not explicitly appear in the Torah (unless Ir Shalem in the Avraham/Malkitzedek story is a reference to Jerusalem), it appears hundreds of times in the Bible. It is our Jewish center; every day, we think about and pray for and toward Jerusalem in the *Amidah* and *Birkat HaMazon.*

Jerusalem is a place of our past, where tradition is that the *Akedah* (the binding of Isaac) happened on Mount Moriya in Jerusalem, where the Temple stood, and so much of our sacred history for thousands of years occurred. However, similar to the Chanukah story, ostensibly about the past military victory and miracle, the meaning is really about Jewish survival today and celebrating and renewing our commitments. So too, Yom Yerushalayim is about the past, but is also the most true celebration of re-committing to the building and fostering of today's Jerusalem.

We are to emulate God who is *"boneh b'rahamav Yerushalayim"* (Builder of Jerusalem through mercy). We are not tourists and shoppers (who just go to the Kotel, a pizza shop, and buy some gifts), although our tourist money is of course very important. We are also not just advocates on the sidelines (although this is very important). We are builders of Jerusalem, each of us in our own unique way.

In the Talmud, Rabbi Yohanan notes the words of HaKadosh Baruch Hu: "I shall not dwell in the Celestial Jerusalem (*Yerushalayim shel maalah*) until I dwell in the Earthly Jerusalem (*Yerushalayim shel matah*)." Thus, the heavenly Jerusalem (ideal) cannot be built until the earthly Jerusalem (the pragmatic city) is built. There is the concealed (intimate home) and re-vealed (model in the world) and the concealed Jerusalem is the reward for achieving the building of the revealed city.

Before we can deal with a spiritually ideal home, we must build an eth-ically sound model society – a paradigm for the world of a just city. We know there are very serious social problems in Jerusalem and broader Israel. Indeed, throughout the Western world, it has been acknowledged that the gap between rich and poor is widening. Consider the following:

- 25 percent of Israelis live in poverty
- 850,000 children and a growing number of working poor are now considered to be living below the poverty line

In comparison, Jerusalem fares even worse. As Israel Kimhi, of the Jerusalem Institute of Israel Studies, said before Yom Yerushalayim: "Jerusalem con-tinues to be the poorest city in Israel." In the Jewish neighborhoods of West Jerusalem (East Jerusalem suffers from even worse poverty), the number living below the poverty line is sobering:

- Nearly one-third of families
- About 45 percent of minors

In addition, only 33 percent of Israeli twelfth graders matriculate, due to the large number of ultra-Orthodox students who do not take matriculating exams.

Jerusalem is also ranked as one of the most corrupt cities in the world, and several former mayors have been arrested for corruption. From dys-functional law enforcement, denial of minimum wages, slave trafficking, torture, and other problems, Jerusalem in many ways is struggling.

These should not deflate our love and commitment to Israel – the opposite!

There is a tremendous moral and spiritual opportunity to help develop our greatest Jewish gift from God and the greatest Jewish project of our time. As a Jewish community, we must get on the same page. The secular culture often does not appreciate the *kedushat ha-ir* (holiness of the city). The ultra-Orthodox culture often does not appreciate the collective responsibility that comes with building and defending the city. The Religious Zionists sometimes isolate themselves from society and become fanatical. In the Diaspora, too many Jews are not pro-Israel and too many others support Israel but are not vocal in their support.

But we also know there are many great things happening in Jerusalem today.

I am inspired to learn about the new wave of Israeli Jewish social justice organizations such as Bema'aglei Tzedek and their Tav Chevrati, MiMizrach Shemesh, Yahel, Zika, B'Tzedek, Kolot, Atzum, Atid Bamidbar, Elul, Bina, and Hillel.

I have been inspired to learn of the growing Israeli social justice culture that is starting to emerge – hundreds of thousands of Israelis in the streets during the tent movement of the summer of 2011, from Tel Aviv and Haifa down to Beit Shemesh and Eilat protesting for *tzedek hevrati* (social justice). This is a very new phenomenon.

I am inspired to watch firsthand that after a devastating earthquake in Haiti, the Israeli medical relief team was first on the scene.

If you have lived in Jerusalem, you know it is a city of *hesed* – great (almost miraculous) kindnesses happen every day, and less violence than an outsider would suspect. In 2010, in Los Angeles, a city of 3.8 million people, there were 297 murders. In Jerusalem, a city of 800,000, that same year there were nine murders. In 2011, there were only five murders. One is too many, but it is nearly unique to have such a low number.

I am inspired by Israel's Declaration of Independence, which states that Israel

> will foster the development of the country for the benefit of all its inhabitants; it will be based on freedom, justice and peace as envisaged by the prophets of Israel; it will ensure complete equality of social and political rights to all its inhabitants irrespective of religion, race or sex; it will guarantee freedom of religion, conscience, language, education and culture . . .

This is a world model, where we can fully embrace religion and democracy. The Midrash calls Jerusalem "Ir Shalom." Shalom is not only a moral attribute, it is also a Name of God. Shalom is not political but a crucial Jewish value about removing physical and psychological suffering. Further, the Midrash refers to Jerusalem as "Ir Tzedek," city of righteousness, since the city should ideally serve as *ohr la-goyim*, a light to other nations.

We recite in our Sunday morning prayers "*Mi yaaleh b'Har Hashem*," who is just enough to be able to confidently enter Jerusalem (Psalms 24:3–4). The only one fit to enter the Beit HaMikdash was one who could vouch that they were honest and ethical and did not cheat other people. The Mikdash is an intensified version of Jerusalem and thus one had to be ethical and fair in business in order to enter. A higher *kedushah* (holiness) demands a higher level of ethical and honest behavior. When people violated these principles and went into the Beit HaMikdash (and into Jerusalem any way), this enraged Hashem. God rejected the Mikdash because it had become a den of thieves (Jeremiah 7) and Jerusalem had been turned from a place "full of justice" to a place of murder and stealing and Hashem found this intolerable (Isaiah 1).

We must restore today's Jerusalem to its true ideals: honesty, integrity, and a spiritual and intellectual center with a foundation of social justice. Jewish survival matters not for its own sake – but because Jews add value to the world. Jerusalem's survival and liberation matters not for its own sake, but because the city can lead as a moral model in the world.

The psalm of the day is "*K'ir she'hubra la yahdav*" – "Built-up Jerusalem is like a city that was joined together" (Psalms 122:3). Jerusalem Day is a day of unity for Jerusalem, for our people, and for peace. We do not just look toward the past; each of us must also look to the future and commit ourselves toward furthering Jerusalem as a model state for justice.   □

ADDRESSING THE PLIGHT OF THE AFRICAN REFUGEES IN ISRAEL

I N JUNE 2012, 120 REFUGEES WERE SENT BACK TO South Sudan, where they face existential danger in the shape of hunger and threat of war. Things have been getting worse in Israel, with militant violence. There is some hostile, intolerant language coming not just from crowds at protests, but also from politicians. Authorities are arresting refugees and deporting them. The Hebrew Immigrant Aid Society has termed this anti-foreigner wave "the largest one in scope and severity" in Israel's history.

Israel is experiencing great difficulties with rising immigrant populations, as are other nations around the world. Significantly, Israel is the only democratic state with a land connection to Africa, so it is inevitable that a large portion of African refugees would seek to go there. These undocumented migrants cross into Israel either looking for work or fleeing from severe persecution. The social and economic burdens are immense and Israel is already struggling with very limited resources. Clearly, Israel cannot be a home for all refugees who wish to come. This is not a fair request of this tiny state already overwhelmed with social and economic issues. However, there is no justification for the racism and violence that some Israelis are showing toward this population.

This crisis has developed over decades. During the 1990s, Israel opened its borders to migrant workers, and about 180,000 came. Only about half were able to obtain the necessary work contract and visa, while the others tended to work at very low-paying, unofficial jobs. On the other hand, since 2006, about 60,000 refugees have come to Israel, mostly from Eritrea (34,000) or Sudan (15,700), and 2,000 more enter every month. The Israeli government has regarded these refugees under the law as "infiltrators," and regards them as migrant workers, subject to deportation. Of the 4,603 new applications for asylum filed by other refugees, only one was approved in 2011.

Ironically, Israel, a nation of refugees, has not fully developed a legal process for non-Jewish refugees. Since Israel did not have diplomatic relations with Sudan, and since Eritrea has deteriorated into a lawless state, most of the refugees from these countries could not be immediately deported. Nevertheless, they have not been given the opportunity to apply for asylum (in contrast, 85 percent of Eritreans who reach the United States are granted asylum, and 70–90 percent of refugees from Sudan and Eritrea are granted asylum in Europe). While Israel has given some of these refugees temporary group protection, this has to be renewed annually, and most importantly, it does not confer the right to work within Israel. The result is that refugees have little access to work, health care, education, or other services.

Who are these refugees, and how are they treated? Stephen Slater writes about his 2007 encounter with a Sudanese refugee, George Kulang, whose wife and children had been murdered by the Janjaweed (armed militia on horseback who have committed many atrocities in Darfur). He fled to Egypt, where he was tortured, so he continued his journey to Israel. When he saw an Israeli flag, he felt that "I must walk to that flag, because the Israelis are good, they have democracy, they will not turn us away." However, as is typical for most refugees, he then spent several months in jail, and (usually when the detention centers are overflowing) was released to an urban center to fend for himself, often working below the minimum wage.

South Sudan won independence from Sudan in July 2011. Israel established relations with the new state, and this enabled Israel to deport Sudanese refugees, even though the political situation there is far from stable, with much military activity. In the spring of 2012, events took an alarming turn. Some Israeli government officials raised a more intolerant tone:

- Prime Minister Binyamin Netanyahu said that Israel had to prevent "illegal infiltrators flooding the country."
- MK Miri Regev called the refugees "a cancer in our midst."
- Tel Aviv Mayor Ron Huldai and the mayor of five other cities called for the imprisonment and expulsion of African refugees.
- MK Danny Danon claimed that Israel now has "an 'infiltrator' enemy state" within its borders, and has called for the detention and mass-deportation of all infiltrators.

In addition, unsubstantiated reports of a rising crime wave among African refugees in South Tel Aviv raised tensions, and then apartment houses (including a daycare center) in the Shapira neighborhood of south Tel Aviv were hit by four firebombs in April; fortunately, there were no injuries. On

May 24, tensions reached a breaking point. Politicians incited the crowd with xenophobic rhetoric, and then the crowd smashed the windows and destroyed goods in stores owned by African refugees, and then attacked Africans on the streets. Fortunately, many courageous Israelis rose to denounce this act of hatred:

- Yair Lapid, as head of the new Yesh Atid party, called the attack a "pogrom" [an extremely hateful term describing the tsarist attacks on Jewish communities in Russia], adding: "They don't understand the meaning of Jewish morals or collective Jewish memory, nor do they understand the meaning of Jewish existence."
- President Shimon Peres said: "Hatred of foreigners contradicts the foundations of Judaism."
- In an editorial, *Haaretz* condemned the rioting against African refugees and human rights activists: "The history of the Jewish people – rife with instances of incitement, persecution and pogroms – does not resonate with the inciters. . . . it is becoming a badge of shame on an entire society."

The statements of the beleaguered refugees supply an added poignancy. One Eritrean who experienced the violence said: ". . . when we try to explain that we fled murder and torture no one is interested. We did not believe that things like this could happen in a democracy like Israel." A Sudanese resident of Tel Aviv spoke in a manner disturbingly familiar to many: "You don't know when you will be taken by the police, arrested and deported. You don't know how long it will be. We're living in an uncertain future. We are living in fear." Others wonder if their neighbors will attack them, and know that the police will not help them if an attack occurs.

In response, some Israelis have gone out of their way to show kindness to the stranger, such as walking African children home from school. Others have pointed out that, according to official police data given to the Knesset in March 2012, the crime rate among foreigners was 2.24 percent, while for the general population the crime rate was 4.99 percent, significantly higher, refuting the myth that Africans are disproportionately involved in crime. Lifting the prohibition on work would probably help lower the foreign crime rate even further.

June 2012 brought many new developments. An Israeli court approved the deportation of 1,500 Africans who were living in Israel. The government then arrested 240, and 300 others chose to leave rather than face arrest.

There was also a spate of bills passed based more on political expediency than coherent policy. On June 3, a law went into effect allowing the detention of "infiltrators" for up to three years, yet another attempt to deter refugees.

On June 10, another bill increased penalties for those who aided infiltrators and for those employers who hired workers illegally. By the middle of June, deportees were being sent back to South Sudan on weekly flights. Since South Sudan looks forward to Israeli investment to build its economy, it is cooperating with the deportations.

Policy on the refugees was one of the issues facing candidates for the race for mayor of Tel Aviv in 2013. In September 2013, the Israeli Supreme Court decided that the mass arrest of the refugees is illegal, and each detainee case must be examined individually.

The government's pledge to enforce a ban on work for refugees will have consequences. Israel is rapidly working to finish its southern detention center, Ir Amim (City of Nations), which will be the world's largest prison for immigrants when it reaches its capacity of 10,000–15,000 inmates. In addition, Israel is building a barrier covering most of the border with Egypt to discourage refugees. However, even this will not succeed in taking all the refugees out of Israel's cities. As a result, there is a plan to set up 20,000–25,000 tents in the Negev, which will probably not have a sewage system and will severely overtax the water and electricity supply of the region. As Ramat Negev Regional Council head Shmuel Rifman said: "I'm told it's temporary, but in Israel the transient becomes permanent" (*Haaretz*, June 12, 2012).

It must be pointed out that the instability in much of Africa cannot, of course, be solved by Israel alone, and that international efforts must be coordinated to reduce the level of poverty and human rights abuses that leads to mass migration of refugees. There must be more international support and collaboration to support the State of Israel and other democracies facing these challenges. It could also be noted that, on many occasions when Jews were persecuted, there were few voices raised to defend the Jews, whereas here there is a significant revulsion against the rioters. Many nations have refugee problems, and few have resolved the issue with humanity. There are no perfect solutions to these immense challenges. Nevertheless, as the refugees themselves have often said, Israel is a place where you should expect something better. Defining refugees from places where murder, torture, and rape are common as "infiltrators" and "criminals" shows a poor example to the world. Up to 50,000 asylum seekers should not be ignored or routinely detained by the Prison Service.

Israeli rabbi and scholar Rabbi Donniel Hartman teaches the importance of embracing our Jewish responsibilities toward refugees that come along with our political sovereignty.

As a Jewish state committed to the continuity of values and as a co-signee of the 1951 UN Convention Relating to the Status of Refugees, the value of Jewish continuity cannot be allowed to cause us either to shirk our responsibility or to be deaf to the needs of others. As a strong and successful country with a clear and sustainable Jewish majority, we have the ability to assimilate thousands of individuals a year without weakening our national identity. Given the size of Israel and the value of Jewish national continuity, however, this number is not unlimited. We need to determine a realistic policy which recognizes both our responsibility as Jews and our responsibility to the Jewish people.

Rav Donniel continues showing how our Jewish response to crises like these determines the future of our nation.

With Zionism, the Jewish people have entered into the arena of political sovereignty with all of its gifts, challenges, and opportunities. We need to defend our borders and defend our national identity. We must also make sure, however, that we do not create a state whose border policies are Jewish but where life within those borders is not conducted with the highest standards of Jewish moral principle. As Jews we have matured sufficiently in our treatment of our border policy but we have yet to do so when it comes to our internal policy. We have created our Jewish state precisely for such an opportunity. It is time for us to embrace it.

Call upon Israeli government officials to ensure the safety of the African refugees so that they not live in fear. The building of the detention facility in the Negev to indefinitely detain refugees should be halted. A thoughtful, ethical, and comprehensive immigration policy needs to be developed for how the State of Israel receives African refugees. Creating a true policy for dealing with refugees in accordance with international law should be a priority. We not only need the Israeli government to stop wrongs done to innocent vulnerable refugees but to fully swing the pendulum to being the global leader to fight the genocides occurring in the world today and to support refugees in all ways possible. Due to our unique Jewish history, we are best positioned to be at the forefront. Israel cannot become just another nation struggling with the refugee problem like other nations; rather there needs to be a distinctly Jewish compassionate response that raises the global standard. Israel, our beloved homeland, is a light in so many ways and this is another opportunity that cannot be missed to demonstrate how we care for the vulnerable.

As Jews, we are a nation of immigrants commanded to love and protect the stranger in our midst. This imperative is highest when we have sovereignty. It is not only our historical condition but also our eternal identity as the children of Abraham, the paradigmatic stranger.   □

A SPIRITUAL START-UP NATION

D AN SENOR AND SAUL SINGER AUTHORED A popular book called *Start-Up Nation* (published in 2009) which shows how Israel has become a mecca for entrepreneurship and business innovation. They show that:

- In addition to boasting the highest density of start-ups in the world (a total of 3,850 start-ups, one for every 1,844 Israelis), more Israeli companies are listed on the NASDAQ exchange than all companies from the entire European continent.
- In 2008, per capita venue capital investments in Israel were 2.5 times greater than in the United States, more than 30 times greater than in Europe, 80 times greater than in China, and 350 times greater than in India.
- Comparing absolute numbers, Israel – a country of just 7.1 million people – attracted close to $2 billion in venture capital, as much as flowed to the United Kingdom's 61 million citizens or to the 145 million people living in Germany and France combined.
- After the United States, Israel has more companies listed on the NASDAQ than any other country in the world, including India, China, Korea, Singapore, and Ireland (pp. 11–13).

Senor and Singer attribute this success to "a story not just of talent but of tenacity, of insatiable questioning of authority, of determined informality, combined with a unique attitude toward failure, teamwork, mission, risk, and cross-disciplinary creativity" (p. 18).

This is really remarkable and something to be proud of. Can we replicate this on a spiritual front?

Can we get to a place where our nation is also furthering spiritual innovation around the world? Millions flock to India, Thailand, and other spiritual centers to find themselves and their place in the cosmos. What do Israel and diaspora Jewish communities have to offer? We have many historical sites to share – arguably the best in the world! – but when it comes to contemporary spiritual practice, our contributions are more parochial and not tremendously accessible or meaningful to billions of non-Jews around the world. Let's change that. We can remain unique and be open and we can be particular and universal. We have much to learn from other communities and many of our own gifts to share.   □

☐ CHILD ADOPTION

11 CHILD ADOPTION

THE JEWISH IMPERATIVE
FOR CHILD ADOPTION

MILLIONS OF CHILDREN FALL ASLEEP EVERY night hungry, wearing an unchanged diaper, and with no one to hold them as they cry themselves to sleep. There is perhaps no greater suffering than to feel unloved, unwanted, and uncared for by anyone. This is the story of the orphan.

In March 2012, the global population surpassed 7 billion, and concerns for the poor in a world with more limited resources than ever before must be a top priority. Perhaps the most vulnerable among us include the more than 160 million orphans who lack love, attachment, and emotional support, let alone homes. Millions of children need families, and we can all pause to consider adopting some of them.

My wife Shoshana and I feel that, as Jews and global citizens facing the realities of the twenty first century, we must consider adoption as a moral imperative. It would not be easy, and there are always risks, but we are blessed with a safe home and with lots of love to give. One need not be rich or be challenged with infertility to consider adoption.

In addition to the moral imperative given the current global state, the Torah strongly condones adoption. The orphan (*yatom*) is prioritized in the Torah along with the widow (*almana*) and stranger (*ger*) to ensure their protection (Deuteronomy 16:11, 14; 24:19–21; 26:12–13). God is described as a "father of the fatherless" (Psalms 68:6). To become a parent to a parentless child is to emulate the Divine.

Jewish law encourages adoption so much that the law even considers the adoptive parents who care for, raise, and teach their child to be the official parents. "Whoever brings up an orphan in their home, it is as though they gave birth to him" (*Sanhedrin* 19b). This is true to the extent that a child's halachic name includes his or her foster parents' names, because "he who brings up a child is to be called its father, not he who gave birth" (Exodus Rabbah 46:5).

The rabbis taught that one who rescues and raises an orphan child in one's home fulfills a tremendous mitzvah, since there is a community responsibility to support impoverished orphans (*Ketubbot* 50a). The Talmud holds the community responsible for the support of orphans, for marrying them off, and for providing them with the means to live economically independent lives. Even further, we must allocate our communal funds to support orphans (*Ketubbot* 67b). We are collectively responsible to find solutions for parentless children in the world!

We all might find our own ways to contribute. At the least, we must find a way to love and support this population. Rambam explains how we must show the highest sensitivity toward orphans: "Whoever irritates them, provokes them to anger, pains them, tyrannizes over them, or causes them loss of money, is guilty of a transgression" (Mishneh Torah, *De'ot* 6:10). We must go beyond avoiding wronging parentless children and be sure to actively show love and care to this population. The great prophet Isaiah teaches us to "Defend the cause of orphans" (Isaiah 1:17). How will each of us heed this prophetic call?

Adopting a child is not only a great kindness, it is also a chance to cultivate greatness in an individual with a rich background who can understand multiple worlds and identities. There is strong precedent for adoption as a model to cultivate greatness. For example, the greatest prophet of all time, Moses, was adopted when his parents could not safely raise him (Exodus 2). His multiple identities as a Hebrew and Egyptian benefited his leadership greatly cultivating deeper empathy towards human vulnerability. Similarly, Mordechai raised his orphaned cousin Esther, who went on to be a crucial Jewish leader. The great Talmudic sage Abaye often quoted wise sayings in the name of his foster mother.

Adoption is not for everyone. There are serious challenges, risks, and commitments that come with such a decision, but given the realities of our over-populated world and the over-abundance of orphans, it is a decision we must all at least consider. There is perhaps no damage greater to the soul then growing up in the world without parents and without being held at night. Every stable family has the opportunity to embrace the most

vulnerable humans on the planet when we give children a home and family.
Let's consider! □

THE MITZVAH OF ADOPTION, ORPHANS IN RUSSIA, AND THE BAAL SHEM TOV

A CHABAD FAMILY IN NEPAL MADE A GREAT public *Kiddush Hashem* (sanctification of God's name) by adopting a starving child. While definitions for these terms vary, what is clear is that there are millions of orphans around the world and we must all do our part.

Adoption today, especially on an inter-country basis, is undergoing tremendous change. Jewish law has always defined an orphan as one who has lost one parent and thus they recite the *Kaddish Yatom*, the orphan's memorial prayer (*Kitzur Shulhan Aruch* 29:19). In the industrialized world, we define an orphan as a child without either of his or her parents. However, especially due to the A I D S epidemic, millions of children in Africa and other areas have lost at least one parent and have been plunged into deep poverty. As a result, U N I C E F now defines an orphan as someone who has lost one or both parents. It estimates that in 2005 there were more than 132 million orphans in the mostly non-industrialized areas of Asia, sub-Saharan Africa, and Latin America and the Caribbean. (Of these, 13 million had lost both parents). U N I C E F promotes international adoption in accordance with the 1993 Hague Convention on Protection of Children and Co-operation in Respect of Inter-country Adoptions. Only eighty nations have ratified this Convention, which is designed to safeguard the interests of the children and ensure transparency for both the children and prospective adoptive parents from different countries.

Unfortunately, due to changing regulations, suspensions of adoptions, the use of surrogates, and the recession's effect on the ability of couples to afford the adoption process, the trend has been to decrease adoptions.

The number has decreased from 45,000 in 2004 to 25,000 in 2011. After scandals involving the selling of children, the United States suspended adoptions from Vietnam and Guatemala (although Vietnam ratified the Hague Convention in 2012, so adoptions from there may shortly resume). In Haiti, where many poor parents bring children to orphanages when they cannot afford to support them, the ambiguity surrounding which children are actually orphans has muddled the picture dramatically. A government survey revealed that about 80 percent of the 30,000 orphans had one living relative (which qualifies most as UNICEF orphans), and as a result some orphanages have been closed.

What happened in Russia was shameful, with wicked legislators denying the more than 700,000 waiting orphans from potential adoption to the United States due to petty political considerations. In 2009, Sergey Magnitsky, a Russian whistle-blower and anti-corruption lawyer, was imprisoned, and then died in a pre-trial detention facility in Russia. In reaction, the Magnitsky Act was passed in the European Union in 2011 and in Congress in late 2012. The act prevents about sixty Russian officials (those believed to be implicated in Magnitsky's death) from obtaining visas to the United States and European Union, and freezes their assets. In retaliation, Russia passed a resolution banning all adoptions of Russian children by American citizens as of January 1, 2013, cynically named the Dima Yakovlev law, after a two-year old Russian child who died after being locked in a hot car by his adoptive parents in America for nine hours. In statements to the foreign press, Russian President Vladimir Putin justified the law as an "adequate" response to the Magnitsky Act, and further denounced America for criticizing Russia for ill-treatment of prisoners while torturing prisoners at Guantánamo Bay. In an interview with CNN, Prime Minister Dmitry Medvedev justified the bans by claiming that Russia had adequate resources to care for all its orphans, and then added: ". . . we know of a lot of cases when children adopted by American parents died or were tortured or lost their health in the U.S."

This was an obvious appeal to Russian chauvinism at the expense of the welfare of thousands of children. Russia claims that nineteen adopted children have died in America, but they neglect to mention that more than 60,000 Russian children have been adopted by Americans. Unfortunately, while the U.S. State Department estimated that about fifty American couples would be able to adopt Russian children (as their papers had been approved by Russian courts before the new law took effect), the remainder of the 1,000 couples awaiting adoption are without legal recourse. We hope that Russia reverses course and stops playing politics in the near future.

Orphans around the world who are not adopted undoubtedly suffer social isolation and miserable treatment in underfunded institutions that often lead to increased risk for disease and malnutrition. In the United States, studies have revealed that orphans who are not adopted have an average IQ twenty points lower than those raised in foster homes, and fewer than a quarter have a high school diploma. Of those who "age out" of foster care, nearly 60 percent of males are convicted of a crime, fewer than half were employed, and half were substance abusers. Clearly, adoption offers benefits to the orphan, the adopted parents, and society as a whole.

The Chofetz Chaim, in *Ahavat Hesed*, tells a tale that illustrates the power of adoption.

> A childless couple came for help to the Baal Shem Tov. They accompanied him to a distant village, where he asked each child's name. Nearly all the boys were called Moshe, and nearly all the girls were Devorah Leah. The Baal Shem Tov explains why with this story:
>
> A village couple – Moshe and Devorah Leah – were childless. In passing by the *beit midrash* (study house) one day, Moshe heard a passage: When one teaches a child Torah, it is as if he gave birth to the child. Moshe proposed an idea to his wife. There was no reliable Torah education for the village children; rebbes would teach whatever they wanted, leading to confusion and more harm than good. Therefore, Moshe proposed that they set up a proper system for Torah study. They found the best *melamdim* (teachers) and paid them well, kept them supplied, and offered this to every village child.
>
> Since every child was "their" child, the couple provided other needs. For some families, they helped with household expenses, weddings, and anything else a child required. Before long, the town recognized the beautiful generation emerging thanks to this couple. In the children's love of Torah, refinement, and intelligence, they outshone the children of their region.
>
> As Moshe and his wife grew older, they wrote a will leaving money to their relatives, setting up a home for the poor and donating the rest of their estate to maintain the children's education. When they died, the town's great affection and high esteem for Moshe and Devorah Leah manifested in a special way. Almost every child born in those

years was named after these "honorary grandparents," who with end-less love and concern brought the town's children into a life of Torah and *mitzvot*.

"Now, let me ask you," said the Baal Shem Tov, "Was this couple childless, or did they have more children than anyone else?"

Let us take this message to heart and remember the millions of needy children in the world whose lives we can make better through adoption.   □

STUCK – THE UNNECESSARY PAINS OF INTERNATIONAL ADOPTION

T HE INTERNATIONAL ADOPTION PROCESS pushes so many people away with inter-country politics, excessive costs, red tape, and sometimes even unnecessary rejection. Instead of pushing people away from adopting orphans, we primarily need to be pulling them closer together.

The deep roots in Judaism for promoting adoption, as discussed above, should inspire us to create a much larger Jewish discourse about our role in responding to the global orphan crisis. The longer these children stay in orphanages the more risk of their suffering irreparable emotional, neuro-logical, psychological, and educational damage.

The must-see award-winning film, *STUCK*, by the Both Ends Burning organization, documents the struggles and rewards of international adop-tion. This quality documentary follows the stories of four orphans from Ethiopia, Vietnam, and Haiti, and their heartbreaking struggles to make it home to their adoptive families.

The subjects of the documentary are just four examples of millions of children around the world who are stuck in a broken system, and the growing outcry in the international community is that every child must be granted the right to grow up in a loving family. We must become more aware and outraged by the incredible obstacles placed in the way of people who are only trying to become parents, and the children who desperately want to have a family. There are an estimated 17.9 million children worldwide who have no living parents. This is probably a low estimate, as UNESCO data indicate that there are up to 150 million street children who spend their days in the streets of Latin America, India, Eastern Europe, and other areas. Some have families to return to at night, some have homes to sleep in, but millions literally live and sleep on the streets. In Latin America, they are called "*los abandonados*" (the abandoned ones), and many spend their days sniffing glue or paint thinner in an effort to get high and forget their hunger pangs. They are also subject to abuse by pedophiles and at risk of being intimidated and even murdered by the police, with little chance of obtaining justice. The idea that many of these children have families that can provide for them is a cruel exaggeration.

For years, liberal adoption policies allowed many Americans to have inter-country adoptions. The U.S. State Department reported that there were 233,934 total adoptions from 1999–2011, an average of about 18,000 a year. However, the number of international adoptions has declined greatly in recent years – from 21,467 in 2002 to 8,668 in 2012.The following factors should be noted:

- Due to increasingly difficult regulations, the number of adoptions to the United States has decreased by 62 percent.
- A 2012 State Department report noted that adoption service providers charged between $0 and $64,357 for all services, with a median charge of $28,425. The median wait takes 896 days; some adoptions have been held up for years due to bureaucratic obstacles.
- Current models predict that there will be even fewer adoptions in 2013, due to the Russian orphan ban. In addition, the State Department is not accepting applications from Cambodia and Guatemala.

STUCK is a film designed to raise awareness – and inspire outrage – over the deplorable practices allowed in current international adoption. Politics, inefficiency, and apathy leave children trapped and uncared for in orphanages around the world while there are loving families eager and willing to adopt them.

I would encourage others to watch the film, to consider volunteering to be part of the STUCK team when the film comes to your city, sign the petition, join marches and rallies supporting adoption of orphans. When we raise our voices and advocate the voices of millions of children, we can make great change.

Counterintuitively, the Skulener Rebbe taught that one should even show more care to an orphan than to their own children. The Rebbe stayed in Europe after World War II defying the Soviets to look after refugees and keep orphans in his home. On one cold night, he found an orphan on his floor crying without a blanket. He went and took the blanket off of his old child and gave it to the orphan child. His son understood but nonetheless the Skulener Rebbe said: "My dear son, please understand. You have a father. You can at least warm yourself with that. That child has no one in the world; let him at least have a blanket."

May we open our hearts to the orphans of the world crying out for homes and for love. ☐

□ BUSINESS ETHICS

FEEDING OUR WORKERS

I RECALL MY EXPERIENCES AS A TEENAGER WORK-ing waiting tables in various restaurants. There was a high-paced energy that was difficult to maintain, but the greatest challenge was constantly being hungry while serving others food. Today, many have it much worse than anything I experienced, because they work long shifts with no breaks at all to eat.

The *Kitzur Shulhan Aruch* (42:14) ruled that we must ensure that the food server also eats from the food being served. The *Biur Halacha* (169:1) went further, arguing that this rule requires the cook to be fed as well. The Gemara on which these rulings are based (*Ketubbot* 61a) actually went even further than these legal authorities, stating that one must give food to anyone who can smell the food being prepared or served.

We have not lived up to these just rulings. One-fifth of all Americans work in the food sector, from planting and harvesting crops to selling food directly to consumers in fast-food establishments and restaurants, but these twenty million Americans face an absurd dilemma: in addition to the 86 percent who receive low to sub-minimum wages, many are literally not allowed to eat during their workday. Consider the following statistics for food workers compiled by the Food Chain Workers Alliance in 2012:

- 8 percent never receive a 30-minute lunch break
- 22 percent never receive even a 10-minute break that would allow them to eat a snack
- 22 percent at times do not receive a 30-minute lunch break
- 28 percent at times do not receive a 10-minute break

In addition to the injustice involved, it does not make practical sense from a health or morale basis to deprive people of food while they are on the job. For decades, we have known that students who eat breakfast perform better than those who do not, especially in terms of attention span, the ability to concentrate, and IQ scores. For the adult workforce, companies such as Google and Facebook have long provided free meals for their employees, and surveys have noted that offering food to employees on the job has a positive impact on morale and engagement. With all the data supporting the idea that people perform better and are happier if they eat regularly, what purpose can be achieved by depriving people – especially those who work with food – of the ability to take even a minimal lunch break during the workday?

On the night of Passover, we declare, "*Kol dichfin yetei v'yeichal; kol ditzrich yetei v'yifsach*," welcoming in all those who are hungry and in need of a Passover meal. This message should not be restricted to our most special of holidays: As we sit in comfort to eat a meal at a restaurant or in our homes, we should think of those whose efforts helped put that food in front of us, and remember that they too must eat. They deserve a right to food for themselves, and ethical, halachic Judaism protects this right.   ☐

VANILLA AND CHOCOLATE SWIRLED WITH COMPASSION: THE CASE FOR BUYING FAIR TRADE

UNTIL 1865, MOST AMERICANS CONSUMED cotton, tobacco, sugar, and other goods produced by slave labor. Some dedicated abolitionists refused to use these products. Today, we face a similar problem, as many products that we consume daily are produced with forced or child labor, with farmers and artisans working for starvation wages, and in an unsustainable manner that damages and depletes the environment.

Fortunately, we now have a better option than merely a boycott: We can insist on fair trade certification.

Fair trade certifying organizations, such as FairTrade USA, are third-party organizations that certify that goods sold in this country meet the criteria for fair trade, including:

- Paying a fair price to farmers and artisans for the goods they produce
- Paying workers a livable wage and ensuring they work under humane conditions, while forced child labor is banned
- Ensuring that these operations are sustainable, i.e., that the crops and products do not directly or indirectly damage the environment
- Banning the use of genetically modified organisms and many harmful chemicals, and encouraging organic production

These principles involve some of our core Jewish principles. Consider Rambam's words in *Hilchot Mechirah* 18:1: "It is forbidden to cheat people in buying and selling, or to deceive them." Halacha demands that all parties (buyer, seller, workers, etc.) are respected. From slavery to colonialism to multinational buyers who dictate prices, the farmers of Africa and other regions have been exploited and underpaid for centuries. We must act to ensure that these farmers are paid a decent amount for their crops so that they in turn can hire laborers at a fair wage.

Consider cocoa, from which our chocolate is produced. West Africa produces most of the world's cocoa, with Côte d'Ivoire alone growing 40 percent. While we may complain about the price we pay for chocolate, the farmers who produce cocoa are paid about $1/pound by buyers who fix the price at this unfairly low level. As a result, after expenses, West African cocoa farmers make about 50 cents a day. This in turn has led the farmers to use forced and child laborers to produce much of their cocoa. In a pattern reminiscent of the era of slavery, farmers have even resorted to bringing in forced child laborers from neighboring countries to fill out their labor force. A 2009 assessment from the Payson Center for International Development at Tulane University found that 15 percent of children in Côte d'Ivoire and Ghana reported that they had been forced to work in cocoa production within the past year. Many work with machetes and lift heavy loads daily, activities which, predictably, frequently result in injury. In fact, approximately 50 percent of child cocoa workers in Côte d'Ivoire and Ghana were injured in 2012.

Activists have centered their efforts to promote fair trade on the Hershey Company, which controls more than 40 percent of the U.S. market, but which has lagged behind many other companies in refusing to identify where it buys its cocoa. In response, the "Raise the Bar Hershey" campaign seeks to persuade the company to comply with requests for transparency and to begin the certification process for fair trade standards. Key to this is a plan whereby one of Hershey's five top-selling bars made with cocoa would be 100 percent certified by third-party fair trade verification immediately, and then one more bar every two years afterward, so that all five bars would be fair trade certified by 2022. You can sign their petition and become involved in their campaign.

There have already been dramatic successes. Serving "Imagine Whirled Peace," and donating profits, Ben & Jerry's, Inc. was already known as one of the most socially responsible enterprises around. Ben & Jerry's announced an expansion of its fair trade commitment. In 2005, the company began to use fair trade cocoa, vanilla, and coffee for some of its products. However, activists pressed the company to expand fair trade to ingredients that comprise much more of the ice cream, such as sugar. Now, the company has agreed to switch to fair trade sugar and seven additional ingredients used in its ice cream products by the end of 2013. This will hopefully spur other companies to follow suit, further expanding the clout of fair trade consumers.

Thanks to organizations such as Fair Trade Judaica, where I serve on the Rabbinic Advisory Council, there are now fair trade certified gifts available such as Hanukkah gelt (dark chocolate from Ghana), kippot (from Guatemala), and Jewish blessing flags (from Nepal). They have helped design at least twenty new Judaica products, including the first fair trade tallit, *tzedakah* box, and paper cut banners. They are working on getting kosher certification on many of these fair trade products. They have created a Jewish Values and Fair Trade matrix. Consider watching a film about fair trade to learn more. There have been studies in England exploring International fair trade labeling and by the European fair trade handicraft organization which operates separately from the food certification process. The movement to certify clothing is reported to be expanding.

Anyone who regards *tikkun olam* and *tzedakah* as guiding principles rather than abstract concepts should act to promote fair trade certification in all areas. Fair trade promises to end the exploitation and poverty that has plagued much of the world for centuries. Remember that poverty is the greatest evil. The Midrash tells us: "There is nothing in the world more grievous than poverty – the most terrible of sufferings. Our teachers have said: if all the troubles of the world are assembled on one side and poverty is on the other, poverty would outweigh them all" (Exodus Rabbah 31:12). We must not exploit the economically weak so that a relatively few beneficiaries higher up the food chain can profit. While we have our economic problems, we can afford a few more dollars a year for our chocolate in exchange for promoting a just world. We must heed the words of the prophets who warn of ill-gotten wealth: "I, the Lord, probe the heart, and search the innermost thoughts, to repay every man according to his ways, with the proper fruit of his deeds. Like a partridge hatching what she did not lay, so is the one who amasses wealth by unjust means. In the middle of his life it will leave him, and in the end he will be proved a fool" (Jeremiah 17:10–11). Isn't true empathy with the downtrodden and a commitment to *tzedek* worth a few extra dollars? We must advocate at local stores, work to expand fair trade certification, and support and promote the options that already exist.   □

PROPER MARKETING AND SELLING

THERE IS A FAMOUS BUSINESS CONCEPT called *caveat emptor* (buyer beware). In secular society, as long as a seller does not blatantly lie or actively conceal a defect, it is the full responsibility of the buyer to exercise due diligence and to inspect what is being purchased. Jewish law takes a totally different approach: It is presumed that no defects or problems exist in a product or property if they are not disclosed explicitly by the seller.

We are well aware of fictional examples in literature and old movies of the quack doctor who promises miracle cures. This goes further back than you might think, and was prevalent in the entire Western world. One of the more famous comic Italian operas is Gaetano Donizetti's *L'Elisir d'Amore* ("The Elixir of Love"), in which quack Dr. Dulcamara ("Bittersweet") touts an elixir that cures everything from apoplexy to diabetes, though it is actually just repackaged Bordeaux wine. In this country, the creation of the

Food and Drug Administration (FDA) in 1906 regulated the drug industry in a helpful way, so that drugs no longer contained dangerous substances like cocaine and opium. However, new marketing schemes have continued to emerge and flourish as long as people were unaware of the deception. In the 1920s, for example, numerous "miracle" cures based on radium were sold to the general public in everything from water to bread to suppositories. Today, of course, companies sell radon detectors so homeowners can tell if there is radon gas (and thus a risk for lung cancer) in their basements.

In looking back to these bygone eras, we should not feel smug about how sophisticated we are today, for we still are fooled by deceptive marketing practices. You may think that that bottled water has to come from a pristine spring in the wilderness, that "natural" is just as good as "organic," or that the FDA has accurately defined and regulated all these terms. If so, you are in error.

For example, many people drink bottled water, unaware that the source of that water is ordinary tap water. Nestlé' Waters' 5-gallon bottles of water come from the municipal tap water of Woodridge, Illinois, while Aquafina (owned by PepsiCo) also bottles its water from municipal tap water. Even worse, a Coca-Cola subsidiary makes "Vitaminwater," which sounds like healthful, vitamin-fortified water, but at 130 calories and 33 grams of sugar it is quite the opposite. To make matters worse, several government- and privately-sponsored studies have concluded that tap water is more closely regulated than the bottled water industry. (Additional benefits of drinking tap water instead of bottled water include less waste disposal and lower spending.) In our search for healthy food products, we see labels such as "natural" as well as "organic." The U.S. Department of Agriculture regulates and certifies the production of organic food, and excludes many harmful substances: "Synthetic fertilizers, sewage sludge, irradiation, and genetic engineering may not be used." For multi-ingredient food items, a label of "organic" means that at least 95 percent or more of the content must be organic.

What about "natural" food? The FDA has this to say about "natural": "[The] FDA has not developed a definition for use of the term natural or its derivatives." Thus, all those pesticides, genetically modified food, and "sewage sludge" that are excluded from organic food may well be in "natural" food, and these are not required to be listed on the nutrition label. Unfortunately, many large agribusinesses have subsidiary companies that sound small and organic, but which use food that have pesticides and other harmful substances.

Finally, many people are concerned about consuming too much sodium, but will "reduced" or "low" sodium products be a better option? Fortunately, there are definitions here, but you may still take in far too much sodium. Of the two, "low sodium" is often the best option, as it means 140 mg of sodium or less per serving (don't forget to check the serving size as well). "Reduced sodium" means at least 25 percent less than the regular product. Thus, if a "normal" soup contains a staggering 900 mg of sodium per cup, the reduced sodium version can have 675 mg per cup, which in a 2.5-serving can would still give you nearly 1,700 mg of sodium, already more than the daily suggested serving for children, older adults, and people with diabetes or advanced kidney disease.

In consumer cases, the Federal Trade Commission sometimes catches the more outrageous marketing schemes. In 2012, for example, they successfully ordered Oreck to stop claiming that their vacuum cleaners could reduce the risk of flu, asthma, and other airborne illnesses, and forced Nivea to stop claiming that its skin cream could make people lose weight. However, the FTC also acted against a more insidious trend to mask commercials as news stories. The FTC forced the cessation of fake news sites such as "News 6 News Alerts" and "Health News Health Alerts" by six companies selling acai berry weight-loss programs. These companies used fake news sites to pretend that major media organizations had aired stories confirming the false claims of weight loss.

The American concept of caveat emptor is unjust, as it presumes that the consumer has as much power and ability to find good information as huge corporations do to spread the bad kind. We should be smarter consumers but the onus ultimately should be, as in Jewish law, almost completely on the seller to actively reveal any problems. If the owner does not disclose problems or defects, they have violated the prohibition of *geneivat daat,* deception (*Hoshen Mishpat* 228:6). If a product has a defect that is not actively disclosed then the buyer has the right to return the item for a full refund (232:3), since the transaction was a *mekah ta'ut,* false sale. This disclosure may not be broad but must be very specific to the problem (232:7). To determine whether or not a certain type of defect needs to be disclosed, we employ *minhag hamakom,* the customs and norms of the land/region (232:6). With the marketplace as complex and convoluted as it is, it is only just to shift responsibility for improper marketing to the seller.   □

EATING STALE POPCORN:
HOLINESS THROUGH
CONSUMER EMPOWERMENT

H OW MUCH STALE POPCORN DO YOU EAT?
A team of researchers at Cornell University
wanted to assess eating patterns, so they gave
movie attendees old stale popcorn in buckets of different sizes, weighing the
buckets before and after the movie to measure precisely how much popcorn
each person ate. The results were striking: People with the *large* buckets ate
53 percent more popcorn than people with the medium-size buckets. While
each movie attendee was equally hungry, and each had equally bad stale
popcorn, those with larger buckets ate the equivalent of 173 more calories
and dipped their hands into their buckets approximately 21 more times.

Sometimes, we don't make real conscious choices about what we want,
what we like, or what we need to be doing, but instead just keep eating
up whatever society gives us, even when we don't like it. Psychologists
have long known that we humans almost always prefer immediate gratification to delayed reward, and this can lead to catastrophic consequences.
For example, according to 2012 data collected by the Centers for Disease
Control and Prevention (CDC), 37.5 percent of American adults are obese.
In addition to a higher risk of numerous diseases and early death, obese
people pay financially for their condition, laying out more than $1,400
additionally every year for medical care than people of normal weight. In
spite of this, Americans continue to flock to fast-food and other unhealthy
establishments, especially if they can get huge portions of high-fat and
high-carbohydrate food. In the financial sector, the past decade saw a flood
of risky get-rich-quick schemes on Wall Street, and a real estate bubble that
burst with catastrophic results. Once again, the lure of easy and immediate
rewards trumped common sense and concern for long-term and societal
health.

The Torah comes to tell us that we can and must become more aware as
consumers. Rambam teaches, based upon the Gemara, that one should only
eat until he is two-thirds full. This ensures we do not fall into gluttony and

that we maintain our health, but also it is a way of maintaining self-control. We do not just consume all that we find before us; rather, we must make choices.

Our sages have long championed the wisdom of considering a delayed but more enduring reward over an immediate but fleeting one. Rav Levi of Berdichev, known as the Kedushat Levi, teaches that there are two months that mark the creation of the world. One is Tishrei, the time of Rosh Hashanah; the other is Nissan, the time of Pesach. How can there be two birthdays of the world? He answers that the first represents the potential in creation, and the latter, the actualization and the purpose of creation (i.e., freedom). This is also true for humans. We are created and have great potential but we must each day fulfill and actualize the purpose of our creation. If we embrace the false, temporary pleasure of instant gratification, we will stumble and fall on the way to a life of unfulfilled potential.

We cannot just walk through life as zombies, eating up all the stale popcorn just because that is what is served to us. Rather, we must process and critically evaluate marketing that comes our way and not just let it control us. We must keep our long-term health and growth in mind, choose the best path to get us there, and stay focused on achieving our goals. On this path, the Kedushat Levi teaches, we can truly be re-born every day. □

☐ SOCIAL JUSTICE – CONSIDERING THE FUTURE

THE PROBLEM OF
OVERPOPULATION AND THE
COMMAND TO PROCREATE

THE UNITED NATIONS HAS DECLARED THAT the seventh billion person in the world was born. Further, they have announced that since 1960, we've been adding a billion people to the earth every 12 to 13 years.

These unfathomable numbers are cause for significant alarm. Our rising population – nearly half already living on only $2 a day – together with a very finite number of resources almost inevitably means that we will have higher rates of homelessness and poverty, more environmental problems and depleted natural resources, and more orphans and neglected uneducated children around the world.

We will need to find more care for the global poor and vulnerable; we will need to consider more alternative energies; we will need to restructure our economies of production and consumption, and we will need to assess global education and incentives for birth control. And of course, we'll need to have faith.

We need to have faith since we have a conflicting message from our first mitzvah in the Torah – *peru u'revu* – to procreate. Quite simply, we are called upon as humans to populate the world to the best of our abilities. The great Prophet Yeshayahu teaches: "*Lo tohu b'raah lashevet yatzara*" – God created the world not to be empty but to be dwelled in!

Yet, we know that Avraham and Sarah had trouble initially fulfilling this mitzvah of *peru u'revu* as Sarah was barren. Avraham struggled to fulfill the mitzvah of *peru u'revu* both in procreation initially and in how he ended up treating his sons once they were born – he allowed his son Yishmael to be sent away and he almost had to kill his son Yitzhak. In both cases, God tested Avraham with the impossible: to struggle having children and then to send them both away alienating them forever. *Peru u'revu* was one of the only *mitzvot* that had been given in the Torah thus far at the time of Avraham, and yet he struggled tragically.

Yet I would suggest that Avraham understood the core value of this mitzvah very well – to perpetuate life and to value each and every life as having infinite value. I believe he valued this due to his personal struggle with family and reproduction, and due to his personal journey as an immigrant which gave him a very acute awareness of human vulnerability.

It was for this reason that he welcomed the strangers to approach his tent who were famished and in great need. It was for this reason, that he argued for the value of every life in Sodom and that they not be destroyed. Avraham truly revolutionized the world by bringing the notion of love for the stranger to the fore. This was, I would suggest, the actualization of the deepest meaning of *peru u'revu* – to give life and dignity to others.

Avraham becomes not only our model of the first Jew, and the first to enter the covenant through *brit milah*, but also our model for the foundation of Jewish values. God loved Avraham and formed a covenant with him because he and his family were "*Shamru derech Hashem laasot tzedakah u'mishpat*" (Genesis 18:18) – guards of the way of God to do justice in the world.

Even further, he is our model for prayer. Twice, with Avraham, we see "*Vayashkem baboker*" – Avraham wakes up early to pray for Sodom (19:27), and he wakes up early to fulfill the *Akedah*, the binding of Isaac (22:3). This becomes the source for our *Shacharit* prayer, the morning prayer. However, the source that the Rabbis teach as the origin for the obligation to say *Shaharit* is not the *Vayashkem baboker* of the *Akedah* but the *Vayashkem baboker* of Sodom (Avraham's prayer for the salvation of the righteous in Sodom). This is our model for prayer (that the masses not be destroyed and that not a single innocent person on the globe be dealt with unjustly). Avraham taught us that a significant, or perhaps the most significant, aspect of prayer is the crying out for and cultivation of mercy and compassion for the vulnerable.

Avraham struggles to fulfill one mitzvah of valuing life, of procreation, but masters another, that of pleading to save the lives of innocent others. We learn that when we cannot achieve a mitzvah for whatever reason, there is always another way to achieve the core value. In life, when we cannot achieve one dream, there is another dream to be cultivated.

Our Individual Callings

Tragically, there are families that break. There are businesses that go under. There are loved ones that pass. There are visions that go unrealized. But there is always another dream to reach for and there is always another calling to cultivate. But to do that we must have one absolute commitment.

To hear our calling as we grow through life – we must be ourselves. We must own who we are since we are the only ones in the world who were created for our unique mission. Each of us is a partner with God in creation in our own unique way.

In the book of I Samuel (17:39), David tries on Saul's armor so that he can fight Goliath (armor made for a king), and yet David says he cannot wear it. He takes it off and goes to fight. Profoundly, David realizes that one cannot go to battle in life in someone else's clothes. We must be ourselves if we wish to win, if we wish to prosper, if we wish to fulfill our personal destinies.

Our individual callings may be professional or existential. The call can be a loud scream or a subtle beckon, unambiguous from the start or shrouded in uncertainty to the end. Some of us feel one clear call throughout our lives and others may experience an evolution. Each of us must find a different way to hear our names called.

The Midrash (Tanhuma *Vayakhel* 1) teaches that each person is "called" by three names: the name given by parents (a name of essence), the name given by others (a name of relationship), and the name one comes to earn (a name of merit). Perhaps the greatest challenge of all in our lives is to choose to open ourselves to who we are and to who we can become.

We're all aware that there are many barriers to hearing and heeding our call: the inability to sit in silence or decipher competing interests, our reliance on serendipitous fate or the failure of courage to heed the seemingly insuperable call. Ultimately, no one can help us face these challenges within the vicissitudes of our daily lives but ourselves and perhaps our closest life partner. We must have the courage to remember that our callings are primarily personal and individualized. As the great Jewish psychoanalyst Viktor Frankl suggested, one should not seek the meaning of life but the meaning of one's own life.

Life is too short to follow someone else's dream to fulfill someone else's mitzvah or to become a cookie-cutter Jew (living the exact same Jewish experience and vision as others around us). Our lives have purpose when we follow our spiritual callings with zealous rigor and commitment. Each of us must be prepared when we hear our own Divine call of *ayeka* (where are you?) and to reply uniquely with our *hineni* (here I am)?

The Kotzker Rebbe explains that the most challenging test for Avraham was not leaving his native country, or sending away Ishmael, or even the binding of his son Isaac. The most challenging test for Avraham, the Kotzker explains, was to come off the mountain after the *Akedah*. The Kotzker suggests that Avraham never really forgave himself for his past, he never really came off the mountain.

How many of us have never come off the mountain? When we got stuck in a rut, trapped in a failure, caught in a regret, scarred in a tragedy, we never came off that mountain. Yet when we are lost in our life path, confused about how to move forward into a next stage in life, there is always a way to come down the mountain and start again to find ourselves.

There are seven billion people on the planet. Over-population is a big problem for us to wrestle with. Yet, we must remember that each and every one of us among these seven billion has been given a gift, each a talent, and each a destiny. We are a complexly interconnected universe with a great collective destiny, but we cannot forget that God brings each individual into this world with infinite value, a unique purpose, and a particular calling.

A story is told of the great Chassidic master Reb Zusha of Hanipol in the eighteenth century, the brother of Reb Elimelech. Reb Zusha laid crying on his deathbed. His students asked him, "Rebbe, why are you so sad? After all the *mitzvot* and good deeds you have done, you will surely get a great reward in *Olam HaBa*!" "I'm afraid!" said Zusha, "because when I get to heaven, I know God is not going to ask me, 'Why weren't you more like Moshe?' or 'Why weren't you more like David HaMelech?' But I'm afraid that God will ask, 'Zusha, why weren't you more like Zusha?' And then what will I say!?"

We do not know what is coming in our lives but if we listen carefully and we stay true to the mission that we believe we have been created for, we can go forth and stay the course with confidence. □

THE MOST IMPORTANT AND DANGEROUS JEWISH VALUE: THE MESSIANIC IMPULSE

"**W**E WANT MASHIACH NOW!" HAVE YOU sung it? What did you mean?

The Torah teaches us about the four stages of redemption (*Exodus* 6). Through God's miraculous interventions in the world (the ten plagues), there was a mass exodus, perhaps the greatest story of liberation and redemption in human history.

But we have to ask ourselves whether this is the historical model for future redemption. Is this the way that we want it to occur? As a miracle of God?

In the middle of the plagues the Torah says, "*Ain kamoni b'chol haaretz*" – there is none like Me in all of the land. It is not only distinguishing God from the belief in other gods. It is distinguishing what God can and should do versus what humans can and should do. In general, we follow *halachta b'drachav* (Imitatio Dei) that we emulate the ways of God, but here there is a limitation. It may be that the text is saying: I (God) can redeem the world through a punishment of the other but do not think that you should emulate this in search of your own redemption. "*Ain kamoni b'chol haaretz*" – there is none like Me – there is no one on earth that may act as I am acting here, for a higher reason than you can understand. Thus, the redemption from Egypt is different from the future model of redemption.

Jewish Messianism is everywhere in modernity, including Zionist, Chabad, and secular Jewish messianists (Karl Marx, Rosa Luxemburg, Leon Trotsky and other Bolsheviks). It seems we cannot take the messianic impulse out of the Jew.

Today, the messianic impulse can have very dangerous expressions. More and more, we see messianism leading to extremism and also to the watering down of core Jewish values; the notion of the coming of Mashiach not only becomes disproportionately important in Jewish thought, but also a justification for lack of responsibility. The concept of Mashiach becomes a religious excuse, a crutch, a shortcut. When it is our collective version of the Tooth Fairy, Easter Bunny, or Santa Claus, we risk religiously remaining children, constantly expecting a supernatural intervention that will instantaneously change all of nature. We interpret a prophetic hyperbole too literally. But there is, of course, a very different model at the foundation of Jewish thought.

In the Gemara (*Sanhedrin* 98a), Rav Yehoshua ben Levi wrestles with the question of when and how messianism works, and asks Eliyahu HaNavi when the Messiah will come. Eliyahu replies that he should go ask the Mashiach himself, who is sitting at the entrance to the city of Rome. Rav Yehoshua then asks Eliyahu HaNavi how he will recognize the Mashiach at the gates of Rome. Eliyahu replies profoundly that he will be sitting amidst the poor and sick, putting bandages on them one by one.

The Messiah exists on the periphery of society (gates of Rome) and is a healer! Rav Yehoshua runs and finds the Mashiach and asks him when he will come. The Mashiach replies, "Today!"

Rav Yehoshua, confused, goes back to Eliyahu questioning why the Mashiach said "today."

Eliyahu replies, quoting Psalms, that it is today – "if you will hear His voice."

The Gemara is teaching us that Mashiach is here already. Messianic possibility is always right in front of us in a very real way.

Rambam explains (*Hilchot Melachim*) that in the pinnacle of human progress, nature will remain as it is, but there will be universal benefit to all humankind, not via miracles; Mashiach is not a miracle worker, but brings about change through natural means. It is through the good deeds of Jews, and as the censored part of what Rambam says, Christians and Muslims will also help pave the way for the messianic time. He explains there will be no more jealousy – all will feel they have sufficient resources due to the human transformation of society. There may be an enthroned king; Rambam calls this the Philosopher King (the one who fully contemplates and clings to God). But in the naturalistic view (as compared with the apocalyptic view), getting to a better place comes from us, not from this miraculous intervening redeemer. For the Rambam, the vehicle is *Halacha*, and he explains that the purpose of *Halacha* is to create a just society (*Guide for the Perplexed* 3:27).

Yeshayahu Leibowitz, an Israeli thinker, explains further, based on his read of Rambam, that Mashiach is not a person or event, rather it is a process. We are always waiting. It never actually comes about fully.

The messianic impulse can be very dangerous, but it can also be very positive, perhaps one of the most important Jewish values – to keep our optimism and idealism intact and to work to improve the world – where we progress but we never quite reach perfection. We improve through our human toil. Rabbi Yohanan ben Zakkai explains that even if you are planting a tree and the Messiah comes, what do you do? You keep planting your tree (*Avot d'Rebbe Natan*). That we are a part of redemption does not exempt us from the work we continually need to do to advance it. "The *mitzvot* of the Torah will never be nullified, not even in the future days (i.e., the messianic age]" (Jerusalem Talmud, *Megillah*).

We have made too many mistakes throughout history, thinking that the Messiah is a person or event. They are called Bar Kochva, Abulafia, Shabbatai Zvi, Jacob Frank, and certain Chassidic rebbes. It was Christian influence that helped further this idea of the single divine human. The Jewish notion, preceding that, suggested that all people are imbued with Divinity (*tzelem Elokim*).

At the end of the day, I would like to suggest that we are Mashiach – we are the ones we have been waiting for.

The Baal Shem Tov, the founder of Chassidut, taught that one does not look outside one's soul to bring about redemption: "All our prayers for redemption are essentially bound to be prayers for the redemption of the individual." He taught that each of us must turn inward and seek redemption through seeking transcendence in all our actions and transactions.

While there are some important things to learn from the Reform movement, I believe that it was a mistake to take messianism out of the liturgy – we repair the world through activism but also through the moral components of all the *mitzvot*. Rav Kook emphasizes the messianic potential of our ethical actions and teachings (*Talelei Orot*, "Essay on Reasons for the Commandments").

As Martin Buber said: "There is no definite magic action that is effective for redemption; only the hallowing of all actions without distinction possesses redemptive power. Only out of the redemption of the everyday does the Day of Redemption grow."

As passionate Jews, we are hopeful – we believe in progress. Mashiach is the name of the value that we can do something that is truly magnificent. It reminds us that we must keep the highest optimism about the human potential to achieve on the highest level.

So we have raised the stakes. The Gemara (*Shabbat* 31a) says that when we ascend and stand at the end of our lives before the gates of heaven, one of the main questions asked of us is whether or not we yearned for redemption. Did we continue to believe in a better world and commit our lives to furthering that vision?

Today, yearning requires more intentionality. We must ask ourselves: what is the redemption we are working to bring about? How is our davening helping us to get there? How are we helping to create a more just society? How are we preparing our children to bring their contribution to our redemption? How are we intertwining our *tikkun atzmi, tikkun kahal, tikkun clal, and tikkun olam* (repair of self, community, Jewish people, and world)?

This is a formidable work, the biggest project that G–d gave the Jewish people and humanity. Perhaps the goal of Shabbat is to pause and taste a little bit of the perfection, the messianism that we never fully reach. Perhaps the suggestion that every Jew keeping Shabbat would bring the Mashiach means that if we were all to taste perfection together, we would be able to unite to collectively fulfill our mission. ☐

ACTUALIZING DEMOCRACY: CAN CHANGE REALLY BE BOTTOM-UP?

NEW YORK TIMES COLUMNIST DAVID BROOKS, writing about today's social reformers, argues that "it's hard not to feel inspired by all these idealists, but their service religion does have some shortcomings. In the first place, many of these social entrepreneurs think they can evade politics. They have little faith in the political process and believe that real change happens on the ground beneath it." Is Brooks correct that we can only create bottom-up change if we address the political process?

President Obama won the presidency on the premise that bottom-up change works, yet now that he is in the White House, the change he can really make is top-down. Grassroots supporters looked to him to create this top-down change and in their confusion over what seems like paralysis in the political process, they often blame the White House. Did the President's grassroots mobilization to gain the most powerful position in the world help our society or set us back?

Saul Alinsky, the great organizer and author of *Reveille for Radicals* (1946) and *Rules for Radicals* (1971), argued that the true democrat is "suspicious of, and antagonistic to, any idea of plans that work from the top down. To engage in democracy for him is to create change from the bottom up" (*Reveille*, 17). Alinsky appears to suggest that nothing productive can come from playing the political game. Yet, as upstanding citizens, should we not enter the political discourse and engage in politics? Is there not a place to rely upon government and politicians as partners and allies?

Moving from grassroots to political conversations can have great costs. Too often we get lost in intellectual and political abstractions that achieve little. Princeton Professor Jeffrey Stout, in his *Blessed Are the Organized: Grassroots Democracy in America*, makes the case for bottom-up change, explaining that "Listening closely while ordinary citizens describe their struggles, victories, and setbacks is itself a democratic act. One of its benefits is to bring the ideal of good citizenship down to earth." True social justice activism is more concerned with human individuals and their personal stories and struggles than about philosophical theories and ideologies, as enticing as they are.

Stout references Alinsky's Rules to show how grassroots activity emerges – ". . . ideals become an ideological fog when they are abstracted from the activities of ordinary people. Liberty and justice are made actual in the lives of people who struggle for them." Stout then quotes Alinsky to show how collective action is the essence of democracy: "If we strip away all the chromium trimmings of high-sounding metaphor and idealism which conceal the motor and gears of a democratic society, one basic element is revealed – the people are the motor, the organization of the people are the gears. The power of the people is transmitted through the gears of their own organizations, and democracy moves forward" (*Reveille*, 46). Democracy is not a philosophy; it is, rather, a way of life.

Grassroots work is really difficult; so many of us just read op-eds about elections and legislators, and debate them as a sport. Is it possible that elections are merely exercises in mass manipulation leading to top-down change, or no change at all? Politicians may declare their allegiance to democratic ideals, but in an age of powerful lobbies, whose interests are they really advocating?

We begin to fulfill our democratic responsibilities nonviolently by voting, learning the issues, speaking out freely for what we believe in, petitioning against injustice, and building coalitions. But this is only the beginning. We hold politicians accountable through our votes, but this step often comes too little, too late. Rather, we need a culture of accountability to ensure the masses hold enough power to challenge politicians when they stray from the values they committed to.

Bottom-up change is possible, but it requires a very significant time commitment in building relationships. Organizing was already draining when it was just about relationships in the local neighborhood, but the term "community organizing" has fallen out of favor since the move to building broader bridges across religion, race, class, and location. It is more complicated and time-intensive than ever. How can we all be a part of such a large complicated process of neighborhood walks, one-to-one meetings, house meetings, and actions?

The facile answer is that we should just get the right person into office to do all the things we want. Yet inevitably the politician gets caught in concessions, abstractions, and political self-preservation, and we get pulled along. Our grassroots idealism then fades into an abyss of political bureaucracy and deception. Brooks tells us we are naïve if we think we can create change without changing the political landscape, but it is unclear which approach is more delusional. Where do the greatest democratic victories occur?

In an age of political corruption, economic crisis, terrorism, and environmental crisis, we have to ensure that we hold those with power accountable for creating real change. Real change can happen through political endeavors, but we must work to actualize the true democratic process of grassroots change. As citizens, we must not allow ourselves to become disillusioned, alienated, or fearful. We must build coalitions that seek to create grassroots change and hold institutions of power accountable. Relying on a charismatic community organizer in the White House to create top-down change is a delusional dismissal of our democratic responsibilities to create change on the ground.   □

THE CASE FOR EPISTEMIC HUMILITY

"**T**HE MARKET IS ON THE RISE!" "WE WILL win the playoffs!" "As President, this nation will be rebuilt." Whether it is politics, business, medicine or sports, there is little news that we read every day that doesn't propose certainty of belief. In the news, we hear politicians and analysts speak with surety about world events, the effects of proposed policies, and the potential outcomes of war. We have been plagued in all sectors of society by a surfeit of confidence and certainty.

The Torah takes a very different approach to human knowledge.

We learn in *Parshat Hukkat* (Numbers 19:1–22:1) that there are commandments that have rational explanations (*mishpatim*) and those that appear to lack any rationale whatsoever (*hukkim*). Rational laws, such as prohibitions against killing and stealing, teach us moral imperatives. Laws without rational explanations inspire humility, reminding us that we are limited and cannot understand everything.

While we must continue to interpret the tradition and make our own meaning of it, we must also remember that we never possess absolute truth. While we aspire to bring God into our lives through our active engagement with Torah, we must always remember that we are human and not divine.

The quintessential *hok* (law without rational explanation) in the Torah is the red heifer, where we learn about its use in an ancient purity ritual. While it is challenging as a modern Jew to imagine how this act might be efficacious today, I try to stretch myself and understand its sacred power for my ancestors. In so doing, I am reminded that my own spiritual practices might not be as powerful for others as they are for me. This humbles me.

People of true wisdom embrace the importance of uncertainty. Is there anything in this life of which we can be absolutely certain? In short, we must cultivate an epistemic humility, a deep understanding of the limits of our knowledge. This idea is said to originate with Socrates (Plato, *The Apology*, 20e–23c). The great Greek thinker was puzzled by how others in his community were so sure of their wisdom, while he regularly experienced uncertainty.

In the early nineteenth century, Rabbi Naftali Tzvi Yehuda Berlin (the Netziv) explains the importance of humility in our approach to the Torah:

> Just as it is not possible for the wise student of nature ever to boast knowledge of all of nature's secrets. . . . and just as there is no guarantee that what his investigations do accomplish will not be invalidated in this generation or the next, by colleagues who elect to study the same things differently, so it is not possible for the student of Torah ever to claim that he has attended to each and every point that claims attention, and even that which he does explain — there is never proof that he has ascertained the truth of the Torah!

Similarly, the Israeli poet Yehuda Amichai, living through decades of strife in the Middle East, writes of the importance of uncertainty in his poem "The Place Where We Are Right":

> From the place where we are right flowers will never grow in the
> spring.
> The place where we are right is hard and trampled like a yard.
> But doubts and loves dig up the world like a mole, a plow.
> And a whisper will be heard in the place where the ruined house
> once stood.

Using evocative, land-based imagery, Amichai challenges us to imagine what might spring forth — even in a war-torn region — when we stop trying to always be right. Certainty can limit our vision and narrow our hearts, not allowing us to respond properly to objections, exceptions, and alternative perspectives. The twentieth century was littered with absolutist ideologies unchecked by humility and empathy, leading to some of the greatest evils in human history.

To be sure, we all hold different levels of certainty and doubt about different issues. I tend to have more skepticism about theological and scientific principles than moral ones. I am confident that certain moral values are fundamental to living a good and upright life. Even still, when moving from general principles to specific lived situations, things always become more complicated.

This is why it is so important to engage in rigorous and open discussion with others – including those we disagree with – about matters of consequence. None of us understands our religions, contemporary affairs, or even our own souls perfectly. We must humbly join intersecting communities in which we can reflect, be challenged, and learn together.

To change the world, we must have strong convictions and act on them effectively, but we must not forget the importance of our doubts. The role of faith is not to move us toward an opiate but to inspire more questions and conversation. □

THE CLOUDS OF GLORY AND HUMAN RESPONSIBILITY

AFTER THE SPIRITUAL INTIMACY OF ROSH Hashanah and Yom Kippur, we subversively break from the walls of institutions and the comforts of home into our modest *sukkot* (outdoor huts). It is in these huts that we rediscover during the Sukkot holiday the religious foundation of our human responsibility.

The Torah teaches that the purpose of sitting in the *sukkah* is so that later generations should know that the Jewish people were placed in *sukkot* when they left Egypt (Leviticus 23:42–43). The Rabbis argue about the meaning of this ritual (*Sukkah* 11b). Rabbi Eliezer suggests that we dwell in the *sukkot* to commemorate the miracle of the *ananei ha-kavod* (clouds of glory) that sheltered the Israelites from the hot sun in the desert. Rabbi Akiva, on the other hand, argues that we sit in *sukkot* to commemorate the actual *sukkot* the Israelites were miraculously provided (in the city of Sukkot) while in the desert.

The great nineteenth century rabbi, the Sfat Emet (Rabbi Yehuda Leib Alter), suggested that both rabbis of the Talmud were correct. He suggested that the clouds of glory (Rabbi Eliezer) represent the miracles at the time when Divine Providence was clearly observed by all. The actual *sukkot* (Rabbi Akiva) represent the miracles of Divine Providence that are no longer openly seen. Thus, in our *sukkot* today we are reminded that we must have more faith and we must devote more human toil to enable that hidden Divine Providence.

Rabbi Yitzhak Aizik Sher also suggested a synergy between the two positions. The clouds of glory represent a miracle that covered the entire Jewish people. The *sukkot* represent the individual providence that God did and does for each individual. We can be appreciative of global, national, and covenantal miracles, and we can also appreciate the blessing of a more intimate and personal providence.

The great sixteenth century rabbi called the Mabit (Rabbi Moshe ben Yosef Trani) asks why a holiday was not created around the other miracles of the desert, such as the providing of manna to eat or the wells to drink from. He answers that it was an extra miracle that God provided the luxury of shelter and not just survival (Beit Elokim, *Shaar Ha-Yesodot* 37). We can never express enough gratitude to be alive and to have food and drink. But we are also grateful for the other "luxuries" that we consider needs, and we emulate God in securing these needs for others as well. One can survive without certain human needs and wants, but one cannot flourish without them. The *sukkot* represent the blessings of human potential and flourishing.

On Sukkot, we commemorate historical miracles and eternal values, national redemption and personal salvation, Divine providence and human toil, the spiritual and the physical, the metaphysical and concrete pragmatism. In the *sukkah*, we are reminded of the peace that exists in the world that we can be thankful of and the need to further perpetuate that peace.

We are not only to welcome the stranger into our huts, we are commanded to once again experience our own alienation. The Torah makes the case on numerous occasions (Leviticus 23:42, 25:23; I Chronicles 29:15; Psalms 39:13, etc.) that all humans and all Jews are *gerim* (strangers and immigrants). Not only are we strangers alienated before our Creator, we are also strangers on this earth during our temporary visit to the world. Rashi explains (Leviticus 23:42) that our *sukkot* must not only include citizens but also immigrants and strangers to ensure we remember our true nature and our temporary corporeal existence.

By reconnecting with our modest hut and connecting with other strangers in the community, we can rediscover our own frailty, our own alienation, and our own human responsibility. □

SPACE TRAVEL: IS IT WORTH IT?

WHILE NASA HAS EMBARKED UPON ITS most ambitious Mars mission, spending a whopping $2.5 billion on the one-ton Curiosity Rover – hoping to find some evidence as to whether or not Mars once supported life – a United Nations report noted that there were 870 million undernourished people in the world (defined as "a state of energy deprivation" for more than a year). Even if all food production and distribution goals are met, 12.5 percent of the world will be under-nourished in 2015. On a planet that also has more than a billion people living in destitute penury, can we justify spending so much on another space mission?

Abraham Joshua Heschel said it well:

> I challenge the high value placed on the search for extraterrestrial life only because it is being made at the expense of life and humanity here on earth. . . . Is the discovery of some form of life on Mars or Venus or man's conquest of the moon really as important to humanity as the conquest of poverty, disease, prejudice, and superstition? Of what value will it be to land a few men on the wilderness of the moon if we neglect the needs of millions of men on earth? The conflict we face is between the exploration of space and the more basic needs of the human race. In their contributions to its resolution, religious leaders and teachers have an obligation to challenge the dominance of science over human affairs. They must defy the establishment of science as God. It is an instrument of God which we must not permit to be misused ("The Moral Dilemma of the Space Age").

Proponents of the space program and NASA's current $17.7 billion budget (and $300 billion collectively spent by all countries) point to technological advances that have come about or accelerated as a result of the space program:

- Satellite television and the mobile telephone
- Global positioning system (GPS) technology
- Virtual reality devices
- Extremely accurate maps
- Advances in digital imaging that have improved screening methods of existing technology (e.g., improved MRI, CT scans, and breast cancer screening)

There are also elements that cannot be quantified, such as the use of the photograph of Earth taken from space that was used to promote environmentalism, or the effect of the space program in promoting science in schools. As astrophysicist Neil deGrasse Tyson stated: "You don't have to set up a program to convince people that being an engineer is cool. They'll know it just by the cultural presence of those activities. You do that, and it'll jump-start our dreams." There are a lot of benefits to space travel and galaxy exploration.

NASA has about one hundred space programs ranging from examining the Earth's atmosphere, measuring the planet's water cycle, and tracking hurricanes and storms, to exploring asteroids and planets. Many scientists consider these ongoing programs to be vital to the advance of science and understanding our planet and the universe.

On the other hand, the American space program grew out of the Cold War anxiety over the Soviet Union's success in launching the Sputnik satellite, and much of this program has had military intentions. Nor should it be forgotten that the United States employed former Nazi scientists who had developed the dreaded V2 rocket (some of whom worked in facilities that starved their slave laborers). While the program had a spectacular success in landing men on the moon in 1969, it also led to the creation of weapons like the intercontinental ballistic missile and multiple independent reentry vehicle. These "advances" enabled a single missile to carry up to ten nuclear warheads thousands of miles, creating the potential for annihilating all human life on Earth. Thus, the space program has had mixed results.

Many believe that we are searching for extra-terrestrial life. This reality is not impossible according to Jewish thought. There is a Jewish theological basis to accept that there are other worlds in existence.

> "There was evening and there was morning, the first day" (Genesis 1:5): From here (we learn that) the Holy One, Blessed is He, created worlds and destroyed them, until God created these. God said:

"These give me pleasure, but those did not give me pleasure" (Genesis Rabbah 3:7).

Rav Saadia Gaon taught that we live in a centripetal Platonic notion of the universe, where everything moves toward the center (toward the human). This is an anthropocentric approach (i.e., that humans occupy the central position of existence, and that everything should be interpreted for its effect on humans). Rambam, however, taught that we live in a centrifugal universe of Aristotelian values. Furthermore, Rambam rejects anthropocentricism with the teleological position that God creates everything for its own purpose (Mishlei 16:4, "*l'maanehu*" – for the sake of God as opposed to for the sake of man), and thus the universe is centrifugal (everything moving away from the center), and the value of all increases as it goes outwards from man, Earth, into the "active intellect," and beyond.

The science of both thinkers is known to be incorrect today, but there is still philosophical value to their approaches. In our own time, an important Jewish philosopher, Rabbi Norman Lamm, follows in the school of the Rambam and writes: "There is no need to exaggerate man's importance, and to exercise a kind of racial or global arrogance, in order to discover the sources of man's significance and uniqueness."

Although "there is no need to exaggerate man's importance" and there is a lot of value in expanding our knowledge of the universe around us both for knowledge's sake and for the forward march of technology that advances the cause of human sustainability, on balance it is clear that the noble goal of reaching out into the cosmos must play second fiddle to the nobler goal of continued life on the only planet we call home. We must be invested in science and discovery and long-term growth, but we must also remember that our main priorities are addressing the human needs of today in this world. □

ADDRESSING FAMINE:
ANCIENT EGYPT AND TODAY

W E DO NOT HELP OTHERS IN THEIR TIME of need by increasing their dependence on us, but by helping them become more self-reliant and independent. This is as true in parenting and primary education as it is in international affairs.

At the end of the Book of Genesis, Joseph and his family are reunited after years of separation. Suffering the effects of famine in the land of Canaan, Joseph's father and siblings join him in Egypt. Joseph, we recall, has ascended from slavery to become Pharaoh's most trusted advisor. Joseph, viceroy of Egypt, has devised an elaborate food storage plan to deal with the "lean years" in the region.

"Give no thought to your possessions," Pharaoh says in his invitation to Jacob and his family, "for the best of all the land of Egypt is yours" (Genesis 45:20). Generous as this offer may seem, it is complicated because the Patriarch and his sons become completely dependent on the Egyptian monarchy; their land and food are the property of the kingdom.

The situation is even worse for the Egyptian populace, who give up all they own in exchange for food from Pharaoh's storehouses. They become so hungry that they actually beg to be slaves. Joseph's grand food aid program is problematic, to say the least.

Even if well-intentioned, one wonders if some of the current agrarian policies of the United States likewise create dependency problems for the countries they are attempting to support.

We have long been taught that American is the world's breadbasket. President Eisenhower established the Food for Peace program in 1954, in which American food surplus was set aside to feed the world. Its supporters boast that this program has helped 3 billion people in 150 countries. However, we should also be concerned by how these acts and programs are carried out.

Since, by law, 75 percent level of food aid must be bought from American agribusiness and shipped by American companies, 40 percent of U.S. food aid money goes directly to American shipping companies, and the price paid for grain is more than 10 percent higher than what could be bought on the international market. It also means that we further subsidize our American food industry while upending the local food industry where the aid is given, by crowding out their business.

Additionally, the food we send, which is very slow to arrive, often does not provide the types of food that are requested but rather the types that we wish to provide. Recipient countries often become dependent upon U.S. aid and end up in an even worse economic situation.

For example, less than a generation ago, Haitian farmers were able to grow enough rice for their population during normal years. Now, after years of American and international food aid policy that distributed foreign grain to the people of Haiti, that nation's farmers have been driven out of business; local farmers now produce less than a fifth of the rice necessary to feed the populace, so Haiti must either import food or depend even more on foreign food aid. It is a painful cycle of dependence that causes long-term harm.

Critics, such as the American Jewish World Service (AJWS), are attempting to change this policy. AJWS believes that American food aid funding should be paid directly to local farmers in developing nations to buy their food, or purchase the available local food that may be temporarily too expensive for the local population to afford. In addition, trusted local organizations could be given funds to purchase this food. Once the situation stabilizes, the local farmers would remain in a position to supply their people with food, and the need for food aid would abate. AJWS has already worked with farmers and organizations in Thailand, Kenya, and Haiti. It reports that the United States could feed 17 million more people, and get the food to the people fourteen weeks earlier, for no increase in expenses if it changed its distribution policies.

There is a precedent for this more efficient and constructive model of food aid. In the years following World War II, the Marshall Plan (1948–1951) provided the nations of Europe with billions of dollars worth of grants to buy their own food, which helped the recovery of European agriculture. This formula ensured that Europe would not be dependent on foreign food aid in the long-term.

Congress continues to debate the Farm Bill, which by law is supposed to be renewed every five years. The Senate version moved toward a more reasonable system that would allow for the purchase of local goods and payment, while the House of Representatives reverted to a less equitable version of this plan. The United States Congress will continue to debate the U.S. Farm Bill. We must speak up to ensure that the final version of the Farm Bill represents the most just ways of giving, and that our food aid program is reformed.

As Jews, we know well the importance of fighting poverty and alleviating hunger. We are like Joseph, blessed with influence in the greatest country of our time. We must use that influence to advance the cause of justice for all.

□

MICROFINANCE, KIVA, AND URI L'TZEDEK

JEWISH TRADITION FOCUSES HEAVILY ON THE importance of *gemilut hasadim* (acts of kindness), and charity. One way today's globalized world engages in large-scale charity is through microfinancing, a way of offering financial services to the poor or those without access to typical bank lending. The movement is based upon the belief that low-income people can achieve their goals and lift themselves out of poverty if given access to loans. Microfinance Institutions (MFIs) help people in developing countries as well as in developed ones, including the United States. Microfinance includes a number of financial services, such as microcredit, micro-lending, micro-insurance, savings, and money transfer. Today, anyone with access to the Internet can join and contribute to an MFI.

Microfinance is not new. For example, a group of fifteenth century Franciscan monks founded community pawnshops, and a European credit union movement began in the nineteenth century. Jews have also been involved in microfinance for millennia. A Gemach (abbreviation for *gemilut hasadim*), interest-free loan fund, is the quintessential example of Jewish microfinancing. The Gemach fulfills the positive mitzvah of lending money (Exodus 22:24) and the negative mitzvah against charging interest (Leviticus 25:37). Jews also established some of the first MFIs in America, referred to as Hebrew Free Loan Societies.

Today, Microfinance has grown into a global movement comprising thousands of institutions, each with its own lending practices. Microfinance currently empowers approximately 160 million people in developing countries.

There are three general microfinancing methods: 1. formal financial institutions, including banks and insurance companies, which have been reluctant to service poor populations due to high transaction costs and other risks; 2. non-governmental organizations (NGOs), such as Grameen Bank (created by Professor Muhammad Yunus, Nobel Peace Prize winner), which currently lend to more than 100 million clients worldwide, and whose safe, secure deposit services make them very popular (though in some countries NGOs are not permitted to collect deposits); and 3. informal organizations, including moneylenders, informal associations, cooperatives, and community-based development institutions, often managed by the poor themselves, which provide flexible, convenient, and fast services, but are highly risky and much harder to study formally.

Do MFIs help people get out of poverty?

David Roodman, of the Center for Global Development, is critical of the microfinance movement's ability to alleviate poverty. He believes that with the rise of large bank participation in microfinance, the world's poor are encouraged to borrow repeatedly, with increasing liability. Instead, Roodman believes that the poor should be offered ways to save money as a way out of poverty. He is also critical of certain microfinance groups that hold groups of borrowers liable for all the loans, thus putting pressure on members to sell or barter all their possessions in order to come up with the money to repay the loans. Kadita Tshibaka of Opportunity International counters by noting that MFIs are beginning to offer interest-bearing savings accounts, low-cost insurance plans, and financial education programs for the poor that will help them start businesses, hire people from the local population, and help the community rise out of poverty. In addition, Tshibaka argues that pooling borrowers (who are overwhelmingly women) does not lead to desperate borrowers, but has led to a 95 percent repayment rate in 4-month cycles, contributing to stability. Thus, while there are still problems with some MFIs, the overall effect is beneficial.

Kiva is the world's first person-to-person microlending website, relying on a network of microfinance institutions to allow people to donate in small amounts and build community in the process. Kiva lenders learn about available loans online. When choosing a loan, they are connected with MFIs ("Field Partners") who find the individuals in need of loans, and then disburse the loans. Thus far, Kiva has made loans of over $386 million to more than half a million lenders in 67 countries. An average loan is about $400, with a 99 percent repayment rate. Find out more about the way Kiva loans work on its website.

Rambam famously stated that the best way to give someone charity is to give him a loan, enter into a partnership with him, or give him a means to an income (Mishneh Torah, *Hilchot Matnot Aniyim* 10:7). Microlending is one of the most important ways we can work to eradicate poverty and empower those in the developing world to build their lives and dreams on their own terms.

Uri L'Tzedek has proudly maintained a Kiva lending team since November 2008, with over 130 team members and 847 completed loans, comprising $28,825.

By joining the Uri L'Tzedek's Kiva Lending Team, anyone can become part of this larger movement. Encourage your community to purchase products associated with microfinance, including goods made in enterprises funded by microfinance or retailers that donate a percentage to support microfinance. For poverty is a solvable problem, and microlending is a great tool to get our world to the point of its complete eradication.

To put Uri L'Tzedek's motivation in Muhammed Yunus's prophetic words: "Poverty does not belong in civilized human society. Its proper place is in a museum. That's where it will be. When schoolchildren go with their teachers and tour the poverty museums, they will be horrified to see the misery and the indignity of human beings. They will blame their forefathers for tolerating this inhumane condition and for allowing it to continue in such a large segment of the population until the early part of the twenty-first century." □

APOCALYPSE?
BUILDING A NEW WORLD!

WHEN A REPORTER FROM THE *KANSAS CITY Star* called me, it was not to ask about Israel, the Presidential Election, or anything of immediate local or global relevance. Rather, she asked me about the Jewish perspective on heaven. I, of course, reinforced for her that the Jewish tradition has a deep eschatological foundation and offers a strong belief in *Olam HaBa* (the World to Come). I also assured her that the Sages of the Talmud could not imagine a heaven that was exclusive only to Jews, but rather that it was reserved for the righteous of all nations. Lastly, and most importantly, I let her know that Jews have felt obliged to prioritize the holy work that needs to be done in this world over speculation about the nature of the next world.

Jewish worldly responsibility trumps any necessity to embrace dogmas or beliefs about the nature of an afterlife. Rambam even suggests that it would be harmful to spend much time thinking about that which cannot be known, such as the messianic era and the next world. He urges us to steer away from more radical cataclysmic apocalyptic thinking (Mishneh Torah *Hilchot Melachim* 12:2).

However, in my reflections, I also recalled the *haftarah*s read around the holiday of Sukkot dealing with the final apocalyptic end-of-days war of Gog U'Magog. In both the books of Yehezkel (38:18–39:16) and Zacharia (14:1–21), a complex picture is painted. These stories have grasped the human imagination for centuries and penetrated deeply into our religious consciousness, since they represent the destruction of our imperfect world, the ultimate full-blown war against evil, and the victory of God and the Jewish people in a battle for truth. Both of these *haftarah*s describe a future war fought against nations oppressing Israel, in which God rises to fight against the enemies of Israel. Rashi argues that both *haftarah*s describe the same end-of-days war with "every man's sword against each other" and God's ultimate supernatural intervention and destruction.

Some modern thinkers have suggested that we have experienced these wars already or are in the midst of them. The Vilna Gaon (commentary on Mechilta Exodus 14:20) said that this Gog U'Magog war would only last three hours and would take place on Hoshana Rabba. Another rabbi pointed out that the U.S. war in Afghanistan against Al-Qaeda had begun on Hoshana Rabba.

Others claimed that World Wars I and II were the Wars of Gog and Magog preparing the world for the coming of the Messiah, started by the Jewish return to Israel. Previously, Chassidic teachers saw the Jewish struggles with France and Russia as the wars of Gog and Magog.

But must we worry? These wars are of the past, not the future, and these stories of Gog U'Magog have not gained prominence in Jewish theology.

An alleged Mayan prediction that the world would come to an end in December 2012 was popularized in the media. Responsible theologians and scientists alike have unanimously repudiated this, along with popular entertainers. As Jay Leno joked on the "Tonight Show": "According to the Mayans, the world is supposed to end in the year 2012. Are you buying that? When's the last time you even ran into a Mayan?" Or as the band R E M once sung: "It's the end of the world as we know it and I feel fine."

Incredibly, many people have given credence to this apocalyptic vision. In an international poll conducted for Reuters in May 2012, fully 10 percent of Americans believed that the world will end by the end of 2012, and 22 percent believe that the world will end during their lifetime. Contrast this with France, where only 6 percent of those polled believe that the world will end in their lifetime. Significantly, the poll revealed a correlation between anxiety over the future and belief in an imminent end of the world.

Contemporary thinkers have echoed the warnings of past rabbis to focus on real contemporary crises rather than imaginary doomsday scenarios. Deepak Chopra has noted that Americans should focus on the changing world, in which nations will have to curtail their indiscriminate use of natural resources, and in which "crude nationalism" and "religious intolerance" were credible threats worthy of attention. He warned against those who focused on the end of the world: ". . . reactionary forces, fueling an undercurrent of fear, promoting a fantasy of America as a perfect society where privilege is a birthright and the rest of the world exists on a plane almost beneath notice."

Since the Mayan doomsday episode is forever behind us, I would suggest that the wars of Gog and Magog are not in the Tanach and in our *haftarah*s in order to strike fear into us or to lay out a perfect picture of the end-of-days. Rather, it should tickle our moral imagination around the possibilities of destruction and creation.

This theme of global destruction is not new. We saw that God destroyed the world with the flood and Noah rebuilt the world. Later, all of civilization was broken once again and dispersed at the Tower of Babel. After the Shoah, the Jewish people needed to recreate a lost Jewish world. We are asked, now once again, to step out of our known world and imagine a new one. If your world were destroyed, how would you rebuild it? How would you change it?

Today, our American discourse is dominated by the details of how we are going to rebuild, as is demonstrated by the political process. About half the country says we need big strong government and half says we need small hands-off government, and a lot of bickering in between. But within the debate of *how* we structure our society, have we lost the big picture of *what* – what is the ultimate world we are trying to construct together. That is much bigger than any individual's pocketbook, any particular policy, any politician, and even any generation. It is ultimately what we leave in this world. The project of Judaism is designed to constantly push us from self-interest into the big picture of society, global impact, and long-term generational impact. What will the world be like after me?

To do that, we cannot go to the woods and wonder alone. To dream, we must do it together. And we must do it with those who have been excluded from the actualization of past dreams. As poet Toni Morrison said: "All paradises, all utopias are designed by who is not there, by the people who are not allowed in." The best dreamers of the future are often those denied the dreams of yesterday.

The stories of apocalypse that we read may tempt us to think about how the world could be destroyed, but our moral challenge is to think about how we will reconstruct the world, how we rebuild after the storms. Destruction stories can divide us in fear. Construction stories can build us in unity.

The eighteenth century revolutionaries in America understood that they were building a new world. In 1948, those building the new Jewish state, understood they were creating a new world. When one holds their newborn child for the first time, they understand that they are holding a new world.

In fact, if we look at Noah after the first destruction of the world, Rashi explains that his name is Noah due to the *nehama*, the comfort he brought to the world. How did he do that? He invented the plow. To build the world, we just have to start plowing. That is our work, to dream but also just to start plowing and working toward that dream.

Rabbi Yohanan ben Zakkai was once leaving Jerusalem. Rabbi Yehoshua was walking behind him and saw the Temple in ruins. Rabbi Yehoshua said: "Woe unto us for the destruction of the Temple, the place of atonement for the sins of Israel." Rabbi Yohanan ben Zakkai said to him: "My son, do not worry – we have another form of atonement like it." "What is it?" "Acts of loving kindness" (*Avot d'Rabbi Natan* 4:21).

That is how we rebuild the world today: turning from a destroyed past and rebuilding the future through *gemilut hasadim* (random acts of loving kindness).

When we read the stories reminding us of the power of destruction, may we rather dream of a new world, and commit each day to doing random acts of kindness to secure this future world that turns our dreams into realities.

CONCLUSION

T O LIVE AS A COMMITTED JEWISH LEADER, I believe that one must be deeply knowledgeable about the issues, trained as an activist, in solidarity with key partners, deeply passionate, and on a constant journey to cultivate a deep spiritual life. A daily commitment to ritual, meditation, reflection, and learning can deepen the impact of one's social justice work, provide new insight, and help to prevent burnout.

It is my hope that this book will open up a broader conversation about our moral and spiritual responsibilities as Jews to repair the world with more urgency, sophistication, and passion.

I believe that the purpose of the Torah and the Jewish tradition is to inspire leadership for the creation of a more just and holy world. As Jews in the twenty-first century, we can and must be on the forefront of the most pressing contemporary moral issues such as poverty, immigration, workers' rights, animal welfare, prison reform, business ethics, and child adoption.

This book opens up a complex process attempting to challenge, support, and inspire the Jewish community to consider particularistic and universalistic moral and social justice concerns through a *halakhic* and Jewish ethical lens in a more nuanced way. These short essays were not intended to be conclusive, but to inspire further discourse, scholarship, and activism. Our community must continue to gain the tools and inspiration to address particular social justice issues from a traditional Jewish perspective in the most effective ways possible.

To all readers, may you be blessed to continue to find your true calling to improve the world in your unique way and may you remain committed and steadfast in your learning and growth and your pursuit in these goals to create the change that is so sorely needed in our world. *Chazak V'Amatz!*

□